THE CHINESE

A gem of Chinese architecture: Loong Wah temple, Tang Period,
700 A.D.

THE CHINESE

By

JOHN STUART THOMSON

ILLUSTRATED FROM PHOTOGRAPHS

見 一 知 不 學 千

"One seeing, however, is better than
a thousand people telling you of it."
—*Chinese Proverb.*

INDIANAPOLIS
THE BOBBS-MERRILL COMPANY
PUBLISHERS

PRESS OF
BRAUNWORTH & CO.
BOOKBINDERS AND PRINTERS
BROOKLYN, N. Y.

TO
L. M. S.

CONTENTS

THE CHINESE

THE CHINESE

I

DAILY LIFE OF FOREIGNERS IN CHINA

The feeling of exile, ever too melancholy in the heart of the white stranger whose lot is cast in this southern land of ten thousand granite peaks which extend along the coast for two days of the sea journey from Shanghai, is nowhere more happily dispelled for a season than at Hong-Kong Island during the "race week" in February. The indispensable Celestial, Ah Chow, arrives from the breeding camps in Mongolia with a motley-colored string of shaggy, hardy Chinese ponies, thirteen hands high, for which he paid at the breeding steppes only ten dollars each, but which he will sell at ten times that price. They are all of such uncertain temper that bets are laid as to whether they will be left at the post or run away before the starter has shouted, "Go." Fat-bellied as they are, some do the mile in two minutes ten seconds. There was a day in China in the reign of Hiao, when the Superintendent of the Stud ranked next in importance to the Throne itself. Then horses were large enough to bear armored men to battle. The history of stock in Japan, as well, since that time has been one of decadence. These ponies are drawn by lot by the staffs of the Scotch firms, English officers and gentlemen, and the Parsee bankers who deal in opium and land.

Native *mafoos* (the same word you meet in Korea as *mapus*), or jockeys, are hired, and you will notice that they mount from the right side. Betting booths for the slow-going *paris-mutuels,* where the book-makers have no chance to manipulate odds, are erected. In this French form of betting each investor puts an equal amount into the pool and those who have named the winning horse share the pool money, less eight per cent. for expenses. The anæmic European ladies do what the Chinese women do, and paint their weather-melted faces. But they do what the Chinese do not, that is, don chiffon and lace, which all too soon is sorry and soggy in a dripping, moldy climate. But what better portrays the spirit of Empire than this very indomitableness of these English women — this determination to have an Ascot of fashion at least once a year even under humid tropic suns, or drizzly gray skies and mist-wrapped peaks, on this one level spot of the island, a filled-in swamp called Wong Nei Chong at the foot of the exiles' blue-walled "Happy Valley" cemetery? Not only are China ponies run on three days of the meet, but enough Walers of thirteen and one-half hands, Arabs, India "country breds," and stray Americans, are gathered together for a fourth day's racing. Frequent gymkhanas are held, even through the hottest spell, when the Polo Club members ride in tent-pegging, hurdle, obstacle and nomination races, and such other horsey excitement as shall keep ladies from ennui and young gentlemen in debt to their shroffs, in a climate which does not foster the memory. The most unique of all, certainly to the Chinese onlooker who is making notes for a book, are the 'rickisha races, where the *Ku-niangs* (ladies) wave their motley-colored Parisian parasols — it would be impossible to hold at arm's length a Chinese bamboo parasol — to urge their human steeds (not native coolies this time, but English gentlemen) to win. The English gentlemen jockies go to the post in the hard sun, with wet bamboo or plantain leaves packed under their helmets, but they are game enough (as the world may always expect of our European Ulysses) to throw these away as the race reaches the keen stretch. As the Jockey Club of Bombay permits the women from Grant Road to attend unescorted, so the Hong-Kong Jockey Clubs permits the denizens of Lyndhurst Terrace to watch the scene from a remote corner of the stands. It would not be that " East of Suez " if exclusiveness had not its startling inconsistencies. At Peking, the foreigners do not adjourn to the famous old course outside the northwest gate, beneath the Taoist and Buddhist temples, until May.

They tell tales that at Mirs Bay and other practice waters, the mess of the war-ship lands, sets cups into the Chinese hills and tees off the first horseshoe gravestone for an impromptu game of golf. I know the courses which are laid among the native graves outside the Porta Cerco of Portuguese Macao, in the Heungshan district of China, and at Ichang are not much improved on this. Hong-Kong boasts of two courses. That at Wong Nei Chong is level, over a race-track twice, one swamp, and made bunkers. Pulling the stroke is costly, because most of the greens lie parallel with the track and ditch, which penalize the player if driven into. The other course at Deep Bay on the south side of the island is reached by climbing over four miles of hills, or by a launch sail of nine miles. The wooded hills are lofty, and the joy of contemplating that you are playing in view of the combing surf of the limitless Pacific is sublime. You

land from your launch by native sampans and play around
the edge of a narrow valley. The fifth tee is in the neck
of a gorge and the chaparral to each side, and the rocky
stream at your feet, are not St. Andrew's classic comforts. Put away your brassey and even your driver, for
that's no brawling burn before you. It is iron work; be
steady, satisfied with the tight, short gains of infantry
in face of fire. One foot off the course is to be enfiladed,
and put *hors de combat*. The nerve that is needed; the
thrill when it is all over! Again, there was that tree
which you learned to loft rather than play past it with
a cleek. On these two sides men who for many a year
in battle's din and travel's mire, have ever been as David
and Jonathan, shall be arrayed in unsettled argument
for ever, in a Service Club on Pall Mall or in a library
at Annapolis.

Here, too, is classic English law punishing by the
astonishing method in these days, of sentence to the
stocks. There must be the trappings of awe accompanying
the means of punishment where only two thousand Englishmen rule three hundred thousand Chinese, all crowded
on the north sloping beach of the island, or on the ten
thousand sampans in the harbor. There has not been a
riot among the natives since the memorable one of October 3rd, 1884. Beside Victoria the Good's statue, a
red-turbanned Sikh policeman stands over Kong Sing,
who sits on the powdered disintegrated granite road, with
his feet imprisoned in boards, all because of a vaga-
bondish habit of greasing his queue and looking covet-
ously at foreign gentlemen's watch chains. No fewer
than seventeen hundred undesirables were banished by
the Hong-Kong courts last year. Sometimes Chinese
mandarins come to the Colony and their victims follow

them to lodge complaint in a British court. Juries consist of seven men, because of the scarcity of Europeans serviceable. In Singapore, natives are mixed with the Europeans to bring the jury up to twelve. A nefarious but amusing trick of the light-fingered natives who operate on the crowded steamer wharves, is to expectorate on their victim's left shoulder and then call his attention to it. While he excitedly removes the heathen affront, the rascal, whose ways are saffron, quickly goes through the victim's right pocket. Natives imprisoned on grave charges have to submit to their queues being cut, as formerly many excited prisoners hung themselves thereby in their cells.

Hong-Kong's bustling port is peculiar in that there are no wharves. Moreover, the anchorage, instead of being well spread out from Causeway Bay to Kennedytown, is all crowded before the center of Victoriatown. Every piece of freight is lightered, and every passenger is ferried. British Hong-Kong is really Chinese Canton's seaport. Two million passengers pass between the two ports annually.

The picture of her tonnage can perhaps best be quickly drawn by comparative figures; London thirteen million tons; Hong-Kong twelve million; New York eleven million tons annually. Hong-Kong's growth to be the second port in the world is in some quarters credited to the fact that she imposes only one charge on shipping, viz.: the insignificant Lighthouse tax of one cent Mexican silver a ton; but Manila, which imposes no tonnage taxes, remains stagnant at a small tonnage. Shanghai, which imposes the highest tax in the Orient of twenty-nine cents a ton, continues to enjoy a large share of shipping. Yokohama imposes seven and one-half cents a ton.

Hong-Kong rejoiced at the close of 1906 to find herself drawn twenty days nearer Europe by the new service, under one management, of thirty days from Hong-Kong to Liverpool via Vancouver and Quebec, and the Colony expects to throw off her alienation in the host of travelers who will visit the port and enter China through the southern gateway, to which she is the key. The rateable values of the city of Victoria have reached six millions, nearly half of which is invested in the precipitous " Peak " district above the clouds. On the mainland at Kowloon, where the railway to Canton is rapidly raising values and where the future of the Colony will lie, rateables have reached two millions. Great as is Hong-Kong's position in shipping and which is assailable by China at Whompoa, her leadership will remain in banking, headed by the noted Hong-Kong and Shanghai Banking Corporation, which is now financing nearly all China's great developments in railways, mines and industrials. If England, through this bank, would only give one-fortieth of the attention to China that she has given in the past to Japan, the harvest would be the more potential, even as the high millet of the former's fields overtops the rice fields of the latter. Hong-Kong and Shanghai bank-notes are the only paper issues accepted in the country back of the treaty ports. The name most prominent with the Chinese in the history of the bank is that of Sir Thomas Jackson, a tall Irishman, whose motto, writ large, was: " Never break your word with a Chinese, for he'll never break his with you."

It is believed that the Hong-Kong government and this bank participated in the loans for the Chinese Trunk Railway line, on the stipulation that China would assist in connecting Hong-Kong and Canton by rail, and thus sidetrack Whompoa for the present. This railway of eighty miles, trestled across swampy country, will end at Kowloon, the British settlement on the mainland, from which Hong-Kong Island lies one mile distant. With railways coming through from Calcutta, Mandalay, Bangkok and Hanoi, centering at Yunnan, and thence turning to Canton, and with rails from Han-kau and Amoy, Hong-Kong is dreaming of the time when she may be the largest trans-shipping port in the world. Land is at steeple prices, and living more costly than in New York City. Tenure is based on crown rentals, the same as the Chinese system.

This wonderful island, which is distant seven thousand miles from San Francisco, supplies the Pacific coast of America with half of its refined sugar. The raw material comes principally from Java, but also from the Philippines and Chinese Swatow. The largest cane refinery in the world is the noted Taikoo at Quarry Bay, owned by Butterfield and Swire. There is also the China Sugar Refinery at Wong Nei Chong, owned by the historic house of Jardine, Matheson and Company. Chinese labor refines two hundred thousand tons a year at three and one-half cents a pound. The coal is brought from Moji, Japan. It will before long come over the Han-kau-Canton Railway from Fa-Yuen and elsewhere in the heart of plethoric China. Up to the present these two refineries have supplied China and Japan. Japan has now put up a tariff wall of six-tenths cent a pound, and is manufacturing her own sugar. She subsidizes steamers to bring the raw product, and threatens to subsidize ships to carry the manufactured article to China. Hong-Kong, with cheap labor and a nearer location to the raw product, is holding the fort so far against subsidy, and is supplying China. For *po-po* or sweetmeat-making, however, the Chinese prefer their own hand-refined Swatow sugar, which goes half as far again as the cheaper imported brands.

The Taikoo refinery is a marvelous study in Scotch sociology. There is a Company reservoir and hospital in the hills; a cable to carry the European overseers five hundred feet over the gullies to the fever-free Company bungalows on the cliffs; Company model tenements at inexpensive rents; a Company loan fund for overseers to bring out Scotch wives; running track; athletic associations, medals and baths; launches for picnics, and a seven-hundred-foot graving-dock and repair yard for Company ships. Employees are encouraged to join yacht, golf, water polo, gunning, cricket and riding clubs, so as to be athletically happy even in enervating South China. You will notice that nothing indoors, such as billiards, has been provided. One looks in vain for the great American firms of forty years ago. Russell and Company, of clipper-ship fame, as well as the Heard, Oliphant, Bull and Archer hongs, have ceased to exist, and the historic hong of Dent and Company, at Macao, has shrunk to an unpretentious and seldom-visited building, hid behind an ancient wall. Kee Chung, the old princely house with its tropical garden, where Russell and Company once entertained Secretary W. H. Seward, is one of the show places of Wanchai, an eastern part of Hong-Kong, now overrun with Chinese coal-carriers.

The disintegrating granite peaks of Hong-Kong may some day furnish *ping tu* or porcelain powder as good as that of the Kiang-si Hills. Cement works have already raised their chimneys over the famous land-locked Kowloon Bay, where Admiral Keppel won Hong-Kong.

An Englishman (few as there are in the East as compared with the Scotch), brings all his sporting and club
impedimenta to the Orient.   In a little vale at Hong-
Kong, between Mts. Kellett and Gough, sixteen hundred
feet above the water, they have placed a bungalow club,
which has a marvelous view of peaks, seas and land-
locked bays.   There is nothing like this view at those
other famous oriental mountain retreats from the heat,
such as Simla, Darjeeling and Namhan.   The luxurious
and hospitable Hong-Kong Club, where I had the
pleasure of staying for a year and a half, would be hard
to surpass on Fifth Avenue or Pall Mall for accommodations and appearance.   It is situated on the Praya Grande
Central, in the heart of Victoria City and at the bay's
edge.   The Emperor of China could not be made a member on account of his color, but I have heard of one
Parsee getting in through the eye of a needle, and it
was said the needle was threaded by the English king.
There will, however, never be another such contretemps.
The question of eligibility for this club is about the hottest question in Hong-Kong.   Imperial politics and
nearer wonders are taken as a matter of course in
comparison, by these widely traveled Hong-Kongites.
To be sent into Coventry by the membership committee is a quietus on the most persistent aspirations,
in a colony where life is in the balance between
great social happiness and keen social misery, made
the more poignant by the feeling that you are so
remote from home that you could not go farther
on this globe without getting nearer.   Porcelain baths;
electric fans; Amoy oysters in season; mango ice-
cream; curries made opiate with powdered poppy seeds,
and the noblest wines of Europe, minus export reduc-

tions, but plus a little salicylic acid, are certainly luxuries, to which a bouquet is added because it is all enjoyed
in the alien and uncomfortable tropics, where miseries
and privations are supposed to reign. The Japanese add
their most famous brand of beer, which they humorously
call Peace, and which name was suggested by their
richest magnate, Baron Mitsui. Perhaps the cuisine has
its wearinesses in the endless repetition of stewed cucum-
bers, sickly *petsai,* and tough fried brinjals, but never a
mortal tasted a richer dish than vegetable marrow when
served hot. Add some golden Dutch butter, which by
the way is unsalted, to the golden meat, and you despise
the namby-pamby " stay-at-home." Then the Australian
steamer arrives once a week with Queensland mutton and
beef, to take the place of the Chinese water-buffalo and
humped cattle from the West River hills. The Chinese
also offer you a turkey, which if lacking in gameness and
color, supplies a soft delicacy of flesh which is a welcome substitute for our bird. The furniture, paneling
and flooring of this club, like in the other fine buildings
of luxuriant Hong-Kong, is all of Siamese or Javanese
teak, which is the most durable, hardest to carve and
costliest of woods. It has a close grain and is polished
in its natural color, which is red. This is the wood which
is brought at great cost to America, to undersheathe the
armor of battleships. The fine carving is done by Cantonese in those wonderful shops of scented chips along the
narrow Sun Tau Lan, Yuck Tsze, Tai Sun, and Old
Factory Streets. The beautiful new Hotel Mansions, at
the water's edge; the King Edward; the famous old brick
Inn, the Hong-Kong, with its roster of ten thousand
world's notables; and the unique Peak Hotel, nursed near
the summit above the clouds in Victoria Gap, are all

hostelries excellent enough to grace the Strand or Fifth
Avenue.   The Peak Hotel is the center of the garrison
social life, and every dinner is a glitter of regalia, braid,
buttons, forgivable swagger and affected intonation.
You will notice the menus have numbers opposite each
item; brinjals may be number fourteen; marmalade, sixteen; vegetable marrow, eight, and likewise with the
wine list; the boy would not know what you meant by
Sparkling Moselle, but tell him number six, and you
will have your wine.   The little cube of ice is removed from your cocktail after it has chilled it, and is
used to perform the same service in your neighbor's glass.
Torrid as is the climate, fleeting as is the life of the cube,
its service is a remarkably long one, for at the bars of
these treaty ports of the Orient the line of customers is
well filled, and be it said that American drinks reign.
When you permanently locate at a hotel or club you are
expected to bring in your own house boy to wait upon
you, the hotel only providing waiters for transients.
How one gets to hate the hot red heathen hills where
never for a moment in the long exile once lies the familiar snow lines of home, and the first sight of snow on
Mt. Ætna fills the returning wanderer with a thrill which
can only be understood by experiencing it.   You believe
then that snow is the sign of the Saxon character.

As the expatriated Chinese sighs for his eel, mullet
and native quail, to be brought alive to him across the
wide Pacific, a thirty-days voyage, so the white man in
China longs most of all for frozen American oysters.   It
is the mess of pottage for which he endures exile, and
with a tin and a cronie, he is able to knock through another twenty days until the next steamer, with a cold storage plant, arrives, when he forthwith hails a sampan, and

with a Lucullian smile, sails to make a studied flank attack on the steward.

Nowhere in the world perhaps are lantern illuminations more indulged in, and certainly nowhere so effectively. The terraced homes all have the mountain peak as background, and whether one looks from the bottom of the cup up the illuminated hills, or down upon the million lights which no factory smoke clouds, to the water, and the fish lantern procession passing through the lower streets and prayas, the view is glittering and multicolored. The natives are especially lavish of lanterns in the time of the sixth moon, when every shop is radiant with a lighted crab, fish, fowl, or dragon, the ingenuity in design surpassing the more classic Japanese fashion in lanterns.

No other race has looked upon the waters, and finding them more level than the land, with quick wit and sense, said that there by hundreds of thousands they would anchor their tax-free homes. Hong-Kong and Canton best present this unique spectacle, and the most moving sight, emotionally and literally, in the world, is when this immense populace is stirred by news of an approaching typhoon. Sails are hoisted, sculls and oars put to work, and a dozen times a year a vast armada sweeps like the scuds of clouds along the harbor, to another place of safety beneath a great mountain peak. How, on their return to the accustomed anchorage, they settle their position by number and lane, no one of us *Wai I* (outer barbarians) has ever yet been able to determine, but sampan and junk certainly drop into position as quickly as if drilled by a fleet-captain. Whichever foreigner can discover the key, will have given proof of his genius to camp an army better than a Cyrus, or shall we say as well as the local Yuan Shi Kai, on whose kind the hopes of militant China rest.

The exile's solemnity is coaxed with the superb music on the Parade Ground three times a week of the several military bands, and indeed one hotel makes a feature of employing the Baluchi's Indian band and pipers during dinner. If nearly everybody else loafs on foreign duty, the band is never idle. Too often it is Saul's march and extra slow step, along the Wong Nei Chong Road past the monument, to the hill side cemetery, for too many a comrade who has died of drink, melancholy, or malaria. The firing party loses no time in signaling among the peaks that another of the king's soldiers has been laid to his everlasting rest in the compulsory land of his exile, only twelve hours after his death. Then it is a piping march back to the barracks at quick step, for the officers greatly fear the effect upon unaroused men. A battle is less depressing to them, with its hastily gathered dead on the field, than the draped gun-carriage and funereal pomp at the door of the barracks hospital. There is, besides, playing in the barracks garden, for officers' guest night, and music for the theater, all crowded into a week, together with countless marches to be played from the landing wharf to Government House steps for many a braided Siamite, Nipponite and other Jebusite, who, by adopting the comity of nations, has perforce bowed to the yoke of our unpicturesque tailors. The German flagship *Hertha* drops into port, and in an evening or two afterward the German Club, established in a beautiful Renaissance building on Kennedy Road, announces that the warship's splendid string band will give a musicale, which is more clannishly attended than the artistic treat warrants.

And whenever Neptune and Mars meet and kowtow,
as they are always doing here, the gunners may be asleep
and the muzzles may be capped, but the Tommies who
"blow their lives out in China" in more ways than this
particular one, must ever be on hand with cornet and
trombone to make admiral and general extra-congratu-
latory. The philosophizing Chinese tax-payer, who
comes down from Canton on these occasions, again
shakes hands with himself, and explains that he instituted the custom of skimping on public works and being
lavish in imposing taxes for ceremonies' sake. None
of the treaty ports equals Hong-Kong in musical luxuries. Manila has one famous Filipino band and Sir
Robert Bredon at Peking has a Chinese band, both trained
by occidental masters.

It is an English colony, this island which dropped
as a first fruit from the folds of the flag of the Opium
War, but Englishmen rule by suggestion more than
compulsion. They endow, of course, but they have
elasticity of judgment enough to adopt, and this is why
they are successful colonial rulers. The water front
they have called a Praya, from the custom at famous
old Portuguese Macao, forty miles away. A walk here
(and every one walks on the street instead of the sidewalk) is a kaleidoscope of dress and a College of
Languages. Here are good Scotch names like Mathie-
son; Japanese like Mitsui; German like Melchers; Portuguese like De Mello; Netherlands like Stoomvaart
Maatschappij; Parsees like Cawasjee Moosa; and Indian like Matab. A European has just got out of
a Sedan chair, which, as rain is threatening, has the cur-
tains down. They are dyed in the familiar *yin-chi,* or
Chinese red. The Hok-Lo bearers are ringing the coin

on the pavement to see if it is good and if a slight tip
is not given them they proceed to berate the unsuspecting
passenger in their twangy dialect. As the coolies walk
off, be sure to notice if the right leg of the trousers is
rolled up and the left down. It is a frequent sign of
membership in an anti-dynastic society, such as the Triad.
Their trousers are of hard Nanking cloth, which has been
dyed black with gambier. Here are Koreans with tiny
black bamboo-fiber hats, perched on their rolled up hair.
Their baggy white trousers flutter in the wind; their
Eton-like tunics are tight. A Taoist priest comes along,
wearing his hair on the top of his head and not down his
back, as most Chinese do. An Episcopal bishop passes
in regalia which concedes something to the East, while
he remains reminiscent also of the Occident; a sun-topy
crowning a black morning coat, knickerbockers, silk
stockings and pumps. His Catholic confrère, who is a
Portuguese by blood, wears the familiar long black gown
of his ilk and a cross, but notice his sun-helmet and that
his beads are of native jade. Belgian monks, who would
crucify the flesh, stick to black Friar hats which focus the
actinic, merciless rays of the sun upon their devoted but
dizzy heads. That gaunt gentleman under a gray Fe-
dora is the best shot in the colony. He has just beaten
the governor at the traps of the Royal Gun Club in the
Wanchai gulley. He is known as a " manufacturer's
agent," but darkly it is said that his real business is the
smuggling of arms into China. Anyway, as he is only
a *cooee* (Australian) he is given the cold shoulder
at the English club on the Praya. When he and a stocky
Canadian there get mad about it, they chum and rub
" Paardeburg " into those whom they call in the hour
of their wrath " snobs," " Pharisees " and " Little

Englanders." The Frenchman who overhears it all
says:

> " Mais en guerre,
> " De meme que freres!"

As your 'rickisha rolls toward the Polo Ground at
Causeway Bay, Chinese boys turn pin-wheel somersaults
and pipe forth a petition for "cumshaw." One of the
four carriages of the Colony passes along, drawn by tiny
Chinese ponies. It contains the powdered and carmined
wives of a native banker of Bonham Strand. There
comes a Dom from India, his tall, thin limbs swathed
tightly in a white chadar, which answers for garment
by day and bed-sheet by night, and his head (all but the
black buffalo eyes) is hid beneath a tremendous red turban. With eyes averted from the Dom a couple pass,
Jyotishi Essabhoy — a silk merchant once of Calcutta —
and his wife, who wears a wonderful one-piece silk sari,
which is caught at the waist and half-looped around the
body. The other half is thrown over the head and
shoulders. She was born in Ceylon, where all the
women learn the carriage of a Venus of Milo from the
habit of bearing water jars on their heads. Soft is her
walk and voice, which latter purrs along with the subdued
answers of her lord, whose race has never learned the
confident manners of those who are used to ruling others.
Following, is an Indian officer of the Baluchis, whose
march is as stately as a column from the Taj Mahal.
You can tell that that other tall, independent-looking figure, swathed in white from turban to turned-up shoe, is a
Mahratta from Bombay, for if he were a Hindoo from
Benares his dhotee cloth would be gay in color. Shorter
than either, comes another, his hair dressed with tortoise

shell combs. He hails from Ceylon and wears a comboy-
skirt of checked cloth, and by trade is a vender of ame-
thysts and precious stones. Truth with him is a pearl
of great price, and he therefore indulges in the cheaper
imitations when he deals with the inexperienced. A Bur-
man, tattooed and looking afraid, steps by in ladies'
shoes and putsoe skirt, but he has a man's voice, which
disillusionizes you. There, too, goes Chang, the coolie,
with his string of goats, which he milks at the doors of
his customers. On the wet stone steps in front of the
Fish Market, labors with the pitch baskets one who has
been a pirate on the *Si Kiang,* and who dipped his hands
in white man's blood when the *Sainam* was attacked.
He will gather water-front news for a season, unless the
lukong of the law meanwhile recognizes and gathers him.
Japanese courtezans from Ship Street, dressed in their
blue-figured kasuri cloth, shuffle by on wooden shoes.
The Chinese *fokis* greet them with Abderian laughter,
screaming "pig" after them, and the Japanese sailors
are ready enough to fight with knives on the pretext of a
harlot for the honor of a flag. A Hebrew, who worships at "Othel and Leah," on Robinson Road, drifts by
on the wind behind the only cloud of whiskers east of
Calcutta. He is one of the daring few who wears a
derby hat instead of a topy. A chimney-hatted Parsee,
looking very confidential in black, and sporting a pink
ruby of faultless water, passes with his secrets of what
fine English young gentleman (all too forgetful that in
this blistering climate a European can be imprisoned for
debt) owes him money, and his nervous fingerings and
whisperings are doubtless a part of the process of mental
arithmetic. The Parsee has progressed in the far East
since the days when he sat on a cotton cloth on the floor

and ate his food from a plantain leaf or a piece of Benares brass.

The mansions of Belilios on MacDonald Road and
those of Mody and Chater are the show houses of
Hong-Kong and the Colony has no citizens who equal
their generosity, a pretty touch of personal sentiment for
the king who has noticed them, warming their public
acts. They are few in numbers, these Zoroastrians, but
an unusual fire burns in their minds and hearts, as well
as in their worship. A people of no country, it is moving indeed to hear them sound with a sonorous earnest-
ness and sweetness the words " our home," when referring to whatever land in which they have cast their lot.
A people of no God, in whatever alien scene, at even they
climb the hills to follow with worshipping eyes and resigned mien the fast dropping orb of the sun, which now
is life-giver and anon their destroyer in the hour of death.

It is against the law to traffic in lottery tickets, but that
oily Fong, whom you see slipping in and out of European
hongs, has a choice assortment of crisp green tickets of
the Han-kau, Macao and Formosa lotteries, and for a few
extra cash he will also sell you the lucky tip on the drawing, which divination he procured for a consideration
from a top-knotted Taoist priest. Tall Sikhs, wearing
the red of the king, march by as straight as fir-poles,
while a stocky little Welsh ".Tommy" remarks: " 'Is
long pipe-ligs might beat hus hup the first 'ill, but 'ead be
flat-blowed in the second valley, when we'd be strong
going the third 'ill; it ain't ligs, it's wind."

With a privileged swing of the free arm, a stamp of
the off foot, and a cry, " Look out for your heels," red-
liveried coolies bluster by. Everybody looks; it is the
British governor of Hong-Kong being borne in the red

Queen's Road Central, Hong Kong, South China, showing side-walks under second stories of buildings so as to afford protection from the sun.

Looking from mountain road down the slopes of Hong Kong upon
mountain-encircled harbor and British settlement of Kowloon,
on the mainland of China. British and German cruisers
and torpedo boats in offing. Union and Christ
Episcopal churches and British Governor's
residence in left foreground.

Hong Kong, Western section, built on the slopes of Mounts Victoria
and Davis. British cruiser "Talbot" inshore. This vessel
saved from drowning the crews of the Russian war-
ships "Variag" and "Korietz," sunk by the
Japanese at Chemulpo in 1904.

chair of a mandarin. Remember that the natives themselves do not use the word " mandarin " (which is Portuguese), but " Kwun." Red of a brighter shade is used
only for Hwa Kiao or bridal chairs. I saw a crowd running to Blake Pier to see the only citron-yellow sedan
chair in town; it was for the late emperor's brother,
Prince Chun, now regent, who was on his way to Germany to apologize for the murder of the German ambassador. Every foreigner whose salary is above seventy-
five dollars gold a month retains a passenger chair, which
is carried by two or four coolies, who are uniformed as
conspicuously as purse will allow. Cæsar in an effort to
extirpate effeminateness among the patricians, prohibited
the use of litters, but the excuse eloquent Hong-Kong
could offer is that it is more hilly than Rome.

During a royal procession the Chinese guard, which
patrols the line of march, turns volte face, for it would
be intrusive for a soldier to look upon the royal chair.
Only members of the royal family may use yellow sedan
chairs. How quickly the Chinese Club of Hong-Kong
got the ochre pot to work, when they heard a royal prince
was coming! Only royalty may have borne before it the
flag with the five-clawed dragon; the people must use a
four-clawed emblem. A yellow Lo, or state umbrella, is
carried before the procession. You will notice that the
Chinese gentlemen and their clerks are vigorously fan-
ning themselves, and the fan is more used by men that
women. A Chinese not only fans his face, but opens his
long silk tunic and fans his body, or bends his neck to fan
his back. The fan is carried in the back of the neck and
protrudes over the shoulder. These cheap paper fans are
made at Nanking, seventy thousand people deriving their
livelihood from the manufacture. The Hakka boat peo-

ple could never get on without fans, for their fires are made of charcoal in a pan, and when meals are being prepared the children stand by on the poop and vigorously work up a draft. But the oddest use is when a host orders his servant to fan a seat so as to cool it for the guest.

Where one's pores, in a most humid temperature of ninety-five, perforce do much of the work of the kidneys, it is highly important that washable white clothes should be worn. A few martyrs to convention deserve renown, however — the governor's secretary, who is doomed to a plug hat and Piccadilly frock-coat, and the aide-de-camp, in braid and pilot cloth.

The Chinese, especially in the West End, is in all the glory of his habitat, and is an unexpectedly dignified entertainer of the many voluble or alarmed looking Occidentals. He has his own splendid banks, like the Yuen Fung Yuen on Bonham Strand, and native hospitals, like the Chung Wah. He frequently loans to the British a countryman as *lukong,* who is forthwith dressed in that wonderful mixture of mushroom-shaped, white bamboo helmet; blue tunic; engineer's white leggings and native felt soles. Who is that peddler whirling a strident rattle around a bamboo stick, and carrying a chest of drawers? He is the embroidery vender. Every girl and woman decorates her own shoes and a visit of the peddler of silk floss and gold and silver thread is a daily necessity. A gloriously carved bright red chair, decorated with kingfishers' feathers, is borne along. It contains a bride and everybody laughs. The chair is kept for nothing else at the livery. China, beyond all lands, revels in colors. Native youths in long gowns of blue, buff and purple; Chinese women in tunics and trousers of yellow, red, black and gold; and Hindoo women in the flimsiest pink

silk from the bazaars of Calcutta and the downiest shawls
from Cabul, make a joyous scene on the wide Praya and
hill-side roads of the oddest tilted-up Colony in the world.
Occasionally a Eurasian, stouter than either European
or Chinese, and whose blood kinship neither boasts
of, with hair hanging loose, passes by, to the un-
heeded shame of the foreigner. It is an evidence of
the vast passive virtues of the Chinese that they
do not rise up and behead every foreigner in the
Colony as an offering of vengeance at the feet of
the unnamed.

To cool his prized Waler under a noble tamarind,
and a cynosure of all eyes because of the unusual sight of
a fine animal, an English officer of the Indian army mess
jumps from the saddle, all jingling with the parapher-
nalia of occidental war. He has removed his heavy topy-
helmet, which is filled with cool plantain leaves, and is
ornamented with a blue- and white-barred pugree. Perhaps (for he has lots of time) he philosophizes how signs
of subjugation soon become cherished customs. The
queue of the Chinese was first a badge of Manchu authority imposed upon the conquered; and the Indian pugree
was originally the yoke which the Mohammedan victor
placed upon his Hindoo subject. It is the only handsome
feature of the absolutely essential but hideous Indian helmet, now coming into universal use in southern China. I
have noticed that in Marseilles they are numerously worn
in the summer months, which is the result of the example
of France's returning Tonquinoise colonists, who use that
port altogether. Topies are beginning to be exhibited in
the show windows of Broadway hatters' shops in New
York City. As an additional protection against the sun's
rays, the British authorities compel their regiments, on

oriental duty, to wear a strip of flannel down the spinal
column. The Oriental's respect for his native sun is
strikingly illustrated in the statue of Dai Butz at Kama-
kura in Japan, where the head of the saint is covered with
brass snails, which in their art represent a cool protection
from the heat.

In Hong-Kong and the Orient, water is king. It
rules for happiness and safety during the short rainy season, which commences in May, when lavish cloud-bursts
fall, as they can do only in the tropics. It tyrannizes by
its stinginess during the dry season of nine months. Imagine the bases of a dozen conical untenanted hills, one
thousand eight hundred feet high, traced around with a
cemented trench. Every drop of water that falls on the
hill preserves is eagerly caught and led to the basins in
the valleys. But the consumption, and particularly the
waste, by three hundred thousand Chinese in Hong-Kong,
is immense. In the broiling summer, the valves are
opened only night and morning, and there is great privation and danger in a colony which is subject to the ravages of smallpox, typhoid and every other disease that
unflushed filth breeds,— not to mention the discomfort of
limited baths where the body sweats without ceasing.

The richer Europeans flock at five o'clock to the harbor,
and in launches seek out a spot where the sewage of Canton does not lie like false lilies on the wave, to enjoy the
refreshment of a dip and swim, returning at seven
o'clock, when the sudden sunset flames without heat
for a glorious half hour, before night, without a
twilight, falls suddenly black. The launches are
abundantly provisioned with tea, whisky, soda, col-
lation, and cigars, and if the native launchmen could
speak with the metaphors of our literature, they would

certainly call us a race of Clodii from all the appearances. The swimming parties leave the Queen's Statue pier for Shelter, Junk or Lighthouse Bays, except when rumors go through the Colony that a shark has been seen in the waters, and all the terrible tales of Hong-Kong becoming as dangerous as Sydney's harbor are told to the terrified griffin. The alarming visitor is only the Peh-ki, or great white porpoise, which has wandered a little from his fishing grounds on the Macao flats for a dash among the shipping and bays of Hong-Kong. Nevertheless for a week the stream of launches that nightly left the Matshed Pier at Victoria Statue will turn their noses toward Sham-Shui-Po Bay instead of Junk Bay. The rivalry of the launches on the long sail is thrilling; national, guild, district, social, and professional feeling all coming into the competition of ten knots speed. Junk Bay at low tide affords the grandest bathing. Not only is the scenery stupendous and the loneliness primeval and alien, but you can leave the cooler water of the bay for a hot fresh-water bath in a sand basin at the top of the beach, which has been heated by the tropical sun all day. Luxuries truly Pompeiian!

Wherever, among the unpreëmpted hills, there may be a spring, the thirsty Chinese place bamboo runnels and lead the trickling silver to the roadside, where patient coolies wait in line for hours to secure their own or their master's drinking water for the day. The bottling (really jarring) and shipping of potable waters is not unknown in China, which land, after all, is really the universal inventor. Near Sam Shui, on the West River, is the large Ting Wo monastery, which is built on the cliff's side. Above it is a waterfall, which the bonzes de-

clare is sacred and possesses healing powers. They ship
the water all over the country. If there is anything a
Buddhist priest loves as an adjunct to prayer, it is a little
of such a dignified and easily run business. The Taoist
priest is not so exacting that the business shall be
dignified.

Water is Tyrant! When he comes again, he falls in
unruly torrents, which sweep away the bounds of cement
and granite which have been placed for him; he drops
over cliffs, and you would not know the arid peaks in this
new land of thundering waterfalls that leap, echo and
roar in the narrow gulleys with the alien voice of terror
and destruction. Visible tongues of water appear from
out the awful mist, which darkens even a tropic day, and
rolls from valley to valley, disguising and anon revealing
every scene.

Droll enough to a stranger, but terribly important to
a resident, is the item in Hong-Kong's Government Bud-
get entitled *Rat Estimates,* where many thousand dollars are appropriated yearly to battle with the rodent.
Hong-Kong has nearly conquered the mosquito by ce-
menting, in the woods, every gulley and indentation that
is near a dwelling, but the rat of subterranean secrecy is
harder to reach, and it is the fad or fact in Bombay,
Tokio and Hong-Kong to find in him, and the elusive flea,
the transmitters of the virulent bubo bacillum. The first
sign of plague in Chinese villages is that of the rats leaving their haunts, leaping around mad and suddenly dropping dead in the streets. Then as surely as the pursuer
of Pharoah, comes the Destroyer. Some say all this care
is as futile as offering rewards for rabbits in Australia
or wolves in Russia; that the treacherous natives breed
the pests for the bounty. At all events, it is not uncom-

mon to see a wily-eyed coolie carrying a dozen live rats in a wire cage to offer to the sanitary board in the balconied yellow building which rises over the Parade Ground, and who, like every hunter, takes his reward in the silence that clothes the brave. Nor is rodent immigration permitted; every steamboat and foreign launch that ties up to the Praya has to submit to funnel-shaped tin guards being placed upon its lines, so that if Mr. Rat intends to come ashore, he must not do so furtively, but decently, as any first-class passenger, down the main gangway, where his credentials will be passed upon. But this is the only restriction at this free port, where everybody and everything comes sometimes, which is the unique characteristic of this truly entertaining port. The natives are much opposed to the dreaded white-uniformed Sanitary Corps, whose members break into the plague-infected houses with disinfection oven, sprayers, brooms and tubs. Lau Chu Pak, in a memorial to the government, calls the corps " those Rat Kings, because of their arrogance in dashing in and out with what they have destroyed, while the owners, in convict-like garments provided by the board, watch with sad faces the touching, and for them, impoverishing scene." So a beneficent and ' wise government, even at the ends of the earth, has its caustic critics.

Another abhorred feature of government is the lime-washing, which effectually destroys the micro-organisms of plague, enteric and cholera, which may settle upon the walls. If an outbuilding is suspected of harboring disease it is sprayed white by the Sanitary Corps, which custom adds not a little to the picturesqueness of the Chinese villages which lie beneath the banyan and tamarind trees, and on the terraces of the black disintegrating granite

hills, and green slopes.   Such a requirement could not be
followed inland in China proper, because the natives fear
spraying with white, which is their color of death.

Government also pounces hard upon the flour shops,
where *fokis* are re-bagging cheap flour in bags of superior brand, and many a war waves to and fro in the
courts as to whether the Three Combed Cock was in the
Red Bamboo bag.

In the " chit " system, the Colony rebels at the suggestion that it is not walled off from all the world.   It
takes three months to establish your identity.   Thereafter all your purchases are signed for by I. O. U.'s, or
" chits," which are torn out of the merchant's stub book.
No one carries the money of the British or Chinese
realms, which happens to be Mexican silver,— it is too
heavy.   Even at the hotel bars, you do not pay for your
liquor when it is drawn for you, for obliging Sam Lin,
whose legend is that " Heaven's smile, like his own, is
wide," hands you an account-book in which you are asked
to make your own entry.   On the irregularity of the
writing, when the chit is presented, hangs many a tale.
Once a month, the various merchants bring these signed
chits to your hong comprador or cashier, who de-
ducts them from your wages or account, and the balance
is brought to you, together with the canceled chits.   Thus
every firm's cashier acts as the private banker of the employee.   No interest is allowed or charged, but if it were,
the credit would be on the side of the patient, kindly Chinese.   These compradors are of course heavily bonded
to the firms or companies.   They act in a sense as the foreign firm's Chinese member, and handle all the diplomatic
dealings with the natives.   Their association or club is
one of the most important sureties of business stability in

each Colony or treaty port. The word "hong" literally is a row, and was first applied in the old days of intercourse with Europe, to the dreary line of windows in the foreign warehouses at Whompoa, near Canton. It is now used to cover a firm, as well as its building. The word "Taipan," used for the chief of an office, comes from "Tai-poa," a village headman, or non-commissioned mandarin.

The premier event of the year, so far as Europeans in the Orient are concerned, is the ball on St. Andrew's Eve, which would make it appear that the merchant princes of the East are Scotch. St. George's Hall is hired,— it is half of the artistic City Hall. Lanterns are hung around the stone verandas. The tramway to the Peak announces that there will be a two A. M. car, and special cars at a heavy premium all night. The three silk hats of the mildewed Colony are sought for and brought forth out of a maze of fungi. Everybody else, who hasn't a tartan, goes in full dress, but wears a steamer cloth cap. The admiral furnishes a string band from his battleship. The British "General Commanding in China" furnishes brass pieces, and the Indian Baluchis send over their pipers from Kowloon, for they have been practising Strathspeys, Caledonians and Eightsomes for half a year in preparation for this event. The cellar is turned into a free wine-room; the theater is turned into a supper-room, and haggis struts upon the stage. A company in a corner of the room are two-stepping to the music of the Eightsomes, and a fluttering comment goes through the hall: "There romp the Americans!" Ladies are contested for in a manner which ruins Chinese good opinion; there are a dozen tartans and a half dozen uniforms and dress-suits fighting for the card of Miss Anaemia, and divided dances prevail. The officers of the society don their kilts and wear a sprig of heather received in the last mail from home by " P. and O." steamer. Here is the brilliant scarlet of the Stuarts, and the greens and blues of the Gordons and Murrays. 'Rickishas and sedans camp in blocks and in the aisles between, the coolies crowd and express undisciplined delight to see Europe in finery pass by to the gala scene, and they jeer all they dare at the exposed shoulders of the women. The hot, moist air holds the perfumes.

For a week previous, practise dances have been held at five o'clock, so the sets are all ready for rivalry and triumph. There is a dais and the " Distinguished Patronage " will mount it, though the merchant princes are somewhat sarcastic that the governor has the interests of the Chinese more at heart than those of the British merchants, but this has always been the keen question of foreign colonies, from Syracuse to the Congo, Macao and Hong-Kong. The navy looks the manliest and has the nonchalance which is popular, but it carries no women. So the army rules the ball, for the officers of the garrison are paid extra allowance for " keep " of families when on foreign service. A German admiral, a French one, and an Italian man-of-war captain come and bring their staffs. It is worth leaving Saigon with its transplanted opera, to attend the great ball of Hong-Kong. It is hot between dances, and you lean over the balustrade of the veranda. There's an oriental fragrance rising from the smoking joss-sticks which the coolies below have lit to drive the mosquitoes away. A lazy and nearly naked fellow is lying asleep in *your* sedan chair. You vow that if you are sober when you get in it, you won't lie back and take your ease as you used to. Down the hill at the water's edge a dozen launches are puffing at the pier, waiting to return the officers to their ships. Laughter is growing louder in the cellar, and everybody's wife is left to her circle of a dozen men friends of her husband. She is in good hands, and he seeks relief with a hundred like himself in the cellar, where a hasty but gushing bar has been installed. The punch counters, however, are erected on the ball-room floor. These colonial women drink less during evenings than mornings; the men seldom drink during mornings, but the evenings are very moist. There is perhaps a famous " Forlorn Hope," called the " Ten A. M. Cocktail Club," which wends its way across the blistering white Praya to the Hong-Kong Club, but that belongs to the business day, and has nothing to do with this ball. There is something about the moist, dreamy tropic night which bids you stay; the flowers and ferns give out a heavy perfume, which the tropic sun would burn up. These are the hours the festive Colony loves, for it can then forget for a while the fear of who will be the next to fall a victim of sun, plague, cholera, typhus, malaria, or death-giving Bal-Tse fly. The day after St. Andrew's rises upon a deserted Colony so far as Europeans are concerned. They awaken to philosophize that the abstemious virtues of the Saint and not his popularity were meant to be followed, and the Chinese overrun the Colony with an expansive smile and similar quotations from native wits who acquired this sort of wisdom before Noah.

Hong-Kong is a dozen higher and grander Gibraltars clustered together. The fortifying of, and the road-building to the strategic heights are rapidly and secretly progressing. Tunnels are being bored, and the rocks still unmasked by fir-trees, both on the island and China

mainland, facing Junk Bay and the wide Pacific, are
beginning to bristle with guns. Garrison life at these
outposts is unusually melancholy; society is impossible,
as the fortifications are eight miles by water from the
city, and communication over the mountains is arduous.
It is not a question of which is the better of the two, but
which is the worse, to be of the British Garrison Artillery
or the Chinese Lighthouse Services.

Here and there are introduced interesting touches of
the conservatism of the old country, for instance, the
Ciceronian motto: " *Esse quam videri*," over the door
of a steamboat office. The boats are Scotch-built, and
indeed " better than they seem," though the appearance
is surprising enough in this outlandish country, where
no such luxurious accommodations for travel are expected
on the heathen waters, which wind between the idol's
hills.

The siesta system has not taken hold of busy Hong-
Kong in the manner that it has at Bangkok and Saigon.
At Bangkok, offices are shut from twelve noon till two-
thirty P. M., and the only things at work in the street are
the rasping vultures, which have swooped down on some
unfortunate buffalo, which has fallen in the white road.
At beautiful Saigon, the work of the Europeans begins
at seven-thirty A. M., and continues till ten o'clock; then
every one repairs home in his *pousse-pousse* (jinrickisha), has a bath, a light meal, and a sleep during the
intense heat of five hours, when even the glorious perfume of the ylang-ylang trees becomes a stifling misery
of cloying sweetness, all too suggestive of the flowers of
death. From three P. M. to five P. M. the offices are
again opened. At five P. M. every one (the majority
being officers of the Infanterie Coloniale), with all the

exotic accoutrement of the joyous *boulevardiers* of Paris, goes driving in miniature victorias or *mababars,* behind tiny black Tonquinoise stallions of marvelous vigor, along the red roads, and God help your eyes if it was noon, for the glare is worse than the flame of Japanese trenches. How sane the French abroad are in matters of comfort! No one in Saigon ever dresses in anything but white, whether for opera, promenade, business or social tea. But at British Hong-Kong, the black broadcloth dress-suit is donned every night for dinner, in a climate which is nearly as hot as that of Saigon's; the hours of work are continuous, and this British Colony therefore takes vitality out of its citizens more than any port of the Orient. Its line of invalids and derelicts who have fallen back for repairs, is a long one, and not all of them reach Glasgow, or even Chifu, Yokohama or Colombo, before the chill ghost-order " Halt " is all too willingly obeyed for ever.

A word in passing on Hong-Kong's architecture, which is the grandest in the far East. Not one coign of vantage has been missed. The whole city is tilted up from the water's edge at an angle of twenty-three degrees under the triple guardian peaks of Wanchai, Victoria and High West, which soar one thousand feet higher than the highest street. The building material is generally brick, double-walled for coolness and also for strength against typhoons; covered with plaster of local manufacture, called *chunam,* and faced with granite which is cut by hand in the Kowloon quarries across the bay. At regular distances apart stand four magnificent Renaissance piles on the water's edge: the Hong-Kong Club; Queens, Alexandra, and Connaught Road Chambers. Swinging round to the right and left of the official city of Victoria

for nine miles, and rising eighteen hundred feet in terraces, and deep into Wanchai, Victoria and Glenealy Gulleys, creeps and spreads the imposing panorama, all the
more striking because you did not expect it at the world's
end. No factory chimneys soil the view; they are hidden
around the curves at the extreme ends. There is a rich,
canopied Corinthian monument to one whom the Chinese
call the "Black Queen of the White British," Victoria
in bronze, and a Clock Tower in Spanish style. For fifteen
hundred feet upward, trees wave everywhere, and if you
desire complete details of the buildings, you must climb
to them. Above that height the peaks are bald, and take
every color in the changing light. In the delicious early
morning they are blue; growing to gray, and in the stillness of the hot noon their climax is as white and insuf-
ferable as the sun itself. Then they change to gray,
green, purple and gold again, as the sun dies quickly at
their crests, from whence you will first view two of the
glittering stars of the Southern Cross. The diamond on
the breast of all this pomp is the Catholic Cathedral on
Caine Road, twelve hundred feet above the water. It is
Gothic, with a Spanish effect in the squat tower. Conspicuous are the great flying buttresses, and very beautiful
is the stone canopy over the entrance to the Nave. All
this stone carving was done by Christian Chinese; at least
they said they were on pay days. Christ Episcopal Cathedral on Battery Path is a West Indian or Colonial adaptation of Gothic. The stucco has turned yellow and blue
with time and damp, and there is no place in the island
where that fern and tuberose smell of the tropics is so
prominent, as here under the tower of Christ's. Mt. Austin Barracks frown down fifteen hundred feet of cliff;
across Victoria Gulley, which is five hundred feet deep,

the admiral's residence holds a similarly lofty perch, while beyond Wanchai and Wong Nei Chong Hills, scores of peaks serrate the unnamed and uninhabited sky-line of this grand, grim island, which holds in leash the three heathen seas for England. There are other things placed fifteen hundred feet high, which could announce themselves with devastating thunder, but there is not a suspicion of them in the view. They are the masked forts which command the unfortunately many landing beaches on the south, and the Green Island and Lyee-moon Passes to the inner harbor, from the West and East respectively.

The new courts on Des Voeux Road, and the Naval, Civil and Tung Wah Hospitals on Kennedy, Barker and Robinson Roads, are as impressive as anything of the kind in Europe. Whole rows of buildings of hand-cut granite line Queen's Road Central. The domed Corinthian pile of the Hong-Kong and Shanghai Bank, with L'Opera at Saigon, are the two finest buildings in European design, in the Orient. Against the granite grandeur of the double pillars of the former, are set double rows of royal palms, and across the way is a glorious unbroken bank of ferns, forty feet high, crested with centenarian banyans. The City Hall, containing the Royal Theater, is a worthy nucleus of the ambitious civic architecture. The sidewalks are unique in that they run under the protruding second stories of the buildings. The effect is not as threatening as the overhanging Elizabethan buildings of Eastgate Street, Chester, or the umbrella buildings of old Rouen, as the second story of the Hong-Kong buildings is supported with pillars which are anchored to the street curb. The use of stucco permits of adding to line the joys of color. There are many yellow, blue and buff buildings which close the eucalyptus, tamarind or palm glades with a wall of color which is delightfully oriental.

Government barracks, severely plain and warlike, are set in extensive stone-paved courts, so that the collection of stagnant waters under windows shall be impossible in this habitat of malaria. The buildings all provide veranda space by the use of double walls. Behind a characteristic fence, half iron and half stone, which you associate with British barracks whether at Halifax, Bermudas, Malta, or Hong-Kong, is a cemetery in miniature, " for pets of the garrison." As the Colony has only one street or praya on the water level, there is an endless necessity for stone bridges and revetment walls. The opportunity is taken advantage of in a manner not surpassed along the Riviera, and the happy Chinese has loaned to the Saxon strength of wall, his ideas regarding the inlaying of tile fretwork and coping of colored porcelain. The Hindoos have raised a beautiful white and canary-yellow temple and the Musselmen have erected a characteristic mosque and minaret.

Sumptuous and commodious homes, all of an Italian sameness, and every brick, stone, tile, and beam of which has been laboriously borne up the mountains by coolies, are planted on the ledges about Wanchai, Victoria and Glenealy Gaps. Some day the gaps between the remaining twenty peaks of the island will also be tenanted. Most picturesque are the zigzag paths, which certify that the chair with four bearers is an indispensable adjunct of hill residence. Over Victoria Peak, facing the south, is perched the Hill Château, or so-called summer residence of the governor, in a land which is all summer. In design it reminds you somewhat of Chaumont; a truly ducal dwelling, but, oh, so melancholy when friends shall have gone down the lonely path homeward, and only the wide, purple, heathen Pacific, with its unreal calm, unflecked by a sail, in view in the morning. The home of the Royal Hong-Kong Golf Club, whose Augustan motto is *Festina lente* (Make haste slowly), is a worthy example in miniature of the genius of a talented local architect, Turner, who perpetuates that grand old-fashioned art spirit of refusing any contract, however lucrative, if the work must be ugly, a spirit which would foam with civic rage to behold that chimney-building of architectural brutality lately erected opposite Trinity Church, New York. The vast Belilios Mansion, with its many domes, reminds one of Byzantine Constantinople. In his old home on Victoria Peak, this Parsee gentleman built an aery outlook where the view sweeps over a thousand heathen hills, with many bays between, while the immediate seat delights with familiar Grecian lines. Surprisingly only one house in the city, that, too, owned by a Parsee, uses lace-like iron grilles in place of windows, in the delightful hacienda fashion of Havana and the hot towns of the Caribbean. Truly this Hong-Kong builds with a taste and confidence, which have made her architecturally the boast and crown of the whole Orient. Britain has never colonized anywhere and in her style of building given any intimation that she ever meant to recede.

Not only the houses are handsome, but the walls and gardens beneath your feet appeal to you along Glenealy and Peak Roads, which are so steep that the attraction is physical as well as odorous. All this is Saxon. A word for the Chinese type. On the Kowloon side of the water, in the bay where Admiral Keppell practically won Hong-Kong from the herded junks, is the delightful

old joss house, double-roofed, with blind walls. Study
its proportions, its ridge, curling eaves, and the use of
color on the outside frieze. Then, most beautiful of all
is the Joss House at Causeway Bay; such feathery mullions in the dainty windows which relieve the heavy
wall; such lavish color; — the arches, the squat pillars beneath the circular balcony, the tiny door ap-
propriately narrow to let only the secrets of the soul slip
out to Heaven, and, of course, the opalescent tiled roof,
which is made the most conspicuous and beautiful part
of the building in Chinese architecture, while we degrade
it. The natives declare that we Occidentals are sinners
to expose what is ugliest to the view of Heaven (Tien)
and keep all the beauty of walls to our little selves, as
though we had no hills where we might climb and see our
faults therefrom. The native coolie has his own names
for the streets: Victoria Statue Square is " Black Empress
Place "; Queen's Road Central is "Typan's Chow House "
or " No. 1 Jade House," because the Chinese Club and
the best native jeweler (Wing Cheong) are located
there; Caine Road, where the Catholic Cathedral is situated, is " Foreign Devil Joss House."

Imagine the entertainment to interject in this modern
city a characteristic procession of the Orientals, such as
that of the dragon lanterns on the evening of the first full
moon. The mythical dragon, called a " lung," combines
the powers, virtues and characteristics of the popular
animals; its belly is soft as a frog's; it has scales like
a carp's, claws like a five-toed hawk; a palm of a tiger;
neck like a snake's; eyes of a rabbit; brow of a camel;
horns of a deer, and ears of a water-buffalo. The purpose of the procession, to a degree, is one of exorcism.
Hundreds of silk lanterns, sized over with a seaweed

Palatial double-walled residence of foreigners on Victoria and Kellett
peaks, 1600 feet above Hong Kong, South China.
Famous Peak Hotel in left background.

Mountain-chair, four bearers, used on peak roads of Hong Kong
Island, South China.

Lovely Shameen Island, where foreigners live, opposite native city
of Canton, Pearl River, South China.

glue, are tied to a long painted back; a wonderfully realistic lantern head and tail are attached, and poles like the feet of a centipede hold up the national monster. The crowd catches these, and the glittering, swaying, writhing animal is borne through the city to the accompaniment of drums, tom-toms and fire-crackers, for if evil spirits hate anything in China as elsewhere, it is public attention being called to their presence. From the Yamen's eaves, in the native cities of the mainland, you will behold the flaming beast slowly gliding around the corners, and a Milky Way of lanterns following to the foot of Pagoda Hill.

On the ninth day of the ninth moon (our fall) the newly arrived European in Hong-Kong is amazed to see thousands of Chinese, gowned in their finery, climbing the exhausting road to the Peak, and jamming the little cable car which is hauled up fifteen hundred of the eighteen hundred feet. If the silks and women were absent it would certainly appear to be an attack deploying on the governor's summer palace, Lawn Tennis Court and the Signal Station. The same ascent is being made by the villagers up every one of those tremendous *feng-shui*, or nature-dominating peaks of the mainland, and broiling work it must be with only the grass-cutters' paths and no shade, for the Chinese long ago cut the trees from all their magnificent peaks. Throughout China this religious ceremony, called locally " Chung Yong " (Ascending on High), is being observed. It is identical to what our idea of the ascent of Ararat by the Hebrews would be, if they desired to commemorate Noah's salvation from the flood. The fête is one of the most beautiful in sentiment, and certainly the most picturesque of the many observed by the Chinese. Joss paper is of course burned, and tossed to the winds, and the boys bring their kites and assail the heavens. It is one of the few occasions when the betrothed among the young people have an opportunity to see one another, and we have very wilfully misunderstood the Chinese on this subject. The same festival is observed by the Cantonese, who leave the city for the White Cloud Hills, where the highest peak is ascended in honor of Cheng Sin, or Fairy Cheng, who has bestowed good luck and safety, historically perhaps as far back as Noah. In all these pilgrimages the Buddhist monks throw their monasteries open as hotels.

When the European stranger takes his first walk on the noble roads of Hong-Kong, one of the things immediately to impress him that he is despite the architecture in a land foreign to his own, is to see the Chinese urchins standing under the banyan trees, with their long bamboo poles, which they carefully work between the branches. The boys are snaring cicadas with a glue which is made of fir ashes and rice paste. This ear-splitting harpist of the sultry day is a stubby insect with no beak and a body as large as that of a mouse. The native children fetter them with strings, and tie straws around their abdomens to irritate the insects to make a constant strumming. They also tie them up tight in foreign newspapers, and exult as the insect, with powerful wings and jaws, bursts its way through.

Whenever the foreigner is melancholy in his exile; when his harp has been hung on the willows or tamarinds for ennui, he may essay relief by taking a walk up Wyndham Hill Road. It is popularly known as Flower Street, for the road is banked solid with the baskets of the native gardeners. In contretemps, the turreted jail, where incarcerated Europeans (unless they soon die in tropical confinement) are forced to make cocoanut coir mats, frowns down from the top of the street. In the damp heat one almost swoons from the perfumes. Branches of fruit trees are sold for their spangles of plum, peach or cherry bloom. There are baskets of yellow and white narcissus in February; the peony, which is the royal flower of China; tuberoses stuck into hollowed-out bamboos; fragrant magnolias, camellias, and calla lilies, which are waxy enough to attract the appetite. All this of white bloom. In July there is the sacred purple lotus, as big as a hat, and in fall, golden and pink chrysanthemums and red and yellow dahlias larger and finer than we ever see at home. Twenty cents will buy what we at home are able to purchase for twenty dollars. The scene is not like that in gentle Honolulu, where the Kanaka women sit behind the baskets and patiently wait for you to choose. This is decidedly a masculine, and it is going to be a strenuous land. The brown and nearly naked flower-sellers raise their guild cries, and charge you with a pannier. You have to buy to escape. Go to their gardens and they will show you wistarias which their great-grandfathers tended one hundred years ago.

Hong-Kong is a world-famous city of the Unroofed, twenty thousand coolies having no place on which to lay their heads each night, and even if they wished to pay for a bed, the Colony has not been able to provide Crown sites enough on the rocky terraces for buildings. On D'Aguilar, Wyndham, Wanchai, Caine, Connaught, and a dozen other roads, when the last chairs of the white gentlemen-taipans are being borne by to their handsome residences on the Peak, the first of the great class of the Unroofed follow along slowly to find a spot of the stone sidewalk in recess, or a pillar supporting the overhanging second story, where to prop themselves, or to lie down, for sleep. With a sigh, they drop to the pavement and contentedly say: "Two meals a day, brother, but one sleep at night, eh?" On their backs, with knees up, and hands under their heads for a pillow, they lie at Wanchai. Against the precious teak logs which are destined to undersheath American battleships; against the sugar barrels at Taikoo; the rope coils at Yaumati; and the gunny bales at West Point, you can discover them in hundreds, with a bamboo near each one, but not for protection, because no man can rob the naked. They are the stevedores; the hewers of wood, drawers of water, and carriers of rice and jute; the men who, without the aid of steam, put all the brawn against the spokes of Progress when the new day opens. Against the blind wall of the jail on Mosque Street, they are propped,— optimists they, who say: "We are, after all, better off than those inside, for the worst work is less than the lightest shame." The Chinese *lukong* and the red-turbanned Sikh *chowkidar* mark the regular patrol of British law, and could belabor every stretched out, upturned foot, but they forbear, in that sanity which philosophizes that "they are torn enough already by honest toil." Fellow sympathy dims the eye of duty, and the steps of authority die away as soft music upon the ears of the most weary of mortals, whose workday is from dawn till dark for a pittance. In front of the new flour-mills at Junk Bay, where the heathen hills have first heard the hum of modern machinery, the dismantled sailing ship, *Maple Leaf,* has been moored and her main deck has been roofed. On the 'tween and main decks hundreds of hammocks have been slung, and here the native mill operatives find a shelter at least from the rains and night-dews.

An amusing feature of life among the Indian colonists in Hong-Kong is their propensity, when unemployed, to betake themselves to the Indian temple in Morrison Gap. Free food is passed at the services, even to white strangers. You are, however, emphatically commanded to take off your shoes. There are always twenty to thirty men loafing within the sacred precincts and a service is called every time hunger gnaws. All is well until rum is passed by some sacrilegious outsider, when war rains from the dim clouds of religion, and Matab Singh and his brother priests wear a worried look upon their generally reposeful features. At the commencement of the service the audience squats upon the floor. On a platform performers sit in the middle of Kyee-wains, dexterously swinging their sticks before and behind them on the metal cymbals. The music begins low, but increases to a tremendous noise, to which is added the clapping of hands, until the swaying worshippers are worked into the religious intoxication in which they delight. The foregoing applies to the Hindoo. The Mohammedans among the soldiers have built a mosque and minaret on the Chinese mainland at Kowloon, next to their vast parade ground. The call of the blue-turbanned muezzin, ringing through the hot oriental night, does not assure peace of mind to the exile on the occasion of his first sleep away from the home land, when the knowledge comes upon him that he is indeed stranded on a foreign shore, and that his ship is now steaming far away from the harbor, bearing onward the last few white-men friends he had made en voyage. Before long, however, he himself will be in the motley-colored throng, admiring the notable voices of the criers, and more contented with his interesting billet in the hypnotic East.

Last summer, an amusing incident stirred the *chow-kidars* or Sikh police of Hong-Kong. A comrade who had enlisted and grown comparatively wealthy in the Panama police service, on his return to Hong-Kong, was seen to drop a gold piece among his comrades' pennies in the alms box at the Mosque. Immediately, like a simoon across the Jetcha Doab of their home land, all the *chow-kidars* marched up Wyndham Street on strike, and vociferated that they must have their wages raised or they would emigrate to the American El Dorado, where the princely price of three dollars gold a day was paid to *chowkidars* of experience, ability to roll diphthongs and the letter "r," and to strike a salute which is as steady as if cast in bronze. The Sikh in India is as disciplined as clock-work, but in China he is a boiler of conceit without a safety valve. Opposite Hong-Kong, on the Yaumati side, the one hundred and nineteenth regiment of Baluchis was quartered. The Sikhs of the famous red-barred Hong-Kong Regiment, now disbanded, who were crazy to get at the Russians at Tientsin in the International march, were never willing to respect the Chinese, and the Baluchis have been equally undisciplined. It is, of course, partly their caste prejudice brought to this Mongolian land where there is no caste. These Baluchis at last disgusted everybody by casting all the honor and discipline of a king's soldier aside, and waylaying the Chinese on the roads and in their shops, and robbing them. It culminated in a great race riot on August 23rd, which was the first Hong-Kong had experienced in a decade. Swagger sticks and clubs were used by the soldiers and bamboos by the Chinese. The thick turbans of the Indians saved their heads, but many Chinese skulls were fractured. Amusing scenes were presented, a thin,

tall Indian grasping a Chinese by the pig-tail, while the
stout Chinese was reciprocating by the equally gross insult of unwinding the Indian's red turban.

On June 11th the fire-walking ceremony of Thee-
miri takes place in the walled court which is connected
with every Indian temple. Weird, sensuous and ghastly
by turns it is, altogether leaving the taste of ashes upon
the mouth. The priests secure some plump young girls
among the devotees, but most of the thirty or forty are
toothless crones and haggard men. For days a fair
is held. Sleek Kling priests offer you tickets which are
torn out of a book in true modern style. Holy chupah
food and sweetmeats are passed, especially during the
playing of music. Incense thickens the air, but does not
exclude the knowledge of fluttering silks, glances of dark
eyes and the clinking of jewelry increasing on every hand.
Wood fires are lit, for by and by the embers are to take
the chief place in the orgy. A pool is dug and filled
with imported sacred water which is poured from kongs.
The devotees begin by bowing, crawling in the dust, and
dragging themselves around the temple. Stirred by their
cries of fervor and pain, the excitement grows, until it is
an easy thing to precipitate the crowd into a frenzy.
Every dark eye leaps now with unmasked fire, and every
dark skin becomes pallid; the clear-cut consonants of
the speech are chiseled even harder by the gleaming teeth
which crown the matted beards. Occasionally there is a
laugh, not of ridicule, but of tension too hard to control.
As the crawlers grow exhausted in their self-imposed
penance of dragging themselves over obstacles, bearers
step forward and assist them. Word is passed that the
first who fell out had fasted ten days, and early exhaus-
tion is taken as a proof of piety. Saffron robes are now

donned by the remaining performers; more priests come forth and surround the gods. Swords are drawn and limes are cut at as the performers turn a double-somer-sault. A cocoanut is thrown on a brass salver, and a somer-saulter deftly cuts it in two and spills the libation of milk. The first of the exhausted devotees throws up his arms; they are lashed with thongs. Saffron dust is thrown upon those who endure, and they are considered as thus "cleansed of sin." The embers of the fire are now spread beyond the devotees, and the gods are carried across the pool. A white goat is brought before the idols and is beheaded. By this time the devotees are in a white heat. They are loosed by the priests; they rush over the coals barefooted; they sweep through the gushing blood of the animal, and dash into the pool, after which devotees and spectators dance around the idols, the whole cere-mony concluding by everybody taking the ashes in hand-fuls and casting them into the air and over themselves and everybody else. The Chinese Taoists of Fu-kien oc-casionally practise a fire-walking orgy.

If the foreigner is a sportsman who prefers less dan-gerous explosives than Scotch-and-soda, he has the no-blest game at his door, for tiger-shooting is possible not far from Canton and is abundant in the long fissures in the rocks at Amoy and Fu-chau. The natives hunt the animal fearlessly with antique weapons and home-made powder. The heart of the beast is eaten, as it is esteemed to be a courage-producer. The claws are sent to Hong-Kong to be mounted in twenty-carat gold and sold as charms. The skin, which is finer than the Indian ani-mal's, generally finds its way to Russia.

There is excellent snipe-shooting no farther away from Hong-Kong than Castle Peak and Deep Bays, along the beaches under the towering brow of old Tai Mo, the king mountain of all these peaks which roof you daily, 3640 feet above the water of the harbor. The favorite name for the dominant peak of whatsoever range is Tai Lik Shan (hill of great strength). Walk inland a little way along the raised mud path between the rice fields until you reach the clumps of banana and bamboo. There you will find surprisingly good shooting of wild pigeon, ortolans (rice birds), teal, wild goose, partridge, and noblest of all, the pheasant in his habitat. When our forefathers were using the catapult and crossbow, the Chinese were making powder on the following formula, and the peasants still use the fizzing stuff within spitting distance of the tiger's teeth: three catties (a catty is one and one-third pounds) of ground rattan charcoal, the expense of which can be understood, for it means so many baskets destroyed; three catties of saltpetre; ten of sulphur; all wet with kaoliang spirits, and stirred to a paste over a low charcoal fire, and afterward dried on paper in the sun. This powder of course dirties the gun barrels abominably, and before ignition has to be packed hard with the ramrod. In Yunnan (the honey land), tigers, leopards, wolves and even elephants afford the king sport of China and perhaps of the world. At Tientsin, trained eagles are used to hunt pheasants and hares.

The British have not interfered with the custom of purchasing servants, or technically, slaves. All the well-to-do native families of Hong-Kong buy at Canton girls of eight years of age from parents who have been reduced by poverty resulting from persecution or opium. Nor has the government with whole heart and open eye set itself against the works of the traffickers in the souls of native girls. The custom is only rife at the treaty ports, where the foreigner has taught the wealthy young Chinese to neglect the example of his fathers and the rules of his religion which prescribe an early marriage. The purchase price of an eight-year-old slave is fifty dollars; of a courtezan slave of eighteen years, three hundred dollars. A deed is given to the purchaser and the parents are prohibited from visiting their child. The idea is not similar to adopting a daughter, for in the latter case no deed is signed. Sometimes in extreme want due to famine, the impoverished one will engage his most precious possession — his son — to his creditor for a stipulated term of service, or a ransom, but papers must be signed whereby the creditor assures the safe-keeping of the child. These things shock us, but suffering has worn off the edge of shame in the minds of the Chinese poor. The act is deemed meritorious in the victim, who serves for his parent's debt. These contracts in the case of girls, run from the eighth to the eighteenth year, if there is a saving clause that the daughter is not to be sold into prostitution, and at the expiration, the parent may arrange a marriage. But if the clause is omitted, the child may be sold into shame by the first purchaser. A promise of a change seems to light the horizon. When Chow Fu was governor of the two Kwang Provinces of the south, he recommended to the throne that the sale of girls should be prohibited, and an Imperial Rescript was issued. The law is good enough; the point is, will it be enforced by China when the corrupt parents decide to succumb to the tinkle of the silver dollars offered by the depraved of a treaty port?

One of the sights of crowded Queen's Road East, Hong-Kong, is the itinerant street barber at work on the sidewalk, under the immense canvas signs of the tattoo-ers' shops. When a customer has hailed him, the barber simply drops his mirror-bucket and basket from his pole, and he is at once set up in business. He finishes the process by shaving the inside of his patron's ears and nostrils, and by giving the eyeball an interior massage, which latter fashion accounts for the prevalence of trachoma. A humorous customer, thinking he would reprimand a careless novice who was shaving the inside of his right ear, asked: " Are you at my *left* ear now?" " Why, no, I have only begun on the right ear; why did you ask?" "From the pain, I thought you were passing to the left ear without taking the trouble to go around."

Some of our occidental brokers are said to do business in their hats, but the Chinese cobbler does his in his basket. He sits on the road and hangs a few shoes on a tripod as a sign. The repairs consisting of pasting and sewing the felt, are done while Chan waits goose-fashion on one leg.

The wealthy Chinese of the treaty ports have taken joyfully to our electric (gasoline being prohibited in the tropical south) automobiles, music-boxes and phonographs, and if the last named plays piccolo or violin solos, it will hold a crowd of thousands of natives under the window. Hong-Kong boasts of two modern jewelry shops, one kept by a German, the other by a Scotchman, where the finest diamonds are on sale. The Chinese are developing a connoisseur's liking for them. Of course pearls have always been their prime favorites. Many of the Chinese curio stores still advertise: " Kruger sovereigns on sale." These dull gold coins were brought to the Colony by the transferred battalions of the Royal

Welsh Fusiliers and Derbyshire regiments immediately
after the South African war. The former regiment is
humorously remembered in Hong-Kong by the black tail
which hung from the collars of the tunics, as a relic of
the regiment's mourning when wigs were taken from the
troops. The Derbyshires, perpetuating the times and
territory of Robin Hood, where they are recruited,
sported a band of Lincoln Green on their forage caps.
Despite the fact that the new land furnishes them the
bread which the old land was unable to do, the Colonists
have not brought all their hearts with them, and find in
these little traits of the troops the reminiscences which
" drag at each remove a lengthening chain." Telephones are in use in about eighty European hongs. The
wires must be nearly worn out by the *fokis* and native
office boys talking to their friends. When office hours
are over, even the chair coolies come in to learn and enjoy the novelty, which they utilize at the top of their
high voices.

The newspapers of the treaty ports are generally set
up by Macaense Portuguese and edited by Scotchmen.
In Hong-Kong, a floating dot of the red Empire, some of
the finest leaders in our language are prepared, out of
pure pride in the profession, for the circulation of the
papers is not large, but the men are. Of course there is
no rush, as in New York or London, and possibly the
heat furnishes (though you would not expect it) hot-
house-growth to some of the finest English that is now
being written, something that it is a pleasure to compare
with the traditions of Addison's day. Hong-Kong is
not without its literary records and is boastful of those
pealing hymns of Christendom which Governor Sir John
Bowring wrote under these frowning heathen hills:

Watchman! Tell Us of the Night, and *In the Cross of Christ I Glory,* as well as his famous literary cameo on Macao: *Gem of the Orient Earth and Open Sea.* China proposes that her Chih Ming Pu (Board of Colonies and Censorship) shall pay better attention to the rapidly increasing number of *Paos* (native newspapers) which employ many Japanese in editorial positions, and whose bias often causes worry to the Manchu policy and dynasty. " *Wo sei lai liao* " (the Japs are coming)— says the Board.

What a striking change has for the time being, taken place upon the once embattled waters of Hong-Kong since the Anglo-Japanese Alliance and the Anglo-Frank *entente-cordiale!* Where once we daily looked through our blinds upon scores of battleships like the *Albion* and *Glory;* four-funneled flying cruisers such as the *Leviathan* and *Crecy;* and low, swift, narrow, telescope-funneled French cruisers of *valeur Superieure* like the old favorites *Montcalm* and *Gutchen,* now we see only a few river gunboats like the *Moorhen* of two-foot draft, so as to be able to skim the creeks which feed the Chukiang and feed the pirates from a four-inch nozzle. There is one startling and epochal exception,— when the Japanese, as they police all the eastern waters from Singapore to Hakodate, in the protection of their new lines of commerce, send down those low grayish-green gladiators of recent fame, the *Asama, Nisshin* and *Kasagi,* and their enrolled captives, the *Sagami, Tango* and *Iki,* whose high foreign lines show that they were once the *Peresviet, Poltava* and *Nicolai,* which vessels were raised from an average depth of sixty feet. America alone of the white nations has maintained battleships (at present two) in Chinese waters and the prospective increase to a much larger fleet will act as the best salesman for American goods. In the franchises granted by their Wai Wu Pu, the Chinese reflect the evidence that they are particularly impressed by these demonstrations of the white powers, and England and France in their anxiety to strengthen home waters politically, have in China lost to Japan certain ground commercially by this action.

In a Chinese cradle, under the mysterious yellow robe, really lies the commercial future of the Pacific States of America. Shall it be rocked by a faithful hand, made steadier because of the backing of a mighty fleet, or shall the nursling be tumbled out to be Ju-jitsued, Bear-throttled, or Stein-smashed? The fleet shall say.

The Chinese prophesy the political union of America, England, Canada and Australia, with America the spokesman of the union, because of their identity in Protestant religion, speech and literature, and that this union can alone save Australia to the white race from Japanese absorption.

At Hong-Kong, blue jays and magpies (the natives call the latter *hi tsoih,* jolly birds) are frequently seen. The magpies mischievously chase the golf balls along the Happy Valley course. During the rainy season, wagtails visit the waterfalls on Bowen Road, and when the dry season comes they retreat to the deep stream which runs from the Peak to Aberdeen at the back of the island. Of course the gorgeous Yuen Yang (mandarin ducks) are in their habitat, and at your comprador's home you will find specimens in his courtyard — not his back yard. In their heraldry surprisingly this bird of gorgeous plumage has to be satisfied with seventh place. Justice has however been done the golden pheasant, which though allowed second place, really holds premier position, as the fung-hwang is only a mythical phoenix.

The government's splendid botanical (they almost look like hanging) gardens, set upon terraces five hundred feet above the water deserve special mention. Tufted Norfolk pines of great height frame the view, and the scene over the islands and blue waters is unsurpassed. As one could expect, the palm section is as royal as Cleopatra's retreat reset. The tea-flavoring jasmines, dahlias, tuberoses, asters, kosmos, and azaleas give this land the right to be called the Eden of Flowers. The whole province of Kwangtung is a spangled meadow of violets. The climate is so damp that no glass is used upon the luxuriant fern house. Merely bamboo wands are nailed on the roof and sides, to afford a chequered shade. Heart of all the bloom, in the central fountain there is a glorious display of purple lotus (Eichhornia speciosa). Your Yalensian friend (a Chinese) hands you the candied root and bids you realize Cleopatra's dream. While you have been talking with him you can measure the growth of that most exquisite of all perfumed flowers, the Chinese sacred narcissus, and also the growth of the giant bamboo. Notable among the flowering trees are the purple Bougainvillea and the faithful Bauhinia, which latter offers you garlands when all else of nature sulks. The Hong-Kong gardens have not the magnificent Assam rubber trees, spice shrubs and other exuberant growths of the Peradeniya Gardens of Cingalese Kandy, or rows of such magnificent waringen trees as the Buitenzorg Gardens of Batavia, but they make more of what they have. For picturesque setting, there is nothing in the world to approach them.

Mouse deer, under government protection, are becom-

ing so numerous in the Stanley and Taitam Valleys of the
island, that they boldly come over the Wong Nei Chong
Gap, and jump the blue walls of the Parsee and European
cemeteries on the Happy Valley Road, and do great damage to trees and shrubs. Lamps have been tied to the
swinging branches of the trees, and the Chinese of the
Wash-house village near-by verily believe that our ghosts
are for ever unlaid, and it takes something steadier than
the Celtic temperament on our own part to investigate
the uncanny thing.

As clothes are never put on a line, but on the lawn in
China, the long, light bamboo pole can be used for dark
purposes. It is affirmed that at night, flags have flut-
tered over one's wall, and in the morning laundry has
been missed. So often has this occurred, that a native
who carries at twilight a pole with a nail in the end, is
arrested as a suspicious person, just as a *lukong* would
have a right to gather in on sight a Chinese whose queue
was greased. There is a custom in Hong-Kong of permitting coolies to sleep on one's doorstep and sidewalk,
and thieves are often entertained unawares within stalk-
ing distance of their snoring victim.

The delightful house-boat trips which the Shanghai
sojourner may enjoy on the Yangtze, or the Soochow
resident on the Grand Canal, where months may be spent
at the cost of one dollar a day for four rowers, are denied
to the resident of south China, for the romantic West
River and the hundred and one branches between the Chu
and Sikiang Rivers are poorly policed, and subject to
piratical attacks. Not since the rule of Li Hung Chang
have these devious waters of Kwangtung Province been
safe, and how often have we of the south sighed for a
rule such as the mandarins of Hupeh enforce on their

waters. However in moving about the districts or Shens of Kwangtung, the foreigner does not experience the insecurity which is felt in Fo-kien and Hunan Provinces, whose inhabitants are the harshest speaking, roughest mannered and most cruel of the Chinese. In Kwangtung we were terrorized in Shum's reign, and hope soon gave way to renewed despair when Chow Fu succeeded him. For a while the British gunboats patrolled the waters, but this worked Peking and the more advanced New China party into a turmoil, and then Britain withdrew. We used to take well-armed tugs and make the trips, but sleeping over the boilers in the tropical night, with its sheets of hot showers, is not comfortable. The house-boat has no permanent roof; only a bamboo support over which mats are thrown, whether for sun, rain, dew or moon. When we spoke of the superstitions of the Taoist priests, the Chinese would retort that our Jesuit missionaries always called for the mats when the moon was up. I found that this could be corroborated, even among the Missiones D'Etrangeres men in Somaliland and at Aden. Some of the boats are nicely carved and lacquered, but for your peace of mind they will be all the better for a simultaneous and reckless attack of buckets of water and soda.

The supply of milk for the white man's infants, who have only one-tenth of a chance for life, is a matter of great concern in the treaty ports of the Orient. At Hong-Kong, a small herd of acclimated American cows are kept on a comparatively cool plateau twelve hundred feet above the sea, in cement stalls, and grass-cutters are sent into every shady nook of the valley and behind every gravestone in the desperate search for green fodder, wiry as it is. The value of the cattle is enormous because of the frequent raids of the government to destroy such animals as have developed tuberculosis, murrain, anthrax, etc. The dairies of Spartan Hong-Kong, speaking generally, consist of a can opener and your selection of Swiss, Highland, Dutch, or American St. Charles labels, according to whichever steamer may be in port.

Where the eastern seas bubble up hot to the flame of an equatorial sun, Chinese workmen, with Scotch overseers, turn out six thousand ton steel ships and do battleship repairing worthy of Woolwich or Devonport. The dividend for 1907 was twelve per cent. after writing off for depreciation in the past twenty years the unnecessarily large amount of two million dollars. Hong-Kong possesses on the mainland at Kowloon and Sham Sui Po, five graving-docks of the Hong-Kong and Whompoa Dock Company, which concern sixty years ago moved from Whompoa Island, near Canton. One of these docks is cut six hundred and fifty feet into the face of a towering granite hill. With all the exertion of the baronial Mitsui family of Nagasaki, and the other private shipyard owners of Kobe and Yokohama, assisted by immense subsidies and national preference, Japan is still behind indefatigable Scotch Hong-Kong, in her maritime product. To illustrate. A bid was opened at Manila to build various sea tugs and launches. The Uragu Dock Company of Japan submitted, for a tug one hundred and forty feet long, twenty-six feet breadth, draft thirteen feet, a price of $109,500. The Shanghai Dock Company bid $105,376. The Hong-Kong and Whompoa bid was $86,280. Situated on the island of Hong-Kong, in the center of expensive Victoriatown itself, is the new Naval Yard Extension, where a battle-ship graving-dock and immense tidal basin, impos-

Carrying black brick tea from Yang-tze river boats to Tokmakoff's "Russian House," Hankow, Central China. River rises 40 feet during Spring floods.

The environs of Canton, South China. The embrasured city wall;
the famous "Five-story Pagoda," visited by every American traveller to China; the treeless hills overrun
by humankind continuously since Noah's time.

Where hundreds of thousands of people live on small boats. "Dutch
Folly" section of Pearl River, Canton, South China.

sible to be reached by shell, have been completed in re-claimed land. At Quarry Bay, five miles farther east on Hong-Kong Island, in a position however that can be shelled over the southern hills from the sea, the Butter-fields have cut in the rocky shore a dock seven hundred feet long, and have erected repair shops, so that, at the earth's extremity, are three ship-building and dock plants (one government and two private) of modern equipment and great size. In addition there are a number of Chin-ese plants which regularly turn out ships of twelve hun-dred tons burden, and install in them copies of European engines. The enforced extension of official Hong-Kong is being carried on by expensive reclamation from the sea, on a scale which is equalled at no port in the world. The money is provided by Parsees. One whole praya, six miles in extent, is thus being added to the front of the island. Across the harbor, on the mainland of China, bays are being filled in, so as to afford sites for factories and native tenements, for surly granite nature has here turned everything on edge on a more gigantic scale than even the Titanic upheavals of our own Greece. By this I mean to say that if the white man means to stay in southern China he must build for himself a foothold from the bottom of the sea.

Coal is brought from Wales and Australia at a cost of six dollars gold a ton, and stored under water as a re-serve for the Admiralty. The carbonic dissemination from the piles as they lie exposed to tropic rains and suns is extravagant. Kyushu Island in Japan mines most of the commercial coal used in that great port, though it is surprising to learn that India sends one hundred and thirty thousand tons a year of her Bengal coal to Hong-Kong.

Just before your 'rickisha whirls around the curve toward the saluting battery and the famous Soldiers' and Sailors' blue Canteen, against which the W. C. T. U.'s of England wage uncompromising war, look up Queen's Road Central at the vast, grotesque canvas sign of the King of Tattooers, who is one of the most unique characters a globe-trotter comes across. He boasts that every royal traveler who has come to the east, including the Tsar, has "sought the charming effects of his absolutely fast colors."

At Hong-Kong I brought to a native shoemaker on that dizzy old Wellington Road, which has not been hollowed out of the natural hill, a pair of low shoes to copy. He did so, but finding the novelty of extension soles, he adopted the "Melican fashion" for every future customer. When the British complained of the innovation he gave his opinion of styles as follows: "I sabee you no likee now, but blymby you likee." Their leather, which is tanned in gambier, saltpetre and alum, is very tender and in so damp a climate, soon gives out. The Chinese tailors on Queen's and Connaught Roads have progressed a little from the romantic days of Perry, and are not now copying the "bombardier's patches and all." They lay the tape with assuring smiles about your person and call out Delphic numbers, but the result still looks grotesque. Unless you watch them carefully they will run around the hem of your garment, for art's sake possibly, a thread one shade lighter than the cloth. They are a decided failure in sponging worsteds and tweeds which they import from England, but in flannel and linen suits, Ah-men-Hing-Cheong and Tak Cheong do some passable work, as well as in the hard, wild yellow silk, called "tussah," which is the product of worms which feed on oak and ailantus leaves in Shan-tung Province. China is a pinless country, as clothes are fastened by holes and buttons, or loops and frogs.

China too produces its gum-shoe men of nocturnal prowlings. It was the hot season at the Hong-Kong Club, every roomer sleeping with only the half door closed. The electric fans worked loud enough to drown the foot of a thief, or possibly he carried a sleeping draft in his handkerchief. Into six rooms he crawled night after night. He doubtless carried the long Punjaub knife. Gold studs were removed from shirts; watches were taken from under pillows, and rings from bureau tops. How could it all be done with so formidable Sikh *chowkidars* on guard at the door all night! Weeks went by and there was no trace. The Chinese bath boys; the older tea boys; every one's private boy, were in turn marched up to be put through no simple inquisition of " Third Degree " behind the stone walls at the top of Wyndham and Mosque Streets. Then Blass, who was on a seven year indenture in the East, and who was a wonderful fellow scientifically, remembered that his ring had a flaw in the ruby. It is a way pigeon rubies have for catching thieves, and that is why Burmans call only the pink gems good luck stones. The pawnshops were again searched, even to distant Yamati on the mainland. The ring was found, but horrors! the Chinese broker attacked our faith in those perfect guardians of our eastern homes, the Sikhs. He identified one of our own *chowkidars* as the guilty party. The latter confessed to pounding the gold to bullion and throwing the watch works in the harbor from a sampan. He also said he knew why he could safely move around our rooms, but that it was " Indian knowledge " which he would never betray. Let the curious therefore debate whether it was ether, hypnotism or mere luck six times unbroken. Those who had studs stolen were of no use as witnesses, for there was no recovered gold to identify, but Blass was witness enough, and the Indian got as fair a trial as a white man. We think less of Sikhs now, but Rasul Singh, behind the jail walls on Mosque Street, thinks more of us.

Crews for all trans-Pacific ships are recruited at Hong-Kong. The Chinese of Canton is the best disciplined and most tractable of all sailors. He never rushes . on shore to get drunk; he stands without flinching, even better than an Aden Arab, a heat which, south of Cancer, fries the pitch out of the deck seams and the marrow out of human bones; he never detains the vessel after its sailing hour because he is lingering ashore, and he never requires the irons to be clapped on him at sea. If he goes crazy he goes overboard without telling you of it, and killing a man on the way. He seldom moves his bunk, signing with the " samee olo ship " year after year, and if he does leave it is because of the Confucian law requiring three years of mourning when a parent dies. The white mates manage the sailors through a native bo'sun or " Number One man." They ask only one privilege, that of gambling with their returning countrymen who have made money abroad, and tawny Jack never fails to see that his landlubber brethren pay due toll to his Neptunic lore. All the way across the calm Pacific, the fo'c's'l head, and the battens of number one hold are checkered over with the cards, chips and cash of poker, pai-lau, fan-tan, and other heathen games. When the typhoons blow, or when life-boats need to be lowered for men overboard, the Chinese act with such coolness that one's confidence

in them is established at once. The blue-gowned waiters, with their long queues swinging dangerously near
the soup, may not be so popular with the traveler, but on
deck these machine-like, silent workers of the East lend
assurance to the long, tedious voyage of twenty-eight
days across the Pacific, when one takes the southern
route.

At Hong-Kong you will notice that when the 'tween
deck ports are thrown open to the stevedore's men who
come alongside to take delivery of the quarter sacks of
flour, bamboo sticks are used in the tallying. The criminals among them must twinge when they recall that
these are the same tally sticks which the judge at Canton
counts out and throws down to indicate how many lashes
the culprit shall receive. Not a few of the Hong-Kong
laborers are deserters from justice at Canton.

As soon as a mail steamer arrives in the busy port,
dozens of smoking steam launches crowd alongside, and
the first to board the ship are the native boarding-house
runners from Elgin Street, who are soliciting returning
Chinese emigrants. The health officer is helpless; the
emigrants toss ropes over to the launches and the runners,
with the agility of monkeys, clamber up the sides of the
ships and over the bulwarks. The crews look like
pirates; they are half naked. On their wide straw sun
hats are painted the names of the houses, so that the emigrants, looking over the rail on the scene below, may behold the merits of their temporary abiding places before
returning to Canton on the morrow. Many of the
signs read: " Fine Gambling," " Auspicious Welcome,"
" Heavenly Thought," etc., the philosophy of all of which
the fleeced emigrant will probably have cause to recall on
the morrow eve. When the steamboats, such as those

from Canton, berth at the few wharves during the night, these boarding-house runners carry lanterns with the same signs emblazoned on them. The overturning of one of these lights caused the great steamer *Han-kau* holocaust in the early morning of October 14th, 1906, when four hundred Chinese were burned to death in their sleep, and a $300,000 cargo of silk consumed.

The Chinese Imperial Customs under Sir Robert Hart and Robert Bredon, Hong-Kong and even Macao, have done something to light the ancient coasts of south China. As the exile walks along Barker Road in the gathering dusk toward the Wong Nei Chong Gap, he beholds Waglan in the south, flashing out an intermittent signal but reminding him in comparison of the more frequent safety appliances of our home waters. Looking to the north, a weird sight is presented in fall along the flanks of the mountains which frown over old Kowloon City, Junk Bay, Yamati and Hang How village, and the Lyee-moon Pass, which shut in the scene. A low running fire sets them off into the buttresses and towers of a heavenly city. It is the grass-cutters, who are thus fertilizing their mountain pastures of wire grass. The hills are composed of a progressively disintegrating granite, which supports only a coarse grass which kills sheep, but the natives use it for pig fodder, fuel for kindling and for vase kilns, fertilizer, baskets and bedding. The tremendous rains wash away into the crevices even what little loam does accumulate. The Hakka grass-cutters are a fiery lot, and the government has been slow to step in and prevent the destruction of the imported Scotch fir growth which would in time reclothe the denuded hills.

The Colony is visited often by the enlightened native lady, Mrs. Wu, wife of the famous minister Wu Ting

Fang, and sister of the eminent Doctor Ho Kai of Hong-Kong, who is a colonial legislator Westminster would be proud of for his attainments and zeal.   It will be recalled that Minister Wu years ago practised as a barrister before the British courts of Hong-Kong, where he was born. His wife, so beautiful in her quiet and sweet dignity to every one who saw her in the Colony and on shipboard, has shown that high thoughts and a great heart throb behind her unassuming mood, or is concealment the wonderful way of a Celestial?   She has given Hong-Kong a great hospital, called the Ho Min Ling, for the women of her race.   Government provided the site.   Already a native hospital existed in the Tung Wah, whose officials surprise foreigners with the avidity with which they send for the bones or bodies of even the obscurest Chinese emigrants who die at sea.   " Prince or pauper, he is a Chinese, and the same worship is paid him by a loyal son." There are besides, the large Civil, Military and Naval Hospitals, and the private Peak Hospital, but all are not too many for this tropical station of sickness where fevers fight for ever under their yellow banner of " No Surrender."

Old Kowloon City, (whose translated name is " Nine Dragons," owing to the nine overhanging peaks) across from Hong-Kong, is beginning to draw the feet of antiquarians.   There is, of course, nothing like the higher, wider scene which appals the ordinary imagination in the north, where the Great Wall climbs peaks five thousand two hundred feet over one's head.   The wall of the ancient city of Kowloon clambers between the boulders of the valleys and over several hills three hundred feet high, which were encircled and used as redoubts. The wall between the angles uses more stone than appears in the construction of the Great Wall in many places. These Hakkas evidently did not believe in jerry contractors, when the safety of their city was to be tested. The guns have been dismantled and cast about the ramparts by the British with the same intent that induced the Assyrians to sow salt and tares in the fields of those whom they had conquered in citadels but were not so sure they had conquered in spirit. On the way from the shore settlements to both old Kowloon and Yamati, the government has cut some remarkable roads through the yellow loess. It packs well, and if you did not test the walls, you would conclude on sight that it was an engineering work which had cost millions. With what a feeling of security once on one of these night walks above the native settlement of Hang How, we came across a British corporal's guard stationed by a four-point-seven gun on the dark road! Hundreds of coolies had dragged it part of the way up in the daytime, but it was too valuable a government pet,— this pointer-nosed beauty,— to be left unguarded, out in this picturesque southern China, where the white man, while he talks mannerly to his yellow neighbor, still keeps his powder dry.

As the curio-hunter saunters into Kruse's, or Kuhn and Komor's, Hong-Kong, a creepy feeling possesses him, in his illegal search after hara-kiri swords, scimitars from Borneo, and dahs and krises from Java, that a Sikh policeman is watching him with hypnotic eye through the windows, to see if the store is selling swords in a colony where arms are interdicted because of the overwhelming native population.

When the hot summer swoops down upon Peking, the foreign resident goes to the cooler hills of Patachu, twelve miles away, and the residents of Kobe, Yokohama and Seoul have relief within a few hours. Think of a commitment for a seven years indenture to an island, where only three places (and those water level), can be reached over Sunday. This is the experience of most of the Anglo-Saxons who contract for service at Hong-Kong. Canton, once known by the Joshuan name of Yang Ching (city of rams), affords the longest trip. This is the city of the empire where it is said every new thing and luxury germinates; where excitement always runs high and box-top orators abound; where the myrmidons of tax farmers flourish, and if it does not equal Nanking in literary culture, it is the Athens of China in conceit, and the Paris or Kyoto of China in art productions. Take lots of money, for the stores will tempt the tightest fist. The boat sails from Hong-Kong at eight-thirty A.M., before foreign life is astir, but long after the alert Chinese have opened the day with firing of crackers and burning of joss paper on the high sterns of their junks. The wharf shed on the Praya is about the loudest in design that can be imagined, and would frighten any Ostend resort of the most bizarre aspirations. But once aboard the modern boats *Fatshan* and *Honam*, one is delighted that the comforts of a Boston steamer are afforded in so remote a country, with the additional unique feature of armed Sikhs patrolling the hatches. The first part of the trip is in landlocked British waters, frowned over by lofty Victoria, Castle and Tai Mo Peaks. Many islands, some of historic interest in the annals of European commerce with the Orient, dot the stream. Half of the native names have happily been retained. Shek Wan Pen is contiguous to Deep Water Bay, and Castle Peaks overlook Cap Sui Moon Pass. First comes Stonecutter's Island and then Mah Wan Island. It is altogether captivating when the captain mixes his new-found learning of the east with your old world names. Little white villages of stone are scattered as far up the great peaks as terraces can be cut to support life, and the foothills look like patterns in plaids with the varied green of the small garden patches which are unbroken by fences. Melancholy Lintin Island is passed, with not a house or tree, and only a few cellars remaining on it. Who would believe that in 1830 it was covered with the stores and homes of men of our race? Great bays five miles deep, open up, and the receding tide uncovers to the waders edible seaweed, shell-fish and eels. Bloated bodies and heads bald in front drift by, carrying tales of the murdered and the beheaded, and the tails of the men themselves in the former case,— the terribleness both of disorder and order in uncanny company. When you are half-way to Canton, the estuary narrows to the Bocca Tigris (Tiger's Mouth in Portuguese). All about are rice fields, banana plantations, and plots where the *canabis sinensis* is cultivated for the famous buff and blue grasscloth. A thousand canals communicate with the East and West Rivers, the most of them extending from the central Pearl River to the West River. Many of them are navigable for the tugs one finds in Hong-Kong waters, and I recall some keen experiences when we followed in the wake of the government cruiser which was catching pirates, and tossing their heads into baskets on the top of bamboo poles, as a deterrent of crime. Soon we pass Whompoa, where the first foreign dock was located, and where Russell's famous American tea-clippers used to drop anchor. Whompoa will come into its own again and make Hong-Kong tremble because of a rival greatness.

Then Canton the ancient and wonderful, Canton the brains of China, comes into view. The wharf is in the old city, and it is necessary to take a dirty sampan to reach the European's island of Shameen (literally " sand face " because of its beach). Across a dirty canal, the Sha Kee Street of the native city faces you with its myriad signs. The government proposes to reclaim land in the canal, so as to make this street two *cheungs* (thirty feet) wide,— something very lavish for South China. Everywhere the boat population surges on the waters, probably three hundred thousand people thus finding a home along the famous Pagoda anchorage. What a contretemps! two marble Gothic shafts of the French Cathedral, where the French and Belgian priests officiate, robed in Chinese costume, spring from amid the low wilderness of tile roofs. The only other tall objects are the square, unwindowed pawn shops; a pagoda or two outside the walls; the towers for detecting fires, and a smooth Moslem minaret, one hundred and eighty feet high, which has stood for five hundred years. The temples are only two stories high, and are hid away among the squat houses. In the zigzag streets, made so for defense against pirates, and also devils who can not turn a corner, with their many steps (for the Great Wall set the precedent that grading should never be done) a guide is indispensable. They wait for you under the palms at the beautiful Victoria Hotel at Shameen. One dollar Mexican silver a day is the fee. Your chair with four bearers costs one dollar more, and one dollar will pay all fees for bonzes who admit you to their temples.

The city has a market history since the eighth century, and is easily the premier city of China. It decidedly is the metropolis of the country, as New York is with us, and it may eventually be the capital if the Manchus are overthrown.

How many places there are to go: the shops of those who inlay silver with kingfishers' feathers, whose work each day brings them that much nearer to blindness; the Chy Loong ginger works, which have candied sweetroots for you and me since we were boys; the Tung Shing sandalwood and ivory carvers; the shops of the jadestone polishers; the Chun Loong matting works; the shops where artists paint on ivory and rice paper; the Yan Kee tea burners' works; the Edible Birds' Nest market; silk and embroidery shops on Sai Loy Street; the fragrant camphor-wood coffin shops just beneath the Tartar wall, where the horsemen ride with panoply of antediluvian war; the venerable Water Clock dripping down the moments of centuries which knew not our white-men's politics; the lazy beggars on the steps who do not even ask an alms, but trust to their professional distortions and their hypnotic eyes to attract pity. The less said about the gaudy Hwa Ting or Flower Boats, and the fan-tan shops, with their huge lanterns along the Chung Sun Street in the western suburb, the better. There are teahouses, like so much driftwood, on the water's edge, with some loose life, bad music and gorgeous robes. A meal there of rice, cabbage, pork and bean fixings costs the dandy three and a half cents. Signs of the Crescent here and there show where Mohammedans have their bathhouses.

The Hwang Han Temple is remarkable for its expansive tile roof and two miniature pagodas in the great stone courtyard. Not much can be said for the Emperor's Temple, which is taudry and modern in style. He never visits these temples, and the citizens therefore spend only enough money on him to conform with the law, which prescribes a place in each of the provincial capitals for the Emperor to worship the One God. In the Fa-ti Gardens, clipped chrysanthemums wear porcelain heads and hands.

The little ancestral chapel of the Tsang Clan is altogether delightful, from an architectural point of view particularly, and partly from a sociological consideration. Two great beacons of three tiers flank it. The railings, friezes, grilles, eaves, the ridge ornament particularly, and the wing chapels are as delicate as the best occidental taste could prescribe. The modern ancestral temple of the Chun Ka Che clan, outside the walls, is more elaborate and the costliest in China. This is the part of the country where a merchant prince dares laugh at the idea that the throne may not be vied with in ostentation. The fretwork of the balcony exhibits the richest specimens of carving. The general chasteness of line found throughout China is here lost in too much decoration.

The Temple of the Five Genii on Great Market Street has a beauty of pillar, a lightness in poise of double roofs, and a length of vista through the halls, that appeal to the imagination instantly. There is little carving and you desire none. You have found what only genius can conceive, proportion, and it is no more plentiful in China than in other lands. The Buddhist monks have set out royal palms on the terraces to fit into the general scheme of columns approaching the cloisters, and the illusion that Nature built the temple easily ensues. A balustrade with pink tile frettings, completes a picture of line and light, so that it is hard to say whether etcher or painter would best essay it.

The curious can go to the Nam Hoi Magistrates' Yamen, where the prisoners are on view in cangues and chains and the unconscionable rascals are the only Chinese who like to be photographed. The Green Tea and the Swatow are the best known of the Guild Halls. Even the beggars here have their Guild Hall. An amusing advertisement of one of the Canton hotels confesses the more of the general conditions: " This hotel is entirely free from obnoxious odors." The rent of the best shops is low enough, but tens of thousands prefer to carry their shops on a bamboo over their shoulders. A Canton adage needs no explanation: " Get rich with a taxless basket, for the tax-gatherer sucks a shop as dry as an empty shell." The hucksters can not carry signs, so they yell their wares, each in the note of his Guild. The barber's note is like a cicada's; the cobbler's like a cat's; while the umbrella man storms like our Themistocles when he roared above the fleets of Salamis. I think a Chinese has the shrillest and strongest voice in the world, and can make the wryest face in ejecting it. But he is quite capable of exhibiting the most infectious smile at the first sight of humor. He shows all the indications of a healthy, well-poised mentality. Two chair-bearers, jostled into by two coolies who are carrying a great load between them on a bamboo, shout back most filthy language concerning the mothers of their assailants. Nothing daunted, the latter retort: " *Mo mi ma wo peen*" (Go on, you tailless horses), which is the most insulting name a draft coolie can be called, and a trail of laughter follows in the wake of the jeered. Everybody else, in the height of manners, is extending the usual morning greeting, " chih kwo fan " (have you had rice), which answers to our " how-do-you-do " salutation. The peddlers are in force; they chiefly visit the homes of foreigners with their baskets of porcelain, jewels, silks, furs, and jade. We remember one of the wiliest who used to bring white fox furs which we suspected had lain too long in the pawn shops, until the fur was molting, for they have no cold storage system in the south of the empire. He would leap like a jumping-jack and vociferate: " No slake (examine) 'em first; you makee buy, then can look see," which was all too good for himself.

The umbrella mender; the cutter of wood seals or " chops "; the itinerant banker with his strings of cash, the load under which he was groaning probably not being worth over six of our dollars; the shoe-man shouting " straw sandals one cent a pair; " the *loaping* or yellow cookie man, for they keep in China the yellow of their eggs while they send us the albumen in crystals; the dentist with his pincers and a string of his horrible conquests; the medicine seller with his dried snakes; the seller of ché (sticks of sugar cane one foot long),— all hurry along with an eye searching one way, and a voice the other, for "good luck pidgin," or the first bargain of the morning. A guided company of the blind in Indian file, with their hands on one another's shoulders, pass near the wall and murmur " *kou lun* " (for pity's sake, a gift!). The streets are so narrow and sunless with signs that the lantern-maker, the fish-man, the dyer, and the housewife all dry their wares on the tile roof, where possibly a small tree may be growing in the ancient collection of dust in the gutterway and spout. The fruit vender will not sell you the orange with the skin. He sells the skins separately as a flavoring for boiled rice or for preserving. The professional story-tellers gather crowds as dirty sugar gathers flies. If you listen you will conclude that the reciters have memorized from un-expurgated editions of popular novelettes, and also added a dressing of their own.   The lantern and balloon seller is in tremendous difficulties, and has the pain of Atlas on his brow and shoulders, for while his long pole lifts his wares above the crowds, it is for ever bumping into the forest of street signs.   Here is a fresh-faced country boy carrying his baskets of water-cress.   His feet are covered with sores, for the water where he works is none too pure.   There goes a band of strolling musicians, out to earn a day's honest wage, blowing furiously on sangs, scraping on tikins, picking at pipas and banging at los. A barber, when he has nailed a customer, backs up to the wall, for " if cutee, no payee."   Every one else traffics in the jostling crowd.   Look! there steps a mandarin from his chair toward the Yamen's steps.   He affects a walk with feet set very far apart, just such as you see copied by a certain class of the jeunesse of the army as they take an airing down the platform at the Horse Guards Parade Ground, London, or at our own Presidio; it was learned in China!

One never sees fisticuffs.   Now and then an urchin spits at a foreigner's chair and shouts, *Fan kwei lai* (See, here's a foreign devil), but his ears are cuffed by the first shopkeeper who can reach him, especially if the American monitor *Monadnock;* the British gunboats *Algerine* and *Moorhen,* or the French *Styx* are in port.   Coal bearers, corpse carriers, idol bearers, all join the rout of the barefooted, but outside of their voices these millions pass in silence along their smokeless streets; no wheels, no hoofs, no bells, no whistles, no leather shoes.   What a difference between the street scenes here and in Peking, the capital of the north!   In

Canton, the capital of the south, there are no animals or carts in the narrow streets. In Peking the most striking features of the street life are the trains of double-humped Bactrian camels and the springless Peking passenger carts in the wide streets. Step ten paces off the street in Canton into the first temple court, like the Hwang Hau, and the hush of the longest recorded centuries of this, our poor earth, immediately closes about you, as though your soul had dropped into space. You who have never thought before in your own land of excitement and danger on the streets, suddenly are awed in this exile among the heathen by your own mind turning about, facing you and saying: "We never met before." This is what you will never forget. This is what you can truly say for ever: "I discovered my identity; I accepted my responsibility in fear in China."

Who are these little Cantonese? Up the Fu-kien pirate coast; up the scented Yangtze; up the shadowy Si River; along the marshes of Malaysia, or under the iron cliffs of Liaotung, always keeping within sound of the thud-thud of the screws of British gunboats, has followed the greatest abettor of British power and British prints, the peerless Cantonese middleman, the real civilizer of the East.

The second excursion is to Macao, of which we will relate separately, and the third and last trip available to a Hong-Kongite is that up the West River (Sikiang). The sternwheel boats *Sainam* and *Nanning* leave Canton for Woochow, two hundred and twenty miles away, three times a week, making the journey in thirty hours. The river was opened to foreign trade as far back as 1897, but its beauties are only lately coming into fame with us. The Chinese have always appreciated

them, but this is not the only thing we have learned they
have been concealing. " Concealment is Nature's first
measure of safety, and half of a man's wisdom," says
their proverb. Where the North River and Fatshan
Branch join the West River at Sam Shui (Three Waters), which you easily mispronounce and say " whisky "
in Chinese, the most beautifully wooded headlands reach
into the water. It might from all natural appearances
be a bend in the Ottawa. Stone temples peep from beneath the trees and you conclude that the Chinese, who
do everything opposite to us, do not place their best architectural creations in cities, but on hills, in woods, or
beside the waters, so that beauteous Nature may be a
propitiator between God and man, for they say true love-
liness and sin can not exist together. As you sail into
the broad waters of Woochow reach, and the moon comes
over Pagoda Hill, and glistens on the porcelain tower,
you have something lovely to remember for ever, and conclude that a country can be beautiful and a man patriotic
in any language.

One of the stops is called Do-Shing, and you wonder
whether you are in Devonshire or along the Danube, until
you separate the name, Do — Shing. There is no
journey equal to the first part of this trip in affording
opportunity to study Chinese life, for the villages crowd
to the water's edge. The Hudson, or the Danube at the
Iron Gate, can not surpass Shui Hing Gorge, with the
Marble Mountains, Seven Star Hills, and How Lek
Peaks, and their many pagodas towering over the water,
which is swollen with the summer's torrents. At Kamchuk the rapids run twenty miles an hour. The river is
more picturesque than the Hudson because of its greater
number of bends. One seems to be sailing into a wall,

One of the three most beautiful pagodas in China. The octagonal
" Flower Pagoda," Canton, 1000 A.D. Native house
of tile, stone, brick and cement such as built
in South China in foreground.

Cargo junks and small residence boats, where hundreds of thousands
of people live, Pearl River, Canton, South China.

The Old and the New—A modern steamboat brought in sections
from Scotland, anchored among the slipper boats and
sampans of Canton, South China.

when suddenly a new reach is spread before the view, with banks where sorghum, indigo, cassia, mulberry, tea, banana, ramie, matting reeds, palm and bamboo grow in varied colored luxuriance, not to speak of fields of that most quiet of all green shades of nature, where the rice and millet patches extend. Now the stream narrows to a gorge, and the mountains again come to the water's edge, and during the torrential rains of summer the bare hills present thousands of glorious waterfalls. Then a turn is made, and a lake covered with boat life extends wide into the fields. A pagoda's thin shadow spears the waters. Great junk sails seem to be moving through the gardens, along hidden creeks, of course. Not all the ports which you pass on the river can be touched at, because they have not been opened by treaty, and the interdiction lends zest to the trip. Now and then a raft of the precious giant bamboo is towed past by launches. Along the Teng Yu Mountains, waterfalls glisten. Decidedly the most unique sight on Chinese waters is a native passenger boat, with the great sweeps and sails, working its crowded human freight up the stream. A first-class ticket costs one-half of a cent a mile. There is no steward's service, for every man eats from his own lunch basket, or rather, handkerchief. At Kamchuk and Shui Hing, the old capital of the province, buildings encroach into the stream on piles. A Chinese seems never to be afraid of water or freshets, though floods, typhoons, clumsy junks, and frail sampans are for ever taking a terrible toll of death among this persistent, patient race. Along the tow path on the right of the stream, human trackers pull freight boats against the current. Tak Hing, on the north bank, shipped you the matting which is laid on the bedroom floor of your far distant home.

The marshes, where the reed grows, extend far inland. Since you have at last made a call upon them where they were working with a will for you, you will doubtless now and for ever have a new heart for the little saffron brothers who are knee deep in the water, whose wage is twelve cents a day, and who, after paying their living expenses, have as a profit on what they sell you, only two cents a day left to save.

II

When Luther, Wolsey and the Pope were the names
that clamored loudest in the world, a few swarthy Lusitanian adventurers in half-decked caravels, had taken so
long a journey that the fame and luxuries of the old
world were of small import to them in their remotest
exile.   From the yellow Tagus and Lisbon they had come
to the red delta of the Canton River, in China.   The colony exists to-day, and I found the dried-leaf charm of
the dim past clinging to the yellow and blue chunam
(stucco) walls of sunny Macao.   The dangers of the past
are also a present reality on these, the most dangerous
waters of the world, from a police standpoint.   A river
trip is spiced with the risk of piratical attacks.   The
creeks and upper reaches of the delta, between the Chu
and Sikiang Rivers give refuge to nearly naked and
bronzed bucaneers, who frequently fire from the sorghum
brakes upon passing steamboats.   All the native junks
which ply on the West River to the silk plantations, are
equipped with cannon of antique pattern, and hand-
grenades.

The handsomest steamboat east of Suez, the *Heungshan,* leaves Hong-Kong for Macao at two o'clock, arriving at sundown.   The trip is to the mouth of the
Pearl River, and across more open water than the voyage
to Canton.   Differing from Chinese and mediæval cities,
for in the spirit of the latter it was partly planned, Macao,

filling up the end of a narrow-necked peninsula, is walled
only on two sides, the north and the south. The sea
itself, providing the moat on the east and west, has always proved to be the stronger barrier. The Chinese at
will have leaped the Porta Cerco wall, but on many occasions the Macaense prevented the landing of the Dutch
along the eastern beach by the guns of Bomparto, Francisco and Guia forts. The city's incorporated name is
" Cidade da Nome de Deos, Nao ha outra mais leal ":
" City of the Name of God, most loyal of the Colonies,"
which honor was accorded it by Dom Joa IV., in 1642.
The Boa Vista is a castle-like hotel on the Penha Heights,
which overlooks the sixteenth century Bomparto fort and
the great half moon Praya Grande bay. It is the most
picturesquely situated and cleanest hotel in the Orient,
and has been a source of national jealousy between Portugal, France, China and England. France has been endeavoring to secure it as an advance post toward Canton,
for if England ever takes the Yangtze basin, France is
going to demand the whole coast from Tonquin to
Fu-kien, including the two Kwang Provinces and Yunnan, to the capital of which she is now sending a railway
from Haiphong. The Boa Vista's fish and game dinners
are famous throughout the East. It also makes a specialty of Portuguese wines, from the light Colares to
golden port. The drive from the band gardens along the
cliffs to the Areia Preta bathing beach rivals Hong-
Kong's noble Jubilee Road, and both of these oriental
roads, hanging over the sea, surpass Nice's Corniche
Road in foliage and color. Through the productive, in-
tensively-developed Chinese truck-farms runs the wide
Avenida Vasco da Gama, as far as Mongha Fort. Over
Cacilhas Bay is the picturesque Montanha Russa Park,

which is graded like a grassy volcano.   All were built by chained convict and impressed soldier labor.   Few now frequent these noble, highly maintained roads, as the courtly dark Macaenses have drifted to Hong-Kong to earn a livelihood, and the historic little colony, Europe's first conquest in Cathay, is lapsing into merely a sanitarium and pleasure resort, from which place neither Manila's Baguio or Hong-Kong's peak promise to displace it. Macao's unique feature in this respect is the steady-blowing through the hot months of the sou-west monsoon. Should this breeze lapse for a moment, death would come to thousands from the awful heat resulting.   As you look at night from the wide verandas of the Boa Vista hotel, you notice lights like fireflies flitting along the Praya Grande.   They are the lanterns of the few who must be abroad late, or of adventurers who are returning from the fan-tan gambling-houses.   The *lukongs* will challenge none who bears a light.   In all oriental cities there are more private watchmen than police.

The hospitality of the Macaense is proverbial.   Their table conspicuously displays the influence the Chinese have had upon them during four centuries: candy flavored with arbutus and haw seeds; laoping pasties made of water chestnuts and flour and colored the popular citron yellow; coagulated duck's blood pudding; bamboo shoots preserved in sugar; and carambola and mango jellies.   As butter is scarce, you can taste the sesamum oil in food.

A visit to the opium farm, as you drive up the tortuous Rua da Penha, affords a curiosity.   The lane which runs along the low, dreary factory smells of the narcotic fumes, and not a green blade grows.   Look through the bars.   They are boiling, stirring and straining the balls from India, which they have mixed with the lower grade pods from their own Yunnan fields, in brass dishes, till finished like brown treacle the mixture is poured into water-buffalo horn cups. These cups are incased in tin, and again in camphor-wood. There is a great park-like, stone-paved court attached to the factory, but none save an Occidental is ever seen in it. The factory boys are more stupefied for sleep than play, after their work. All the opium brought to America is made at this farm. The ships lie twenty miles away, just off the edge of the smuggling shallows, at the famous Kowhow-Yang anchorage, where arms are dealt in at night over the sides of phantom ships, for pirates and the Young China party. Old-fashioned Portuguese gunboats, like the *Diu* and *Goa,* with low waists and high bulwarks, and Armstrong guns on wooden carriages lashed to the deck, escort the prize-laden, high-sterned junks from the crowded inner anchorage to the mail steamers. I once returned on the gunboat with the tanned Legionaires of the romantic little kingdom. The men could recite the epic of Camoens with that pathos which is possible only by those who have a proud past, but no possible future. The shippers of the opium are quite justified in their fears that pirates may dash out for the million-dollar cargo from behind Taipa, Don Joao or Lapa Islands.

Lonely Portugal, the relict of a great race, sits in her ancient palace surrounded by portraits of a famous past. The names she whispers in her melancholy are Da Gama, who gave the world the sea-link to India; Prince Henry the navigator, who suggested to Columbus his ambitions; and Camoens, who was the Chaucer of the Portuguese language, and one of literature's five great epic writers. He was the greatest genius of Portugal, versed in the

Oldest ruin (1594 A.D.) of European association in China, façade
of San Paulo Cathedral, Macao. The Chinese classic,
"Ming Shi," lauds the architecture. Quaint bronze
statues were cast at Bocarro's gun foundry
at Macao in 16th century.

Macao, looking from Penha Height to Cape Sao Francisco. Famous
Praya Grande drive facing water; Guia lighthouse in right
distance, and Monte Fort in left distance, both
first of their kind in China.

Macao, looking from Cape Sao Francisco to Penha Heights.
Hotel "Boa Vista" in distance.

classics like Milton, a warrior of Sydney's stamp, a
dashing courtier, and a traveler of Cervantes' wit.
Portugal may be notable again, when Brazil, her offspring by blood and literature, dominates in South
America.   She exists to-day as a tragically discontented
decadence in Europe; a sunny spot in China; a group
of forsaken cathedrals on the Malabar Coast, and a neglected blur of uninhabited territory under the blue-
and-white flag-of-the-castles, in Africa.

Half-way between Hong-Kong and Canton, on a narrow peninsula of canal-veined Heang-Shan district of
Kwangtung Province, between the Pearl River and the
sea, is the settlement of Macao, holding in its arms, toward the cool sou-west monsoon a flashing blue bay,
which dashes its waters over the long walls of the circling
Praya Grande.   It is the Naples of the Orient in appearance, color, joy and carelessness.   Here in 1557 came
Camoens, a political exile, and here he wrote half of *The
Lusiad,* thus producing in China a supreme work of
European literature, in days when the American hemi-
sphere loomed like cliffs of wonder in the uncertain mists
of early discovery, and when the morning star of Shakespeare had not yet risen on the minds of mankind.
Camoens' luxuriant garden and grotto overlook the
inner and outer harbors, which were covered in his day,
as on the golden afternoon when I saw them first, with a
forest of yellow and brown matting sails of junks.   Little,
however, was the poet's heart fed by the argosies of
silver, golden brocades, ivory, pearls, porcelain, camphor,
and silk, passing homeward to his cruel Lisbon.   He was
weaving another web, and his heart, bitter in exile, was
wounded to produce the poetic pearls of a second
Odyssey.

Blue, yellow, red and brown, the squat buildings of
Macao crowd on rising, uneven ground, and present, with
their roofs of heavy tiles, a color scheme worthy of the
brush of Velasquez. The streets run a zigzag course,
so that from house to house defense could be made
against the Chinese, or against the Dutch in the later
days of the Colony. These houses are popular with the
Chinese, whose superstition it is that a devil can not turn
a corner. The shutters of the buildings have fish-scale
and pearl-shell windows, which soften in the rooms the
intense light of an oriental day. High against the sky-
line is the distinguishing ruin of Macao, the windowless
Renaissance façade of the burned San Paulo Cathedral,
with its three rows of Corinthian pillars, superimposed
on ten Ionic pillars. The antique edifice was erected early
in the sixteenth century. The magnificent flight of one
hundred stone steps, as wide as the edifice itself, is bound
by Time's hand in plumes of grass and bright oriental
blooms, and the night alone swings lamps of worship
over the old roofless altar of four centuries ago. In the
Se Cathedral I heard a military mass, reminiscent of the
cavalcades of Da Gama and Cortez, the host being saluted with presented swords. *The Miserere* of Gounod
was played by a military brass band in the church loft.
Little swarthy soldiers, uniformed in blue, swung along
the dazzling streets to a march played by the bugle.
They wore rimless caps, these reckless ones, suited more
for the Estrella Mountains of their homeland than the
pitiless suns of the East, but with the impulsive Latins,
as with the Chinese, appearance and old customs must
never be sacrificed for a mere thing like climate.

The government ration to the soldiers included good
Colares wine, poured desecratingly from a tin pail into

pewter cups. The native-born Portuguese, called Macaense, dress in contradistinction to the usual oriental custom, in black, which uncomfortably attracts the actinic
rays of the sun. The small ruling class from Lisbon
seems out of place in the exotic gowns of European
fashion. The Chinese shuffle along the excellent concrete
military roads in their gorgeous blouses of purple, yellow and blue, and they look to the manor born. They
gather in knots before the wax-model and lantern stores on
bright Rua Felicidade, and discuss progress in the ear of
the unprogressive. The blue-and-white barred turbans, with
long streamers attached, of the imported Sikh police make
the most attractive head-gear one could see the world
over. The sound of clanking chains approaches along
the road, and a band of native prisoners, linked together,
who have been working on the highway, are escorted by.

Filled with the piety of Xavier, and following his steps
on the same sunny roads, the little Colony is most characteristically solemn and impressive in its Santa Croce
procession in June, which reminds one of the Paso processions of Seville. The Legionaires are as disciplinary
as the soldiers of Da Gama; they compel the Protestant
stranger at the points of their swords to remove his hat.
The music is doleful and fitful sobs fill its pauses. The
procession is slow and halting; its color is black where
the small number of Europeans and Macaense lead, and
purple where the long line of Chinese converts follow.
Down the Rua da Se, named from the yellow, Spanish-
style cathedral at its head, it winds to the Praya Grande
which skirts the ocean. Camellias, carnations and leaves
are scattered at the nine street stations of the Cross.
Two children robed in white, and winged as Raphaelic
cherubs, lead and regulate the kneeling and the march.

The whole Colony is out upon the harbor street; the women veiled behind their Do cloths are in the windows of the single line of houses which face the bay; the rest of the city is deserted. The Chinese come to wonder especially at the gaily dressed band of converts who are nearly all girl slaves who were purchased in childhood. The Casa Misericordia, the Church Lottery, is strongly represented by liveried officials. Finally a heroic-sized figure of Christ, bearing His cross, is brought forward upon the shoulders of the troops. The flare of the trumpets assails the heathen air; the draped drums roll out the gathering thunder; the emotion of the onlookers contributes sobs, and the little band of Catholic exiles take every thrill of courage possible out of their famous fête. High above the Areia Preta Beach, behind the square walls of the Protestant cemetery which is smothered in a vast foliage, lies the body of Robert Morrison, the pioneer Protestant missionary and translator, whose name is at last coming into its own in a great fame, now that the Christian scriptures are leavening China.

On the fifth day of the fifth moon, the Chinese hold their religious procession of Ken Yuen, their greatest democrat whom they have canonized, which ceremony, however, takes place on the water, and the Macaense become the spectators. Flimsy bamboo stands, bound together with rattan only, are erected, and their not infrequent precipitation in the excitement causes vast loss of life. The island communities of Taipa, Joao, Lapa and Heungshan send boats, very like our war canoes, only that the bow and stern are carved into the form of a dragon. The ceremony includes the casting of gifts and sacrifices into the water, which was copied by the Venetian doges when they heard the tales which Marco

Polo brought home. The festival closes with racing on
a vast scale. The boats are all overmanned, sometimes
with sixty paddlers, and the gunwales are often only five
inches above the choppy water. A platform is raised in
the waist, on which stands a naked man who beats the
stroke on a gong for his bareback crew. Native women
are, of course, kept at home. In the exciting finish I
have seen the stroke raised to seventy-five. The irregularity of the paddling as much as the collisions is responsible for the swampings. The whole world has leaped
in alarm when telegrams have come from Yuet Shing on
the Kau Kwan reach of the West River, of the loss of one
thousand lives through the tumbling of one of the stands
during the wild finish of the races there. After the
races, the boats paddle to all the villages of the sea
delta. Wafted into your room on the Penha Height at
Macao by the sou-west monsoon, far into the night, like
the classic echoes of the strokes of Jason's crew, come the
sounds of the gongs and the paddles of these dusky boatmen as they visit and challenge for the morrow among
the bays of Taipa and Joao.

Once a month, on a Sunday, crowds from Hong-Kong
repair to Macao, to a classic little building with white
barred windows, on the Rua da Se, to witness the drawings of the Misericordia Lottery, which is the most extensive in the East and has given Macao the name of the
oriental Monte Carlo. The officers are in uniform and
have just come from special benediction for the drawing,
and mass in the Se Cathedral close by. Inside a railing
the costumed committee sit, with a smile upon their
countenances, which is half between the cupidity of a
gambler and the satisfaction of a virtuous judge. A
trumpet is blown for eclat. Around goes the great brass

globe, while every breath is held. The dice-like number, which falls out only one at a time, is passed to three persons, two of whom witness the number, and the last steps forward and theatrically announces it to the assemblage beyond the rails. This lottery draws from Manila three hundred thousand pesos annually; from Hong-Kong six hundred thousand dollars, Mexican. For its franchise it is compelled to maintain Macaense charities, including a college named for St. Joseph, under the direction of the church; hence the religious name of the lottery. It also pays a heavy tax to the " Governmento Leal," half of which assists to maintain the fine local roads; a quarter goes home to Portugal to be lost in the aristocratic halls of the white Ajuda palace on the cliffs of Belem; and a quarter helps to support the poorer Portuguese colony of Timor near Sumatra. In comparison with this lottery the largest bank of Macao, the Po Hang, hides its diminished head.

In the arch of the half moon bay at Macao, between the forts of Bomparto and Francisco, just before you turn up the street by the park where the Portuguese bands play on Sunday afternoons, you will notice an unusual house for the East. It faces the purple bay where the fishing junks are drying their brown nets on yellow mainsails. The windows are of imported stained glass, and the grilles are painted white. It is the only house you have ever seen in China where the blue stucco is not scaling or lichening like an architectural leper. You are told the owner is a rich Chinese, or a Tsai-shu, and that his country place is among the Heungshan Hills where he was born in poverty, ten miles away on execrable roads, which pass through acres of graves, underneath wonderful tamarind trees, and past the golf course of

the navy and outdoor staff of the Imperial Customs Service, where the holes are earthen cups hammered into the
stony hillside.   I took a 'rickisha, with two pushmen and
made the trip, which is one of as many ups and downs as
a Gulf Stream passage when the wind is against the tide.
It would have been better to have taken a barrow, especially between Passaleao and Chinsan.   At the Porta da
Cerco, where the soldiers are drinking imported Colares
wine, and lolling under the trees, you leave Portuguese
territory, and enter old China.   The truck gardens smell
noisome, but are luxuriant in appearance.   The chow
dogs are barking like a side-battery.   The tillers never
leave their fields to look at you, a Fung Kwei, and the
coolie, though weighted with two heavy pails hanging
from a bamboo borne upon his bare shoulders, steps off
the road into the swamp to let you pass, but he does not
look up.   The manners of China, by the Tao Li code, are
self-effasive.   At the outskirts of a village, you come to
the country seat.   Hand-cut granite walls inclose a lawn
where horned black water-buffalo feed.   The tea-house
at the gate is open for you to step in and rest.   You pass
through doors which are always open, to the rock garden,
the lily pools, the fir forest, and the flat gardens of clipped
chrysanthemums nearer the house.   Cool stone seats are
everywhere, roofed over to hold off the great sun.   The
master sends you tea, even though you have not sent in
your card, you being only a hurried foreign visitor of no
significance, who has heard that his grounds are open
to every one.   In our land the seat would cost a million.
There is not an establishment in the village worth twenty
dollars, but the religion of China requires that a man shall
return to his birthplace.   The remarkable man whose
homes these were, died at the Praya Grande house in

September, 1906.   His name was Ah Fong, and he had
been living in retirement for fifteen years with his homely
village relatives.   Forty years previous he emigrated to
Honolulu, where he amassed millions in sugar and labor
contracting.   He married there a half white and half
Kanaka woman, by whom he had thirteen daughters and
two sons.   When he left Honolulu he gave his wife and
daughters, who did not want to go to China, one million
dollars.   One of the daughters married an admiral in
the United States navy, and the others made marriages
with white men of some prominence in the territory.   Ah
Fong brought his son Anthony to China, and to him he
has left the greater part of this romantic fortune on the
stipulation that he shall follow the religion and patriotic
teachings of Confucius.   China has had no emigrant
whose career has been more picturesque; she has had no
son who was more loyal; at home among his people they
merely tell you that he did his duty to his forefathers and
his country, and that he will therefore never lack a male
heir to bow before his tablet.

The doorways and gateways are a mine for the illus-
trator, in their quaint lines of stucco.   Through many
a gate of ancient wrought iron work glimpses were had
of luxuriant tropical gardens, hid behind high white-
washed chunam walls, which glistened like a porcupine
with their armor of green, broken Munchen bottles stuck
in the plaster.   From ten A. M. until four P. M. the almost
breezeless, burning streets are deserted.   In the silent
night the native watchman drags his wooden sandals
noisily along and strikes his drum as he goes his rounds,
so that thieves and evil spirits may know his whereabouts,
and work elsewhere.

When England, in the days of Henry VIII. was war-

ring no farther away from home than France, Macao,
at the end of the earth, was strenuous in daring struggles.
The Dutch attacked St. Francis Fort, but drew off their
battered boats in defeat. The old copper cannon still
glisten on the picturesque ramparts, and beneath the white
stucco sentry boxes. At the Monte Fort they cast cannon, and when war of their own was not on, turned a
penny by selling the armament (the institution of manufactures in China), as in 1651, to the king of Cochin
China. In 1622, two hundred Spanish infantry, and
some cannon arrived from Manila to help the Macaense
against the Dutch. In Macao of to-day, opium is taxed
and gambling farmed, to feed the depleted purse of a
decaying Portugal. Macao was the emporium of Southern China until 1840, when she was superseded by British
Hong-Kong, which lies forty miles eastward, and that
the feeling of resentment toward the British still rankles
in the Macaense breast on this account, is evidenced by
Montalto de Jesus' history of Macao, published as late
as 1902, when every one supposed that the remembrance
of the slave barracoons and opium had been lost long ago.

In this old city of China, once lived and wrote the
illustrious poet whose name reads like a jewel, and is
sounded with the rich vowels of Greece. Camoens was
over forty when he completed his epic. He died in
Portugal, alas a victim of the Black Death, which, in its
own melancholy haunts, he had defied a thousand times.
The bubonic plague which was then attacking Europe,
originated in the territory of Camoens' exile. It exists
there to-day, and is the terror which arises every May
in Hong-Kong and Canton, alarming the ships that ply
therefrom to every European port. In Camoens' time
the plague went overland from mephitic Yunnan to Bur-

mah, following the Moorish traders from China to India, and the Red Sea, and by Arabic caravan to Constantinople and Venice. To trace its dire sweep through Milan and London, we need only read the terror-stricken pages of Manzoni and Pepys. Camoens, like Cervantes, in the fashion of the time, was soldier before being poet. He was a Hermes in regular features and curly yellow hair. In those days statesmen were poets first and courtiers afterward. Such were the talented and gallant Sortelha and Conde de Vimiosa. The Infanta, Donna Maria, led her court in epigram and sonnet. Portugal in the days of Camoens was a forerunner of what England was to become in the time of Raleigh. Arms, adventure and literature danced the measure, and the actor played equally well all three rôles. For a while Camoens was the favorite of the Lisbon Court, until that unfortunate day when his admiring eyes fell on the golden-tressed Donna Caterina, kneeling at prayer in the Church of the Chagos. Then his woes began, but with his woes upgrew his character, his interest in mankind of all colors and religions, and his fame. The Donna Caterina was of the queen's household, and the court opposed a suit, which was beyond his station. But this temerity also was the fashion of the time, for poor Tasso had similarly loved at Ferrara.

Camoens was born in 1524 at Lisbon. The world had almost forgotten classicism. The Renaissance and Boccaccio were long asleep. Chaucer had died in England, and all seemed dark again. It was yet a long cry to the births of Shakespeare and Milton. The Renaissance had sown the seed of ideals, but the seed was slumbering. In Camoens' time, Portugal was to rise, thrilled with the new life, and her glory it was to give India, South

America, Asia, and the seas of all the globe to the vision
and touch of marveling men. It was a generation of
gods, but as ever the gods whom men make have feet
of clay. Greece's clay was State's rights politics;
Portugal's was ill-distributed wealth. Camoens' fate
drifted into a current that bore him far from his sun, the
Donna Caterina, and a rival Andrade de Caminha, who
could also touch the lyre, but dressed in a more fashionable livery, displaced him. Banished by captious royalty
from the court, Camoens fought under his country's
flag in Africa with no diminution of patriotism, which
showed the man he was, because in those days there was
no democratic sentiment to laugh with those whom society snubs. In leading a boarding party over the bulwarks of a Moorish galley off Ceuta, he lost his right
eye. With the dauntless spirit of the traveler, but with
the broken heart of a lover, at twilight on a day in March,
1553, aboard the San Bento, he put out once more from
the golden Tagus. He was then twenty-nine years of
age. In nine months he was in Goa, on the Malabar
coast of India, and it was here on his way home with his
immortal poem, *The Lusiad,* seventeen years later,
that he was to hear of the death of the inspirer of his
youth, the Donna Caterina. Life for a while was adventure only. The feats of arms were considerable,
sometimes two thousand being slain. In winter there
were Moors to pursue at Ormuz, and through the summer
heat, in dissipated days for most of his companions, they
dreamed at Goa. Owing to a satire of Camoens, who
was engaged in more intellectual if not more tactful work
than wine-bibbing, Governor Barreto banished him from
Goa to the little colony of Macao in China.

When the discouraged poet first saw Macao from the

sea he wrote: "In this lonely, sterile, sun-scorched land did fortune will that my life be passed, and in fragments be scattered throughout the world." Here he finally found the cords of life pulling taut, and the breeze sure and full, with a course laid which he might sail, unpursued of enemies. He had a luxuriant garden; a small competence as "Trustee of the Estates of Those at Home," for the faint-hearted soon left if they might; and a devoted Javanese slave. The angel of fame, as present in the ends of the earth as in the temple of Delphi, gave him a language to seal to a people, and an epic whose theme is the widest man has sung. In the yellow matting junk sails of the Pearl he dreamed that he beheld the argosies of classic song, and the gong of the Confucian rang in his fancy as the cymbal of Bacchus. Without the accommodating temper of the soldier, the poet's imagination in him would have sunk in despair. Courage held him up in his lonely life. Poesy was the bread of his soul. His theme was his nation, and patriotism was held by him almost in a frenzy. His was that refined patriotism which sees one's country, not as she is or has treated him, but as she would be when he had in love remolded her.

I have seen the proud Macaense gathered about the poet's bust at the famous grotto at Macao, while an orator, tearful with emotion, recited the proud cadences of the great song of his dying race. Camoens was the Homer of the Portuguese, and Da Gama and Albuquerque were his Ulysses and Eurylochus. Almost within his lifetime, Portugal was the shore that abutted on the sea of oblivion. Within his memory, the African coast had been ventured along, Good Hope rounded, Azores found, Brazil discovered by accident, India linked by a sea route,

Macao, the Inner Praya. Curious house with bamboo roof garden,
oyster-shell windows, brick, tile, and stucco work;
architecture showing Portuguese influence
of the past five centuries.

The beautiful marble and teak Royal Palace, Peking, where the Emperor Kwang Su and Dowager Empress died in November, 1908. The grotesque lions attract sculptors from the whole world.

Shanghai, the metropolis of East Central China, looking south into the French and native quarters. Shanghai, situated at the junction of Soochow Creek and Huang Phu river, is 16 miles inland from the mouth of the Yang-tze river.

and Lisbon displaced Venice as the capital of the world
and the hub of luxury and fashion. The "celibate of
Sagre," Prince Henry the Navigator, in his court at
Cape St. Vincent, was the brother of these greatest of
discoverers, this "Company of Captains." Vessels were
then half-decked, and carried thirty-six sailors. It was
with four of these caravels that Da Gama took a year to
reach India. Not only to the south went the intrepid
Portuguese, for Martin Lopez discovered Nova Zembla
on a search northeast for Cathay. Evora's caravans
ventured the dreariest, hottest and widest desert of the
earth, then called Guebla, as far as Timbuctoo. Andrade
reached fabled Peking in 1521. Magellan, bowing under
the auspicious sign of the Southern Cross, parted the
violet veil that concealed the Pacific, and Pinto landed in
quaint Japan in 1537. Little Portugal is the grand-
mother of the world. In every glass of her famous wine,
that breathes the richest boquet at our dinners, she
should be toasted by the nations on whom she has bestowed her heritage of discovery. The vast, world-
encircling commerce of modern times was founded by
Portugal in the fifteenth century. Some day a baron of
British, American or Japanese shipping, who has a taste
for history, may desire to perpetuate gratitude by erecting
at Sagre, in old Portugal, a monument to Prince Henry
the Navigator. In St. Francis Xavier, who came to Goa
in 1542, Portugal instituted world missions. In the
noble De Castro, invincible in battle and pure in life,
she has given a hero to song and story. From the Moors
and Venetians in the Red Sea and India, this soldier won
dominion for the Portuguese, and died in the arms of
Xavier, bequeathing to his son "his only spoils and
riches, a sword unrivaled and spotless of shame."

These are the antecedents of Camoens and the heroes of his epic *Os Lusiadas,* which was published in Lisbon in 1572. The French Montesquieu wrote: " It makes us feel something of the charms of the *Odyssey* and the magnificence of the *Æneid.*" The English Hallam called it " the first successful attempt in Europe to construct an epic poem on the ancient model; it is the mirror of a heart full of love, courage, generosity and patriotism." Doctor Johnson contemplated the translation of the poem, but afterward invited Goldsmith, with his larger sympathy and understanding of travel, to do the work. Voltaire called Camoens the " Milton of the Portuguese." The first translation in English of *The Lusiad* was made by Richard Fanshaw, a literary diplomat of Charles II.'s reign. It has been translated into English by Aubertin, Sir Richard Burton, and Thomas Musgrave. Mickle's translation, made in 1776, is probably the best known. The stately iambics of that translation do not do justice to the sprightly dactyls and silvery rhyme of the original. The metaphors are luxuriant, as about our classic forms the poet twined the colored vines of oriental fancy. Camoens had been first a lyrist. The purity of form of the Italian sonnet had influenced him. He was profoundly educated at the University of Coimbra, then at the height of its renown, in the Greek and Latin poets. In *The Lusiad,* he broke from the severe classical style of his compatriot Ribeiro and the Italian influence of Miranda, which looked to the past only, and founded a virile Portuguese language, which adopted the best of what was new and strong in the experience of the traveled, of whom he was the chief. His poem is the bond of the Portuguese at home, in wide Brazil, Goa, Mozambique, Macao, and Hong-Kong. Virgil was his mas-

ter in elaborating a theme.   Voltaire pointed out that a
serious fault of the poem is in the commingling of Christian and classic imagery.   In Camoens' epic there
breathes a similar religious purpose to that which consumed Milton.   Milton exalted his story to the heavens.
Camoens chose a theme all human, which trailed its in-
domitable course over the most dangerous paths of the
world in the half-awakened morning of the newly discovered planet.

This is the theme of *The Lusiad;* the history of Portugal at the acme of her glory, and the spirit and past of
ancient Macao, where the conception of it all was nursed,
and where it was brought to bloom.   It is the greatest
epic of travel; the history of the feud between Moorish
caravan and Portuguese caravel for the first sandal-
scented oriental commerce.   The arena spreads from the
arid plains of Arabia to the dancing purple waters of
India.   The rounding of the Cape of Storms (Good
Hope) with the frail vessels of that age has probably
been the most awesome adventure in the imagination of
mortals.   India by overland route had been reached;
South America had been discovered; the Atlantic was
ferried; but the demons of the lost were believed to have
placed an insurmountable barrier, reaching into the turbulent unknown, between India and Europe.   When the
Portuguese captains first set sail, Europe was mist-
wrapped and demon-haunted off shore, like Turner's
painting, *Ulysses Deriding Polyphemus,* only here and
there a galleon, after the blessing of the waters and unc-
tion for the sailors, braving a narrow sea; Venice ven-
turing along the Mediterranean shore; Flanders assailing
the Baltic, and England smiting the channel with her
Viking prows.   From the dark Moors, who, it was

rumored, had sent out adventurers on waters mysterious, Prince Henry the Navigator learned that Africa probably extended to the equator. Henry's first salvage from the deeps was Madeira, and upon that success he sent out captain after captain, like one possessed of a universal vision. Probably the most ecstatic thrill of the human imagination has been accorded to this famous prince who was as scientific as he was enthusiastic, though history has not so credited him.

The Lusiad's hero is Vasco Da Gama, and its story, his adventures from Lisbon to Calicut in India, during the two years and two months which it took him to make the voyage. The Moslems were masters of the Eastern waters and Calicut was their emporium. The first canto of the epic is fresh with new pictures of the new-found far East: "The sails they hoisted were of matting made, woven of leaves of palm trees." Canto Three contains the famous romance of Ignez de Castro, which secured Voltaire's enthusiasm, and is one of the most celebrated in all literature. The gentle Ignez was maid of honor to the Infanta, and was clandestinely married to the heir, Don Pedro. When this was discovered by the ambitious and cruel King Alphonso, he ordered Ignez to be murdered. When Pedro succeeded to the kingdom, he ordered his bride's remains to be disinterred and placed on the throne, and the homage of the people done to her, as a saint who was queen even in death. The figures of the story are woven with the luxuriousness of Keats:

> *Estavas linda Ignez, posta em socego;*
> *Mas ella os olhos, comque o ar serena."*
>> "Behold her, fair Ignez, deep-bosomed in quiet;
>> Soft-turning her eyes, e'en the cruel air she calmeth."

Adventure, classic allusion and romance, succeed one another in limpid and alluring verse, and strength is not lacking, as witness the stupendous battle masterpiece in describing Aljubarota. Voltaire, cynical concerning the poem as a whole because he hated the joys of the imagination not less than the confident truths of experience, was carried away despite himself with the vision of Adamastor in Canto Five. The pictures of storms have the true sweep of typhonic nature, from the experience of fearful months of privation and danger by the poet himself on the yellow Chinese seas, in days when ships were merely shells. It is interesting to know what the Lusitanian thought of his less cultured neighbors. He calls the Teutons " all pride, rebels to creed," and the English through whose taciturnity few Latins have ever penetrated to discover any real idealism or vivacious enjoyment of achievement, he called: " hard, in Hyperborean winters walled." Canto Nine contains the bewitching allegory of the Isles of Love, which Venus brings from the sea. Here Camoens has shed the adorning fancies of the Orient on the forms of Greece, and every line revels in coruscating color. Thus through strange lands and beautiful story does he bring the Lusians back to Lisbon, and lays his poem at the feet of the nation. He is buried in the Franciscan Church of Santa Anna at Lisbon, and upon his tomb are the lachrymal words where Fame charges Life with treachery: " He excelled all the poets of his time; he lived poor and miserable, and he died so."

The poet's fame is more beautifully kept at Macao. In the grotto of his exile, the world's poets, among them the exquisite English hymn-writer, Governor Sir John Bowring of near-by Hong-Kong, have carved in the enduring granite of the Chinese hills, their gentle lines of praise about the poet's bust in honor of their pilgrimage, which is the only one in the Orient of European literary association. The banyan, the tamarind and bamboo keep shade in the poet's garden. The tuberoses, camellias and azaleas make the air dense as with censers. Still does the Chukiang (Pearl) roll beneath his seat and whisper the old lullabies. The yellow matting sails still drift with the returning tides, as in the evenings long ago, when they were borne slowly from the poet's vision into the wide oriental sunset of cloudless gold. Soft oars beat by in the dusk, as though the poet's spirit passed along. A silver gong from a belated junk strikes the first stars into being, as once before in a land where there is no twilight, they showered from the fingers of a Southern Night, to teach their music of the soul to a lost one at last attuned to their purposes, the exile Louis de Camoens.

III.

Lives there a land which has no political parties? Then look there for the secret society in all its rank luxuriance. China abounds in it. Socially its curse is that it upholds its members in private evil more than in the public good at which its charter loftily aims, and from the exercise of which it is prevented by the present stunted constitution of the country. At Tientsin there is a house known to foreigners from its door as the " Society of the Red Door." To the initiated it is the " Society which Meets Injury with Retaliation." The branch at Hangchow, known as Hung Pang, or Red Association, is constantly fomenting rice riots between the villagers and the up-country boatmen who arrive from the Grand Canal, as a pretext for political risings. Only recently they captured a prefectural city and it was necessary to call upon the reorganized Imperial troops to dislodge them. In Che-kiang Province the Chiu Sik Lun (Earthen Pot Society) murdered a governor in August, 1907, for discouraging the principles of the New China party, and the effect has eddied at last as far as Peking, in the institution of the new Supreme Council, whose duties are proclaimed to be the educating of the country toward representative government. The echoes of the fourth century rescripts of Honorius, or the nearer melancholy of the Chinese edicts of 1898! Unless China does more for real representation, dissolution is not staved off for

ever, any more than it was during the lingering centuries
of the Roman Empire. Advance and a partial reaction
divide history, and China has had her share of the latter
during the Manchu tenancy of the throne. The most
famous secret society is the Triad (Sam Hop Wui), the
members of which are supposed to go armed for private
revenge, in addition to the great aim of their body to
enthrone a native dynasty. They are ruled by a Master
of the Red Stick, who sets the penalties. The " Society
of the Sword " is also anti-dynastic, and strong in the
central provinces for the new patriotism. During the
New Year celebration of two weeks, all secret societies,
as well as the guilds, whose rivalry also is often very
bitter, declare a " Truce of the Gods," when no man may
attack his brother. This is generally respected. Both
the hunter and the hunted are glad of a relief, when they
may feel free to travel, or be careless in the use of their
samschu wine.

The statute books contain the unrepealed death penalty
for belonging to some of the secret societies, such as the
Gee Kung Tong, which also is a Freemasonry vowed to
the work of driving from the throne the Manchu house
of Tsings and establishing thereon descendants of the
Mings, but the government does not dare to enforce the
statute. They would have to depopulate the kingdom
if they did. The Ko Lo Win is a similar anti-
dynastic society. The branch of the society among the
emigrants in Malaysia is called the Orchids, and lines
of their poetry are breezy enough to dispel the ennui of
exiles. "We are strong and spread everywhere, command hills and rivers; despise us who dare. Lo! In
Fu-kien, a black flag flying; Attention! Kun Su is the
place for gathering."

Candidates are sometimes rushed for election by being kidnapped in bags and brought to the lodge room. Meetings are called by split bamboos being left at the residences of the members. Since 1845 in Hong-Kong, and a later date in Singapore, the British government has prohibited meetings of the Triad Society. Where murders are committed, the sentence of death is passed upon the local leaders, whether they are present or not. In a trial at Sarawak, Straits Settlements, under British law, in April, 1906, a jury composed of eight Chinese towkays, three Malays and one European (foreman) passed sentence of death upon eight leaders for the murder of one victim of the Triads.

The Buddhists have a temperance society called the Tsai Li, which has effectively adopted the anti-opium crusade, and its enthusiasm is stimulated by certain secret society rules, which are so dear to the Chinese heart. In the same way religiously, Buddhism got her roots safely in Chinese ground by adopting ancestor worship. The Oriental distrusts iconoclasts.

That a hidden tide is undermining educational China is most marked in the discontinuance, in their old form, of the triennial classical examinations which have been in vogue thirteen hundred years, and whose three degrees of Hsiuts' ai (Budding Talent) answering to our B.A.; Chujen (M.A.), and Chin Shih (D.C.L.) for which a yellow diploma with red characters was issued,—alone opened the way to political employment, which is considered the highest profession in the land. *Nien shu tso kuan:* "Get education and position will get you." Examination for the higher degrees included reëxamination in considerable of the lower. No such feats of memory have ever been required of students, and where this faculty alone is required, the oriental student is invincible in American colleges. Where our students speak of "ponies" and "cribs," the oriental student jokes about his "skin paper," but so cumbersome is the language that a crib, to be of any use, would be detectable. A red sash is worn from the right shoulder to the left waist. During the examination, the student in his cell recalls that at home, and in the pagoda, his family have hung lamps before the idol as votives on his behalf. Even though the successful scholar enters business he is considered of the Shin Kin, or gentry of his district, there being no landed titles. A branch of the olive is waved over the winner's head, and frequently he is hazed and "run" for secret societies. Like the Campanile of St. Mark's, without immediate warning, this famous institution has tumbled in Kwangtung and is being reërected with the Tsin Tsueh or new learning taking the place of one third of the old. The first blow at the old system was really struck by the lately deceased emperor, Kwang Su, in his famous reformatory edicts of 1898, when he was disturbed by the shocks of and the reasons for his defeat by Japan. Every village is now striving to possess a Hok Tong (day school) which will conform with the new standards of the Board of Education, whose requirements include military drill. The most radical decrees in the history of the throne, those of Kwong Su in 1897, were addressed to mandarins and "schoolmasters." The new text books use illustration to the fullest advantages. These books, as well as the maps and globes, are at present all prepared in Japan. Many Japanese teachers are employed, and numbers of them as professors in English. Education and property will equally be the qualification for suffrage

A merry market party floating down a tidal river in South China.

A fine view of river life, Canton, South China; temple with gable carvings in foreground; three pawnshop towers in distance.

North Wall of Canton and "Five-story Pagoda." Note in foreground marble graves of two native rich men, set in bare hillside.

in electing the proposed provincial parliaments, which are suggested for trial two years hence by the Kiun Ki Chu, or new Supreme Council.

In 1905 China sent ten thousand pupils to Japan, in 1906 she doubled the number, which has been increasing right along. When America in 1908 waived rights to half of her share of the Boxer indemnity of 1900, China enthusiastically reciprocated by recruiting scholars to go to America's colleges and schools. The future will show that this move was one of unusual brilliance on America's part. Hong-Kong for some time has possessed a medical school for Chinese, and Singapore, through the generosity of the towkays, has afforded similar opportunities to natives. Canton is soon to have bestowed upon it a medical college under the auspices of the University of Pennsylvania, which with the branch of Yale College called " Elegant Proprieties " at Changsha, Hunan's capital, have here the opportunity to seize an influence and do a work with the more intelligent natives, which missionary societies have failed in because of the suspicion attending purely religious auspices at the present time. Prophetically, the first patent issued by China was granted to a Nankinese for an electric light, which of course adopted a poetic name, " the new moonshine." As you enter the palace at Peking, the new and the old display themselves in an unusual fraternization. The lacquered teak bars have been displaced by plate glass doors, on which the word " Sho " (long life) has been emblazoned in immense red characters. In the new schools in Kwangtung the provincial government is offering the high salary of thirty dollars Mexican (fifteen dollars gold) a month to native teachers. Those who have had experience in mission schools are preferred, for this province remembers that other wonderful mission school pupil, the famous Hung Siu Tsuen who nearly reached the oldest and widest throne of the ages.   It is to be hoped that the sacred Kings, and the Confucian collection of prose and verse, will always retain the place in the culture of the nation that is held by Greek literature in western refinement.   Chinese travelers say: "When you seek culture go to Canton; when you seek its opposite, go to Fuchau."

The proudest procession of the clan is the marriage procession, and in it the highest of all the banners are those naming the men who have won literary degrees. A graduate erects a flagpole before his home, and his proud father nails on it a triangle.   The ten thousand stalls in dreary rows at Wuchang across the river from Han-kau, the seventeen thousand brick booths in the western capital, Chingtoo; and the fifteen thousand cells at Nanking, stand empty, like our fair-ground booths between seasons, and down the walks blow the leaves of the old examination papers,— a literary Vollombrosa in autumn.   Many of the ten thousand stalls at Canton, which every traveler will recall by the fine camphor-trees in the sixteen-acre park, have been razed to provide a site for a modern university.   Students who fail to secure the highest degree recall as an ill omen the name of the examination hall at Peking, that of " Intense Mental Exercise."   In these stalls the candidates remain for days, until they complete their papers.   Their name is pasted within a fold of the paper, and the pocket is not opened until the examiner has perused and marked the answers.   The students are expected to bring sufficient food, tea and covering to last during their occupancy, and they may not hold conversation with soldiers on guard, or with other candidates. The booths are rough brick constructions like sentry boxes, and are often daubed in blue with some classical inscription. While the lowest peasant may compete, four classes are debarred, in this most democratic of countries, where there has never been a nobility in perpetuity, except the direct line from Confucius. The tabooed classes are court eunuchs, barbers, actors and keepers of opium dens (i.e., a class who answer to our saloon keepers). As in every university, it is found that the higher education emasculates the character and independence of a small percentage. Certain students who pass high, and are the sons of poor men, advertise that they offer themselves as the sons-in-law, or adopted sons of rich men who have daughters but no sons. There is not a Chinese, however poor, who will endure being without some one to carry his name, and sacrifice to his manes and tablet. He could not otherwise face death with composure, or what is harder, he could not face this obloquy of fortune during life. Even the beggars and the lepers search the banks for some human driftwood to adopt. This motif takes the place in Chinese novels of our theme of love, and is also the incentive for most of their humor. The Chinese have furnished historic proof that an eastern race being founded on Thought, does not disintegrate when its men of action, like Genghis and Kublai Khan, pass away. It is quite a different thing to endow with Thought, and thus make permanent a race founded on Action,— and so have passed away, when their leaders fell, Nineveh, Macedonia, and the Empires of Charlemagne and Napoleon.

England and America jointly contribute five million

dollars a year toward the education of China, in the salaries paid missionaries, colporteurs and medical men, but this is a very small tax, considering the trade which the two countries enjoy with China. As a trade measure alone, not to speak of a humanitarian one, let there be more missionaries,— especially medical,— sent out, and do not hamper them by confining them to didactics; let them put their hands to anything civilizing for the precarious present.

There is something marvelously authoritative in the clang of the cantankerous gong. Sleepy China, and even the sport-pursuing foreigner outside the gates, are obedient in an instant. Insistence is shown by the rapidity of the strokes. The gong saves China policemen. It is the flare of the short sunset. At the southern gate of one of the ten thousand walled cities of dragon land, one hundred strokes are rapidly struck by the watchman. Every one becomes his brother's policeman, and shouts to his neighbor to hurry. There is a pause. One hundred more strokes are rained upon the gong, in the fort which is built upon the wall over the gate, where the instruments of the bonzes indicate that the sun has gone down. Not all the gate towers are beautiful, Peking's having little curl to the cornices and the structures being too heavy. The Chien Mun gate, which the expeditionary force blew up in 1900, was as plain as a gunny godown. At Mukden, and indeed the deeper you go into Manchuria and Mongolia, the more the artistic wanes and the colder, older and sadder the forts and everything else look. At Hang-chow, the gates are too low and long for such heavy walls, though the cornices have the grace that you expect in the happier south. But at Kialing Fu is a beautiful gate-fort of splendid proportions, with lofty sweep to the cornices, grace in the lattice work, and adornment in the frieze. The farther you go up the Yangtze, a kindlier sun and sweeter air warm the heart and foster into flower the artistic dreams of the native architect. The two story guard-house on the wall over the low grim north gate of Canton, is more ponderous than beautiful however. One exception to the general stern style of the north is the chaste and truly delightful pentagonal gate with frieze through the Great Wall at Nankow.

Within a few minutes after the clangs of the last one hundred strokes have died away, the crowd,— all but the thief who is greasing his body and filling his rolled-up queue with needles so you can not hold him by the tail,— has divided between those who will remain in the stone sheds among the vegetable and rice terraces, or stay within the clamorous city, where half the traders keep shop (not in their hats for they have none), in their umbrellas. The ponderous iron-bound gate is dragged shut with much laughter, chaffing and jeers at the gate-men, who with earnest faces, excitement of manner, and shouting *san* (get out of the way), drop the long fastening bar into its socket. The clamps are padlocked with enormous quaint brass locks, which any peasant could pick with a rice-hook. The piratically inclined have been known to use a little palm oil to lubricate their exit, after the law had posted its warder. Outside the gates, Leong has been jostled by Cheong. They drop their bamboo poles and baskets; rush at each other, plant their feet in each other's stomachs and tug at each other's queues. Nearly every southern Chinese is subject to enlargement of the spleen, and therefore the western method of fisticuffs has fortunately not been adopted. The gate of a city is considered as holy as a temple, and it is sacrilege to paste posters upon it. If you would not invite bad fortune, you must leave a city by a different gate from the one by which you entered it. It is the hurried close of the race-meeting outside the northwest walls of Peking in May. The evening shadows are growing longer beneath the thirteen story Buddhist monastery, and the roofs of the Taoist temple. Some one announces that it is about time for the gongs of Peking to sound their warning. The Chinese begin to race home on foot. The last races are hurried, and the mafoos hardly wait for their badges. Foreigners mounted on mules, Mongol ponies, and India breds; in chairs, in Peking springless carts, in 'rickishas, and on foot,— all vanish into the advancing cloud of loess dust, which swallows them, and move on to the Anting gate just before it is closed for the night. Thus far at least has our Occidental in exile become orientalized.

Half of the false hair used in America and Europe is gathered in China. It is not uncommon for the river pirates who infest the delta about Canton, to burst upon a village, and after kidnapping for ransom all they can conveniently convoy, to cut off every other queue they can lay hold of. Rats are eaten by the extremely ignorant in the superstition that the queue will grow longer. In Shansi, human hair combings are collected and woven at home into large over-socks for winter use.

The queue fills not only a roll of honor, but sometimes comes in for dishonor. On a March evening not long ago, at Fat Shan on the delta of the Pearl, the silk shop of my friend Tai Cheung, on Sui Tsun street, was attacked at night in back and front. Four pirates, with stones tied to the ends of bamboos, broke a hole through the adobe wall at the back and entered. The eight *fokis* (shop tenders) who were sleeping on the premises, rushed to the front bars to escape from the shooting in the rear. There sixteen other desperadoes alarmed them with torches and drove them back. The robbers herded the *fokis* in a corner, where they were all tied, queues together, with wire to a post, where these inglorious Celestial Samsons were later found by the amused villagers. To complete the consternation of the poor *fokis,* the thieves exploded bamboo bombs, and with their arms full of bolts of silk, and shouting *San* 桑 兵 (scatter) to one another, they safely decamped. There are also bands who make a specialty of robbing the mulberry trees. A company recently stole upon the Shun Tak community near Canton, with shears, ladders, and bags. The villagers awoke to find their only wealth, the lusang trees, denuded of every branch and leaf. It is pretty hard to prove ownership of a mulberry leaf, but the worms of the adjoining Sai Kwan district proved to be exceedingly productive that season,— so that the Shun Tak people retain their suspicions for a retaliatory raid next season.

Some of the rich unquestionably eat fried silkworm grubs which are fed on oak leaves, and some of the poor eat non-poisonous snakes, cats and dogs. The last mentioned are sold slyly even in the British colony of Hong-Kong, but this taste is not unknown in Europe. The price of dog flesh in Hamburg, on July sixteenth, was quoted at sixty pfennigs. In the cities of Cassel and Chemnitz last year fourteen hundred dogs, and throughout the German Empire about eight thousand dogs in the same period, were slaughtered for food purposes.

Au Yang Kang, a butcher, recently made unblushing

application to the Sanitary Board of the British colony of Hong-Kong, for "permission to sell deer, snakes, cats and dogs for food in the petitioner's shop on Temple Street, Yaumati," on the Chinese mainland. Their dog is stockier than the Esquimaux, which it most resembles. Its plumed tail is curled well up on its back, and it has a noble frill and mane. The color is either solid black or solid tan. Those of black tongue and black mouth are considered the purest in lineage. The black dog is preferred when used for food. Its characteristics are an absolute unfriendliness to every one except its owner, and freedom from hydrophobia even in so hot a climate. As a watch-dog it has no superior, never attacking but barking like an irrepressible string of fire-crackers. Its power in the shoulders makes it a useful and most unique adjunct to sail and man in propelling the barrows along the narrow, raised, country paths.

The Chinese seldom build oblong mounds over their *fens* (graves). The rich of the southern provinces adopt the conspicuous horseshoe brick work, in the toe of which the urn or coffin is sealed. These spots are chosen for the view they afford, which is an important consideration in Fungshui geomancy. The poor build merely a cone of earth over the urn, and into this is inserted the wooden stick with its black letters. The cemeteries cover a larger area than the cities of China, which is an indisputable visual evidence both of the age of the country, and the stability of its customs. Around the mounds beyond the Porta Cerco gate at Macao, I have seen the Heungshan farmers permit their water-buffaloes to crop food. Who that has stood on Kwan Yin Hill, beyond the north gate of Canton, and looked into the necropolis of the ages which extends up the acclivities of the White Cloud Hills, wide as the eye can sweep beyond the walls, can for a moment feel that the living speak as vastly as do the honored dead of this city, which was sending out funeral processions two centuries before Christ, while to-day those graves now being dug are for the bones of Kwangtung men who died in Africa, Australia, Panama, Saghalien and Demarara, where they formed the advance guard of our occidental civilization, Orientals though they were by blood and birth? The white captains of steamers who are known to exercise care that no Chinese emigrant dying en route is buried at sea, are remembered by the guilds at Hong-Kong with handsome silk banners testifying to their "Honorable Benevolence" so truly Confucian in practice.

In the first part of April, when the earth and air is joyous with oriental color, the hills around the cities are crowded with those who come to perform *pai shan,* or worship on the hills. Five foods are laid at the tomb: duck, goose, fish, fowl and pig. Cousins come from distant points, and the festival is really their Christmas in the sense of reunions, rejoicing and feasts. Part of the ceremony is called *Siu Fan Tai,* "sweeping the tomb" clean of leaves and dust in preparation for the kowtow. The worshiper raises up his voice, invoking his ancestor, and declares: "Lo, I have swept thy tomb." But the heart of the foreigner is touched by a closer chord of pity for his own exiles, when his eye beholds the white man's cemeteries on French and Dane's Islands in the Pearl River.

In the funeral procession, the white lotus is carried as the badge of mourning, and a sprig of growing bamboo, to signify that the soul sprouts again in another world in another form. Pretty enough for any faith! The red census slips on each side of the door are taken down for a season, and white ones are pasted up. A white lantern instead of a gaudy one is hung out at night. White cord is braided in the queue. Indeed, if you point to a funeral procession and ask a yokel what it is, he will say "a white affair." Two conical incense mounds are carried on a tray to be burned; they are called Chin Shan and Yin Shan (gold and silver mountains). No procession is accorded to those who have not been married. Such are hurried to the grave unescorted, save by the two melancholy bearers and the parents. White cakes are taken so that the soul of the deceased may inhale their fragrance. The priests are gowned in white. The only legitimate widow, (the first), wearing white flowers in her hair, is hurried along, led by a child. She is expected to cry aloud, and should seem to make endeavor to break from the throng, so as to commit suicide in faithful grief. Professional mourners, called " dogs of the devil," wear white sheets over their shoulders, weep tears and howl uninterruptedly, except when they explode us Westerners by quickly changing to a smile and nod for some passing acquaintance. A white pall is thrown over the coffin, which is trotted along by two or four bearers. Arriving at the grave, the bier is approached by near friends, who call out the name of the dead. Flowers are not sent, but friends contribute banners on which are emblazoned the offices and virtues of the deceased.

The Chinese are always dramatic. There is a considerable stretch between the sections. This is intended to magnify, by repeating, the impression, so that the word shall be passed several times down the streets:

Golf in the Graveyard of the Ages, Canton, South China. The spot
where all the Chinese of America state in their wills
that their bones must lie.

Sheep grazing in a graveyard of the poor, in the suburbs of Peking,
North China. Ancestor-worship has preserved these cemeteries to the clans, safe from intrusion by agricul-
ture or building for thousands of years. Two
topes to dead llamas in background.

Canal between native city and Shameen Island, where foreigners
live, Canton, South China.

"It is Hip Tong — it is Hip Tong — it is Hip Tong, who is released to his ancestors." A wooden tablet with the name of the deceased is stuck in the pot of ashes in the toy spirit house. In this tablet resides one of the three souls of the man. Pirates steal these sacred tablets for ransom. The Imperial family use blue for anniversary mourning, though white is *de rigeur* for first mourning. The largest grave section in the south is at Chek Wan, situated on one of the branches of the Pearl Delta, near Canton. Excursions are run by steamboat in April, and one hundred thousand Chinese from Hong-Kong and Canton make the pilgrimage. The festival is a religious one and is called by the Hakkas *Tsing Ming*, or "saluting of the hill." The exact date is set by the emperor, who thus comes into intimate fatherhood with the poorest of his people, his office as priest often protecting his weakness as king. The Board (Pu) of Rites, realizing however the inadequate means of rural transportation, and the inconvenience and sanitary danger of throwing a crowd of scores of thousands into one cemetery on a certain day, permits pilgrims a latitude of two days before and after the official day, to pay their worship at the tombs of their ancestors. A burial in the small villages near Hong-Kong, like Lyee-moon and Ngan Kok, costs twenty cents excluding the coffin, and where the body is sculled to a cemetery a mile across the bay, the cost is two dollars and a half. The desecration of a grave is a capital offense. The mausoleums of the rich, with their terraces and Yunnan marble stairs, are even more striking and costly that what our own cemeteries have to show. A native will not pass a cemetery at night, without a lighted lantern. The Mohammedan Chinese of Yunnan have a unique custom of whitewashing their graves, which point south. In Shensi remain evidences of great dome-like mounds which are either the graves of emperors, or the victims of famine from drought or flood. So you may guess whether one man or fifty thousand lie under each mound. Knowing what I do of famines in China, I prefer to believe in the larger number under each mound.

One of the saddest sights in the world is a clan's charity cemetery. This is walled around, in contrast to the ant-hill graves of the vast open hillside. Against the middle of one wall is a noble shrine. The chasteness of the design is not surpassed by any architecture; walls strong as the Egyptian, a colored tile roof with heavy eaves, a façade pure as the Doric. There is only the curved line of the ridge to suggest what is characteristically Chinese. Receptacles are made for the deposit of prayer papers, spirit food and incense, the rites being similar to the early Greek. The melancholy view is of the stern field of death, with its closely placed conical mounds which are built over the urns. At the foot of the center path is the one stone, with the name of the clan and the purpose of its charity for its poor members. There is not a tree or a plant in the vast enclosure; only the silhouette of the white and green altar to the gods of the clan, which has not moved from its countryside for thousands of years. The baby towers, about which so many misstatements have been made, are erected by clan charity to " save the face," that is to say, to keep the poor parent's pride from the humility of formally asking charity from the clan. When the child dies, the parent drops its body in the tower of silence, where it is taken charge of by the clan officials, and a proper funeral is given it, the parent mixing in the retinue, and it is not altogether unknown whose child it is. There is a great deal said of children being strangled and thrown in the towers, but there is probably as much parental affection in China as elsewhere. In contrast with this austerity are the elaborate topes to dead Lamas, erected in Shansi, Pechili and Thibet.

Much has also been written of the dangerous habit of leaving bodies above ground, for it certainly is very common to see coffins scattered upon an open lot for months, waiting for the lucky burial day (Fungshui), and the exact spot that the geomancers are to choose. But as the coffins are from six to eight inches thick, the joints cemented, and the body placed in lime, they are as harmless above ground as under it, and one never hears of pestilence resulting from the custom, except in a hurried tourist's sketch. But China is now establishing newspapers, and will prove the truth of what is written about her.

In the futile ostentation of pride and the contumely borne by poverty, the Chinese are not exempt from our own experiences. In the ward of the coffin makers beneath the walls of Canton, near the Five Story pagoda, is a Buddhist sanctuary for the dead. According to the rent paid, a coffin and room are hired, and emblematic food for the spirit and appeasing incense for the contrary spirits, are offered every day by the monks. Some of the coffins like that of the Viceroy of Fu-kien or the Tartar General Chung's which all retain the convex shape of the tree, display the most gorgeous yellow lacquer ever executed. As long as the family of the deceased remains wealthy, this display is the envy of the townspeople. When poppied time passes, and the fees are not paid, another body is installed in both coffin and room. But this

is exactly the custom followed in our French and Spanish cities, as in the brick pile of rented tombs at St.
Roch's, New Orleans; in the tiers which adjoin the old
pit of ejected human bones at the Cristobal Colon Cemetery at Havana, and in the long white alleys at Barcelona,
where trouble is not taken fully to obliterate the names
of the defaulting tenant before the new initials are painted
on the door. A foreigner (and I have known a mean
humorist to do it to sell his wares) who makes it known
to the mandarin and native community that he has bought
his grave plot in sacred China, at once secures irresistible
influence and affection from a people who see in this
act the highest proof of a feeling of brotherhood with
them.

The rivers of China bear an unusual alluvial richness to
the seas. Where America has one mile of river, China
has ten. The deltas and fishing banks around Canton
and Woosung are feeding grounds for innumerable shoals
of fish. The fish as they are caught are thrown into
flooded compartments (the Chinese invented the compart-
ment boat really for fishing purposes), and sold alive in
the markets of Hong-Kong. Your comprador learns to
judge by the dorsal fin as he chooses your dinner, and
your coolie dangles the struggling pomfret, garoupa, or
mullet from a grass thong as he marches behind your
'rickisha. The natives too often insist on the scales being scraped, while life is still pulsing in the victim. For
transportation inland, great sunfish, perch and ling are
salted and sun-dried. The Chinese is nauseated by no
degree of piscatorial decomposition, but he gets a good
deal of leprosy, according to some critics, from the dried
fish indulgence. In the higher country, northwest from
Canton, the peasants in the spawning season pull the

reeds, on which the eggs hang, from the rivers, and throw them into pools. In this way their ponds are stocked with carp. The silt of the Chu and Si Rivers has built a vast fishing shoal about famous old Macao. This emporium of the far East during the fifteenth century lies now like a stranded ship, melancholy in isolation. "*Magni nominis umbra.*" The red land dragon has clutched her from the grasp of the green sea dragon. In twenty-five years, seventy million metric tons of alluvial deposit have been silted around the doomed port. Her custom-house entries of clearances for Europe suddenly closed sixty years ago. No fitter place could be chosen than this blue-walled city, for a Goldsmith of the Sea to sing the stanzas of a " Deserted Harbor."

The widest beach in the world is the famous half moon beach between Ke Tae and Cacilhas. One can walk out two miles at low tide. On the silver strand at high tide, native fishermen dry their nets, which they have dyed with an infusion of mangrove bark or gambier, to preserve them. Others are poling their way along a net, and darting into the water at the end of a bamboo, an inverted half cocoanut, to frighten the fish into the net. Tremendous vigor is exercised in the animating scene. In the fish market, below the three-storied stone building which has a picturesque fourth story of bamboo, on the Inner Praya, you can purchase a different species of fish every day of the year, brought from the feeding shallows around Joao and Lapa, particularly the delicious samli, and among the others, hammer-headed shark, electric torpedo, cuttle, gorgeous parrot, red sturgeon, eels, and anchovies. While there are no lobsters in oriental waters, the Lung Hai, or giant crawfish, affords a good substitute, and efforts are now being made to transplant it to the American side of the Pacific. For river fishing, both cormorants and otters are trained,— the latter, however, only being used to drive the fish into the nets. Prawns are caught in vast quantities all the way from Canton to Hong-Kong, along the Ladrone and Lantao Islands, and even back of Stonecutter's Island in Hong-Kong Bay, and the paste is shipped to European purveyors. At the green and slippy old stone wharf in front of the Harbor Office, Hong-Kong, you will notice the black oysters of Amoy and Fu-chau being landed, but don't eat them if you value your life, except in December, when they are as delicious as the dark oysters of New Orleans. You will notice that the bones of the pike are green and the chickens' bones dark. There is no doubt that the fish, feeding in the estuaries of the Canton and West Rivers, are affected by the mineral matter, in the loess, which the rivers carry down from the heart of the country.

If forests were planted at the headwaters to stay the floods, and equalize the flow during all the year, China would add to her wealth in soil half a billion dollars a year. But there was an instance where a sudden increase in the wealth of the agriculturists of a land, troubled in other directions, made possible a revolution, as in the days preceding Cromwell, and there might be a repetition of this condition here. As soon as the American western states fifteen years ago threw off their farm mortgages, which had been oppressing them for twenty years, the propaganda which flowered in Roosevelt's criticisms began for the elimination of the usurious oppression and discriminating legislation from which they had suffered during those " twenty years of Egypt."

In metal and wood work, the native artisan sticks to

his bow drill.   He draws the cord to and fro with effectiveness, but at a painful waste of energy, as he applies the
weight of his chest for pressure.   The Chinese are entirely without steam circular saw mills.   The great logs
of teak which come from Siam, and pine from Oregon
and the Yalu, are tilted up, while a man standing on the
log, and one crouching under it, push a hand-saw.   I
have seen concrete double walled buildings, six stories
high, and taking up a square, being erected in Hong-
Kong, with the sawyers alongside preparing the teak
beams in this ancient and picturesque fashion.   The English architects brought boilers out, but they always have
and always will grow wheezy in the hands of the Sawyers'
Guild, even in treaty ports.   Joiners use a saw having
a blade fifteen inches long, and widest at the end, where
it measures five inches across.   It tapers toward a bamboo handle.   One edge is set for cross-cut, and the other
for rip.   The dust is drawn with the upward stroke,
which is the thousand and first tiring instance, given by
the telescope man, that " everything is opposite in China."
Smooth and able racing boats are built at about half what
they would cost in America, and the clerk who in England was elate with a whirl in the Tupenny Tube and
a 'bus ride to Hampstead Heath, here blossoms out as a
boat owner in his second year of indenture.   The Royal
Hong-Kong Yacht Squadron turns out a respectable fleet
of thirty half-raters, and several two-stickers and yawls,
all erected, and many of them designed, by Chinese boat
builders like Ah Kee.   In the cup-like harbor, set about
with the lofty Hong-Kong and Kowloon blue ranges, the
dipping sails and bubbling scuppers of the fleet make a
picture a little more animating than porcelain, and certainly dearer to the exile, because it has that touch of

home which made Fong, the Chinese emigrants' poet, say:
"They love home most who never have one."

The meal of the Chinese *bon vivant* (the effete treaty
ports have them all) begins with *samschu,* rice wine,
served hot. The cups must be inverted with some emphasis, as they are emptied. The cup is not lifted by
the fingers, but is rather placed in the hollow of the
hand, and then raised. The wine contains only fifteen
per cent. of alcohol. Soups, which close the repast, are
of the delightful birds' nest, brought from Moscos Island
in Burmah, sweet lotus, fungus, sprouted bean, and
pigeons' egg. Between are served *Sam See Chee,* a
hash of shark, pheasant, chicken and bamboo shoots;
yauk, a jelly of pounded rice and oil; *wo ap,* bone-
less dried duck which has an Egyptian taste of mummy
wrappings; *Mut kim ghet,* a preparation of Chinese
golden lime; *boh loh,* made with pineapple; *lichee
gon,* the Imperial nuts with a raisin taste; sedge root
and water chestnuts. Raw fish and legs of frogs, called
Ye Sang, taken from the flooded rice swamps, are
not infrequently eaten, now that ice is obtainable to make
them appeal to the gourmet. Eggs are preserved in a
paste of saltpetre, soy and earth for periods so long that
they are blackened with their sulphur, and taste like our
high school boy's experiment in sulphurated hydrogen.
In Che-kiang Province hams are pickled in soy sauce.
Hoi Shum, or sea slug from Korean waters, is first
dried, then steamed, and served with pigeon. Cakes are
made of fried grasshoppers. Of all gastronomical delights to the foreigner is the Chinese shad or *samli*
of the Canton estuary, a fish half between our shad and
pompano in taste. Nearly equal as a prandial delicacy
is the *pih fan yu,* or white rice fish, which is breaded.

Your army officer at the club will call for salmon; he means polynemus. It is like our salmon in taste and is the only pink fish in the far East.

Oranges are skilfully opened, filled with various colored jellies, carefully sealed and brought to the table again *au naturel*. The dwarf kin-kew, or golden orange, popularly known as the kumquat, is preserved whole, and is a delicacy which immediately makes you declare you eventually will love the country despite much. The tart loquat tastes and looks like a cross between a grape and an orange. The green, curling fern and seaweed from Korea, are prepared as we serve spinach, and plum kernels are fried in oil. Tea is drunk as the Germans in the East handle cocktails; i. e., the cups are raised in salute and drained simultaneously. A guest receives his cup with both hands. Should an invited guest be absent through illness, the meal is sent to his house. Among the gifts is a beautiful basket, which is filled with rice, and a selected branch of arbor-vitæ or pine is inserted to imitate a potted tree, beneath the branches of which nuts and fruits are spread on the white ground.

A Chinese never takes his politeness humorously. Therefore I have not entered the following anecdote among the humorous paragraphs. Their unlucky number is fourteen. A host found himself, because of declinations, with thirteen guests at his table. To relieve his consternation, Li Chong spoke forth: "Never mind, I shall be the one who will keep his drum head slack in patience; from sweetmeat to soup I shall not eat at all, and therefore I am not here." Native gentlemen generally hire for their dinner parties, a large restaurant, or club, which has facilities for histrionic presentations. Sometimes these festivities last two days, and the bill includes cost of lanterns, presents to bonzes, and 'rickisha hire. A man's love for his women folk is proved by the number of times he sends "regrets" to a banquet, for the meal comes home. Hats are worn throughout. They are generally silk skull caps, to protect the shaven heads. Melon and sunflower seeds, and green cayenne pods are continually passed to the company of singing girls, who come to recite and dance, if the banquet is an official one. Cassia, mushrooms, fish gills, pheasant, partridge, snipe, and reed-birds in abundance, prawns, carambola fruit, almond custard, orange wine, steamed sharks' fins, chicken cooked with rice wine, ginger, soy, sesamum, peanut oil and herbs,— are all drawn upon by these versatile cooks in preparing their menus, especially when a foreigner is to be invited. Whole roast pigs and hares are brought on gilded, just as was the Milanese custom in the fourteenth century. The meal ends with a draft of hot *chook* (rice soup), and a towel, dipped in hot water, is drawn across the face. Hot as is the climate, its lassitude seems to create a craving for hot foods. The foreigner probably over-indulges in spiced Indian chutneys and curries, and the native in the betel-pepper leaf.

So much of the imported liquors and comestibles for the white man's consumption in the tropics (canned goods, claret, beer, champagne, etc.) are preserved by acids, it is now not uncommon to see in the papers an advertisement like the following: "Tuborg beer, ten dollars and a half Mexican, forty-eight quarts, guaranteed free from salicylic acid." Despite the discouragement, the foreigner in the treaty port does not seem to forsake foods which have the acid, and if he ever returns home he brings to his physician a stomach as useless as a sponge.

Ice is now fully appreciated in the household menage, and at Ningpo the heavily thatched ice-houses are conspicuous along the river front.   At Hong-Kong, of course, the ice is made by machinery.   If your native cook gets a fowl which he believes will be a tough problem, he hangs it among the papaw's branches over night, in the belief that the exhalation from the leaves will have a mollifying effect.   Few Chinese comestibles are immersed in the water and boiled.   They are placed in perforated vessels above the water and steamed.   We who are used to the pasty manner in which our cooks destroy the beauty of boiled rice, will be surprised to notice this article of food cooked on the meanest sampan in a manner to keep each grain light, separate and dry to handle.   The rice is made appetizing by taking with it portions of *kumchi,* a sort of sauerkraut.   Economy in fuel and in the use of the chop sticks have created the custom of cooking meats only when they are cut up in small pieces.   When one has eaten heartily, and the affable host inquires if the meal has been sufficient, it is quite polite to use the idiom: "My stomach is as tight as a marshall's drum head." Spartans, too, are they on occasion, for they have a proverb: "He only is a man who can exist on petsai stalks."   Outside of the treaty ports, beef is a flesh untasted by even the rich Chinese, because one hash would cost as much as the whole animal.   The poor could not afford to pay the price; the few well-to-do in the village might not have the beef appetite on the one day, and the owner of the carcass could not keep over what he did not use, as ice can not be procured inland.   A Chinese, in expressing how much land it takes to support a man, says: "One acre for six mouths."

Where we raise whisky and tobacco smugglers, the

Chinese discover opium and salt evaders of the Imperial Customs. First a pirate at Canton; then a salt smuggler farther up the Pearl, is Ng Po's descent to civilization, for later we shall find him buying out a degree and a squeeze mandarin-ship, say on the West River (now become the most notorious pirate waters of the world), not too far from his former haunts, if he ever wants or needs to return to them. Visitors to Canton and Macao will recall the well built British river-boats, *Heungshan, Fatshan,* and *Honam,* and the Chinese built *Tai On,* with thousands of coolies battened like cattle in the 'tween decks under bars; the barred ports; and the uniformed Sikh and Portuguese guards, bristling with rifles, bayonets and pistols, parading by every hatchway on the saloon deck, where the foreigner is accommodated. Glancing up at the pilot-house, your eye is met by a rack of glistening rifles at the quartermaster's back. It used to be quite common in Cantonese and Macaense waters for Chinese pirates (they are nearly always natives of turbulent Kwangsi Province, and have aboriginal blood in their veins) to come aboard as passengers, and when the vessel had got under the lee of Lantao Island, to swarm over the saloon deck, and compel the quartermaster to run for the Ladrone Islands, or into the hundred and one creeks of the estuary of the Sikiang, where the boat was robbed and perhaps scuttled, and pursuit as effective as following quicksilver uphill. The world was first startled by the *Namoa* tragedy on December 10th, 1890. A British motor-boat has been looted within the shadow of the bund at Samshui. The American launch *Comet* was boarded in 1906 within sight of the guns of Whompoa.

Only lately at Lapa Island, across Macao's inner harbor, three hundred pirates withstood government troops at Naiwan Mun. The quaint unpainted junks of Macao all carry old-fashioned cannon in the stern (they mean to run while they fight for it), and stinkpots (bamboo fuse grenades). It is hard to tell when the marauders are pirates and when government troops, and when the Chinese are criticized concerning this delinquency in patriotism, they ask us where in our own civilization, American as well as Russian, notorious detective organizations draw the line, when receipts are low, between blackmail which they manufacture, and crime which they pursue. As the steamers from Wuchow come down the Rhine of China, the Sikiang, they are often fired upon from the sorghum brakes by these marauders, who wait until the native and foreign gunboats, like the United States monitor *Monadnock,* are out of echo. Some years it has been necessary to convoy merchantmen with the two British, two French, one German, and one American gunboats which make headquarters at Hong-Kong. Underwriters are declining risks on the river. It is now proposed to equip the gunboats and merchantmen with Marconi, and allow Robert Bredon's Customs Service to police the river with part of China's new navy, transferred for that purpose. Only during the Viceroyalty of Li Hung Chang, with Cromwellian severity, has the Sikiang (West River) been safe from Canton to Wuchow, and Hong-Kong asserts that the Kwangtung government can, if they desire to, police the Sikiang as satisfactorily to foreign commerce as the stern Hupeh government polices the Hun River. The traveler on the West River ten years ago will recall the three pirate chimneys on Spike Hill, just past the old capital of Shui Hing. The pirates were thrust in the chimneys heads downward, and the tops were bricked in. Canton indulges in a little bit of ceremony in beheading its criminals, but in the smaller towns, as at Wuchow, the pirate is hastened out from the bar to the hillside, and in the presence of a few, including one mandarin on a pony (which must be turned backward for superstition's sake), the victim, who is opiated, is made to kneel while his feet are tied; a rope is put around his neck, and when the swordsman is ready, the neck is quickly drawn out; there is a flash of steel and all is over.

It must be remarked that the irreconcilable attitude to the foreigner, so noticeable at Canton, has been fixed there since the opium war of 1840, and the pirate attacks are not the only evidence of it. The desperation of poverty is the cause of the pirates' ranks being increased in times of famine. In 1906 at Canton the silk crop failed, owing to unusual floods, and the tea crop on the hills was also poor, because fertilizer was not brought up owing to flooded paths. Cotton yarn dealers failed because consumers could not pay or borrow. Piracy grew stronger and bolder, and the *Sainam* tragedy on July 13th, where foreigners lost their lives, ensued. The pirates brought five narrow snake-boats alongside for an hour, to take off the valuables. The marauders burned their clothes forward on deck. The crews of the snake-boats were also naked and painted, all for the purpose of outwitting identification. The *Sainam* is a pretty little stern wheeler of five hundred and seventy tons. The British minister at Peking, incited by the persistent clamor of Hong-Kong, vigorously demanded the transfer of Viceroy Shum from Kwangtung Province. It was granted and Chang Jen Chun sent, as another evidence that Hong-Kong is as yet master over growling Canton in matters

of the peace, and who shall say she will not some day
complete her ambition by purifying Canton's debased cur-
rency and sanitary conditions, and expediting her railway
building.

As piracy of this sort is not infrequent as near Europe
as the Straits of Bab-el-Mandeb, unpoliced China can
perhaps be treated leniently, for, as a rule, she furnishes
more spice than danger to travel, so far as the foreigner
is concerned. Who is there who would not rather cross
China unaccompanied than brave Turkey with a caval-
cade? Only as long ago as Buckingham's régime,
piracy in English waters was tolerated for a fee, two
hundred and forty-eight ships having been seized between Dover and Newcastle in one year. We can not
condemn Chinese mandarins and their civilization of this
time, without condemning English statesmen, judges like
Sir Henry Marten, and the civilization of our great-
grandfathers' time. The day when authority will walk
with modern emphasis and frequency up and down the
path of commerce is not far off, even in so vast a country
as China. She has first been gathering money for lighting her night walks, and it is satisfactory to state that
the recurrent flash of historic old Guia at Macao (the
first lighthouse in China) was followed by Robert Hart's
provision of some sixty lights along the coast, which has
made the rapidly increasing navigation wonderfully safer.
The Imperial Customs paid for this improvement, making
the sea-going nations, as well as the Chinese, double
debtors to this the most thorough foreigner who has ever
given his life service to China, a veritable Daniel working
for the people of Darius.

When you pass the pickets of your native friend's compound, it is a sign of superior breeding to cough purposely

(we may even say, conspicuously to expectorate), so that none of the opposite sex may linger longer than the time necessary to discover that the visitor is a man. When the women have escaped you shout " Li," which is an order for the house coolie to come and receive your long red card. It would express the lowest breeding to ask your host: " How is your wife? " Wife and daughters must remain unmentioned; their privacy is like their honor, inviolate; they live only in the husband's and father's eye. Mixed social gatherings never occur. There are no women on the Chinese stage. Among the better class, the boys and girls of the family are entirely separated after the age of six. There is nothing among their middle class of that curse of American and European cities, " a street education " after school hours. Whatever may be the result of the Chinese system in individual development; however narrow the wife's social sphere may be by reigning alone in a feminine world, the intent is sincere, and based upon the lofty desire not to soil women even so much as with the opportunity for temptation. No modern novel has been written in China, because no fingers have been scorched, and in their measures for prevention and severity upon offenders, the Confucians say they only agree with the compilers of the Pentateuch. As soon as a child rises in the morning, the first duty is to repair to the parent's room, and inquire as to his or her health. And so through life, the filial service and ceremonial broaden, to be looked forward to by the son as likewise his privilege through the long golden evening of age. The saddest story in our Scriptures to the Chinese is the tale of Jacob shorn of his sons, looking Egyptward. Relationship is called a " joint "; i. e., second cousin is " second joint."

Womanhood for the first time has been addressed
in an official document. Viceroy Chang Chi Tung
of Wuchang has compiled an elaborate legal book
(meddling missionary propaganda, take note!) of
the cases from earliest times between the Chinese,
missionaries and converts. The book is inscribed
to "The fathers and *mothers* of the people."
The great port Yochow, at the confluence of the
Yangtze and China's greatest lake, translated means
"Mother in Law." The culture of women is repeatedly praised in the histories, novels and works of
philosophy. A mother is expected to teach her boy until
he can go to school, and most of the education of the
daughters devolves upon the mothers. Mixed schools are
abhorred, and girls are not permitted to leave their
mother's sight. Chapels of missionaries have a curtain
down the middle of the room, so that neither sex may
intrude upon the other but may at the same time hear
the speaker and join in the singing and responses. The
native text books for girls set forth that the culture of
Mencius, their second greatest writer, was due to his
mother's teaching, and one of China's lesser classics,
dating back to B. C. 120, is the Lieh Nu Chuen (History
of Cultured Women). Chinese literature has its Jeanne
d'Arc heroine in the warlike virgin Wha-Mou-Loh. In
some homes, paintings of the Mother of Buddha are to
be seen. Prince Ching of the Imperial Household, and
Governor Chow of Mukden, in their support of the new
educational system, advocate its extension by sending girls
abroad, or at least to introduce foreign college bred governesses.

Throughout the empire, the *pai-lau* (memorial
arches) are the most conspicuous architecture next to

the pagodas. Many of these are erected in honor of chaste or learned women, and widows who would not marry a second time, or, as their epigrammatists say: "The lady who the second time married the white flower in her hair," referring to the fashion of widows. As these *pai-lau* monuments take an important place in the education of the people, the choosing of the inscription is reserved for the throne, through the Censor Pu (Board). An important class in the community are the *mei-jin* (between people), who arrange marriages. The mother of the family has a hundred and one conferences with them, and on them, in her seclusion, she relies for the dainty bits of gossip of the town, all the more colored by an imagination removed, because one could not go and prove the facts. An important present from the youth to his betrothed is a ham, of which she sends back the foot for good luck, the idea being the same as our darky's esteem for a rabbit's foot. When the *samschu* cups of bride and groom are raised, you will notice they are joined by a thread, which should on no account be broken. It often is, however, for there is rough teasing, *lao-shing-fang* (bride-baiting) of the bride of fourteen years. February with them takes the place of our June as the popular hymeneal month. Only the office of *hien-pi* (first wife) is recognized by the ancestral religion, and the children of the *tsieh* (concubine) are enrolled on the family tablets as though they were the issue of the *hien-pi*. This differs not essentially from the ways of patriarchal Israel.

The Chinese insist in their critical moods that there are fewer concubinage marriages in China, under the law, than there are clandestine double households without the law's pale, in the life of the Occidental. High buildings, and the Tangerian custom of mounting to one's roof, are abhorred by the Chinese as the grossest kinds of intrusion. One's wall can on no good account be looked over; it is the protection of women from the unchaste and forward, and is therefore thick and high, and often stronger than the house itself. The women of China have a more cumbersome ménage to run than our women have, which speaks for their patience, industry and cleverness. They have no ready-made, automatic providers, such as laundries, abattoirs, schools, department stores, telephones, daily mail service, etc., to assist them in attending to the wants of the men and children, and yet, at the temples, on the street, or upon evenings in the garden, it can not be said that their families bear the evidence of household neglect. It must not be considered that the Chinese do not think themselves good-looking. You can frequently hear their women, when they are commenting on a foreigner, whose face conforms somewhat to their standards, remark: "Why, she is nearly as good looking as we are."

In every hong (office); in every rice and fish shop; in the stern of every sampan, the brewed tea is left handy, and the porcelain from which you drink it always has a painting of Mon San Gun, the god of longevity, so that you may drink to your own "long life." The Chinese of the south pronounce it "chah," and say: "It is as sweet as a sparrow's tongue." In the theater, and fan-tan gambling-house, it is brought to you as a gift from the management. I suppose the Chinese average a gallon a day. They seem utterly indifferent to its toxic qualities. In India and Ceylon, tea is manufactured entirely by machinery, but in China the opposite is the case. In some parts, where they have learned the habit from the

Russians, Mongolians grind their tea, as we do coffee, and make an infusion of the powder. The indulgence has one good property, in that the malarial waters of the land are not used unboiled. The wells of all the walled cities are revolting. In the country, however, the drawers do not soil the spring, but lead the stream along cut bamboo troughs to a roadside, where it trickles without unusual contamination into the buckets. The bush, being of the camellia family, likes a loose, hilly soil, such as the ranges of Nganwei, where the green tea comes from; damp heat; showers; fog and sun bursting through with tropical intensity, all of which south China is ready to furnish to the letter, Nature being more anxious to produce tea than men. The leaf of a full-grown tea-bush is larger than Westerners would think, viz.: two and one-half inches long. The flower is white, with petals set like a cherry's, but the bloom is not thickly sown in the bush.

The translations of the familiar brands are interesting: *oolong* meaning black snake; *souchong,* small leaf, being picked before the February rains; *pecoe,* white fur, from the fuzz on the leaf of the season's first crop of the three-year-old plant, and *congou,* well rolled. The plants from the famous Dragon's Pool Garden have been successfully transplanted to South Carolina. The second picking takes place after the first light rains of June. After the last crop, the clippings of the stems and branches are saved and sent to the poor of Japan, who use it for a tea called *bancha.* Each crop affords about four hundred pounds of dried tea per acre. The curing of black tea is tedious, every leaf being opened by hand four times after each passing over the charcoal fire, three times in a latticed basket, and once in a metal pan. It is called *Ki* (flag), when it easily unrolls, and

Country scene 400 miles inland, tea district, Kiang-si province. Tea bushes on foothills; rice (paddy) fields in meadow. The modern houses are erected by Russians to store tea.

An irrigated valley of rich Hunan province, Central China, 600 miles
from the coast, where natives are patriotic for a modern
China and are most unfriendly to foreigners. Hunan is
ruled rigorously by Viceroy Chang Chih Tung.

Flat, rice-growing country of North sea coast, outside Tientsin.

Tsiang (awl), when through perfected fermentation, it keeps its dry, tight curl. Expert knowledge is required to know how much fire the leaf will bear, the object being to get the last particle of moisture out, and as this is undertaken in a moist climate, the tea workers have an arduous task. The leaf ferments between the first and second firings, with the result that some of the injurious tannic acid is turned to sugar. This rehandling and fermentation is not done with green tea, the leaf of which is allowed to dry after one firing. In the final drying a room called the " human oven " is heated, into which the workers rush with covered mouths for a minute each time to rescue the laden bamboo baskets.

The success of the Chinese tea is well known. Only their leaf keeps strength for long periods. Moreover, the Chinese tea has the largest percentage of theine (the exhilaration and perspiration principle), with the least proportion of the poisonous tannin, the toxic principle, so abundant in Ceylon tea. The Assam leaf is larger and coarser than that of China proper, and is only fit for black tea of an inferior grade. The blackness of some brands of tea is brought about by arrested fermentation. The Chinese themselves secure a stronger effect from their tea, as there is no necessity for them to brew the highly dried varieties. They use the greener uncurled leaf, just as we might take six leaves of an ash tree, and put them in a small cup. These bunches of uncurled leaves are tied into pretty packages with silk. The infused leaf is also eaten as a salad. The different aromas of tea are produced by azalea, orange, jasmine, or tuberose petals, according to whichever bloom may be out at the time of the tea-picking. Last spring the price of tea materially increased on account of the scarcity of the jasmine flower. An astringent tea of delicate odor is prepared from the tea flowers. The oppressed tea growers of China are assessed an export (loti) tax as high as twenty-five per cent. of the value of the tea, and this five years ago nearly throttled the trade.

Though Russians have the name of being the largest tea patrons of China, Australians really lead with a consumption of eleven pounds a year per head, against two pounds in America, while the vinous French are at the foot of the procession with three-tenths of a pound. China sells Russia sixteen million pounds of black tea each year. A vast deal of it is ground and pressed into bricks at Tokmakoff's Russian factory at Han-kau, where you will find a dominating colony of Russians. The bricks are an inch thick, and nine by twelve inches across. Some Americans who have lived in China long enough to become tea-soaked find on returning home to their trying climate that they can not touch the cup at all, especially if it is the tannic green tea, a few cups a day soon producing tea-poisoning with most distressing feelings. Indeed, those who are thus sensitive are compelled to give up every excitant for years, whether alcoholic, drug or tannic. The strongest tea known to the Chinese is grown at Pu Erh in Yunnan, and is warranted to curl a novice up as though he were the fired leaf itself. Perhaps the strangest of all the tea preparations is the Thibetan's. The infusion of tea is poured into a wooden bowl. Goat's butter and barley flour are added, and all are beaten into a dough called "Jamba," which is eaten warm. This, with uncooked powdered mutton (even lumber powders in high, dry Thibet) are the mainstays of the daily meal. That China teas are coming into their own again was evidenced last June at the opening of the Canton market, when the highest bids of ten years were recorded. Emphatically, the difference between theine and tannin is important, and no physician, who works upon the Chinese plan of being paid for keeping his patients well, should fail to enroll himself on the side of Chinese teas against the world.

I picture a tea scene, which may be upon your porcelain saucer, but in reality is among the famous Sunglo Hills of Nganwei Province, where the able late Empress Dowager was born, though she was of Manchu blood. The slopes and peaks rise everywhere. Here and there you can discover the huts of the pickers, nestled below the cultivated terraces. It is just dawn when the women (the older ones with untidy hair) come forth with their crates to essay their long tasks. The girls wear yellow pomegranate flowers in their hair, and are as merry as the birds which dart among the bamboos which have been set for wind-breaks. There is little light or view, for the mist still delays to rise and roll. The workers call out to one another in falsetto tones, as they cross paths, and inquire which hill they have chosen for the day. They separate into couples, who take turns in holding down the top branches for the other to pick the leaves. The tops are picked first; it makes selected drying. The gatherers are working with speed, hot as it is, for the rains threaten. Jokes are passed: " I've picked enough to make a Hung Mao's (Englishman's) head go round like a bamboo water-wheel." When the baskets are heaped, so that the cover is put down with difficulty (it is too windy on these uplands to rely on a stone for weight) the pickers do not wait for the collectors, but wend their way back to a receiving hut set beside a lotus pool, where willows grow. Do not be irreverent, Hung

Mao, and say the willows are there to supply adulteration! Banter is the diversion of those who are resting. As through all the world, when women become manual workers, their talk verges on masculine humor. The branches and stony hills have torn their feet, clothes and hair, and the wind, too, has added his derision. The poor mortals look miserable enough. Until sundown they work on the hill, staying longest at the southern portion, for there the leaves are thickest. Until midnight they labor in the firing rooms, which are lit with smoky nut-oil lamps. Before the jasmine bud has spilt its matutinal libation of attar beneath the window of their sleeping rooms, the bronzed toilers have arisen, and gone forth again with laughter unto the hill which never sleeps, because it must work for a foreign world which never ceases to thirst.

The most gruesome feature of the fatalistic Chinese and Japanese character,— the quality which makes them terrible as well-led soldiers,— is their stolid view of death. The Japanese *hara-kiri*, imposed for political or battlefield failures, has done more to ostracize the Japanese from occidental sympathy than our jealousy of their success, or irritation at their trickiness. In China a coolie anywhere can be bought for two hundred dollars, paid to his family, to jump from behind a mound, and take the place of the quail or pheasant, when the authorities wish to cause a scandal, and stop shooting by foreigners in the grave districts. When China's first railroad of twelve miles from Woosung to Shanghai was built in 1876, we all remember that a native, whose business of tugging boats along the river was threatened by the new enterprise, deliberately walked in front of the train. His death, of course, accomplished the purpose of the manda-

rins in starting an effective boycott against the innovation. The repetitions of this sacrifice on the national
altar (as they see it) on the Yuet-Han, Peking-Han-kau,
and other railways, have been frequent. The Chinese
method of suicide among unhappily betrothed girls is to
take an over-dose of opium; among men, the larynx is
opened, or the victim hangs himself, which last is the
method official Peking favors for the political *non
gratas*.

Tientsin and Mongolian larks are matched to sing at
daybreak. To the open field, even to the lawn under the
English Club's windows at Hong-Kong, the cages are
brought, and set out on the grass by the native silk merchants, who are not too dignified to run after grasshoppers
to reward their pets. Over the dewy lawn the owners
saunter and enjoy the only refreshing coolness of the
tropical day. As the sun bursts out in his glory, the
birds are set free and matched in song. The gentry take
infinite delight in the conquests of their prized singers.
Some cost as high as twenty-five dollars each, which is
a fortune in China. Who can gainsay that something
patient and good lies in the hearts of a people, who can
find that such pastimes, even to full manhood, afford
untiring pleasures?

The youths of thirteen to seventeen, gathered on the
Praya in groups of six or more on a side, dexterously use
their feet in back and side kicks as a battledore, to keep
a shuttlecock in the air for minutes at a time. No boxing
ring ever trained so well for shiftiness. The boys excel
in kite-flying. In the ports like Hong-Kong, where there
are overhead wires of a modern civilization, there is a
ludicrous hanging out of all kinds of derelict air-ships
and their tangled cables. Dragons, hawks, larks and fish

are all represented in the shapes. Faces of the gods are painted on round and oblong disks. On the strings are hooks, blades, and pasted ground glass. Great skill is shown in the mid-air battles, as the kites are manœuvered into conflict. A hook tears out the body of a dragon, and the wreckage comes to earth to the great delight of the assailant. Or a string is broken, and a god goes soaring cloudward. It is considered an ill omen to allow the possession of the heavenly being to evanesce into the ethereal again. A Chinese nurse teaches her charge that it is auspicious to dream of a mountain, an eagle, an egg-plant, a funeral, a snake, a horse; or to meet a priest the first thing upon the road. It is lucky to be erroneously reported dead, and a mirror hung over the door keeps away bad fortune. It is obviously ominous to trip in a cemetery. When Chinese children wish to express de-rision, they do not make faces, but catch up the corners of their tunics and shake them.

The Chinese, with his paint brush, takes twice our time to execute his letter, but with his swanpan or abacus, he counts twice as quickly as we do, so that clerical honors are even. In recording time, the year of the sovereign's reign is generally used, though there is a cycle system among the Buddhists, based on every sixty years as the length of a good man's life, in which modesty of allot-ment the race confesses its inferiority in medical science, as compared even with the times of the Psalmist.

About two hundred thousand people live in boats on the river at Canton, and fifty thousand at Hong-Kong. It is this custom which makes it possible for such losses of life to occur in typhoons, as in the catastrophe of Sep-tember, 1906, at Hong-Kong. The passenger steamer arriving at Canton from Hong-Kong has an exciting passage through the narrow lane which is cleared through the sampan fleet. The fleet must anchor at night in regular lanes, each boat having a stated place. Tens of thousands of the people never go ashore. Doctors, priests, mendicants, traders, artisans, gamblers, and strumpets (*shoi kee*), all ply their trade by boat throughout this floating village. At night each boat is compelled by law to hoist to the masthead a light, which generally burns nut-oil. As one looks from the city walls, the view is that of the Milky Way turned upside down. The panorama at night, especially during the Moon Feast, from Hong-Kong's signal staff on Victoria Peak, fifteen hundred feet directly above the Colony's sampan fleet, is even finer. The boat women all carry their children papoose fashion, and as the repetition is frequent, the girls of eight must carry their youngest brother but one, to aid the mother, who with one hand holds an infant, and with the other guides the sampan's tiller or handles the sail halyards. The younger children sprawling about the decks, have dried bottle-gourds strapped to their shoulders to assist in supporting them, should they fall overboard. A Chinese goes overboard feet first, and not head first in his dive.

It is to take the wings of Aeolus, to step into one of these passenger boats when the wind is on the quarter. The boats are flat-bottomed, eighteen feet long, with a narrow racing prow, latticed rudder, single square sail, no jib, and ballasted heavily. The bamboo battens, stretched across the sail, enable the crew to haul their sampan somewhat on the wind, but the performance at best is a sorry one. Such a sail of course reefs itself instantly, and upon this quality in a storm, the crew depends more than on the ballast. When the wind is untoward, the woman sculls,

and her husband in the bow has to exert himself with
oars long enough to clear the wide waist of the boat.
The passenger crouches in a bamboo coop, and from the
second hatch in front of him peep the tenantry of children, chow dogs and chickens, while as company for
himself, he hears the metallic scampering of the cockroaches along the three seats around him. On the
larger junks, when the wind is adverse, the long spliced
sweeps, made from whole fir trees, are unshipped. The
rowers, like gondoliers, push them, walking forward on
a cleated wale which projects over the stern. The passage of the lime and cement boats across Hong-Kong's
harbor is a characteristic sight, ten to fifteen sweep
pushers on each side standing out yellow, naked and
brawny against the white-heaped cargo. The sails seen
in a treaty port are a curiosity. A Hakka never believes in mending until a thing is near ending, and this
applies also to his patient politics. The sails are half
holes, quarter matting, and the remaining quarter a
motley of American cotton flour bags, with the brands
favored by the local trade emblazoned: "Duck Lily,"
"Golden Pheasant," "Tiger Lady," "Twelve Pigs," etc.
While speaking of brands it will be interesting to recite their favorites in the cotton piece trade: "Rat,"
"Sitting Tiger," "Heaven Girl," "Eighteen Sons,"
"Twelve Geishas," "Ox Plows in Field," etc. In
Kwangtung Province the fisher folk bring to the shore
in October an offering unto the sea of a pig and a sheep.
These, cooked, are set upon a table in the sands, and
prostrations are made by mandarin and bonze before a
paper effigy of a ship. The junks all have an orlop deck
in the high stern. Caulking is done with rattan, which
is cemented down with oil and gypsum. In them, you

behold the famous vessel which invented water-tight compartments, centuries before the West adopted the idea.

The foreigner of the treaty port is agreeably impressed by the cordiality of their New Year holiday time, when on every hand ring the words: "*Kung Hai Fat Tsoy,*" (Congratulations; may you collect wealth). The commencement of the New Year week may vary a month between a period of years, as the festival begins with the first new moon after the sun has entered Aquarius. It therefore occurs in our January and February, and is observed by at least a week of closed shop. It is the only time of the year when the Chinese really close their shops. In the ports, the greetings seldom go to the extent of the kowtow, where the knees and forehead touch the ground. This being a busy world, and becoming so even in China, the *kung shao,* or joining the fists and raising them before the heart, while the word "*tsing*" (hail) is repeated, are made to suffice. The name of the New York state penitentiary, Sing Sing, therefore means " Hail, Hail! " literally, or idiomatically "Happy New Year," to a Chinese. Our Mott and Doyers Street brethren of the Tong societies are vastly amused, when they learn that their crimes are to take them to such a felicitous gateway. Of lesser significance are the Feast of Lanterns in February; the Dragon Festival and Regatta in July; the Moon Festival in September, and the Winter Solstice in November. These feasts are the periods for financial settlements.

Fighting of crickets is a favorite gambling game. The little combatants are placed in straw cages, and carried to the circular miniature ring. One is distin-

guished from the other by a painted white band across
the wings. Scorpions and lizards are also matched, and
bets are made whether the former will commit suicide by
stinging himself to death when he continually misses the
more alert lizard. Fires are built by the more brutal of
the jeunesse on the backs of tortoises, to incite them to
race, and cockroaches are made drunk so that bets may
be made which side of the ring the foolish insect will roll
over. Where there is a river praya, or court large
enough, the booth gamblers suddenly set up shop from
within their umbrellas, and a crowd immediately gathers,
just as a stone thrown in a stream collects foam instantly. Often betting is going on around a fruit
wagon, to count the seeds of a coolie-orange. The skin
is not given to you when you purchase the fruit;
it is sold to the skin-candiers and the makers of fever-
tea. Until the government stopped the immigration,
Canton used to send to Hong-Kong ship-loads of
its prisoners and gamblers. The bare-shouldered
coolie, on his way from hoisting or sawing great teak
logs, or carrying coal in baskets, loves nothing better,
as a diversion, than to gather around a street fakir's
basket or a gambler's booth. He howls in glee when
the dissatisfied crowd turns the booth over, and the
lukongs, with their glistening enameled helmets bearing the feathers of British law, swoop with padded
feet silently upon the mêlée; or the red-turbanned
Sikhs hear too great a commotion in a coolie boarding-
house on Elgin or Mosque Streets, and rush in to catch
the rascals red-handed at a game of pai-kau, or " Sap Ing
Wui." The runaways, with their padded shoes, think
nothing of jumping thirty-five feet to the ground.
There are many deaths however from contusion of the

brain, because the Celestial Icarus is unable to keep his feet when he lands on them.

King of all their games, especially at that oriental Monte Carlo, Macao, is fan-tan, where a large handful of bright " cash " is taken from a heap at one end of the table, and covered with a cup.   This table is at the bottom of a well.   A two-story gallery rises above the table, and the bets of those looking down are swung in a tiny basket to the cashier.   Gamblers also sit around the table, and closely watch the drawer.   When the bets are all placed on numbers one, two, three or four, or divided on two numbers, the drawing begins by picking from the pile under the cup, four cash at a time.   What remains at the last draw, wins.   The Chinese seem able to tell, when there are ten to thirteen cash undrawn, what number will remain, and you hear the shouts of the winners becoming clamorous: " Hi Yah, three wins, three wins."   The croupier takes out ten per cent. for the bank.   The winners never gain higher than eight to one.   The bank is never broken.   Free cigars and tea are passed around by attendants.   The lanterns outside of the gambling dens of Macao are the gaudiest the world over.   One may feel safe while in the vicinity of their light and the *lukong's* whistle, but the way back to the hotel is a threatening and dark one through streets as crooked as an earthquake's edge.   Chai Mui, is the betting game of feasts, when the open fingers of the hand are thrust against an opponent's in a gamble on the total.   The loser must empty a cup of hot *samschu* rice wine, their humor lying in the effort to get every one drunk but themselves.   The roulette-like game of Po Tsz is popular among the Hakka tribes at Kowloon.   Betting in the temples on the Vi-seng, or examination lottery, has been prohibited by the government, that the dignity both of religion and literature may be maintained. China is so vast a body, in territory, in numbers and in history, that it is hard to believe it is moving until surveys like this are set upon various fixed marks in its social habits. As Japan is running a Formosan lottery, and Portuguese Macao, the famous religious one of the Casa Misericordia, so China has lately licensed drawings at Hankau, where the Russian tea colony is a large patron of it.

Number three and its multiples are recognized as the numerals of honor and good luck. The Emperor's sacred mythical dragon, on which he rides in life and death, has nine times nine scales. At the funeral of an official, " nine times nine virtuous Buddhist priests " offer up prayers for his absolution from punishment, and for his purification. The great marble altar at Peking for the worship of Shangtai, (Lord of Heaven, and answering to our word God) is of three terraces, each three times the size of the one above it. The top terrace is three times thirty feet across, the slabs being laid concentrically in multiples of nine, and the steps are nine in each of the three series. Beside the white marble altar rise three red poles which suspend the lanterns when the Emperor makes that most solemn worship, from a picturesque point of view, of all the earth's kings, just before dawn, uncanopied save by the stars, and mysteriously unwatched by the wide sleeping world. There are " Three Manies "; many years; many joys; many sons, which it is enjoined may be engraved on jade charms. Kowtows are done by threes. Pagodas are of six or nine stories. The entrances of yamens and temples are triple. Poets in adorning their rhyme, speak of the "pagoda's lamps illumining the thirty-three heavens." The shares of the Yuet-Han (Canton to Han-kau) Railway are for three dollars. The Guild of the Nine Hospitals of Canton is famous for its charities and leadership in finance. Then in contradiction, birthdays are celebrated on the odd number period; i. e., the thirty-first, the forty-first, etc.

The Chinese are very fond of using numbers as we use rhymes, to remember related facts and names, as the " five virtues "; the " ten moral duties of men "; the " ten treasonable offenses " of the *Ta Tsing Liuh Li* (Book of Laws); the " five metals "; the " five essences "; the " three powers "; the " five colors "; the " eight immortals " of the Taoists; the " three bonds, of law, filial duty, and marriage "; etc., etc. Although they employ alliteration and rhyme, they prefer to express emphasis by numbers. It is very common to observe even the most stupid looking coolie, who has been reviewing boycott caricatures, wake up, and warmly say to a clansman who proposes going to the treaty port to ship as an emigrant: " Ten thousand times I say it, don't go, they will sell you like a pig." The Chinese day is divided into twelve shins (two hours). These parts are not known by numbers, but by poetic names. Their lineal measure is the *chih*, equaling fourteen of our inches. Their liquid measure, the *tao*, contains one and one-tenth gallons, while the *sheng* contains nearly an English quart. Distance is computed by the level lee, which is one-third of a mile on the flat. One-sixth of a mile up-hill is talked of as a lee, to express the ostensible difficulty of the road. One *cheung* is fifteen feet. Land is measured by the *mao*, or one-fifth of an acre at Canton, and one-sixth at Peking. Their system of weights is more familiar to the foreigner who is compelled to use them at the treaty ports; viz., *tael,* one and one-third ounces troy; *catty,* one and one-third pounds avoirdupois; *picul,* one hundred thirty-three and one-third pounds, and *tan,* two hundred forty pounds. If your ship breaks the native merchant's flour bag or box of'abalone, he will bring to your perplexed, last imported "griffin" clerk, the claim papers figured in catties, and leave him to reconcile the pounds of his manifest.

All the cattle used in Hong-Kong and Manila come from a little river port named Do-Shing, far above Canton on the Sikiang River. The animal is small, with buffalo characteristics as to hump, and is a near relative of the wild anao of Celebes Island. The horns are wide. The sight of lifting these animals from the junks by the ship's hoist, attached to a gunny band about their bellies, is a characteristic view of Hong-Kong's unique harbor life, as strenuous as the West, although under an X-ray tropical sun.

The water-buffaloes (*shui-niu*) of the rice tillers are used to pull a wooden plow through the flooded fields, to turn the loam around the roots of the transplanted rice. A threshing floor is rolled out on the open earth, and men, animals and flails are used to beat out the grain. When the animals are off duty they wade out into the sea to escape the gnats which torture their hairless hides. The droves of these animals which wade into the bay off Kowloon Point is another of Hong-Kong's interesting sights. They have vast strength, and thick, almost circular horns. While docile with the Chinese, to whom they are used, they viciously and suddenly attack foreigners and horses, trusting to

one fell sweep of the horns to disembowel the victims.
The buffaloes are sometimes baited. The animal will
defend his muddy lair. The challenging beast is brought
up, when the defender rushes to the fray. The animals
are seldom goaded, and the fight is never to the death,
as the mild-blooded Chinese seem satisfied when one
animal turns tail.

To speak generally, man is the beast of burden in
China, although there is this notable exception: at
the salt wells of Szechuen and Shansi, one hundred
thousand water-buffaloes are used to work the primitive
pumping machinery. In Korea one sees many black
bullocks. Not a Chinese city, except Peking and Tai
Yuan, has laid its streets wide enough for carts. The
founders expected that men always would be the carriers.
A stout bamboo is thrown across the shoulder, and if
a coolie has a pig to carry home at one end of it, he
balances it with some other household necessity, or at
least a pail of water which always comes in useful,— not
necessarily on the person, for before that luxury the fertilizer pit is selected. The almost naked stevedores of
the treaty ports are magnificent fellows, the proudest
examples of a vegetarian diet the world over. If you
doubt their power, it is sufficient to watch them empty
a junk full of the immense India gunny bales. No
cranes are used. From the bottom of the hold, planks
are laid, and up these from tier to tier, the sure-footed,
bronze-colored coolies carry their monstrous loads, which
are suspended from a bamboo laid upon the bare, smoking shoulders of ten men. Literally they are mighty
men of metal, for one seldom hears of a sore shoulder,
or complaints about the burden. The chanty song is
continually in use, and the possessor of the leading voice

gets more pay than the foreman. The Kowloon coolies who drag teak lumber into piles, and those who saw it, are even more famous for their longer falsetto chanties, which are decidedly the most musical thing to our ear, in the far East.

Where one would say the "roast beef of old England," here it would be the "stewed hog of old China." All eyes look upon him with a deep intent, even though few can afford a piece of him. The golden bamboo is woven about him, and he is laid, one on another, on a two-wheeled cart which protrudes to great length before and behind the axle. The load is arranged about to balance itself. Ropes are attached for ten coolies to pull, and ropes are stretched behind so that four coolies may retard when the course is on one of the many declivities of Hong-Kong. There are few steam whistles even in the treaty ports, but, as always, Nature rushes to fill the vacuum which she is said to hate! As soon as the silent occupants feel their carriage moving, and their pedometer-legs hit by the spokes, one unending screech is set up in a falsetto truly Chinese, which draws to each shop door along the route every grinning *foki*. To make it more amusing, not a smile spreads upon the dumb faces of the stalwart drawers whose shoulders labor under the long cable. Then the shopmen hoot at the procession. This is also the exact procedure when the courtezans, wearing their hair down their backs as a sign, walk the street to advertise themselves. Every coolie jeers, spits and shouts "pig." The Chinese attack shame with its most dreaded enemy, derision. Devotees present pigs to the Buddhist shrine of Honan, opposite Canton, and subscribe a fund to feed the animals until natural death ensues, thus rescuing what is doomed to death, which affords a merit mark in their religious practices.

Who can juggle like a Chinese conjurer! There he sits where the narrow streets widen into a stone court; like a stone thrown into a stream, immediately there is turmoil about him. He draws fire from his mouth, or a snake from your pocket, and all is accompanied by a falsetto jargon which makes you creep. These conjurers also perform the miracle of the mango tree. The mango fruit is planted in a spot which the performer's wand touches. The circle gathers round, and shortly a mango tree, forty feet high, is seen in full bloom and fruit. As this appears slowly, and indistinctly at first, there is no doubt that it is the hypnotism in which his guild and the Thibetans excel, and which enables them so to influence their audience that the performer seems to climb up a rope, vanish from view in the sky, and when the spell is broken, he is first seen on the outside of the circle. This work is all performed while he incessantly talks and fixes his eye on any recalcitrant subject.

The most sensational performance in the all-wonderful East is the act entitled: " The Murder of the Child Lo." I witnessed it on the mountain lawn of the Royal Artillery mess at Hong-Kong. There was certainly no subterranean passage. We hemmed in the performer. First he proceeded with snake and other tricks, until in the high quiet above the city, the attention of all was riveted. Near him on the grass was an upturned empty hamper. Seated at our feet was one stray Chinese child. He called him; seemed soon to quarrel with him; — some one said it was the conjurer's ward. His temper rose as the child seemed to be obdurate. With a growl of a tiger he grasped the boy and threw the basket over him. Holding it with one hand, he muttered solemnly; he was swearing the clan vow of murder. Before we realized it, he drew a sword, and thrust it again and again through the basket, the most heartrending, smothered cries beneath gradually dying to the death whimper. From the sword seemed to drip blood. The conjurer's mad eyes gleamed. He leaned on his sword, as satisfied with his work as one possessed of a fiend. In the awful silence, we looked from the terrace to the heathen hills where rules the Abrahamic code that a child always belongs to its parents, even for death if so decreed. There was a general sigh, and a flutter like leaves as he released us from the spell of hypnotism. Returning reason made us try to reach him, to avenge the brutality. He anticipated this; he kicked the basket over. There was nothing beneath it. A terrible silence settled down and held our hands. We looked at one another, all believing that this was a magician, instead of a rascal, like unto whom there was never an equal. The child had vanished like air, and the dry wicker was as empty as it first had been when we gathered round it on the lawn. The magician had no assistants among us. Suddenly the child, with a cry of joy, burst from our midst into the arms of the wonder-weaver. We had seen the most famous act of legerdemain in the world, and understanding it not, but having experienced it, declare it to have been hypnotism.

Off the banks of the many canals little basins have been cut, which latter are private property, though the government furnishes the canal water free. There are one hundred cases in the Yamen courts on water rights to one of any other cause. The basins are fenced off

with bamboo lattices sunk to the bottom, and are used
for duck and fish pools, and lily-root farms.   Species of
lily are highly esteemed articles of food; the roots are
also candied as bon-bons for the ladies.   The stems are
used in medicine, and the leaves for packing, or for
adobe plastering.   Nothing of nature's productions
escapes the grasp of the utilitarian Chinese, except the
fragrance of the flowers.

The Imperial color is red, and to impress the Colonial
Chinese with a sense of royalty, foreign governors, as
at Hong-Kong, Macao and Saigon, have uniformed
their chair bearers and 'rickisha runners in this color.
The calling card is red, to signify joy within the bounds
of dignity.   Sometimes a mandarin will paper a room
with these cards, to show his popularity with callers.
Throughout Kwangtung Province, both Hakka and Pun-
tei women affect black or mottled headgear, with white
and pink robes, but in Szechuen white headgear with
blue robes are almost universal.

If you own a godown (warehouse) on the waterfront,
and appoint a native godownman to live on the premises,
you will be surprised if you visit your property after
working hours.   The cargo junks, with their loads of
gunnies, have sailed, and the gangs of laborers have gone.
A dozen *karojels*, or dip nets stretched on bamboos, are
in operation from the Praya wall, and your godownman,
in a new rôle, is walking behind the operators taking his
toll of fish from each as his cumshaw (commission).
When the net is dropped, bread and bait are thrown into
it.   The fish swim over the net, which at first is raised
very gently, and at last with a rush.   The catch sometimes consists of the green and gold, mosquito-larvæ de-
vouring, Athorinides minnows, which are destined to

play a wonderful part in cleansing the Orient of its dreaded curse, malaria.

All Chinese music is weird and screeching. They say their pleasure comes in exciting, not in soothing the nerves. They have flutes, horns, violins, *peipas* (guitars), *shengs* (mouth organ with thirteen reeds), and table harps to be played with a loaded feather, which last make delightful music akin to our mandolins. Every business hong has its musical corps (just as we organize company baseball clubs), who, in the evening, are supposed to amuse the *typan* (master), who lives on the story above the comprador's apartment. Seated on the counters, which at night are also their beds, the *fokis* essay with a vengeance discords which are unquestionably disturbing to occidental nerves, but for that reason the phlegmatic Chinese find them exhilarating. It suggests to them untamed passion, and all the savage things their race could do if they willed, and which they have not tried since Hung Siu Tsuen started to march from his Kwangtung village to Nanking, with stops by the way which are ensanguined for ever in history.

Stoutness is rare, but is considered honorable in a man and beautiful in a woman. The most noticeable thing on entering the Flowery Forest Monastery at Canton is that the statues of the five hundred disciples of Buddha were given to corpulency, and the god himself has a line like the equator.

At the time of an eclipse, the villagers deploy into the open with drums and every other instrument that will stand pounding, and make an incessant noise which is intended to frighten the earth dragon from eating up the celestial man in the sun. It is very important to frighten the dragon back to his lair, because his quiescence means

Best taste in dress. A small-footed woman of South China.

A Club for wealthy Chinese; members watching a play. Teakwood
tables with tops of marble from Yunnan province;
water-pipes; teacups; fans.

Mothers of rulers of China. A group of Manchu women at Peking,
North China. Note peculiar hair-dressing; long one-piece
tunics, unbound feet and high wooden shoes.

peace on earth and prosperity for the individual. The
Li Pu (Board of Rites) considers the " Saving of the
Sun or Moon " a matter of sufficient moment to occasion
an Imperial decree. Now, whether this is holiday-
making, humor, paternalism, or superstition, is open for
choice. My own observation, taken even among the very
ignorant, supports the belief that there is not so much of
the last named in the occurrence as to warrant our utter
despisal of the proceedings.

Some of us, when the old monarchic past of our European forefathers haunts us, boast of our Norse and Nor-
man, our Mayflower, or other descent, but members
of the simple Hakka tribes, who live opposite Hong-
Kong, keep with care and can recite veritable trees that
root back infinitely previous to our oldest families, and
when you look at a Hakka woman, with her quaint handkerchief, instead of the otherwise universal bamboo hat
over her head, you have a feeling that she is unchanged
from the woman, who, from a higher peak, saw Noah
disembark!

Though they have hookah water-pipes, the most popular form is chibouk-shaped, with very small cups, which
only hold enough tobacco for a few puffs. Matches are
not in general use. The smoker puts the bowl of his pipe
directly into the smoky nut-oil lamp that is for ever burning on deck, counter and before the family tablets. The
best tobacco is grown on the uplands of Szechuen. It
is of a mild quality. Kwangtung is developing its acreage, as Chinese, versed in the more expert culture and
curing in Manila, return to their native land.

The word home in the Chinese ideograph 家, represents literally a place where a full dressed man may
kneel to his ancestral tablets under his own roof. The

native house is generally of one story, built around an open court (*yuan*), and which is also called by the fancy name of Tien Ching (heavenly well), because the stars look into its pool, where the owner has placed the gold and silver fish from Lake Tsau. In making an arch, an adobe support is first built up. In country places, walls are built higher than the roof so as to serve as a parapet when the owner protects his home from pirates. You will notice at every door that the red Mun Pai (census) tablet is pasted up to conform with the law, and in the kitchen a red slip is pasted calling for blessings from the god of homes, Tsao. Indeed, a mandarin's red Yamen, with its placards, looks like an overgrown valise back from a Cook's tour of continental hotels. Cats are more tolerated than loved, the natives calling them the despised name of Kia Li (house fox). The most expensive breed is from Yunnan, and is tailless.

Shrubs and chrysanthemums are dwarfed and pruned into freakish shapes, sometimes like gowned humans, with porcelain heads and hands stuck upon the extended branches. The effect is pleasing and unique. Greater luxury of bloom could not be developed than their royal lotus and peony. Azaleas, oleanders, jasmine, camellia, tuberoses, and orange are abundant in season. In the moist climate the scent of the flowers is cloying, some foreigners in their ennui calling it "the eternal funeral of the south." The natives excel in several branches of horticulture, attacking the various destructive scales of fruit trees with parasites which die as soon as the pest which they live on is dried up. Parasites to attack our purple, red, and Florida scales have recently been imported into California from China. At night, lanterns are hung in the garden to delight the eye of the master and guest. In the adobe houses of Kansu and Pechili, niches are cut in the solid wall to hold the porcelain or metal lamp, which merely consists of a wick hanging from the bean- or nut-oil in the basin. The two rooms are bare of cupboards. A bar where clothes may be hung, stretches across one end. A long shelf near the ceiling holds utensils, vegetables, etc., while great jars (*kongs*) hold various pickles and soys. Outdoors, small low tables are set beneath mats spread on poles to afford shade, and in contrast with Japan you notice the use of chairs made of bamboo.

In a rich man's house, there is a chapel or room for the ancestral tablets, for a Chinese father is both patriarch and priest. There are no idols in the home, and from their domestic life you do not feel that you are indeed among the heathen. You are really won to the simplicity and honesty of their ancestor-anniversaries and remembrance, for we Occidentals do a little bit of this kind of worship ourselves when we have a general in the alliance or a Covenanter in the blood. Though this is the home of silks, none of the furniture has hangings or upholstery to hold dust. Everything is smooth, cool and cleanly. A bat is worked in the panel of the frieze, between the rooms, to signify *Sho* (long life). Cooking is done outside the house, either in the open under a lean-to, or in a separate building attached to the coolie quarters in the compound. The Shanghai bath, so called by foreigners because they first used it there, but really made at Nanking or Kau-chow, compels the sitter to double up like a jack-knife. It is of brown or yellow porcelain. The stopper is a cork set into a hole placed in the edge of the bottom.

When the weather is cold, brasiers or hand flues are brought in, and in the north a permanent brick or adobe flue (called a *kang*) is built half beneath and half above the first floor. On this the members of the family sleep with wooden pillows under their necks. If the cover is short, it is pulled over the shaven head and not the inured feet. At Hong-Kong, which was comparatively chilly in February for us who were enervated by the awful south, when we had occasion to go back to our offices at night to despatch a ship at daylight, it was amusing to apprehend a dozen of our coolies, and their friends called in from the open highways, sleeping upon our desks and counters in this morgue-like fashion. There is need for the *kang* in the northern provinces, and even as far south as Hupeh, three inches of snow will lie on the ground. In the larger inns a special room, curtained off, is reserved for the *kangs*. There is an aisle in the center, toward which the sleepers place their heads. Oiled paper is used to facilitate the entrance of some light. Reeds, castor-oil plants, and matting are squeezed into the walls to hold the exceedingly poor plaster. The floor and outside covering are generally adobe. The *kang*, which is frequently fed and drawn from out of doors, is used mostly in Manchuria, Pechili and Shansi. South of Chili, the people depend more on brasiers and clothes, although at Ningpo the thermometer drops as low as twenty-four degrees. At Hong-Kong, it was known only once to go to thirty-two on the Peak, but the rawness of winter in the south is as uncomfortable as colder weather in the drier north. The southern Chinese have no word for snow. The Kwang-tung emigrant, who is the man we have in America, writing home, calls it "sky cotton." As we use a hot-water bag, a Chinese uses his charcoal stove, inserting it in his *pu-kai* (mattress), under his vest, or up his sleeve, as need may be for temporary warmth. Like the Russian, the Chinese peasant, though sleeping, can sniff asphyxiation within an inch and yet save himself. Abundant as coal is in Shansi and the north, the dust is utilized by being worked into balls with clay and camel's dung, and used as fuel briquettes in the small hand-cooking stoves which are made at Han-kau. In contrast, consider our waste of sawdust and coal-dust.

The Chinese sojourner at an inn exercises his humorous propensity. You will always see scribbling on the walls, and the subjects generally are: "Guess as to the weight in catties of the rats in this house;" "Enter your name here for the competition as to which guest has risen with the most flea or bug bites." The roofs in Kiang-si and the two Kwang Provinces are made of tiles, but in Hupeh reeds are used for a more picturesque thatch. Mural decoration is done by the use of wood or inlaid tiles. Scroll and screen work are abundantly employed. The Chinese love privacy. The first indication of growing wealth, is to add another foot to the compound wall, rather than an addition to the home itself. A son meeting his father, kowtows to him three times three, with his fists closed together. The superiority of their filial devotion, they attribute to the great superiority of their literature for children. The word *must* is even more emphatic than in the discipline of a Covenanter, or a Cromwellian Ironside. When about to depart on a journey, the lord of the house stands in the midst of his family on his threshold, and looks back. A cup of tea is handed him by his *tin-fong* (second wife), if he has one, or by his wife in her humility as servant to her lord, who is acting as priest. He raises the cup as a salute to Tsao, the god of home, and a prayer for return. He drinks it as an obeisance to god Tien of the heavens, if he wills that he shall never come back, according to that perfect Confucian Golden Rule: "Perform each act and use each day as though they were thy last." If it is a guest who is leaving, the host does not say "good-by," but "*hohang*" (go slow), which is a little commentary on the condition of their roads. Instead of building a proper foundation for the road, the stone blocks are fastened with iron clamps. With the action of rain, or frost, what was meant for a road becomes often a veritable cheval-de-frise!

Rich merchants frequently leave provision in their wills for a monumental gate, bridge, inn or theater, to be erected in their memory, the guild being trustee. All these works are considered to draw trade and travel to one's native town. The Chinese figure of speech expresses the significant fact that their home-maker, and not the bachelor lodger, dignifies the urban population, and composes the beauty and safety of their society. You do not ask: "How many people in this city?" but "How many kitchens within these honorable walls?" Upon entering the house, you do not elect where you shall sit, but advance to the great hall. At the left of the teak guest table, which is against the wall under the longest Confucian motto, you take your place as of right,— the host sitting on the right, since we are reversed in all things. There are chairs down the hall on the left and right, where you gradually ascend or descend, according to the rank of the departing or arriving guests. Thin mother-of-pearl shells are set in wooden frames, and used for the windows of the saloon of the mandarin's house-boat, and for the windows of the better class of houses, the hinge of the window being at the top and the prop at the bottom. The glaring sun is softened wonderfully, and the heat is tempered somewhat. Marble and even granite are cut in slabs, and set in the seats of their black-wood chairs, not only for ornament, but for coolness. At the same time that the foundation of the home is being dug, a spot is selected where to dig in the center of the court, before the women's hong, a lakelet for the goldfish.

Outside Tsianfu, the capital of Shensi Province, is a bluff of cliff dwellings where Tartar families live, and which they fortified against the last Mohammedan rebellion. It was not preference but safety which chose the location, which may throw light upon the *raison d'etre* for scattered cliff dwellings, whether in Africa or New Mexico. In the great drought famine of 1901, when the treacherous Hoang-ho dried up like a bone, three hundred thousand starving Shensi people came up to the provincial capital, and on being refused admittance to the overcrowded city, they dug with their hands caves in the loess cliffs, so that their emaciated bodies might lie out of the way of the feet of men and camels. Let us admit the analogy,—cats, dogs, and even human bodies were as scarce in the streets of Tsian Fu as they were in the streets of La Rochelle in 1628, and the obvious reason shows again how men are all akin under any color of skin when the same kind of trouble meets them. The red banks of the Min near the capital of Szechuen, and down the river as far as Sui Fu, also show cliff dwellings. The valley of the Chu Lung River in Pechili Province exhibits similar dwellings, set as irregularly in the cliff as swifts' nests.

Doors are not made to open on hinges but along

grooves. Into the farthest nooks of China, our clocks, called " iron crickets," have gone. They do not attempt to regulate them, for the sun only is relied on for time. Our clock is appreciated as a toy, for the sake of the revolution of the hands, the ticking like an insect's, and particularly the bells, whose striking apparatus they call the " Melican lark."

In the south, bars are set perpendicularly in sockets, instead of a door being used on the street, and the *lukong* on patrol is afforded a view of the inside of the closed shop. The windows, however, are closed with shutters. These door bars are often beautifully lacquered and gilt. This use of bars, set farther apart, however, is conspicuous at the great prisons, such as at Canton's Yamen, where the prisoners in cangues look like so many zoo inhabitants on exhibition in their various kinds of torture. The purpose is to admit air, or there would be no prisoners for the coming Assizes in so hot a country. Flat locks are not manufactured. The Chinese lock is a brass padlock, long, narrow, and with the keyhole in the end. When shut, it looks like a miniature ark. It snaps without the use of a key. The long key which pushes the spring out, is either our double " L," or letter " E." The security of the lock depends on the length of the key, a three-inch insertion being necessary before the springs of the smallest locks can be reached. The lock is never cast, but is made of seven pieces, carefully joined by interlocking, sweating and solder. A collection of these locks is worth while, for the sake of the artistic brass hammering. The key is a cumbersome affair. It sets into its case like a jack-knife. Each key has a ring. When a *foki*, having locked his master's camphor-wood boxes, door-bars, and window shutters, wends his way homeward, he is undeniably a literal illustration of the Paulist man of " sounding brass and tinkling cymbal," but from his excellent accord with his neighbors, and his long patience in family matters, I have no doubt he eminently possesses (heathen though he is) that charity which was in the same scriptural verse recommended to the Corinthians instead of metal.

The Chinese taste in spectacles demands a wide tortoise rim around the glasses, and for the ear bridges, so that your distinguished and learned friend is a perpetual caricature of a walking chauffeur.

Social letters are marked on the envelope with a character indicating whether the news is of social felicitation, business fortune or condolence, so that the recipient is immediately prepared. In Thibet the custom is more elaborate, silk ribbon being attached to the missives to indicate both the message and the rank of the sender. Between regular correspondents a motto, mutually understood, is affixed instead of the name, a significant commentary on the courier and postal service. Your Chinese merchant is a born conservative.

It is considered social and business manners never to refuse a request directly, but to give a conciliatory reply, and the following day to send an excuse that something untoward connected with the gods, or one's relatives, prevents a compliance. Occidentals call this lying, but it is the national code of politeness which has fostered the custom which they call: " respectfully saving your face." They would never think of asking you to pay a debt in set language, but rather for a " return loan." The manners of the servants constantly lead them to be misunderstood. A coolie never resigns your service; he asks for leave to visit his father's grave. It would be impolite to tell you direct that he was leaving. He sends you a substitute without your asking him to do so, which means, if you understood him, that he has secured better employment, and that he has a cousin to whom he wishes you to teach English.

As the elephant is sacred in Siam, the tortoise is sacred in China, but it has never secured the popularity of the mythical beasts, the four-clawed dragon and the grotesque lion, which one sees sculptured in stone at every temple stairway throughout China and Korea. The blue spot on the Imperial standard set just before the ravenous teeth of the dragon is the famous mythical pearl which he is said to be always striving after, but never secures. This is not meant to convey the futility of empire, but rather our idea of "*Exsertens, perpetua.*" In the lantern procession a round transparency, to represent the same idea, is carried in front of the wriggling beast, which manœuvers on human legs.

Curiously like the Mosaic and Romaic customs, the fixed laws of China are carved on stone and set up in the streets. Chinese criminal law, which is founded on the " Chau Kung," or Ritual of Chau, is based upon the accused confessing, and no punishment can ensue until this is brought about,— all so far removed from the humaner English law, where even the Bench advises that the prisoner need say nothing to incriminate himself, and the action of our juries in throwing out of court confessions obtained by private detective agencies, working for " secret " rewards, through starving and " sweating " the prisoner. Until the late courageous reforms of Wu Ting Fang, torturing was resorted to in all cases before much trouble was taken to collect evidence, and naturally a starved and persecuted victim confessed to anything.

Before the condemned are decapitated, they are offered all the *samschu* they desire to drink, and in most cases they are allowed to choose whether they will ride in a 'rickisha or be carried in a sedan.

No spot of the earth has drunk so deeply of the blood of criminals as the execution court near the Yamen at Canton. It is only a blind alley, not much larger than the back yard of one of our tenements. In the Taeping rebellion, the government beheaded fifty thousand men here. It is stone-paved and sand-strewn. Piled against the walls are immense stone jars, which are reserved to hold the pieces of the bodies of the next dozen victims who are *lincheed* into a thousand pieces. There are also bamboo baskets, in which will be carried away the heads of executed pirates, to be stuck on poles, and exhibited in the districts where they were a curse. The shade of Robespierre would bloom here as a violet in comparison with the ghostly flower of this human shambles. At Peking the execution ground is merely a part of the public highway, in the southwest section, near the palace chrysanthemum gardens, which is blocked off by soldiers for the gruesome occasion, and is afterward immediately given back to the passing of travel. When Vah Kah Der, the notorious outlaw, was executed at Soochow on October 15th, 1906, the new foreign drilled soldiers filed on the parade ground, and took position with true occidental precision around a ring. Then, moving slowly because of the robes worn, came a procession of high officials, who seated themselves on chairs within the circle, the leading officials taking places at a long table under a tent. A deep gong sounded from the Yamen building. At the double quick, a company of Chinese braves or viceroy's retainers, was seen advancing, and in the midst was the chained criminal, carried high upon a wicker tray, and with flags pinned to his new tunic, which the State provides for such occasions, denoting the murders he was found guilty of. The circle opened, and he was cast to the ground in a heap, his neck pulled forward by the queue, and all was over apparently with unseemly haste. The short, thick sword, Tai Fo, is first heated in water, before the single stroke is given. Political executions in Korea as late as 1882, were performed by bullocks tearing the victims asunder.

Oaths are of three kinds, the most solemn being to go out in the open air and kowtow to the skies of god (Tien), and to the earth, when the blood of a white horse and a black ox (Fan Niu) are spilled from cups, as a libation to god and to creation's telluric principle respectively. Outside some of the villages, in a clearing in a grove, a low, wide stone altar is built for this ceremony. The other oaths are breaking a jar, which is a vow by the earth, our mother; and chopping off a cock's head, which is swearing by the blood of life. This last is permitted by the English law courts of Hong-Kong and Singapore. The shedding of a cock's blood is sometimes used to solemnize a curse. In Hupeh Province a cock whose throat has just been cut is dashed against the bow of a vessel going down the ways at a launching. In the service of the secret societies a white cock is killed and the following execration repeated: " May the unfaithful and disloyal perish like this cock." An amusing answer was made in Pidgin-English in the Hong-Kong courts where a Chinese was asked concerning his preference for the Chinese or English method of taking the oath: " Oh, allee samee my, kill 'im cockee; break 'im jugee; smell 'im bookee! " The oaths of secret societies are in addition written and then burned before the god's image, that he may in the spirit world punish perjurers. The most solemn altar is that of the Temple of Heaven at Peking, which is dearer to the Chinese because of its many ravagings by foreigners. Here the High Priest, the Emperor, bows before the High God, or " Shang Ti." At the foot of the altar are iron censers, in which are burned the names of all executed criminals, as a witness that the law of Heaven has been enforced on earth.

China's hope of abolishing the usurpation of her courts by foreign consuls and judges in extra-territoriality régimes, depends entirely upon the success of Wu Ting Fang and his successors in their enthusiastic work to bring the country's code (Pai Yang Kuan), and the new Fah Pu (Justice Board) to approach nearer to occidental practices. In this work Wu was assisted by the advice of Professor Magozo, D. C. L., of Tokio University. The code now in use, and older than Solomon, is not lacking in statutes. If anything, the laws are too severe. In the aim to deter crime the Justinians of China overstepped themselves by making the punishments so severe that the mandarins, fearing the local *fuyins* (people's mayors), and the populace, do not dare to apply them. What is wanted in most cases is a less severe punishment, but its unfailing application. It was the severity of the laws of Leviticus which nullified their application. The following peculiar punishment was inflicted at the assizes of Chantseun in Kwangtung in September, 1907. A military official who had blackmailed a boat captain, was compelled to wear for three days in full view of his fellow officers an arrow which had been run through his ear. Afterward he was committed to jail for ten years, in the laudable endeavor to drive injustice from the rivers, and gain maritime Hong-Kong's approval, for she is rapid to complain and pull diplomatic turmoil around the ears of Peking. The mob has been known to resent an unpopular decision by rushing upon the magistrate and pulling off his long boots, or placing his official chair on the top of a bonfire, as a dare for him to resent it. The old code covers fourteen thousand incidents and precedents in the following divisions: Criminal; Sumptuary; Defense; Military; Public Works; Ceremonial; Judicial; Religious; Fiscal and Family. It is proposed to separate the civil and criminal procedures. The changes in mandarins are so frequent that the law is really interpreted by a local hanger-on of the court, who is not in the Civil Service, and who receives fees from both judge and criminal. Here is the bed of the bribery system. Judges should serve longer. District attorneys should be appointed by the municipalities and barristers should be registered. Juries should be instituted.

The most serious crime in the old code is that of striking a parent, the punishment for which is Ling-chih (cutting into one thousand pieces), but then the Semitic law (Exodus 21; 17) prescribed death as the penalty for cursing a parent. Ling-chih is practised throughout the stern south. In November, 1907, two women were thus cut to death at Swatow, and it is a weekly occurrence at Canton. The lightest punishment is wearing the cangue all day, while being starved. This wooden collar weighs twenty-six pounds, and soon throws the victim head downward, where he lies as a prostrated, exhausted wretch. When we inveigh against the many causes for beheading in the Chinese criminal code, we should reflect that no longer ago than Tudor times, London Bridge not infrequently had two hundred heads ex-

posed at one time on its piers. Wu fought to introduce
trial by jury in capital cases, and the Hong-Kong British
jury of seven is exerting a powerful example in the matter. From juries to parliaments and parties, the steps
are short, and then shall not men wonder if Liberty has
any more fields to conquer, but let us not worry. Liberty
is a thing that rusts, and it is nearly as hard to keep the
pan clean as to buy a new one. If China gets juries, she
will in this excel Japan's judicial system, for Japan has
none. We can not altogether disbelieve in China when
we consider that in the long run that government which
does wrong, falls, and History never raised her voice with
such approval as in this case. The fat old days of official
corruption when a viceroy like Li Hung Chang, clothed
like a beggar to deceive the assessors, could die worth
a billion, and when mandarins would steal the soldiers'
grain to the last *tao,* and then burn the granary down to
obliterate trace of the loss, are departing, never to dawn
in China again in such lurid shame. In the draft of the
new laws, it is prohibited for newspapers to recount crime
at length, as sensationalism is believed to inflame more
crime.

It is not likely that China will yet abolish capital
punishment for the purloining of fiduciary funds or for
bribery. It is also probable that the court eunuchs at
Peking will be dismissed. The intriguing of these effemi-
nates has always been dangerous to crown and ministers.
A native wit advises: "Keep your spirit out of hell,
and your face out of court." The people hate lawyers
as they now know them. They have many a sobriquet
and witticism concerning their calling: "Rats under
the Bench;" "Cash drops into a lawyer's paw as a sheep
falls into a tiger's claw;" "Those who, when they pluck

the bird's feathers, take the skin too," etc., etc. It is among this class that China's poverty and misery have groveled. Ever too poor, with her low taxation, to equip her courts with lictors, clerks, marshals and pleaders, the hangers-on offered to do the work for the privilege of settling the fee privately. They have been the tax gatherers. Has this privilege corrupted them and better than they? What did more to corrupt the great Equites class of the Roman Republic than this opportunity for extortion? A State can not shirk to class its responsibilities, and at the same time be sure of delegating its honor. The result has been "squeeze," blackmail and bribery, and the mandarin, in the poverty of his equipment, has been forced to be satisfied with enunciating the law,— not enforcing it.

The notoriety about offices being purchased does not apply to China's civil service. The tax gatherers and unlicensed counsel would prefer their own purchased opportunities, to the salary of a mandarin. When their purse is low, these pettifoggers hire rascals to charge their fellows with crime and contempt, and see to it that the mill of shame has grist come to it from the blackmail of their fetid imagination. It is these so-called lawyers who have blindfolded Justice in Kwangtung in her search for pirates, and therefore America and Europe have an interest in encouraging China to clean up the Augean stables of her courts. From ten thousand villages where the barns and tax receipts are burned by these rascals; from the bleached bones in the mountain passes of those who were decoyed and murdered to obtain the rewards offered by rich brutes who laughed at the law of their country; from ten thousand litigants whose cases have never reached the judge but been bandied from one lawyer to another; from thousands of daughters, kidnapped by these lictors to keep strife and sorrow active; from the relatives of the murdered, and the ravaged homes of the plundered everywhere in the patient land, swells the plea that the courts be equipped, even at increased taxes, and that the lawyers' clique of extortion be extirpated for ever in a vitalized patriotism among their successors. A similar condition of lawyers studying the law's evasion for the fattening of certain money-changers existed in Palestine in the time of Christ. Success then to Wu and his successors in their radiant-hued reforms in judicial ethics.

Yung Ching writes: " Happy are we when the judge can sleep undisturbed in the court, and when the villager's door is no longer pecked at night, as by a hungry hawk, by the collector of double taxes. What joy is equal to that of seeing the backs of blackmailing lawyers and lictors passing through your outer compound? Litigation is suing a flea and getting a bite for justice." What could better prove that the hearts of this people are attuned to trust law, than the following? In October, 1907, a white explorer, one Deminil, killed a Chinese soldier who was resisting his entrance without passports into Thibet at Batang. The mob, even in this wild country of the Kincha Valley, where they will probably never hear that justice has been meted out, suffered the prisoner to be taken by the military mandarin two thousand miles away, to stand trial in the extra-territorial American court at Shanghai. If we admit that the Chinese people are the poorest the world has known; that they have borne that poverty the longest with perfect philosophy and orderliness, and not out of ignorance or dullness; that they never neglect the old and are charitable even to giving their all repeatedly in their lives, yet never rebelling against the barbed confines of an inexorable duty which is sterner and wider than the Greek's idea of the virtue, we must admit they are the grandest race the Creator looks on, and that it is a greater spectacle than a man rising from poverty to affluence in a land of greater opportunity, such as ours. It is what we bear, not what we win, which is greatness.

In the government of the four hundred clans, and the village and district life, the elders over sixty years of age, and the graduates (of whatever age) of the literary examinations, form one council or Shan-sze, under a *fuyin* (mayor), or *tepao* (dean) of their own, and China in this way has been under democratic rule from time immemorial, for the mandarin seldom interjects his authority. These elders are to be addressed as *laoye* (sir), which is the respect paid a low judge. The *piko* of the kindred Mongolians takes charge of the clan councils with the power of a chief, though in his case, confirmation must be obtained from the " Board of Colonies and Censure " at Peking. The government tax is paid, and the land is divided up among the highest bidders, by the council. Taxes are evaded, especially by mandarins, by a concealment of wealth. Li Hung Chang was notorious for this lack of patriotism. Said one of his kind: " Would the otter have been killed if he had not shown his rich hide? " The *Shui-li* (land tax), which is now five cents a *mao* (six *mao* an acre), the government hopes to raise to eight cents, in conformity with a plan submitted by Robert Hart, lately their adviser. In comparison, the Japanese tax on poorer land is at present fifteen cents a *mao*. We need say no more to reveal the potentiality of dormant China. When drought visits the

Chinese bridge at Soochow, Kiang-su province, East China. Wash-
women and houseboats.

Chinese justice for theft of fiduciary funds, bribery, etc.: Criminals suspended by chins in bottomless cages, until dead. Outside Viceroy's Yamen, Canton, South China.

A funeral procession with honorary banners, passing a forage cart on the street which runs inside the outer wall, Peking, North China. The dark vault of the gate through the wall can be slightly seen on the extreme left of the picture. A soldier of China's modern army is at the right of the picture.

land, oftentimes the peasants carry their plowshares to the plaza in front of the yamen, and cast them in a heap as a mute intimation to the mandarin that it would be inhuman to levy the land tax, when the share, sowing and sweat have brought no harvest. The land tax in Szechuen Province, by an ancient agreement at the time of its repeopling, is the lowest in China, and the province is the most populous and richest, which is a glorious illustration of the wisdom of not taxing necessities, but rather reaching out after luxuries to support government. Family disputes, debts, wayward youths, village works, wells, lawsuits (most of them on water rights), celebrations, processions, and the clan's policy toward other clans, and the government as represented in the mandarin, Taotai and viceroy,— are all controlled by the council. Six clans send all the emigrants to America. Their names are Sam Yup; Yung Wo; Hop Wo; Yan Wo; Kong Chow, and Ning Yung, known to us as the famous " Six Companies " of San Francisco.

Speaking generally, emigration from the village to the city is discouraged. It is the family pride that the sons', and the sons' sons' houses are all within the parent compound. A popular story which the 'rickisha coolies chant from their pamphlets, while they wait for their masters, is about " Chang Kung and his nine generations all within one wall." China has yearned over its children like Isaac. She has loathed the emigration barracoons of Macao, and the blue-funneled coolie ships lying off the Prayas of Swatow and Hong-Kong. An exception is the emigration to Mongolia, where all taxes are remitted for five years to Chinese, the government considering this the most effective way to restrain the vexatious and uncertain Mohammedans, and the troublesome Mongols who have acquired their wayward habits. The clan polices its fields from the depredations of Hakka and Miaotse vagrants. You will notice warnings pasted on the sides of shrines and on bulletin boards. Some of them warn you not to fill in a disused well, as that would be unlucky. The clan law or custom prescribes certain gleanings of grain and cotton which must be left by the reapers. The stubble of sorghum must not be cut below a certain height. Rice is caught in the hand and cut by the sickle half-way down the stalk, while in the northern provinces the whole straw of the millet is left standing, the ears only being cut out. A gong is rung from the temple porch to announce that the clan fields are open to the gleaning of the poor on the day following. Trespassers convicted by the council are consigned to the cangue for various periods during harvest time, and as they are generally the poor and opium degenerates, the punishment of being incarcerated during gleaning days is a severe one.

In the more complex life of the capital or Fu cities, and the smaller cities of Ting and Chau ranks, of course Governors General (Tsung Tuh) and Lieutenant Governors (Liang Kiang) rule. Altogether the organization of departments, districts, provinces, cities, towns, villages and circuits is thorough and admirable. The literal translation of *chichau* (district mandarin) is " knower of his district," indicating the sympathy expected between ruler and ruled, from the Tsung Tuh down to the lowest official, the *siunkien* (justice of the peace). A relic of barbaric clan life exists in the Yeung Kong district of Kwangtung. On the fifth day of the fifth moon, the men of two villages meet in a valley and line up on each side of a stream for an all-day battle with stones and

slings. The battle is witnessed by visitors from surrounding villages. As men are struck or injured, they
are carried or ruled off the field. Sometimes one thousand men are engaged and deaths are occasional, though
not more die than if one thousand men played football.
Similar stone-throwing contests, set for stated times and
the settling of accumulated clan feeling, are not uncommon in Korea. At Seoul, different wards of the city, and
in Yunnan, some of the Shan tribes engage in these
fights.

The paths outside of the treaty ports are too narrow for
even the 'rickisha, and so the wheelbarrow is the passenger equipment. It is not an infrequent sight for a small-
footed woman to be balanced by a live pig securely
strapped to the other half of the barrow. A sail is raised,
the shafts are lifted, and down the path between the quiet
rice fields the comical freightage races, for the sooner
the journey is over the better for the one to whose
shoulders the shafts are tied. As no iron is used in
north China in the wooden cart wheels, which are mor-
tised, dovetailed and wedged, after one has washed his
face in a pan at a Gobi desert well, the precious water
must be poured on the wheels to swell them, so that they
will not fall apart. Vehicles bearing the yellow flag have
the right of way; they are carrying Imperial supplies. It
is a marvelous country of the honorableness of little
things. No man has much, but every man has something, and is drilled to find that something a little more
than sufficient, for little pessimism is reflected in the country's literature.

The elastic, easeful methods of the race will be understood by their having no word to express hour, minute
or to-morrow. They can say night and day, but they

must use a metaphor from nature or custom when they express anything shorter than *kih* (fifteen minutes) "The time it would take a turtle to crawl a *li*" would be half a day. "The time it would take a lark to swallow a grasshopper" expresses an instant. "The time you would get shaved" indicates half an hour. "The time it would take to swallow a good-by cup of tea" expresses two minutes. The word "to-morrow" can only be expressed by an affix of "future" to the active verb.

They call their whisky "the liquor that has three fires" (*samschu*), and the inventor of this distillation of rice, Ih Tih, is referred to as "the partner of the devil" by the school teachers. The liquor is always taken hot, and the idiom for saying, "I have taken a drink," is "I have painted my face." The propaganda against the use of wine has been sedulously and effectively pursued since its institution by the second king of the Chau dynasty, who was contemporary with David. Their effective crusade against drugs (opium) belongs to a much later date, even the twentieth century.

IV

CHINESE HUMOR

Three races, and three races alone,— the American, the Scotch and the Chinese,— appreciate and constantly use humor. The American, divining the point like a prophet, begins to laugh ere the incident is fully related; the drolly slow Scot does not chuckle until he has first rounded the humor in his mind, and satisfied himself that it is true coin. The stoical Chinese laughs not at all, before or after, but next day in sincerest flattery, in his wide charity, he will pass your story along, and he and his will trust you for evermore, because for a moment you have lightened the load of care of a fellow mortal. All three races live life very seriously,— even religiously, — and welcome that forgiveness of attitude which clothes human defects with the smile of tolerance. The Chinese of course chiefly selects such characteristic subjects as the disappointment of the father of ten daughters and no sons; the husband henpecked by his last wife as much as by his first two; the bonze who added to his geomantic threatenings and discoveries, as famine kept the people from supplying his coffers; the discovery of an honest tax-gatherer; the pig trying not to laugh as he balanced the proud beauty on the other half of the wheel-barrow; Truth changing the inscription on a mandarin's honorary pailo arch; the professional mourner saying a cheerful " hello " to a friend, though his purchased tears continued to flow; etc., but in moods like those which follow he approximates close to our points of view.

173

The Chinese padlock is composed of a long, thin brass rod, on which a clasp slides. The usurer of China's treaty ports is generally a Parsee, who intends to go home to Bombay when he has heaped his stack of exchanged sovereigns high enough. Into Restonji Jamshedj's shop on the water Praya of Hong-Kong came Ng Tso Sui, a debtor in whom humor ran alongside of dishonesty. Overpowering the little dark man in the black skull-cap, he took out his large ear-ring, clapped in the brass padlock, and then offered to exchange the key of the latter for his canceled note. No Parsee would dare to admit to his caste that a heathen had ever soiled his person, and that vagabond and boaster Ng, while his fellows lean against their fish poles while the nets are drying on the Lamma beach, again and again descants how a locksmith after all makes the best fisherman.

The Hakka boatmen of Kowloon enjoy nothing better than to foment their women into ancestor-villifying "Billingsgate." The tongue of these women has won for them the captain's position in the family sampan. Off Douglas Pier, Hong-Kong, I saw two of the boats lying sterns together, while from the end of each the respective queens of vituperation jargoned and altercated. When the wrath was at its height, and a hundred sampans crowded about to hear the contestants extend their curses to the seventeenth ancestor (the living having been consumed early in the conflagration), the two husbands quietly took up the oars. Jerking the boats, they precipitated the Protean warriors overboard. With one wild yell from the departing audience, the fray was immediately over, and rescued Peace settled herself in the bedraggled nest of humiliation.

The Chinese valentine which expresses the greatest insult is the one in which a sea-turtle is represented. Mandarin Chang has been superseded by Mandarin Chuen. Thereupon Chang mails to the yamen a picture of Chuen's chair borne by four turtles standing erect in insolence, instead of turbanned and sashed coolies. The Chinese consider the turtle the most contemptible animal, and Chang thereby insinuates that he considers only the lowest of animals,— much less a human being,— fit to be near the person of his rival Chuen.

A hungry priest is not averse to adopting the useful side of humor when his homilies fall on stony ears. Buddhism teaches that the souls of men come back and inhabit animals. The priest betakes him to a parishioner whose fears he knows he can work on, but it must be one who owns a duck yard. Selecting a conspicuous bird, he exclaims that he knows the sainted soul of Farmer Lun's father has come back and inhabited that bird because of its peculiar shuffle, " just like the literary old man's." Immediately pious Lun asks the priest if he will not keep the bird where it will hear the monastery's bells of prayer, to which request Pastor Humor accedes, and later introduces its victim to the bell of a useful doom.

But the Chinese with all his courtesy, which is by the book, can enjoy a little humor. When Abbe Huc, the learned Toulouse monk, was traveling from Peking to Thibet in 1846, he was occasionally ill at the yamens of the mandarins. They invariably rolled up their gift of a yellow lacquered coffin and told him to " forsake sadness and behold in what glory he would die away from home."

The *East Asia News* of Canton, printed in the native character, having cause to denounce the Taotai's policy in the Yuet-Han Railway matter, capped their argument by calling this high official: "for ever a dizzy-headed fish."

A cynic argued with a humorist that even the holiest of men had some sinful secret, and to prove it, stuck haphazardly in a bonze's private incense pot, a tablet with the words: "Alas! all is known," and for once the humorist was defeated by the bonze decamping in the night for parts unknown.

On the long bamboo wharf at Wanchai, coolies in line bore coal in scoop-shaped baskets to the launches which were made fast to one side. The early fish boats had just brought in from the Lamma shoals their supply for the Hong-Kong market, and the fishermen were busy balancing on their shoulders buckets filled from the tanks with live fish. These two lines of men worked to and fro from coal godown to wharf, and from market to boats, until some water from a fish-bucket splashed on the sooty leg of a coal coolie. His leopard spots brought out the jeers of the fish clan, for the labor unions are generally made up of one family. Jeers led to names, and curses to vituperation, until the lines of men dropped their burdens, and faced each other for a battle, first of grandfathers' adjectives. Then there was a rush, and of course the fishermen were the Achilles with the vulnerable heel, for the fish were precious and the coal was not. The coal coolies took the kicks and queue-pulling, while they emptied their filthy baskets into the fish-buckets. A score of wide Hupeh grass hats were left to the grinning ebony victors, while the defeated rushed to their boats to laundry their eels and garoupa.

When a Chinese beggar thanks you for an alm, he always says *"Taipan"*; that is, "May you be the

general manager of your firm," and it is noticeable that
these beggars require from your chair coolie the address
of "*Laoye*" (Sir), before they will get out of the way.
The coolies give this term of respect willingly, for there
is nothing native servants dislike so much as profane
or abusive language; but the smile on the face of the
beggar shows that he is enjoying the humor of the salutation.

A little Hakka girl, who was carrying her brother
papoose-fashion on her back, was asked " Is he heavy? "
and she replied: " No, he is my brother." She was
not thinking of the humor or the humanity of it, but
merely questioning the adjective used, but the grin on
my 'rickisha men's faces showed that they had seen the
other phase.

In the Buddhist monastery of the Goddess of Mercy
at Canton, I asked a native idler for an explanation of
the gilded statue of the goddess Kun Yam, and he replied: " Oh, she Chinee woman who not eat rice ever,
but can eat money any time."

Victoria College, an institution for the education of
native youth in Hong-Kong, while reaping glory the
world over with its graduates in the diplomatic service,
is sowing humor abundantly through its sophomores.
The college paper, *The Yellow Dragon,* contains the
following letter from a pupil to his father at Canton:

" Don't take any anxiety for me gambling and wandering about in bad habit places. I hope you will not
forget to send me those few dollar for to pass the New
Year here alone. I find my body very weak this year,
but I bowl and play cricket much for strength. I begin
to go to bed at eleven P. M. I am sorry I spent so
many money, but all's well. You are an old man,

father! and ought sleep in earling and rise in late. Drink your tea stout and not thin now. Try amuse your tedium and look some humorous."

One laconic diarist entered as follows: "This day an Englishman came to the school and gave a disposal of delivering on the Southern Sea."

A Yaumati cook, who must have had a preceptor cousin employed as a lawyer's errand boy in one of those brief-smelling offices up one flight on the south side of Queen's Road Central, addressed the police of the Colony across the bay the following petition to search for his lost brother:

" To the Generals of the Charge Room:
" The humble petition of Tam Sing, residing at the ground floor, Upper Station Street, Yaumati, sheweth: That your petitioner can not find out his brother, who has been put to be lost after his being abroad from the above address at three o'clock afternoon, Friday last. His name is Tam Noo, with a flat face, sloping eyes, and common size and height as to his body; he has a yellow feature, and is a man belonging to the Dong On district, and his dresses are all black, but his coat was made of cloth, with brass buttons. His feet are bare without any shoes or stockings. And your petitioner as in duty bound, shall ever pray."

A native draper's clerk of Shanghai, as a result of his visit with a package to be delivered to a European hong, where he had seen a calendar which attracted his attention, stormily resurrected his mission school English as follows:

" Excellent Sirs:

" The Calendar in your Company is glance in looking to be sure surpassing all the others; and also it is gigantic beyond example in connection with its fine spectacle, while I look at it, and appreciate pieces for oblige."

As an example in homiletic English, I offer the following effort of a colporteur: " Him sorrying his foolish, and having ashamed it, he was forgave."

A friendly Chinese operator in the Imperial telegraph service at Kalgan, thus wrote a missionary during the famous Boxer siege of Peking in June, 1900: " We have ordered our lineman to go to Peking to peep the condition. In accounting he shall come back in a few days when must have a reliable term from him. With kind regards to yourself and all your combinations."

Cheu Fat, a gourmand, was boasting that as for him, he could digest anything, even to the wild, oak-leaf silk of Chifu, when his physician Su replied: " The trouble is, a man never gets a chance to digest his coffin cloth."

Huan had refused to join the local Triad Society in organizing opposition to an unpopular but powerful magistrate. He thereupon was asked for his reasons, and replied that he had " ten." And what are they? " Two wives and eight children."

The native humor for that prosperity which evidences itself in good living is " Blown tight as a drum." The letters make a rather pretty monogram to look at. The artificers in silver of Yung Yan Lane, Canton, who make belts for European visitors, sometimes mix a little humor with their art in working together the ideograms. They are now being exhibited on the waists of many of the primest of our ladies, who imagine that they are displaying a pearl, all too unknown, of Confucian truth, which emphasizes again the wisdom of being beautiful only in one's own language, especially if one is attending a five o'clock tea at the Chinese Ambassador's.

Shopkeepers seldom put their names on their signs, but announce their stores by a flowery trade mark. Some of the lucky legends so used are: "The shop of Heavenly Peace, dealing in collars and silks; " The shop of Emulating the Phœnix, dealing in ivories"; "The shop of Extensive Harmony," etc. A white man generally catches the pronunciation of Chinese before the meaning, and will swear to you that the Chinese are the most affable of people, for did not every employee stop work when he entered, look up, and follow him through the shop with streaming smiles. The reason of it all was because Mr. Reginald Thusly, "Griffin," lately from Eton, but now Colonial Cadet, walked into the collar shop and inquired patronizingly, "if Mr. Extensive Harmony was in."

The poetical names of the race are a constant source of amusement. An irate mandarin came upon our missionary, who had good reason for never taking him seriously, to "bluff" him out of town, and announced his name as "Yuen Chuen"; i. e., Sweet Spring.

The Peking *Gazette* of August 16th, 1906, after going at length into the charter of the Canton-Han-kau Railway, and expatiating on the latitude of the franchise, concluded with this reserved admonition to the directors: "Think honestly, but act only when you have asked us how."

The *Sin Wan Pao,* a native paper, referring to the signed agreement between the Wai Wu Pu, and the

British minister concerning the Canton-Kowloon Railway, states: " In addition, the viceroy of Canton has been instructed to see that the governor of Hong-Kong understands these clauses in the same way that they are understood at Peking," possibly the first time in a legal document that the text may be amended by the interpretation.

Even the most serious man in all human history, Confucius, was once known to bow to humor. In the Chia Yu (Family Traditions) classic, the Duke Lu asks the Sage if any act was more shameful than a man forgetting his wife, to which the Sage replied: " Yes, when he forgets himself."

An amusing case of wits saving wind occurred August 24th, 1906, on Southbridge Road, Singapore, where they were erecting iron standards to support wires. A lunatic butcher with a cleaver was rapidly gaining on a Celestial, whose eyes fired up with a merry twinkle as he skinned up the pole like a monkey. From the cross-arm the gleeful prey very easily kicked down the pursuer, until the exhausted wretch let his rage froth out in chopping fruitlessly at the iron pole.

Puk Luk was an unemployed coolie of Hong-Kong, who had a humor to toy with trouble and bon mots. He spied another coolie on the walk, sitting on a box with his back to the street, and combing out the feminine locks of his queue. Puk took to the outer edge and in passing the tonsorial coolie, he reached out and purloined a brush. Pursuit was given, when Puk fled to a pile of laundry baskets and hid beneath one. When the *fokis* and *lukongs* were overturning them, Puk bit their fingers. Questioned by the magistrate why he acted in this manner, in addition to being a thief, he said, " I was teaching fool *fokis* to turn only baskets which had smooth edges."

Clans dare not come to blows in the British Colony, and therefore they ransack their heads for practical jokes. A man of the Ng Clan comes to Lok's stall in the Praya market and orders a dozen fowls' heads to be chopped off. When it is done, Ng facetiously says: " Now enter that on my account; I thank you for doing what I told you," and scampers for the street. Lok infuriated immediately pursues, when a confederate Ng clansman steals what he can from the pile. ,When Lok comes back, if he can not sell the remaining chickens at once to foreigners, he loses them too, for he can not afford to keep ice. If Ng's family are rice merchants, Lok hires a loft for a week in a godown at West Point, immediately under Ng's rice bins, and gets to work with his augur. So the humorous war of clan spite runs its merry round.

The wife of a military man of Hong-Kong, the glossiest of the silk in her dignified dealings with American and European society, had occasion to hire a new house boy, but the following dialogue explains why the applicant, who probably had sharpened his wits in the environs of Queen's College, failed to get the place. What is your name? " Oh! my name belong Gao Kung Loy." That is too difficult for me to remember, I will call you just plain John. The Chinese asked, " What now belong your name, Missee?" My name is Mrs. Colonel Errington. The suave Celestial who may yet lead a retaliatory army, felt up his sleeve, and drawing down a smile, in a triumphant long lisp drawled: " Oh! Missee Kulnel Ellington too muchee long for my; maskee, I callee you plain Tom."

I do not know whether the following incident is yellow or white humor. The consulate had a hurried call to match Piccadilly pomposities against visiting martial braid at the landing wharf. The silk hat needed smoothing and master gave his orders. The house boy was a griffin and sought the aid of the cook coolie, who stepped into the breach with an alacrity which later proved to be heroic. When master's frock-coat was brushed, he was handed a silk hat, well daubed with plumbago, to complete the amenities.

The manner in which your house servant appropriates your rights and chattels is humorously pervert. He knows that your knowledge of him, his land and his language, is compassed by two dozen words of Pidgin-English. He waves his occult wand in a realm apart and watches you perform, which perhaps explains his everlasting grin. To illustrate. Mrs. Colonel Blank, very English and lamentably un-Colonial, had just arrived and with that suddenness of the military in things social, after her month of receiving calls, and with her effects from home still a month away, determined to relieve the accumulation of obligations and ennui by giving a dinner to some one " high up," to commence with. It should be something *pukka*. The General Commanding His Majesty's Forces in China, (how the Chinese resent the scope of the title) but located at Hong-Kong, was chosen as the lion. Going to her " Number One boy," or comprador, she said: " Boy, I give dinner this night, belly finee lady, belly finee man, six piecee; splosem you clatch everything best can do; sabee "? In the evening the Number One boy called his mistress from the enlivened company which was drinking Scotch and Schweppe appetizers on the veranda, and announced that dinner was served. The Number Two boy, attired in a long blue tunic, and with his pigtail tucked in his waist cord so as not to whip the soup, swung open the folding doors. Apprehensive, the hostess looked upon the magic scene; cut glass and silver galore, an expanse of occidental and oriental richness. Upon the face of the general's wife hung that pain which is born of knowledge suppressed for kindness' sake. When she could be excused the mistress hastened to the head servant. "Boy, by all your heathen gods, where you catchee; what side; what fashion?" "Oh," said the bland one, "that all plopee easy; I sabee flend who talkee how his piecee master go out topside to eat chow tonight; so he pay (lend) my silver dishee, alee samee you talk clatch everything best can do." From which it appeared that the general's boy and the colonel's boy were fast and reciprocating friends; the former had advised the latter that his master was going out to dinner that night, which gave the colonel's boy the opportunity of his life to ingratiate himself with his mistress for wit, and to make his master's apparent wealth the wonder of his guests. The motive either sprang from pride, or that vast well of humor which is deeper in their hearts than we Westerners have yet plumbed. Which it was, judge ye, as you know them.

A humane mandarin of Sing Yuen, who was more of a statesman at heart than a tax-gatherer, when asked by his viceroy why he did not "comb" his district finer, replied: "We should make soup of the eggs, and not of the hen."

The Chinese petty thief greases his pig tail and also his bare shining shoulders, so that he may be as hard to grasp as a jellyfish. A bland-looking, furtive-mannered individual, with a resemblance to a native who was once deported, promenading in Hong-Kong with a finely oiled queue, is enough for the wary Sikh police. The smile is at once transferred from the Mongol to the Hindoo face, as the suspect is led by the slack of the knickerbockers to headquarters up Wyndham Hill, to explain why one so poor should be so extravagant in pomades.

The southern Chinese recite this proverb: "Why is a pig fat? So that he can not travel far from his mud and learn that he is a pig. It would never do for him to go to Tientsin and see larks. He would then not even be willing to be a thin pig."

The Hakka herders of Kowloon have this witticism on stubbornness: "The proper way to drive a pig is the opposite way."

V

CHINA, POLITICAL AND PICTURESQUE

Despite the reiterated epithets that she is the Eternal, Imperturbable and Impenetrable, during the last five years China has made more comparative progress than any nation, and to her will belong the twentieth century, as the nineteenth was distinctive for the development of North America.

Japan, and the model colonies of Manila and Hong-Kong, have not alone influenced China's politics in these latter days. We may understand somewhat the political lethargy of the Chinese in the past if we frequently call to mind that they seldom contemplated their country as China (the pure country of the Tsins who built the Great Wall), but as Chung Kwok, or the Central Kingdom, which could not, from its position, but be an example to the whole world. Out of vast indifference to and ignorance of travel, of course grew this colossal and stultifying political pride. One of the central provinces, Hunan, first gave itself the name, until the whole people have long learned to use it in the belief that their nation occupied the earth's center, and was accordingly the most important and self-sustaining, which latter assumption was perhaps justified. What we call Thibet, the residents thereof call Bod. Next to themselves, the Chinese ranked the Nui Fan, or internal foreigners, as the old tribute-paying tribes of Szechuen were called.

186

In order, follows the Wai Fan, external foreigners, or wandering tribes of Mongolia; the Nui I, or internal barbarians, like the aboriginal mountaineers of Hainan Island; and the Wai I, or external barbarians like ourselves and other irredeemable strangers. Their distinguishing word for Englishmen is Hung Mao, men with red beards; for Americans, Hwa Ki, men of the Flowery Flag; for Portuguese, who were the first Europeans they met, Si Yang, men of the western ocean; and for Japanese, Wu Jin, dwarfs. Merely their locality or appearance, and not their intellect or history, in the foreigner, appealed therefore to the self-satisfied Chinese of olden days. But things have changed.

When we say that they have been influenced, we do not mean to convey the impression that the Chinese to-day are astounded at the achievements of the Japanese, for they consider that Japan lacks that essential of permanent greatness, population. Numbers have always impressed the Mongol, who learned with respect from the missionary Buddhists in ancient times of another great people numerically, the Hindoos, and forthwith showed them honor by giving their religion a place at the altar.

That it should be possible in recent times that the great hordes in Russia should experience a political upheaval, has induced the discontented and ambitious among the Chinese, in their organization of the patriotic Young-China party, to bestir themselves from despair and torpidity, in the hope that they too may have a government which will be more intimately in touch with the desires of the common people, and achieve that worthy aim of diplomacy: to be valued as a friend and feared as a foe. The Parliamentary Commission, sent

to Europe and America in 1906, reported that they were
most impressed with Japan's constitution, and after that
with France's, as the Japanese, when in a similar embryo
state, modeled their constitution after Germany's, but the
report of a Manchu Commission is far from being the
opinion of leaders like Kang Yu Wei, who look to America as a model.   Trained in obedience to his father during a whole life time, as was the Roman under the
Republic, the Chinese by character offers a steady foundation for the responsibilities of representative rule.   The
Commission suggested that a trial of provincial elective
parliaments should be instituted by 1910; these parliaments to choose a provincial executive, who shall be
subordinate to the viceroy now named by the Emperor.
The Progressives, who are asking for more independence
than this, promise that they will soon turn to contempt
Curzon's prophecy of twelve years ago concerning their
race: " *Sedet æternumque sedebit.*"

China has been easy thus far to govern because she
has been an agricultural people, and not a manufacturing
or urban one.   She has no cities the size of ours.   The
Clan life which they love, and which has given the nation its peculiar strength, never could have survived if
its vitality had depended on an urban organization.

Nowadays one often hears the ancient prophecy repeated: " When yellow snow falls in Peking, the dynasty will end."   Such a phenomenon occurred shortly
before the fall of the Ming dynasty.   China is coming
to the judgment.   If the Manchu successor of that
famous conquering " General of the Eight banners," of
three centuries ago, can not rise to the emergency and
adjust himself, as he did in Kang He's progressive
reign, he must retire, but it is not certain that he will

miss his opportunity of rendering better service any more than the Samurai in Japan neglected his, always remembering that in the fall of rulers, history records incapacity as great a fault as injustice. Peking is now divided between the Moderate and Conservative parties; there is really no advanced section, as there was after China's war with Japan, and what remains of the last named party is at Canton. It continues to send delegations to Peking, asking for an immediate constitution, Upper and Lower Houses of a Diet; juries; freedom of speech and press; the spread of schools, factories and foreign books; pardon of political exiles; a sane criminal code; an advanced railway, foreign and maritime policy; the widening of secret society and guild walls into those of political parties; etc. How every one dares to laugh now at the old edict pasted up in the tea-houses "*Mo Tan Kvo shih*"; "Don't talk politics, By order."

Of course rule by delegation is not perfection in the respect that government should be exercised by the people, but if the Manchu improves in his rule as the men of Satsuma have, something will be gained. When the Chinese criticizes the airs of his Manchu ruler, his idiom is: "He wears his hat on one side." It was the Manchu, and not the native Ming dynasty, which taught the Chinese the doctrine of the exclusion of foreigners. The Manchu has made some concessions to Chinese criticism. Last year the ancient ban against mixed Manchu and Chinese marriages was removed and this year saw the last of the Manchu generals withdrawn from the provinces, thus leaving the Civil Viceroy, who is often a Chinese, free. Is it prophetical that the Manchu has not called his legal city the capital of the land, but only the capital (*Ching*) of the north (*Pei*)?

Peking is really a poor location for a capital, as it is removed from the center of population. On this account, Yunnan Province has never really been governed from Peking. The old capital of the Mings, Nanking (literally, Capital of the South) was a much better location, and Han-kau would be better still. Now that railways are opening up the land, there is no reason why the capital should not be at Choong King, or Ching Too in Szechuen. It would be the center of population and bind Yunnan and Thibet and the greatest and most ambitious of them all, Kwangtung, closer to the throne. There are precedents for something apparently so radical, for we must remember that in so-called changeless China, there have been thirteen changes of capital.

There are only five million Manchus among the four hundred million Chinese. Even in Manchuria, the Manchus who cut only enough cedar and arbor-vitæ wood to warm them, and fish and hunt only what will barely feed them, when their pension is spent, are dying off, and thrifty Chinese emigration from Shantung is filling the land, which is revenge enough for the capturing of Peking in 1644 by the Manchu Dor Gun. In the same way the Chinese are peacefully conquering Mongolia by squatting on the lands of the roving Tartars, who are pushed farther into arid Gobi, or compelled to sober up and settle down among the new tillers of the soil.

Much has been made abroad of the Wei, the " squeeze pidgin," or peculation of the Manchu officials, who are scattered throughout the empire. The Mongolian, who has suffered more from them, does not say " he has squeezed me," but " he has eaten me." In the first place, it must be observed that this is not a charge against the great Chinese people. It will be found, as it is among

China's best-known statesman, Li Hung Chang, in his Vice-royal
Yamen at Tientsin, September, 1900.

Li Hung Chang, with the American General Ward, and the British
General Gordon, saved the Manchu throne in the dangerous
Tae-ping rebellion of the Southern provinces in 1865.
From that year until 1901 he was the late Empress
Dowager's right-hand statesman in her deal-
ings with foreigners, and the internal
reforms which the trend of the times
forced her to adopt.

Marching Home! Gallant 6th U. S. Cavalry after brilliant relief
of Peking, North China, siege of 1900. The allies admitted
that the Americans were the best marksmen and
brainiest open-order fighters in the allied
armies. This is the first time fine
cavalry horses were seen in China.

American section of captured wall of Tien-tsin, North China, siege
of 1900. Soldier of 14th U. S. Infantry on guard.

other people, that small salaries for large responsibilities
led to this obnoxious practice, which came in with Manchu rule. For instance, the governor-general of Mongolia receives on the pay-roll five thousand dollars, and
the residents of such centers as Koren and Kashgar average only eighteen hundred dollars, while the greatest effectiveness is expected of them in diplomacy. Sir Robert
Bredon, their foreign director of the imperial customs,
receives only twenty-five thousand dollars salary. When,
through systematization of collection, China's revenue
is greater, as it is becoming, " squeeze " will die out, as
no race,— ruled or rulers,— are more inclined to be honest. They have never had parties, with a rotation of
plunder, in China. The Chinese Triads differ from the
Japanese Samurai in this, that they do not believe liberty
will be a gift from a superior class, as the Japanese nobles
endowed the clans with a partial constitution. This was
the only time in the world's history when political rights
were so established, and they do not think it has proved
satisfactory. They believe they will have to win from
the higher powers their liberty in the good old Anglo-
Saxon way, by argument all the time and arms part of
the time. Reform really began at the close of the China-
Japan war. Now that the obstructionist Dowager Empress Tse Hsi is gathered to her ghostly traditions, doubtless the Cantonese Kang Yu Wei will return, and the
brilliant Yuan Shi K'ai of Pechili, stubborn Shum from
the south; tried and solid old Chang from the central
provinces; the Columbia College bred Tang Shao Yi;
Viceroy Tuan Fang, the Manchu who, in Shensi, saved
the Christians in 1900; the Yale graduate Liang Tun
Yen; the Cambridge graduate Shen Tun Ho, and their
like, will gather around the new Regent for the renewal

of the militant and reform plans so suddenly and disastrously dropped in 1897.

Who are the men of the hour in China, on whom
Americans should keep their eyes? Who are the strong
characters, a study of whose modern personality will
make China far more interesting to us henceforward?

First, because he held high offices, let us mention Yuan
Shi K'ai, lately deposed by the new Regent from his
viceroy and chancellorships. Yuan is the best equipped,
most practical, most modern, and most popular with the
foreigners in Peking, of all Chinese statesmen. He is
the organizer of China's modern army of the north.
He succeeded in what his predecessor Li Hung Chang
tried to do, in establishing mills, mines and railways in
the north. He is the best financier in China, and a believer that honesty is the most economical fiscal policy,
when you come to borrow again or refund loans. Contrary to the Empress Dowager's orders, he saved the
Christians from the Boxers when he was viceroy of
Pechili Province, but there is always some flaw in the
jewel. By his betrayal of reform in 1897 he made Box-
erism possible. While till lately he was high in the
Manchu councils and offices, he is a native Chinese by
blood. He was dismissed by the Regent, Prince Chun,
in 1909 on the excuse that he had disastrously relapsed
once from reform and betrayed the extensive modern
plans of the late Emperor Kwang Su to the inexpressible
Dowager Empress, thus bringing on the reactionary *coup
d'etat* of 1898, which postponed reform for ten years.
He may be restored if Manchu jealousies cease to attack
Chinese officials, and one hope of his return lies in the
fact that he had an eye for choosing the most capable
subordinates available. These men are a powerful col-

lege, devoted to his personal cause. He is a conservative rather than a radical reformer. He believes in the power of the press, and is not averse to bribing it. He is extremely unpopular with Kang Yu Wei, also a native Chinese, their greatest and most radical reformer, the Roosevelt of China, who is now in exile in hot Penang Straits Settlements, under the protection of Britain.

Who is this Kang, who, like Roosevelt, shows his teeth as he eagerly prepares to attack his opponent with a spring, back of which is the whole incorruptible soul of a leader whose impetus is as weighty as that of a host? He *is* the New China,—has been it since 1897, and it was the example of British organization at Hong-Kong which inspired him who came out of Canton near-by. Had he started north overland with another army of Taepings, he would have won the throne and held it. No, he rather chose education and sought the Emperor for a pupil. He is hated by the old conservative Manchus, and even the literati of the disbanded Tsung Li Yamen (Foreign Office) of Peking, who are as skilful and unprincipled " disappearance artists " as a doge's cabal, or the private metropolitan detective agencies, fed by corrupt millions, which have grown up in some of our western civilizations. He was joint author with the Emperor Kwang Su of the shower of reform edicts of 1897, on which China's hopes of modernity to-day rest. His name spreads like the spirit of an informing angel over the whole of China, and every new official, especially those educated in America, who has seen a light, goes sometime to the Oracle Kang to feed it with oil.

Perhaps the Fates have ordained it that he shall keep his light pure, and never trade in the spoils of office, thus the better to inspire those who must soil their hands

in active politics, pure as the intent of the best may be.
But he chafes at this, for he is many sided. He wants
to be as active as Yuan, who adopted his ideas and betrayed them once for office, though Yuan, from 1898 to
1908, returned to moderate reform, and steady, conservative progress. In America, of course, such spirits as
Kang could not be side-tracked by intrigue, and that
more than anything proves the balance of our constitution and institutions. In China it is yet possible, and
even Yuan has at last suffered by it. Kang is not an
ultra reformer. He proposes to absorb the Manchu and
not to eradicate him. He speaks well of the late Kwang
Su's powers, and he hates the memory of the late Dowager, in which we agree with him. Kang is more sentimental, sensitive and versatile than any Chinese leader.
The very dangers of poison and dagger that beset him;
the necessity for a circle of iron to guard him, show best
the need of our sympathy with these men who propose
strongly to attack the old political literati of China in their
ancient privileges and prejudices. Kang's power from
his remote retreat is shown in the disgrace of even so
august an official as Yuan. Kang's name is the one most
spoken by all Chinese within foreign borders, and
it is these returning Chinese who leaven their country's
institutions, and every American who can should take
a Chinese student to his bosom and impress, ere he departs for home, the vitalizing spirit of liberty. They will
never forget, for, after all, they are as capable of great
enthusiasms as they are of undying forbearance, which,
till now, has been their distinguishing characteristic.

There is also Sun Yat Sen, a neighbor in exile at
Penang. He would go straight to the core of the trouble
with the sword. He is a reformer, of course, but called

a revolutionist because he does not know whom besides himself he would enthrone after the leader had won the cause. He likes republics. Unlike Kang, he would oust the Manchu. He is one of our men of mark, because he represents the eventual force which will come into play if China does not reform, and he deserves respect for his sincerity. His influence is potent. He has no Boxer spirit, for he appreciates the foreigner, but seat him in power and he could be an uncompromising Boxer, for he is exceedingly patriotic, and lives within far narrower mental lines than Kang.

Liang Chi Choa is the writer of the reform party, also at Penang in exile, who selects leavening foreign books and fills China, notwithstanding the frantic Censor Pu (Board), with their translations and his applications of them. He would make a splendid secretary of state if China ever became a republic. We have no idea what an *imperium ex imperio* this company at Penang is in influencing the aspirations and opinions of the younger officials throughout the empire.

Wu Ting Fang, so well known to Americans, by right should claim the longest review. He assuaged our fears in the anxious days of the Peking siege, for he alone, for two excruciating months, in all the world knew that our legations were safe. How he knew he will never tell, and I would not steal the secret from his code if I could. He is the redoubtable, the learned and the true. What he has done for scientific, civic and legal reform in China, at great personal danger to himself, can hardly be recounted. He is as well known at Hong-Kong as at Peking and Washington. He is no leader of arms or politics; he is a quiet deep molder of methods, perfect in his judgment, a chancellor *facile princeps*. Watch

him as he works from year to year for Chinese and
American progress and approximation, as well balanced
as a Waltham wheel. We are rather discussing strong
men at their mighty work, and it is therefore a light
thing, perhaps, to add that Wu is also the Chesterfield of
China in all the graces of speech and manners.

The Regent Chun of the royal blood of longest reign
of all the world's thrones, belongs to this new set, which
is in the ascendant. He is a Manchu, of course. I have
seen him face to face at Hong-Kong and studied him.
He obeyed Kang and took revenge on Yuan for betraying
the plans of 1897. The Regent is the pivot on which all
now turns. He has the opportunity of the Chinese ages,
a John the Baptist to usher in the new era. He is the
youngest of the leaders, the unfortunate perpetuation of
the Chinese system of the last fifty years of having an
infant as titular ruler and a spokesman in its place. It
is a bad system, growing out of the greed of politicians,
but it is not Chun's fault. He loved his brother Kwang
Su, and no doubt sympathizes with his reform plans,
which he is now putting in force. He is to be pardoned
somewhat if he should yield now and then to the bitter
attack of the reactionaries. He is to be pitied, for attack him they will, and a long list of greater than he
have fallen, even the mighty Kang himself. But reform
is here, and he is with it,— reform both in Manchu and
Chinese circles.

There remains at Peking Prince Ching, an uncle of the
Regent, the old Manchu watch-dog who has been the
power behind three Manchu thrones. I do not mean to
say that he displaced the Dowager in late years, but his
growl was often heard. He has not a modern education,
but if sanity, strength and steadiness count in reform,

Ching is still to be reckoned with, and his old force will make itself felt. He does not want a fool China any more than the reformers do. It was Ching who advocated sending Chinese girls abroad to study, and bringing foreign governesses into China. This is the most surprising recommendation that has been offered at Peking.

Then there is dear old Chang Chih Tung, who never betrayed a foreign friend, but who is by no means a sycophant of the white man. He is now a reformer, for he has always been one. Let him tell you at the outset that he will never consent to a jot of reform in Chinese classics or religion, and you will trust his honesty for ever and grant his demand. Yea, he has written a funny book on the subject. It is funny because it is unnecessary. But he will follow you nearly anywhere else. He was building mills, arsenals, opening mines, running railways and ships, while Kang was still at his books. He has a modern army second only to Yuan's in efficiency at the targets and in manœuvers. He knocks hard at our tariff wall, and says, " Take it down a little lower and I will put my Han-kau iron in." He has already landed two cargoes of pig at Brooklyn, and is every week landing cargoes at Japanese ports. He makes all the rails for his own railways, and he has more railways in operation than there are in the whole empire of Japan. In industrial organization, he is the J. Pierpont Morgan of China, but he gives his fortune back to the State, and doesn't own a review, pulpit or newspaper to tell about it. Your interview ended, he will call you back again and emphasize: " Remember, put me down for no reform in classics or religion." What can you do with a man like this but grant him all he asks and love him, though

you lose all your sacred ambitions for western missionaries and books. Chang won't read a line Liang Chi
writes, but he has been doing for years exactly what
Liang, you and I have been recommending in what we
have written. "An old fogy," is he? rather the "Grand
Old Man" of China, marching steadily with the youngest
and carrying the largest knapsack of deeds done.

These are the representative leaders of China to-day,
and they are as diverse as our own leaders in the talents
which have been committed to them, but underlying their
characters, with one exception, are the world-wide essentials of courage, singleness of purpose, devotion to
country, unselfishness, and hate of graft, which is the
prevailing tendency of our age, as absolute as it is hated
by the God of all men, yellow or white.

You will notice that the Manchu has been diligent in
one thing, to place his Uigur character, of corkscrew appearance like the Syrian, opposite the Chinese character
on the copper coin, but this is the whole of his literary
conquest, for even the Manchu officials, scattered throughout the Kingdom, are devoted to the Chinese literature
and language. Over the East Gate of Mukden, in a
large plain tympanum, a Confucian motto has been cut
in Chinese and Manchu characters. However, other con-
siderations have now a certain bearing there. Around
the Black Stone of Mukden, which the Manchus consider
the center of the earth, circles a new influence,— that of
the Japanese. Whether this will drive the Manchus into
the arms of the Chinese, as the loss of Hanover endeared
the Guelph house to the British, remains to be seen.

There is no caste question to fetter the race, as India
has been retarded and disrupted, and if China is only
now approaching a constitutional government, she has

long been preparing for it by the most wonderful democracy of letters which the world has ever known. The old divisions of society fall into Scholars, Farmers, Artisans, Merchants; the Soldier and the Priest having no standing, and being called the " Trouble Makers." The new divisions are to be, Literature, Politics, Trade,— which is probably one more division than we have in our own.

An emigration of one million a year is rapidly filling up Malay, Borneo, Java, Siam and Burmah with Chinese, and sealing them in bonds of blood, literature and commerce, to the home land. As compradors, bankers, merchants and laborers, they are spreading over the whole Orient, just as the Roman did from the Pyrenees to the Euphrates, and theirs is none the less a conquest, though it is peaceful. But whether or not the Home Rule " Ming " flag that last floated over the moat of Nanking flutters free again, the spirits of Hung Woo and Hung Tsin are marching on with the progress of the Chinese race. Only may it be that the feet of nationalism in her frenzy may not be directed in bloodshed against the Si Fan, or white foreigner. This is our prayer, but we must expect some disappointments as progress develops her ups and downs. Shall we take seriously the rapid development of the " Restorer of Rights " party, and articles such as the following written by a student in the Hang Chan *Pehoa Pao,* or *Courier:* " O! White Faces and red-bristled barbarians, when we of the Flowery Land shall march forth to war, then shall you be brayed even as are drugs in a mortar? " The East has always been like its Thibetan glaciers; when any movement warms it, it moves in a mass, and therein has been its danger to opponents since the time of Kublai Khan.

We recall the following manifesto, written during the Opium War with England: "There is that English nation, whose ruler is as often a woman as a man, and which devours Southern peoples, first peeling the fat off their estates. Their island is a petty one; they trust entirely to wooden dragons (ships). Could we reach them, we should hurl them over as the blast does the thin bamboo. If we let them settle on the Pearl (Canton River) it will be like opening the door and bowing in Mr. Wolf! In the hour of our patriotism, even our wives and daughters, finical and delicate as jewels, have learned to discourse of arms. The high gods clearly behold; fight till the golden pool is fully restored to honorable peace." *Pou Toun Kiao Li* (one religion or another, we Chinese are all brothers) say they, when they think of those who criticize or challenge them.

This stolid but revengeful enough race has been stung until they have struck, and may strike again at all foreign domination, whether Manchu, Macaense, Mikado or Missionary, in their striving after the extinction of what, since the viceroy of Che-kiang drove the Portuguese out of Ningpo in 1542, they have considered their greatest humiliation, viz.: the sacrilege of foreign colonies on the mainland of their sacred country — Kiao-chou held by Germany; Shanghai by triple occupation; Kowloon by Britain; Macao by Portugal; Port Arthur by Japan, and Kwang Chow by France. This feeling particularly manifests itself at present over the decisions of the extra-territoriality courts. They claim that they should judge a foreigner who breaks their laws just as Japan does; he, of course, to have the privilege of appeal by his consul if the punishment exceeds what the foreign law would adjudge. They cite the precedent of the strangling for murder of an American in 1821 on the little execution ground between the pottery jars, back of the Yamen, Canton, where so many Americans have stood since then, little dreaming of this particular history. How differently they do it in Japan is hereby illustrated. One, F. J. C., a British subject, was sentenced in April, 1906, under Article 402, by Judge Satomi in the Yokohama District Court, to twelve years' imprisonment for arson, in an attempt to collect two thousand *yen* insurance on his household furniture, and five days were allowed for appeal. It is largely this extra-territoriality occupation by foreigners which is precipitating Chinese patriotism, just as the shelling of Kagoshima by the British in 1863, and the occupation of Shimonoseki and Yokohama by the allies in 1864 precipitated the patriotic clans upon the weak Shoguns, and evolved the new, proud, united and powerful Japan.

Another cause which is solidifying Chinese patriotism is the lucrative concessions, far more opulent than at first imagined, secured by foreigners at little cost. I refer particularly to the Peking Syndicate in Shensi; the Franco-Belgian Syndicate in Honan, etc. In other words, the central government practically gave away provincial concessions, which the newspapers are telling the people are invaluable, in fact the richest in the world, as Richtofen long ago prophesied. Neither are the bitter memories of Peking in 1900 forgotten in this connection. Popularly translated, the significant comments run about as follows: "And why does the foreign soldier shoot? Just to loot, loot, loot!" The soldiers of Yuan Shi K'ai will tell you how the Russians in 1900 piled precious blackwood furniture outside the walls of Tong Tchow, and set fire to it just to warm their hands, and how they dug up the native cemetery of Tientsin, to exhume the valuables buried with the dead.

There remains the bugbear of the Chinese Exclusion Acts in America and Canada, which the Chinese would have been entirely patient with, had not the Japanese been accorded an astounding preference. It ought to be a very simple thing, considering the higher standards of living and education in the white countries as compared with the yellow, and the high tariff burdens upon the poor in the white countries, to exclude once for all day laborers from emigration across the Pacific.

A popular fête of the people held in July throws a pleasant light upon a phase of their patriotism. To the foreigner this festival seems to be a pretty boat carnival, which originated at Chang Sha near the Tung Ting Lake, but the races are preceded by the religious ceremony of searching for the body of Ken Yuen, a famous popular minister whom the Emperor dismissed for urging reforms, and who thereupon committed suicide by drowning in the year 450 B. C. The dragon boats came to be used because, the legend is, the gifts were stolen by a fierce sea monster. The fishermen therefore adopted the all-conquering dragon's head and tail for the bow and stern of their long, narrow racing boats. Here is a national ceremony of patriotism continued uninterruptedly for two thousand three hundred years. In the blue Hangchow cemetery is a remarkable iron statue of four officials loaded with chains, kneeling before the door of the tomb of the patriot, General Yoh, the leader of the Sung forces whom they murdered in treacherous alliance with the Tartars. It is probably the only monument condemning official infamy in the world. Respect for the antiquity of the human race must grow in our minds

when we consider that in conversing with the Chinese of
to-day, we are really conversing, because of their unchanged customs, laws and physiognomy, with men exactly similar to those who were contemporary with the
men of Babylon. China has another interest for the
dwellers on the North American continent, in that the
coal deposits and range formation reveal a land geologic-
ally speaking contemporaneous with our own, which
starts some inquiries as to the age of our Indians, and
their possible descent from the Chinese, whether via the
Aleutian isles, or junks drifting via Honolulu.

It is owing to the following command of Confucius
in the Li Chi (Filial Duty) that the nation has so long
remained passive: " I would teach people justice, benevolence and virtue; I would lead them not to build walls
or moats, but to turn the weapons of war into instruments
of husbandry." But now behold the alarming change.

Japan has taken almost entire charge of China's military schools and army, or Chang Pei Kun, which is
assurance of its advancing effectiveness, and the minimiz-
ing of hampering traditions. The modern military
schools at Canton, Nanking and Peking turn out three
hundred officers a year, and Japan's schools add seven
hundred Chinese military graduates a year, so that the
provincial " armies of the Green Standards " are rapidly
being officered on the most approved lines, especially in
the Artillery, Pou To; Engineers, Kung Chung To; and
mounted Infantry, Ma To. It is perhaps premature to
say that there will be war, but there could certainly at
any time now be a war in which China would be as difficult to humble as Japan would have been ten years ago,
but the comparison between these two countries will end
shortly, when railways join the provinces, and make

China unsubduable, because united.. How little the provinces have known one another can be judged by the fact that the Yangtze River, "the girdle of China," has a different name in each of the nine provinces through which it flows. What a vast body of soldiers, already inured to marches on little food, would the wheelbarrow men of Honan alone make, and Honan sent ten thousand troops to Viceroy Chang's last autumn manœuvers, which covered an attack along the line of the Han-kau-Peking Railway. Moreover, Japan is desirous that China shall raise an army of five hundred thousand men, which will permit of Japan reducing her force necessary to guard the East from those whose land hunger she most hates, Russia, Germany and France. She will officer this army for a while, but she desires that China shall pay its cost. She wants another half million of her own men for ten years to lay by their rifles for spindle and steam hammer, and make her rich enough again to set to and take what the Treaty of Portsmouth did not give her.

No more does the gong beat the romantic call to arms under the East Gate of Canton and in the Kwan Tois, or State Temples of the God of War. The bugle call has been learned, and its windings are heard in every plain of China, from the sandy parade ground outside the Anting Gate at Peking, where it first caught the sound from Japanese lips a few years ago, to the military common beneath the parapet of the ancient metropolis of the south. The former Chinese formation was the Ying, i. e., a division of five hundred in Infantry and two hundred and fifty in Cavalry, as the horse was considered to be equal to a man in those humorous days of Demonstration, when the triangular banner was anointed before the battle was formally opened. Soldiers built the Great Wall of

The now disbanded Board of the Tsung-li-yamen, Peking, which
advised the late Empress Dowager in her dealings with foreign
powers for 33 years of evasive diplomacy. The Board is
now reorganized in the more enlightened Wai-wu-pu.
Two members of the Board are Manchus
and two are Chinese.

Chinese officials at Amoy, Nov., 1908, entertaining officers and
crews of American fleet. Admiral Emery proposing
health of Empress Dowager

The famous American Legation building on Chiao Min Hsiang
Street, Peking, which went through the two sieges, first by
the Boxers, and later by the foreign allies, in 1900.

China, as they probably did the Pyramids. Soldiers in China have always acted as masons of public works, street sweepers, and grasshopper catchers in country districts; but under the new system, their respectability is enhanced by release from these duties. There is an old proverb of theirs which describes the past: " We make our soldiers from our worst men, just as we make our nails from our worst iron."

These efforts of China should be looked upon with friendliness, for government must now become more effective, and there should be fewer causes for altercation under the more thorough régime of a newly centralized government, with viceroys powerful in their provinces by coördinate law and arms, and not by corruption, all of which will give place in time to power directed by provincial and national deliberative assemblies. A China which will not allow any or every nation to camp on the edge of her robe, just because she wears a long one, and take a bite off her rice-cake and persimmon without asking permission, just because they look appetizing, a China more responsible because she is encouraged in self-respect, should find extended to her the friendly hands of the nations. This has really been the intent of the friendly policy of America, and the coercive diplomacy of England for sixty years. When China understands it so, she will rank Elliot as her friend above " Chinese " Gordon. China at last is doing her part toward ending the régimes of bluster and international bad manners, and binding the last link around the globe of arbitration as the means of settling disputes, because none dares try any other. When it comes to standing up like men, and taking that most bitter of medicines, the payment of a national indemnity, history records the fortitude of the Chinese on every occasion. The opium war indemnity of twenty-one millions was paid promptly, and the indemnities to Japan and the allied powers are of recent liquidation. What volumes this speaks for the sincerity, patience, and lack of false pride of this race! In the West, right consists of dying rather than admitting you are nationally wrong.

There are, of course, those in China who fear that the new armies will become the State, as it is becoming in Japan, and as it was in Rome in the days following Sylla. China's foreign wars have, till now, been carried on by the provinces separately, Kwangtung fighting England in the Opium War, and even as late as the China-Japan war, in which one province and a dependency (Chili and Manchuria) took part against the invader without the assistance of the other provinces. The extension of railways and newspapers are therefore prerequisite to united, militant China.

There is indisputably something seismic at present disturbing this great people, something probably comparable to the forgotten upheavals which ejected Kublai Khan, Attila and Cyrus into history. Only the other day, in this country where as yet news travels slowly and where railways are few, fifty thousand men arose in the extreme south, and started on their way to the extreme north, to the wheat fields of Manchuria, where the government, remembering the successful repeopling of Szechuen from Kiang-si after the Ming rebellion, offered each man ten *mao* of land free of taxes for five years. The movement was certainly not political, like those we constantly hear the Triad Society is launching, with foreign missionaries as an excuse, but riots at Canton and Chifu eddied round it, men longing in their strength to be as effective or as troublesome as other mortals who seek new things because they are disgusted with past things. Their orators pointed out the black breath of war-ships on the horizon, and the white battleship of the United States, the *Wisconsin,* in the offing, and said: "We too could own such, only we would paint it yellow." We who heard them, felt that they, too, could pick up the word *Jung* (glory) and follow it as terribly as other races have done, or as their Genghis did. Strict surveillance is kept at the treaty ports that no arms are smuggled in, but somehow or other the astute Japanese, especially through the port of Macao, are getting rid of their obsolete guns throughout China, where the students by tens of thousands are eager to possess a rifle. There is something of a nuisance in this, internationally, as it is found that the pirates of the West River, who previously have been poorly armed, are now more than a match for the government gunboats.

The power of the viceroys or Tsung Tuhs, who rule without legislative assembly or Censor Board, may be judged by that exercised by the late Chum in the Two Kwangs, who had his own army, navy and mint. With headquarters at Canton, he led in the anti-foreign boycott of 1905-6, and in all the new movements of reviving Chinese pride and patriotism. He it was who conceived the idea of a port at old Whompoa, and railway connection to Canton, in order to displace Hong-Kong as the emporium of southern China. Viceroy Tsen Chum Hsuen, known to most foreigners as the "unpopular Chum," was not a native of either of the two provinces which he governed. He not only headed the civil and judicial service, but commanded the army and navy. Twenty million people bowed to his unquestioned authority. His aim was to drill in the south an army of one

hundred thousand, which should reach the recent creditable performance of the Pechili army of Yuan Shi K'ai's
(also a Chinese and not a Manchu), which the Han-
Yang arsenal equipped with "wireless" wagons; rifles
of Mauser pattern; field-guns painted gray; Japanese
kits weighing fifty-four pounds, which included acces-
sories for "first aid," field-glass and blanket. The German goose-neck step and swinging of the left arm are
practised on march. In September last the Kwang-si
branch of this army, in order to suppress a rebellion at
Limchow, made in one day over bad roads through
mountainous country, two hundred *li,* or sixty-five miles,
in forced marches. Uniforms are of red-trimmed khaki.
It is interesting to recall that the uniforms of the Boxers
were red and black. The southern army carries triangular banners; the northern square.

The bugle, and not word of mouth, is now used for
command, and regimental songs, patterned on the Japanese style, are taught with the idea that the *esprit de corps*
is raised thereby. For a while the Tartar general's
troops in residence were added to Chum's forces, but he
returned them, as he desired to appeal to local enthusiasm. The Tartar troops are paid two dollars and ninety
cents Mexican a month. Chum paid his provincial troops
eight dollars Mexican a month. The ribbons were
taken from the men's queues, which were rolled tight
under their caps. Such is the force which Chum turned
over to his successor, Chow Fu. Chum was removed
largely because of the protests of Hong-Kong over the
piratical attack on the *Sainam.* He will be heard of
again when radical things happen in China. He and his
sort have been emboldened by their dream of awakening
national possibilities, and engraven on their hearts is

the recovery of Formosa and Manchuria from the Japanese and Russians. We must not despair of Chinese ambitions and liberties because the new leaders, in driving the chariot of progress over the narrow barrow roads of a past civilization, constantly find one wheel either lost in the fetid ooze, or jolting upon the rocks of the ditch.

There is on the other hand the Japanese version of the future of China, which is a division ten years hence of China's " invalid sovereignty " into spheres of influence, until such time as Japan is able financially to gather all the spheres into her own bundle as she did the Korean, Formosan and South Manchurian. The persistent humanitarian tendency of the Chinese crops through even the soldier's armor in the following Mongolian maxim: "What was the most magnanimous act ever known? When General Tso burned the unread correspondence of the implicated in the tents of the vanquished."

Again there is the American and British version, that there certainly must sometime be a conflict on the Pacific for leadership, which Japan now arrogates to herself. It will then be necessary for America to destroy Japan's navy, whenever Britain, Russia and America agree on the integrity of China; the evacuation of Manchuria by Japan and Russia; the retention of India by Britain, and Korea by Japan, and the patrol of the Pacific by America, just as the Atlantic seas must be delegated to British fleets. The sooner this comes the better, from a humanitarian point of view. It alone can save to the white man that distant empire which fronts the Southern Cross, and that Canada, which for one thousand miles looks out on the broad blue swells of the portentous Pacific. In their scheme to impress the Chinese that they alone are masters, socially, the Japanese working in

China resign from any work when a European is placed over them, saying: " Shall the torch of Asia bow to candles; has the East not hurled back the phalanxes of Alexander, the legions of Rome, the cavalry of the Crusaders, and the artillery of Russia?— and we can renew the lesson to Europe any time."

In the East we constantly observed in print the name of Mutsuhito, Emperor of Japan, and we continually heard *Banzai* (I wish you a myriad years) called out by the fervid Japanese at mention of his name, but seldom in China did we hear the name of the late Kwang Su, the Tsing Emperor and High Priest of China, who had been reigning thirty-four years at the time of his death in November, 1908. This was largely because of the banyan-like shade of the skilful but hated Empress Dowager Tse Hsi, the patron priestess of the Boxer movement, whose ability was so exceptional, especially in intrigue, that she far outranked Catherine and Elizabeth, and some dared to call her a Jezebel. She was the virtual proprietress of all the pawnshops of Peking. When the Emperor was physically weakened and with no hopes of recovery, decrees in 1906 began to bear the superscription " Their Majesties," so as to allay some of the criticism. Petticoat politics (to be exact it is trousered politics where women are concerned in China) might appropriate presents to the throne, as under the Dowager they overrode the rights of the ministers, but the Chinese far and wide love the office of even a Manchu emperor sufficiently for every guild at New Year's time (in February) voluntarily to send gorgeous gifts to his Majesty, whose personal name of Tsai Tien was veiled in his poetic title which meant " Illustrious Succession."

It is to be regretted that at the intriguing and inhuman instigations of the late ambitious Dowager, Kwang Su was drugged and shelved during his formative and closing years, for the hearts of the people, in a land where men are considered alone interested in public affairs, called for a strong, male crown head, instead of the comet-like ascendancy of this effeminate or unscrupulous viceroy and now that one, or one eunuch or another, who might at the time flatter the queenly ear. Among the students, who were trained in Japan, is swelling the longing to cry for a purpose "*Lo Wan Hun*" (Hail the victorious leader of a myriad of men,) of course preferably a Ming and not a Manchu, if the change were convenient. Kwang Su was married to his first cousin, who was older than he. She is a woman of ability and refinement, and more typically Chinese than the late Dowager. Poor Kwang Su was a slight, sallow king; in height not a Manchu; mysteriously contemplative; by nature impulsive when he saw the right; when withstood, sulky instead of determined and patient; a reader; the most Buddhistic looking man in his empire; punctilious in sacrifices and ceremonies; fitter perhaps for a temple than a throne; in short another " Edward the Confessor," lovable enough. The changes appointing Kwang Su's brother, Prince Chun, as Regent, and Chun's son Pu Yi, renamed Hsuan-Tung (Proclaimed Succession) as infant Emperor of three years of age, only corroborate the power that was wielded by their creator, the late Dowager Tse Hsi. We in Hong-Kong in 1901 closely observed Chun, then eighteen, when he was upon an apologetic mission to Berlin. He is now twenty-five years of age. His real name is Tsai Feng. He has not the culture nor the humanitarian refinement of his brother, but he has more experience, force and health; is wider traveled, and he is unhampered by the old intriguer and plotter, and her cabal of eunuchs. The Manchu Tsing dynasty therefore still sits in the saddle, but not so steadily as of yore, for it is bickering with the Chinese appointees, as in the dismissal of Yuan Shi K'ai.

The Chinese in the south and center of the empire resent another infant Emperor and another regency. However the ministry is stronger and more enlightened than it ever was. The path before reform is wider than in the past, and the fruit of to-day, let it be now recorded, was the seed sown by Kwang Su in his liberal and courageous edicts of 1897. It was the only famous thing he did, unless it be more famous to be a martyr to his own courage, for it was owing to those edicts that the Dowager and her cabal persecuted him for eleven years unto his death. China's great future will largely be founded upon these edicts, and therefore the unfortunate Kwang Su's name will not be lost as though " writ in water." At all prefectural cities once a year, the officials, gathered at the temples just before daybreak, place a tablet bearing the Emperor's name between Buddha's feet, and kowtow nine times nine.

The Chinese are not only capable of national enthusiasm but have already experienced one type of it. I refer to classical examinations, where from village to hamlet, and from court to remotest district, the nation has acted from immemorial years in one spirit to one end. This is a unification Japan never experienced in the preparation for her great upheaval. Given a more virile subject to be presented to the people than the book lore of Confucius and Mencius, the government is quite equipped to make it permeate into the last recess, with of course

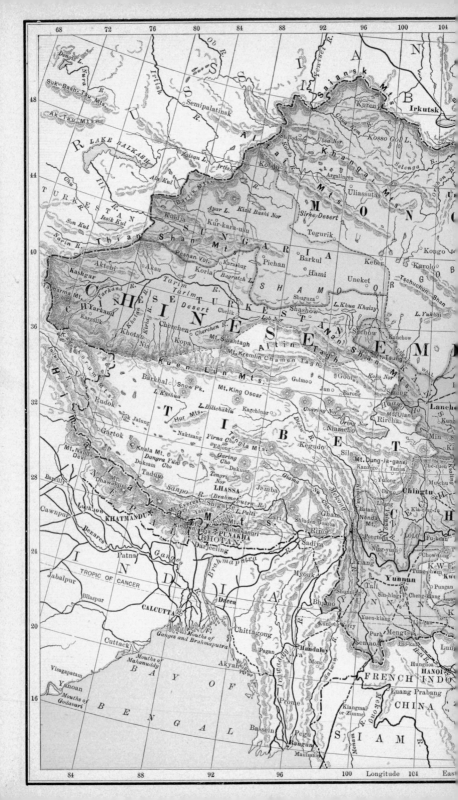

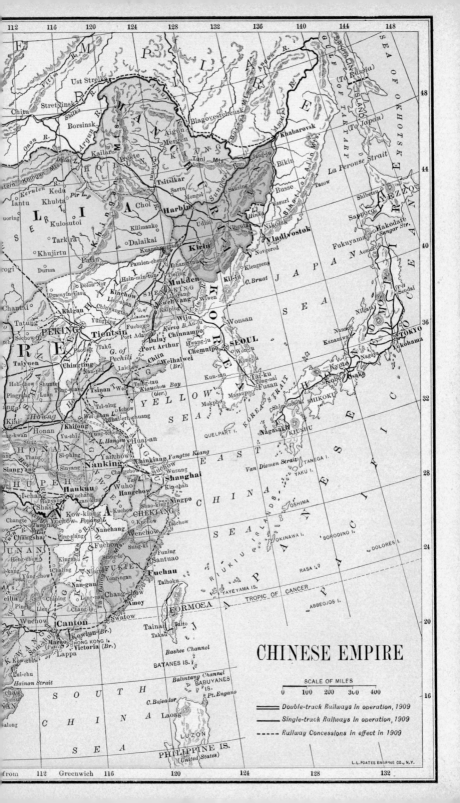

CHINESE EMPIRE

SCALE OF MILES

0   100   200   300   400

—— Double-track Railways in operation, 1909

—— Single-track Railways in operation, 1909

- - - - Railway Concessions in effect in 1909

L.L.POATES ENGR'NG CO., N.Y.

results that will surprise the race itself and shake the world.

That public spirit is growing in China may be judged by one of the Tsou Ku (invite subscriptions) meetings of the guilds of Canton and districts which Chum called at the Wan Shao Kung, or Imperial Presence Temple, to decide whether the first funds for the Yuet Han Railway (Canton to Han-kau) should be raised by taxation throughout the provinces crossed by the line, or by subscriptions among the Canton guilds. Two of the seventy-two guilds subscribed five hundred thousand dollars on the spot, and promised one and one-half millions in the immediate future. This is the first time Chinese have held what was practically a business Witenagemote and it would not have been possible now, had not the boycotts unified the guilds, and brought them over to the New China party's ambitions. While the meeting was in progress, a rich Chinaman named Lai Kwai Pui, who was incarcerated for a political offense, sent word from the prison that he would subscribe for fifty thousand shares. Redivivus, the spirit of Eliot breathing from the tower! No race responds more readily to appeals for subscriptions in humanitarian causes. Voluntarily the Chinese of San Francisco, themselves afflicted by earthquake and ruin, cabled ten thousand dollars to the sufferers by the Hong-Kong typhoon of September, 1906. The shares of the Yuet Han Railway are for three dollars, so as to be within the means of the poorest. When this railway called for tenders for certain cars, a foreign firm was successful. It was proposed by the latter that the contract should be signed at the consul's office, as had been the invariable custom, but Chau Kung Ying, the manager of the railway, stated that the agreement must be drawn up in Chinese, and signed at the railway company's office in Canton. This marks an epoch in the commercial relations between China and the nations.

The constitution of Canton's business community may be judged by the inclusion of the following: "Guild of the Nine Hospitals"; "Pawnshops Guild" and "The Smaller Pawnshops Guild." In the Emperor's decrees in the Peking *Gazette* concerning the railway, the "Nine Charities" take precedence of all other guilds in the enumeration. Again think of a share-holders' meeting attended by thirty thousand people at the governor's Yamen. For the adjourned meeting there this characteristic proclamation was issued: "We respectfully ask the Merchant Guilds, the Charitable Institutions, and the deputies to assemble. All gentlemen are asked to bring their personal jade seals in order that the regulations may be signed, and to state their age, dwelling and occupation." The most popular guild at Canton is the Carpenters', whose Lu Pan procession is the finest given by the guilds. Clan and guild opinion have been developed as in no country. What has been lacking in the nation in the past has been the newspaper, with its facilities of propaganda. The hundreds of thousands of those who have secured the lower literary degrees, and the millions of those who have been unsuccessful in the examinations but who are widely read in the classics, have created a conservative body, influential among the illiterate in uplifting the nation, and on the other hand, they stand as a restraint against the possible oppression of the throne and ministers, which latter body, coming from their number, fears their criticism.

Following these demonstrations of the boycott at the Hoy Toi Monastery (mark you,) and the railway, came a third and a fourth. When the commissioners on representative government returned from abroad, the students and guilds made the streets echo with their shouts of welcome and approval. Now it is parades deriding opium. Banners are carried, showing pictures of the misery introduced by the foreign drug. White ribbons with blue inscriptions are worn on the hats. The opium dens are visited by these Chinese Cromwellians, and the stupefied victims are jeered. I once saw a long procession sweep around the Canton Bund. The students were dressed in white, and threw into the crowds leaflets reading: " China, wake up, cure yourself of opium, and take your right position among the powers." This is the first fruits of the new schools. The Japanese teachers have struck in this something practical and concrete. The procession was led by a boy whose skin was dyed brown and who was masquerading in a red turban, and an immense opium pipe, as a Hindoo. Most of the banners were white, to signify the death-dealing drug which was brought first from India.

Another indication of public spirit was noticeable at Amoy in August last. It was the Emperor's birthday. The native shops were decorated with the Imperial dragon flags, festoons of flowers and branches of shrubs. Never before has the national flag been so conspicuous and popular in one of their own ports.

It must not be concluded that the many advances shown by China are altogether creditable to the students, who have returned from Japanese colleges. The railway policy was conceived and carried through by the gentry and merchants, before the foreign educated students were numerous. The students are fire-crackers in the flame, and add éclat to the demonstration, but the steady fuel and heat are furnished by the conservative element, which is the seriousness of it for those who shall make light of it. In August last, the Canton Municipality decided to inaugurate the Hong-Kong custom of registering chair coolies (the streets are too narrow for 'rickishas). Four hundred coolies gathered at the Hoi Tong Chee Temple on the Honam side of the river, to protest against the tax and tariff. The meeting was an exceedingly lively one, and it can not now be said that a Chinaman can not think on his feet. It is not the same sleepy, satisfied Canton. These things never occurred before, and they will not stop, in greater causes, now. The flames of rebellion could be stamped out in the Kwangs and the central provinces perhaps with the aid of the present railways, but it might be a different thing if Yunnan, which is poorly policed, should catch this spirit of protest, and have time to start the furnace roaring.

A great deal of amusement has been afforded the nations by the vanity of the Chinese in their dealings with foreigners who have sought them, since the settlement of the colony of Macao by the Portuguese in 1557, in the middle of the Ming dynasty. They have long assumed that theirs was the Hub kingdom, and that others were merely satellites. They called their king "the Son of Heaven," and demanded that European embassies should proceed under yellow banners bearing the motto, "Tsin Kong" (tribute bearers). There is however much in fact to support China's pride; that during the longest history of any race, she has taught various civilizations around her letters, arts, and sciences, and has preserved them from Sikh, Vandal and Slav. She gave birth to Japan, and threw that people safely into a glorious orbit of its own, the heat of which now is reciprocally warming

a new spring into being, as it swings near its parent orb.
She has maintained immemorially the security of her
southern valleys from invasion, and her culture uncon-
taminated during a period when southern Europe has
known countless obliterations and denudations, intellectually and ethnically. Flood and famine have visited her
more cruelly than any race has suffered, but to-day she
points to her four hundred millions as a testimony that
she has abhorred the murder of war, and in deeds, if not
in letters, has practised the sacred teachings of the Occident's "Son of Heaven," while we have lusted after
slaughter, so that none of us of any blood can show more
than a tenth of her population.

Very interesting divisions of the Chinese race are
illustrated on the island of Hong-Kong and at Kowloon,
one mile opposite on the mainland, these divisions numbering throughout the nation, sixty millions each. For
instance, the women of the Hakka race, some of whom
can be seen employed breaking stones on the military
roads, wear broad hats fringed with a flapping veil, and
immense rings in their ears. They do not bind their feet,
or wear prominent nose ornaments. They are not so old
a race as the abler Cantonese, and other Pun Tei
(ancient) races of Kwangtung, and Szechuen Provinces. Sometimes they are called Highlanders, especially
in Kwangtung Province, where they never succeeded in
dispossessing the plains people. They, of course, have a
dialect of their own. If one hears two boat-women
screaming ancestral anathemas up and down the gamut,
from legendary grandparent to tenth cousin, at each other
from their respective tillers, you may be sure they are of
the Hakka, or "Guests" tribe. They are the highest
tempered and most argumentative of the Chinese. They

largely compose the armies of the viceroys, and are responsible for most of the rebellions of the last two hundred years. A large proportion of the emigrants to the Straits Settlements are Hakkas. They are not so insistent about marrying within their race as other Chinese. Those who emigrated to Formosa married the wild hill women, and incidentally drove the brothers of their wives out of the camphor business. At Singapore they marry Malays, and at Honolulu, Kanakas (as in the case of the famous Ah Fong family there,) and in New York may we say they are credited with offering themselves to expatriated Hibernians! The bloody Taeping rebellion was led by a Hakka from the vicinity of Canton, named Hung Siu Tsuen.

During the water famine in August, the government of Hong-Kong turns the taps on for only an hour. I have seen Hakka bands from different streets approaching with their pails or Standard Oil tins, dangling from stout bamboos. A fight easily ensued over the precedence in drawing. When the home gang was worsted, their women retreated to the gardens on the house tops and threw flower pots on the invaders, who charged repeatedly up the dizzy stairs, until the Sikh police, and mushroom-capped native *lukongs* came up on the double. It is noticeable in these rows that the Hakkas never cry "help" or "murder," but "save life." The Hakkas are more settled in the land than in former times, and recent disturbances have occurred mostly among the Sang Miaotzes (unsubdued children of the soil,) likewise a roving tribe who have forced their way into Mongolia, Szechuen, Yunnan, Kwei Chau, and the mountains of Hainan Island. In their own dialect this race is called Ba Bu Ren. The great general and Viceroy Ts'en, who crushed the bloody Mohammedan rebellion of Yun-nan, and who incognito would cut rebels down himself, was a Miaotze aboriginal of Kwang-si Province. " As sulky as a Lolo," is a proverb referring to a trait of a wild tribe of the mountains of Szechuen, who declare that happiness consists in being let alone. This race acquired its name in its days of wandering, for " lolo " is a bam-boo basket in which they carry everything, from ancestral tablets to knives for avenging their honor. Among the Iu aboriginal tribes, those Ishmaelites of the mountains of Kwang-si and Che-kiang, you will notice that queues are not worn. The hair is bunched on the head, and beards are not shaved. The women are large footed. All these races are fragments of the rule of the great Genghis, and to a similar leader the Nomadic Tartars and Mongols would again respond.

The people of Szechuen Province are short and stocky; those of Shan-tung tall and bony, while the lithe Kwangtung men are notable for their vivacity and well-fed sleekness. The Tartar of the north is paler than the bronzed Cantonese of the south. If you believe in the aphorism that the land, and not the politics, makes a people, come to China and see it exemplified. The Chi-nese have emphatically assimilated certain families of European blood. To recite three instances. At Macao in the south, the descendants of the original one thousand families, while retaining their Portuguese names and re-ligion, are now nearly all Chinese by blood through inter-marriage. At Kaifong in the central provinces, a colony of Jews has lost names as well as religion, and near Peking are the names, but little of the blood, of the fam-ilies of the Russian prisoners who were captured at Al-bazin in the time of Peter the Great, and who were first corralled in the famous " Russian House " at Peking.

While nearly all the emigrations to America, Singapore and the Philippines have been from Canton in the south, it is remarkable that the emigration to Africa, recruiting for which ceased in November, 1906, was from Shan-tung in the north, where the coolies are taller and handsomer, but not so intellectual as the Southern Chinaman, who has more of the aboriginal Highlander blood in his veins. Behind all the new counters in the bazaars of Chemulpo and Mukden, stands the Chinese emigrant, with the business future of those countries largely within his power.

The honor of the Chinese has seldom received a more significant tribute than in the arrangement for foremen over the laborers in the Rand, and wherever large gangs of Chinese have been employed. Among the Huns in the coal mines; Italians in street work; and our own people in building, there is no gang of laborers larger than a dozen under one foreman. When Chinese are employed, a contractor estimates one foreman for every one hundred men. Give this race a task which they can comprehend, and the sense of duty appeals to them as to no other people. It is the exclusion of Chinese labor which has retarded the progress of the Philippines. Japanese labor prefers other fields to the enervating tropics, although a limited number of Japanese are permitted to land in the Philippines, where they become 'rickisha coolies. The soil under such amorous suns yields too abundantly to compel the Filipino to arouse himself. The Chinaman, whether from the hot Kwang and Fukien Provinces or from cooler Shan-tung, works like a beaver in the tropics. He is reclaiming Siam, Java and Malay, and if he were permitted he would create of

Luzon, Mindinao and Panay the most luxuriant garden of sorghum, hemp, cocoanut, banana, and mahogany that the world has ever seen. Nothing will ever be made of the Filipino, and schools will be wasted upon him, as they have been upon the "ignorantly read" Bengalese, who spouts dangerously and ungratefully of home rule, because sedition and a little learning easily run to adjectives. Sheer need would ultimately compel the Filipino to follow the example of the Chinaman, when the emigration of the latter could be stopped, until such time as the native backslid from his acquired ways of industry. In all the world,— Kaffir, Somali Arab, Mexican peon or government-rationed Indian,— there is nothing that can wear the folds of determined laziness, without creasing them, so long as the Filipino. A stalwart friend of Chinese emigration from an educational standpoint, was Secretary Seward. As the returning emigrants are enriching Italy, so the Chinese emigrant brings modern enlightenment back to his native land.

Here is an interesting tale of the emigrants for a Chinese Boccaccio, and one quite unusual for China where women are seldom faithless. Outside the village of Fatshan only a day's walk from Canton, in an ancestral, tiled, stone farm-house, where a brake of millet stalks whispered peace from generation to generation, lived a patriarch alone with his young daughter-in-law. The son was absent in America, where a Chinese wife might not follow him according to our law. Regularly the old man came in to Canton and stayed with a friend until the *Han-kau,* with an eye for "good josh" painted on its paddle wheel, sailed in the morning for Hong-Kong. The next day he went to the Hong-Kong and Shanghai Banking Corporation, sur-

rounded palatially with royal palms on Queens Road
Central, to cash a draft from his son, and with so great
a fortune to support himself, he retraced his steps to the
Fatshan, which sailed in the evening. From Canton
he started out, between the rice fields and duck farms, on
his joyful tramp homeward, where the "Comfort of
His Age," his daughter, awaited him. Alas! The in-
auspicious shade of the papaw seemed to lie long upon
the threshold. A Lothario came upon the scene in the
person of a farm-hand, seeking work under an alias that
frightened the old man, for it was not a clan name. The
daughter-in-law fatefully interposed, and the worker was
given the *petsai* field to till. Being a married woman, the
daughter also aided in the field. Shortly an elopement
was planned, and fortunately wits rather than murder
were used to secure the four hundred dollars, which the
old man had saved. Paper, ink-stick and brush were secured, and the absent husband's white-wood "chop" was
resurrected from the camphor-wood chest. Chinese characters are easily forged. A letter from the son was prepared, begging the fond father to give money to the
daughter to go to America to join her husband. She
should come if possible with some clansman who was
emigrating, and with whom he could communicate at Victoria regarding a plan which he had for circumventing
the Exclusion law. The old man stepped into the trap;
the farm-hand had always been desirous of emigrating.
For his kindness in the dilemma, the old man would advance him the remainder of his funds. The three arrived
at Hong-Kong. The sea was of course too rough for age
to take the sampan trip to the great ship which lay like a
black dragon cumbrous on the stream. Tears and good-
byes were exchanged on the Wing Lok wharf. The

usual shouts of *shao* (long life) and *fuh* (happiness) were wafted to the rapidly receding boat. The shameless plotters took a devious course, and re-landed in Hong-Kong, much to the amusement of the boatmen who said they were *ying* (mad). The patriarch went home, and shortly afterward received a genuine letter from his son, stating that he was about to return home, and requesting his dearly beloved, the Pearl of Fidelity, to meet him at Hong-Kong on the ship's arrival. Father and son met at Hong-Kong, and with the clan ire mutually inflamed sought the culprits. The native boarding-houses on Elgin Street, which have harbored so many secrets, at length gave up this comedy to the courts, and that is why Wong Chik, alias Cheung Yam, won't bother the Cheung clan any more; nor will the grocery that he was about to open on Rua da Se in Macao deal in credits, opium and rice for a long while. What became of the woman, not all China can reveal, unless the Cheung clan will sometime be willing to tell; the millet is still whispering secrecy around the old stone homestead when father and son talk.

We hear much of the Great Wall, certainly the world's most memorable sight, but that other peculiar defensive work of the Manchus, the Willow Palisade, now in poor repair, which begins where the Great Wall ends at Shan Hai Quan at the sea, and sweeps around the sacred tombs of Mukden to the sea again, has attracted less research than its uniqueness merited. The best preserved and grandest city wall in China, encircles the city of Tsian Fu, the capital of Shensi, which province was the cradle of the race. The wall was built in the fourteenth century, and is seventy feet in height. The towers are notable, which can not be said of Peking's ugly towers.

China's navy is divided into the Pei Yang and Nan Yang, or northern and southern fleets, and also the Customs Cutter service, which includes the Lighthouse fleet. The Chun Chih (War Board) is congratulating itself that China is not without a naval reserve trained at the expense of its critics, for every American, British and German mail and tramp ship, which plies from her ports across the Pacific, or Indian and Red Seas, is entirely manned with a Chinese crew. The capable Yuan Shi K'ai, renowned already for his ambitions for the army, was until his recent dismissal drilling the nucleus for two navies, which since the war with Japan have been used chiefly as arms of the Customs service. The bases for this navy are Changchew and Miao-tao Islands to protect the gulf of Pechili and Peking; Chusan to guard the approach to the Yangtze Kiang and Shanghai; and Hainan, to protect the south, and be within call of Canton. He proposed first to make China great commercially, to have an unexcelled army of half a million within five years, and then to build a modern navy when his people called for that final flourish of patriotism. The Customs receipts and Robert Hart's new systematization of taxation taken up by Robert Bredon are to provide the money.

As Japan by edict and example is endeavoring to improve the stature of the race by inducing the children and women to sit on chairs instead of squatting on mats, the viceroys are founding throughout China, Tientsin Hui or Mutual Feet Societies and encouraged by the Regent and the scientific Japanese, as well as our own missionaries, the movement is spreading. It can affect only the rich and the apish among the middle class, as the poor and all of the Hakka tribes never bound the feet. No candidates are now taken into the Civil Service whose wives or daughters practise the custom. The Board of Education has stepped in with an edict prohibiting the manufacture of small shoes for the *kin lien,* or golden lilies, as bound feet are called. The traveled Chinese are quite argumentative that disgusting as binding the feet is, it can not affect the health of offspring as does the western custom of lacing, nor has it ever affected so large a proportion of the population as has the western distortion. Moreover, the Chinese reply that the binding of feet has no voluptuous motive of revealing the lines of the figure, which in their women rather they conceal, even to the extent of binding the breasts down, and they are accordingly insistent regarding their superior personal purity. In this argument between Paris and Peking, the impartial probably must regret that the third party eligible to judge, the Atnah Indians of British Columbia, who bound their heads, has passed into oblivion.

On approaching Shanghai on the broad yellow flood of the Huang Phu, one wonders if this can really be the threshold of crowded China, for not a soul or a hut is to be seen in the brakes along the shore. The low flooded fields east of the Huang Phu are impossible of cultivation until modern engineering skill wades in and saves the sunken but extremely fertile meadows. Bile-like and unpromising is the approach to Taku, on whose flat shore a few thin birches and willows fail to relieve the scene. But in the south is the grandeur which one expected of the north, making the coast-line just the opposite in appearance of America's eastern shore. Particularly stern is the landscape of much of the eastern part of the province of Kwangtung. The Hakka grass-cutters have burned everything, excepting a few firs of ten years' growth, which the British have sowed on the granite hills of Kowloon. The houses are of granite blocks, and are thatched or tiled, in comparison with the bluish brick huts of Shan-tung Province. In contrast, think of the mud hovels of Mohammedan Kansu Province and of Pechili, or the cliff dwellings of Shensi Province, or even the bamboo and thatch huts of Szechuen Province.

Here and there a person of artistic soul, or a monk, will have protected a wide banyan, whose branches lean like a bowed patriarch upon many rooted canes. Sometimes a wind-break has been preserved of evergreen orange and loquat, yellow syringas, or cotton-trees with their large red flowers. Now and then you see a shining green camphor-tree among the rain-smoothed rocks. Where it is not tapped too often, this tree grows to a magnificent size. The wood is in great demand in the extensive pawnshop towers of the southern provinces, where it is used to make trunks for clothes. The odor is a powerful defense against the attacks of moths and white ants. The wood is a golden yellow, clouded with one wide brown vein, and when polished is silky smooth and gorgeous enough for even the exactions of an oriental connoisseur. Because of the dark vein, the wood is not used for carving, but at Ningpo they find a white wood which holds the knife well and takes a polish. In the northern provinces the familiar ailantus tree, willow, and roseate rhododendron are frequently seen, and in the valleys of Che-kiang Province the deep green leaves of the arbor-vitæ cast shadows over the pale green rice patches. In Korea the ranges remind you of turbulent Atlantic seas, suddenly fixed in stone. All coastal south China and western Szechuen are an array of white granite peaks, the oldest formation of the country. Indeed, three hundred thousand square miles of China consist of lofty ranges. Can any land, which at the same time supports a vast population, so boast of affording her toilers the uplift of stupendous scenery, when labors are laid down, and the eyes of the worker raised above the toil at his feet? These are they who work indeed as in the sight of God. In most of the foot-hills are cut the horseshoe shaped and blue-painted graves of the wealthier Chinese, many of which graves ancestor worship and clan organization have preserved to ages hoary in comparison with our oldest monuments. "The dead must see farthest," is a Chinese saying, when they explain these scenic locations.

In every valley of Kwangtung, hid behind barricades of palest green, brown-plumed millet (*kaoling*), tufted *muk-kwa* (papaw), or needlewood fir-trees are huddled the low stone houses of the villagers, that they may be near their rice swamps, and *shan-yu* (sweet potato) terraces. The women who do not have to work, are dressed in colors which rival the flowers about them for brightness, and it is from nature altogether that they have taken their styles of color and ornamentation. You will notice that the rice is not sown broadcast and harrowed into a field, which is afterward flooded, as is our practice in Louisiana; it is transplanted into an already flooded field, which custom leads to many skin diseases of the feet, and to rheumatism, on account of the human fertilization placed in the water. Over the tilled patches flutter showers of white streamers, for the purpose of disturbing the foraging magpies. More people live on rice than on wheat in this world, so one can imagine the aggregate acreage extending from Cape Cambodia to Shan-tung

Promontory. Fringing the rice swamps are bulrush shallows, where the peasants gather a triple harvest of food, fiber and down. The Chinese farmer only essays a few acres, for that is all his machine-less toil can irrigate and secure fertilizer (mostly human) for, and accordingly the vast unreclaimed districts, even in so crowded a land, are astonishing. In Ceylon, where the conditions were the same until recently, the importation of German patent fertilizers, made largely from Florida phosphate, has greatly increased the area of productive land. With the railroad era now really begun in China, we may expect a similar transformation. In only two of the provinces is irrigation not depended upon for the crops, i. e., at the headwaters of the Yellow River in Kansu and Shensi. The bamboo water-wheel, turned by the buffalo, is in universal use in the country districts, and will not be supplanted soon, though in some of the cities the merchants are introducing foreign steam pumps for wells and reservoirs. Where the village owns the water-wheel and buffalo power, the toll of water diverted from the main ditch is measured at so many marks of a joss-stick, which is set burning.

The pig, the chow-dog, children and old women, alone roam along the large flags of the streets of the small villages during the day, while in the distance the peasants, dressed in blue Nankeen knickerbockers, toil with bare sweating shoulders at the tank-sweep and bamboo wheel, in their primitive irrigation and abominable fertilization methods. The oriental sun burns up all shadows, except the violet silhouette of the tall pawnshop tower, the roof of which is heaped with large stones, for ammunition against the attacks of invaders. Here Cheong, and his wife Chai, have

their winter tunics in pawn, while they venture the
ten *tael* in a lease of neighbor Loong's six terraces (it
would not be lucky to choose four or seven), where
petsai, cotton, ramie, beans, maize, rice or sugar-cane
are sedulously cultivated. Or possibly he turns the land
into peanut patches for the sake of the fifty per cent.
yield of oil. When Cheong redeems the pledge, he not
infrequently secures a life mortgage of leprosy for himself. All land belongs to the government, and tenure
is evidenced more by the last tax receipt than the original
crown deed. Loong pays a tax of six cents a *mao*, or
twenty-five cents our acre. If the pirates make a rush
from the banana and papaw brakes, the children on watch
start a chain of yells, which sets the village streets in
uproar and echo, and the men and women rush to the
fray from the fields with their two-pronged rice forks as
weapons. Sometimes an annoyed farmer's vengeance
is orientally extreme upon the foreigner who disturbs
his soil. Europeans tramping through the paddy fields
after the gorgeous colored and succulent rice-birds, or for
snipe, are, for a deterrent example, apprehended, and the
indispensable sun helmets, or Calcutta topies, are taken
from their heads at midday. There may not be a tree
or shade for miles, and the sun quickly prostrates the
victim.

China owes her vast population to her finesse in truck
farming. Nearly every family raises part of its food.
With machinery, draft animals, and the resultant fertilizer, she can conquer wastes which will support even
double the present population. The present farms average two acres, and support eight persons. Where the
desert has encroached upon the land, and sifted a
blanket of sand over the soil, the peasants can be seen

cutting cellars so as to reach the fertile earth and till it. On some of the towers of the Great Wall, hanging gardens have been planted by the Tartar guards amid scenery of mountain, pass, rivulet and cloud, with which storied Babylon could only have been simple in comparison. In passing, we might remark that no woman is allowed on the wall, as that would be a challenge to the God of War, Kwan Ti.

The three provinces of Pechili, Shan-tung and Kiang-su present scenes of waterways and small farms that are richer in their beauties than even Holland's fertile borders. Theirs is that gentle beauty that warms the heart the most, because it least touches the sublime and imaginative. Everywhere the peach, plum and pear are in bloom as of right royal, for this is their first home. The golden Grand Canal, or Chah Ho (river of flood-gates) flows through plain and village, to connect all things with the Father of Life, the Yangtze River. The cribwork is of stone, or of millet stalks, mud and cord, and miles of the canal run above cities, which could be at the mercy of the rebellious waters. Heavy stone bridges, with balustrades adorned with lions, dragons, monkey and elephant heads, leap from the plain and over the canals, with that mounting sweep which we thought was created in, but was really stolen by Venice when Marco Polo whispered in her ear. The arches are pointed, semicircular and Omega shape. They really look more like picturesque gateways that usher in the stream. Some are white, and others are clothed in green and purple with bean vines and convolvulus.

The Venice of China is Soochow, with one and one-half million inhabitants, dozens of islands and hundreds of canals, all bridged and walled in for ten miles in circumference. Over the Wan Hsien stream, at its junction with the Yangtze, is the famous single arch bridge, pictured so often, which leaps from the bank forty feet high. On the top of the arch is a three-storied guard-house, with panels of white stucco and braces exposed, the eaves of each story all curling gracefully, and a decorated frieze under a fanciful roof. From your boat in the stream you behold through the arch far away a framed purple conical mount of Szechuen relieved on the wide flaming West. At Fu-chau, over the Min, until the flood of 1897, stood the famous Wan Sui Kiao (Ten Thousand Ages) bridge, with its forty piers of monolithic stone; its roadway of stone blocks forty feet long and three feet thick, and its balustrade of stone blocks forty feet long. Tiny shops used to line this bridge, which was only fifteen feet wide. In its bridges, gates, walls and pagodas of stone and tile, China boasts of ruins worth going all the way to see them. Japan has no ruins, for she built in wood. Military boat bridges, some with earth and even brick roadways, are in frequent use on the tidal rivers, and rope and chain suspension bridges join the dizzy loess cliffs in Szechuen.

Nearly every village and city of the plain provinces is crossed with a tracery of glistening canals, most of them beautifully pure from their stillness and the absence of manufacturing, in contrast with the swifter rivers which hold the yellow loess in suspension. Through every field of palest green, such as only the rice blade can display, flows the empurpled flood in joyous contrast of color. Innumerable high-pooped boats are poled along, and as their sails, which are stretched upon twenty bamboo battens, are not taken down when the

wind falls, they become lit up with every shade of
brown, red and gold upon their oblong surfaces in the
hushed sunset time. The hulls of the boats are hid
by the rice and sorghum, and the moving sails, especially
near Soochow, remind one of the Norfolk (England)
Broads, or the Hackensack Meadows, only this scene is
the finer and more animated. One of these junks, the
Wang Ho, lately crossed the Pacific to San Diego in
seventy days, and is the first to fly the Chinese flag in
American waters in historic times, though the Chinese
have legends of the Pacific being crossed. There is no
place in the world where you can see so many sails together as on the Hung Tsih Lake on the Yellow River.
Scattered everywhere, far away, human beings are hur-
rying noiselessly, and before each is thrown the shadow
of a cross. In the center an enormous flat grass hat,
made in Hupeh, hides the face, and at the ends of a long
bamboo, borne on the shoulders, are two large buckets.
These features stand out prominently in the violet sil-
houettes of those who are for ever nailed to the tree of
bondage, but who have ever had the least to say of that
bondage, and the term of it.

Everything is done at a trot. Wherever there is a
spring of water near the paths, the country people erect
for the convenience of wayfarers, Tings of four posts, up-
holding a roof of thatch or tile to shade a cool stone
bench. There are few large forests, but sufficient sophoro
locust, willow, cypress and orange trees, artistically
placed, to contribute adornment and relief to the view,
and rising to heaven with their airy towers, are scores of
balconied pagodas, and monasteries with wide, sweeping
eaves. Heathen though it all is, the peace of God rests
over the scene more palpably than anywhere else in the

world.   The noiselessness, the smokelessness, and the distance account for the impression.   It is conspicuous that there are no fences, one reason being that wood is unprocurable.   When our traveler returns to America, you will notice that he has brought his strange gods with him; that he is a wood and water worshiper.   Let your faucet run, and he will rise mechanically to turn it off.   Injure a tree and he will hunt a magistrate!   Moreover, the borders between Chinese farms must work while they watch.   If they must be marked, mulberry trees are set out and the leaves divided between the owners, or bamboos are similarly planted.

Most of the rivers roll along like the Mississippi in a steady flood.   Only the Ciamu Nu and Mekong Rivers of Yunnan have numerous great rapids, and answer in that respect to the St. Lawrence, as they fall from the Thibetan plateaus to the rice levels of the coastal provinces.   Roaring up Hang-chow Bay and the Tsien-tang River as far as Hang-chow city, at ten knots an hour, flows the world's most famous tide bore.   The maximum height of twenty feet is reached in March and August. Tourists should behold the wonder at moonlight, as well as daytime.   It is an animating sight to see the heavy junks turn their bows to meet the great wave, and then wheel round and follow it to a new position on the bund or wharf.   What a commotion there is among the matting sails, all weighted with their bamboo battens, as they batter their thin masts!   The Yangtze has lesser rapids in its upper reaches, and one long rapid, the Hsin Tan, where it is one of the sights of the world to see three hundred to four hundred men tugging a boat up-stream. These tow-men live near the Red Life-Boat Station at the foot of the rapids, in a dull cluster of brown huts.   From their work they stand as noble models for a Discobolus of Myron as you could see anywhere. They pull high up, with the bamboo hawser drawn over their shoulders, and the tug comes upon biceps, shoulders and calves. The government appeals to their esprit by offering rewards for lives rescued. Min is a favorite name for a river, another well-known one being as far west as Szechuen Province, where it empties into the Yangtze. This Min River is famous for its high-prowed hurdling boats, which are employed to slip over the smooth, large stones of the rapids. The rush is tremendous. Another peculiarity of these boats is the hinged sail, which at night is let down over the boatman's family for a roof. The only sails which they ever furl are the studding sails, and these are the only boats of the Chinese which employ studding sails.

In China, as in India, though there are vast mountains, the topography is without plateaus to such an extent that there are no waterfalls, such as Niagara, Montmorenci, or the Victoria Falls of the Zambesi. Nor are there great lakes, the Ting in Hunan, two hundred and twenty miles in circumference, and the Po Yang in Kiang-si, ninety by twenty miles, being the only ones worth mentioning. Accordingly, when Gaekwar or Viceroy come to America, their first rush is to see Niagara and Superior. The Po Yang is studded with beautiful islands, but the silt of the Kan River has made the shores marshy. The scenery of the Tung Ting Lake, and the eighteen rapids of the Kan, will only be one and one-half days from Canton when the Canton-Hankau Railway is opened shortly. Only three days by camel from Peking lies the least known portion of the globe, Gobi Desert, one thousand miles square and four thousand feet elevation, where men once lived and prospered until the feuds of Mongol and Tartar left the gardens to be sifted over with sand by the winds. Almost undiscovered, China's great chains of mountains lie north and west, with the tales still whispered about them of mines which supplied Khans with their jewels, and which will probably be found based to a great extent on fact when Japanese engineers get the railways to the foothills for the advance of prospectors.

The real dragon of China is the Yellow River or Hoang-ho, but called by the more reflective, "China's Sorrow." In one thousand years, he has drowned more Chinese than all the wars of humankind have slain during that period. His back is arched five hundred miles, as he doubles on his course into Mongolia, and his tail writhes here and there from changing banks for six hundred miles, as he lashes into misery and death the inhabitants of Honan and Shan-tung, who never know when the new foundation for their moving huts will be chosen for the path of their destroyer the following spring. A less rapid river would deposit its loess higher up its course, and thus fix its bank below, but here is a suicidal river which silts up its mouth, and is eternally strangling its middle body. What the suspended loess looks like, every traveler who has taken the tender at Woosung from his steamer to go to Shanghai, will remember; it makes the heart sick at once, for these are not the blue or green waters of home. Any who have lived at Peking or Tientsin know what the dust storms of April are like, when the dry loess is caught up by the winds that sweep down from the hills of Pechili. The Orient sun glistening from every particle makes the whole air scintillate with yellow flame. The loss to the poor each year, through flood devastations, is five million *taels* and ten thousand lives, and besides there is the impoverishment of the soil as the loam is sifted into the sea. In the same manner, the Menam is scouring Siam of its fertility. We have nothing at all comparable in color to these rivers, excepting, perhaps, our arch-thief of alluvial richness, the "Big Muddy" Missouri. What the loess, or *kwang tu* (yellow earth) can produce with rain, is illustrated in Shensi, where three crops of grain are brought forth each year. No fertilizers will be needed for years in the northwestern provinces. When one layer gives out, the loess cliffs can be pulled down, and powdered over the worn-out land.

The Government is in a quandary how to bring relief in the valley of the Hoang-ho. Even to the top of the Sin Ling Mountains, in ancient times, the destroyers climbed eleven thousand feet and chopped every tree all the way up. Reforestation of the upper courses, to mitigate erosion of the yellow terraces, would produce no results for a generation; neither would levees at the mouth, on the Mississippi plan, work, owing to the exfiltration of the waters through the permeable bed of the river. Reforestation would eventually hold back the snows of the denuded hills of northeast Thibet and Mongolia, and the waters of the only rainy province, Kansu. This would diminish the release of the tremendous spring torrent and vast suspended cargo of loess, and provide a steadier and longer flow, with some hope of the banks being fixed long enough, first for binding by vines, and for the later afforestation. It is the most awful lesson in the world of the individual and national crime of forest destruction, and the innocent descendants are paying ten thousand fold for the ignorance and sins of the

unscientific fathers.   The first motto to be written in the
new Chinese copy-books should be: " He who chops a
tree without planting ten is a red dragon to his son, and
a white dragon to his son's son, and his grave shall be
unswept."

The Yangtze, although rising near the Yellow River,
with a greater fall of fifteen inches to the mile, carries
the bulk of its loess well out to sea, although it probably accumulates less loess than the Yellow River.
So strong in flood time and so shallow in the rainless
season is the current of the Yellow River in Mongolia;
of the Han and of the upper Yangtze that many
native boats make only one trip down-stream.   They are
broken up for lumber at the end of the journey.   China,
influenced by poorer Japan spending three millions a
year on a forestry policy, is now willing to spend millions for the control of the Yellow River, and the vastest
scheme of reforestation ever instituted by a government
may soon be put in operation.   The reforestation will
probably be accomplished with the China fir (Cunning-
hamio sinensis), known in China as the " Sau Tsoi "
杉 木; and the Pinus massoniana, both of which produce a commercial timber, the latter having the additional quality for the southern Orient, of withstanding
fairly well the insidious attacks of the white ant.   Germany found the hills of Tsing Tau barren, and in a few
years she has clothed them with a young forest, so that
an ancient mariner returning there would hardly know
his old bearings.   Britain, the great preceptor, has set
forth the same object lesson on the twenty miles of
hilly territory between Mirs Bay and Chung Point, opposite Hong-Kong.   There is a religious sect in Honan
the members of which preserve forests, and at their festi-

vals, which are observed at night, they hang lanterns among the branches.

China could support even double her population if the arid stretches, especially in the northern and western provinces, were reclaimed by irrigation, and now that her credit is improving, and her resources being developed, these great works are sure to be advanced. More hemp should be cultivated, and even in the rich plain of Honan this important product is not developed as it could be, and as the Ching Too men would work it. They are the most scientific farmers of the race. What the Chinese can execute in the way of dikes is well illustrated at Kai Fong, the capital of Honan, where the great Yellow River has been turned from its uninterrupted southern sweep of seven hundred miles. In the battles of the Mings against the Manchus, these dikes were once broken, and three hundred thousand inhabitants of the capital drowned, but there were no newspapers then, and the world has forgotten and forgiven. The Chinese are not altogether unscientific; they so respected the first engineer, Yu, who successfully diked the Yellow River, that they called him to the throne. This was when the nation was emerging from the pastoral to the agricultural state, and admired and needed a Joseph instead of an Abraham. If ten thousand square miles in Japan can support forty-five million people; if the Mormon father could turn deserted sage-brush Utah into a garden, the Chinese without a national debt, can when they will convert their northwest into valleys which will repeat the story of the prolific Ching Too plain. Their coal lands alone would be security enough for any dozen schemes of irrigation, public utilities, naval, etc., that the government could conceive; and the surprises of modern industry and finance can easily occur in China almost any year after the Canton to Han-kau portion of the north-to-south Trunk Railway is completed. You will notice where the new Peking-Han-kau Railway passes through the sand plains, that the government has in a small way begun its afforestation work by planting willows to protect the railway embankment from the winds. The same improvement has been made on the North China Railway, from Tientsin to Newchwang. The object lesson was acquired when the Chinese commissioners looked through the port-hole of a P. and O. liner, which was passing through the Suez Canal, and beheld the sands of El Giser fixed at last by the roots of Scotch shrubs.

Second as a devastator to the Hoang-ho is the Han River, which rises higher than its width, and which drowned only as late as June, 1906, ten thousand people, and in April, 1908, five thousand people. The visitor in Han-kau may notice in the autumn that the houses and booths along the river bank are built on piles thirty feet high. At Yching the waters of the gorge rise fifty feet. This will tell all you may care to know of what the spring flood is like. Confucius ranked as the fourth virtue the cultivation of the mulberry tree, and we, the outer barbarians, have accordingly been dressed in finery from the product of the worms which fed on the leaves thereof. If he had enjoined upon his countrymen the planting of the camphor and the fir in the mountains of the West, he would have saved in the last three centuries alone the lives of ten millions of his race who have been drowned, as the waters of the Hoang-ho and the Han reared themselves forty feet above their banks. Because of the floods in Kiang-su in 1907, four hundred and fifty thousand people had to be fed in concentration camps, each averaging one thousand families. This is the first time China organized against famine. The camps were patrolled by the new draft of soldiers. Some features of the camp life were amusing. Cheese was sent by the Canadian government, but the unsophisticated people preferred even grass to this new food. Only the Thibetans have any knowledge of milk foods. In the relief contributions, America headed the list for the first time in charity accorded the Chinese, and attracted the favorable comments of the officials, who announced that they would influence students to be sent to American institutions. The absence of trees also causes the Hoang-ho to drain itself too rapidly through its porous loess bed. In the first six months of 1901 a drought which dried up the crops of millet, mountain rice, corn and *shanyue* (sweet potato), came upon Shensi Province. One third of these most ancient people of China (three hundred thousand) died before food could reach them, though there was sufficient elsewhere in the land. Nothing can prevent a recurrence, except a railway from Kaifong direct westward to Tsianfu, four hundred miles, so that supplies may be hurried in.

The Min River at Fu-chau, as scenic as the Gunnison of Colorado, contrary to the general conditions in the south, is rich in woods, which wave on cliffs seven hundred feet above the waters. In a grove of gigantic Liquidambar, oak and water plum (myrica rubra) stands the famous monastery of Fong Kong Tse. Immense quantities of paper are produced here, as the bamboo grows in great luxuriance in the dank and shady gorges of the Min. Fringing northern Mongolia is a region one thousand six hundred miles long and three hundred miles broad, where the giant firs curtain in an uninhabited

night, and to which fastnesses Genghis Khan, the Charlemagne of the Mongols, once made his retreats. The
Kara and Tula Rivers have washed from the forest-
clothed sides of the hundred peaks of the Ulamgum and
Khangai ranges a dark loess called rine, out of which
the life has been far from lost, but there is not a soul
now to till it on steppe or in valley. It seems to have
stood since the time of Genghis Khan as a debated land
between Tartar and Mongol, Russ and Manchu.

Where the rice field is not the source of wealth, on
higher ground (for China is three-quarters mountains)
the mulberry growers' huts are grouped. Between the
trees, tobacco is planted as a second line of defense
against crop failure. The great drawback here is the
scarcity of fertilizers, for phosphates are as yet un-
mined. The mulberry trees are stunted to six feet in
height for eight years, after which the shoots and leaves
are cropped for the worms. If the terrace is near a
foreign settlement at a treaty port, Cheong adds a ruby
persimmon tree, a glorious pumoloe, a scarlet-blossomed
pomegranate, or a luscious lychee to his grove, which
latter explains why foreigners grow boils in China.

The province of Shansi has been neglected, but will
come into its own. It is that great loamy plateau of
three thousand five hundred feet altitude, buttressed by
granite hills, which have pushed the destroying Hoang-
ho five hundred miles from its course. Here at Ping
Ting are the beds which used to supply the camel pack
trains with coal for Peking. The colors in the great
loess ravines, four hundred feet deep, are of all hues
and remind you of the cañons of the Colorado.

There will be a day when Thibet will be the mountain
resort of the world. Travelers will take the swift Mes-

sageries Maritimes steamers, about twenty-two days in the voyage from Marseilles to Tonquin; from Haiphong they will take the French railway now building, and in two days run up to the capital of Szechuen, Ching Too, and from there enter a more hospitable Thibet than via the Himalayan gateway. You will realize that your stay can not be long the first time. Think of standing by the toilers as they swing the sickle in the silvery light on plateaus high as Pike's Peak, while as high again rise the mountains that are the ridge pole of this, our mundane habitation. How quickly the panting toilers work, for all too soon comes the long winter, and the silence far above the clamor of the nations at the foot-hills of the world,— Indian, Chinese, Caucasian.

China, too, has its Thousand Islands, scattered along the rocky coast from Hong-Kong to the Gulf of Tonquin, and a trip from Canton to the French concession at Kwong Chou Bay is one of the most thrilling in the country. So silent, majestic and apparently uninhabited is the scene, that you would not believe you were at the gates of the world's most populous country. The rocks which are more seismic than volcanic, assume every shape that the imagination can conceive, and rise purple above a quiet yellow sea, which rims their base with one thin line of white foam. These were the gates the Arabs came to in unrecorded days long before Vasco da Gama and Albuquerque, and with surprised dusky faces, peering from under the long lateen sails, asked questions History would now give a good deal to know, for we might like to reset some mile-posts of Progress.

The voice that wins the wanderer back to the East, the spirit ever calling, is the remembrance of the absence there of smoke, noise and hurry. This is the peace of

Cathay: the promise that there ever is a to-morrow, and never an enemy, and the charm of it never departs.   Vast valleys open up with ten thousand at work, from the pagoda-topped hill where the golden ginko-tree, shaped like an immense maiden-hair fern, drops its red fruit, to the soft green paddy at your feet, and the loudest noise ceases when your barrow's wheel stops creaking in its wooden journal.   Tombs, monasteries and hamlets stand half-shaded by trees, and nowhere does smoke or steam rise to soil the blue.   A country it is, inhabited the longest by man, yet looking the youngest, because its breast has not been torn by mines, or the insult of chimneys been raised against the ever-vernal innocence of its vales.   The flora of all climes are mixed in its luxuriant valleys.   The rubber, apricot, peach, pumaloe, banyan, arbor-vitæ and fir trees blend their shades; and hemp, honeysuckle, cotton, poppies, tobacco, maize and indigo wave together.

The sailors of China, but not of Japan, still cling to the use of the high-sterned junks.   Without keels, these drifters rely for their course on the deep, latticed rudder which towers as high over the water as it sinks under it.   They are helpless, close-hauled, but off the wind, or on the quarter, they make splendid passages.   Chinese waters present an exceedingly picturesque appearance with these junks displaying tremendous oblong mainsails of yellow and brown matting.   They have no jibs, but often carry a jigger mast.   The old Amoy junks were never launched without two tremendous wooden eyes being fastened on with wooden bolts, the purpose of which the sailor explains in his Pidgin-English, " No eye, how can see?"   The foreign steamboat most popular with Chinese was the old *Hankow* of Hong-Kong, which dis-

played two great eyes upon her paddle boxes. The
Chinese commissioners were accordingly humored with
the Central of New Jersey ferry-boats on New York Bay,
which have a circular eye painted upon their funnels, and
the Erie Railroad ferry-boats, which bear the white
stripes of the battleships of Japan. It was a reminder
of the home, which, with all its oddities and superstitions, is still the dearest place to them, despite their
widening experience in affairs. The Canton River junks
have a low bow, fore and mainsails, but no jib or jigger, and from both mastheads they fly triangular red
dragon flags with many tails. In ancient days they hung
a red tablet over the rail amidships when they were con-
veying an ambassadorial mission, but in this case a
green instead of a red dragon flag was broken out aloft.
Most imposing of all, with their lofty carved sterns, are
the junks from Kiang-si Province. Until the Japanese
fleet whipped Kublai Khan's fleet despite the latter's use
of powder and cannon, these were the vessels which swept
the seas from Borneo and Hawaii to Japan and Korea.
Not only the Chinese navy has nailed up its romantic
honors, but in earlier days, in the reign of Chung Ti, A.
D., 80, Chinese armies marched in victory to the shores of
the Caspian, where the eagle of Rome and the dragon of
Cathay saluted and parted in mutual wonderment without fight.

The worship of high places is prominent in the Chinese
religious system. On a given day once a year every
man, woman and child who is able, ascends the highest
peak in the district, dressed in the choice of the silky
wardrobe. It is the festival of long life which was assured to a philosopher who was saved from a flood
thereby, and wrote that all his wisdom afterward came by

taking a survey once a year, of life from an exalted overlook above his former haunts.   It is at once a Thanksgiving, a Good Resolution and a Noah Anniversary day.
The Buddhists build their pagodas on the highest mounds,
and you will hear at even the welcome of the tiny bells
which are swung in the eaves by the wind.   Every traveler
is familiar with the rambling granite monastery above the
fish pools at Macao, and where the alluvial rice fields
spread a green ocean of grain around a peak called oddly
" Lean Dog Mountain," which was once an island in the
delta of the Canton River, there rises another pagoda.
All the storied way across the province for two hundred
miles along the West River from Canton to Wuchow,
pagodas mark the view.   At Han-kau, from the top of
Han-Yang Hill, a white temple signals across the broad
Yangtze's flood to the hundred-eaved Yellow Stork
tower.   Outside Peking, one of the most beautiful of Chinese pagodas, with its nine tiers, commands the view, and
one hundred miles farther, at the Emperor's vast country-
seat among the Ching Tih (hot river) Hills rises an elev-
en-story pagoda of alternating colored stories of yellow,
blue and green tiles.   At Soochow rises an octagonal pagoda with nine stories and sixty doors, which open on airy
balconies that look over the violet bends of the Grand
Canal, as the oriental day deepens from dusty gold to
purple.   On the summit of Kinshan Island, as you approach Shanghai in the early morn, rises another yellow
pagoda of renown.

Speaking of pagodas, and recalling history's curse on
destroyers and thieves of art, one can not but repeat the
fame of that gilt and white tower two hundred feet high,
and four hundred years old, of priceless porcelain, of the
Recompensing-Favor Monastery at Nanking, which the

frenzied and burlesque Christian Taepings destroyed in 1853. Even now its one hundred and fifty tinkling bells seem to sound for the dreamy traveler, from under the green tiled roofs along the dreamy canal at even. A few large golden tiles of this pagoda are among the treasures of the pottery rooms of the Metropolitan Art Gallery, New York. The most visited pagoda in China, and the ugliest, is the " Five Story " one at Canton, built in the fourteenth century, which is not round at all, but merely an oblong building, with five verandas on one side, built upon the Tartar wall. It is mendicant infested. The pagoda has no particular interest or history, but it gives the best view of the city, and of the famous grave district extending up the White Cloud Hills, outside the walls. The octagonal nine-story " Flowery Pagoda " at Canton, built in the sixth century, is less known, but truly superb. The proportions are chaste, and the cornices are not exaggerated. The yellow walls contrast with the darker roofs of the stories. A square non-tapering pagoda, showing Burmese influence in architecture, at Yunnan, has twelve stories; the balconies all being unusual for narrowness. It is the most ponderous pagoda in China. The best proportioned square pagoda in the land is the seven-storied one at Chu Siung. Its unique grace consists in the height allowed from the ground before the first story begins. Then there is another noted one outside Ychow, the eaves of whose nine stories whisper a forest full of Aeolian music, or maybe forbidden secrets about the Tsing Emperors buried within its shadow. On Mount Omi, in Szechuen, there is a temple which, partly because of the difficulty of ascent, has acquired a name of pre-eminent holiness. The temple is placed four thousand feet up the twelve thousand foot mountain, and is reached by ten thousand steps, which were cut in the solid rock by pilgrims. Nothing more aptly reveals the unsatisfying portion of China's religion than these agonizing feats prescribed for the faithful, in their efforts to find surcease of inward unrest. In no land, under the exactions of no religion, are the penances so terrible, or the efforts more sincere, and therefore, if humankind is to be judged only by motives in the Great Day, the Chinese will not be found wanting.

Chinese architecture can readily be adapted to our country. The house should be at least two stories high with a cupola, to balance the parallel curves of the rising cornices of the veranda. The heavy roofs with wide decorated eaves, glistening tiles, and upward sweep of the wide cornices, are infinitely grander, warmer and safer looking in our mountains than the Swiss chalets, and the plain surface of the walls can be sufficiently relieved in summer with awnings, which contrast well with the ponderous effect of the roofs. Another advantage is that every inch of space within the walls is available, as there is nothing of the execrable gingercake style in anything Chinese. German architects are fast ruining the appearance of Japan with their architectural productions. For summer homes anywhere, the Chinese style affords as no other does opportunities for steps, terraces and veranda posts, where potted plants in bright vases can be placed against a dark colored house. The plain Chinese garden which trusts more to the individual effects of flowers and vases, will reach the heart quicker than the conventionalities of Italian styles, which make you think the gardens need a roof and are not for outdoors. Such a home as I have described has been built by a New Orleans gentleman, Raul Villon, and is worthy of wide imitation.

VI

CHINESE ART AND LITERATURE

China ushers the visitor into her art life with delightful surprise. From the bright wide streets, bordered with tamarind trees, of Shameen, the island in the Pearl River, where the foreigners dwell in English and French concessions, to a crowded and dirty bund, over a shaky camel's back bridge, you cross to Canton, the center of the artistic production of the nation. In your blue-curtained chair, borne on the bare shoulders of speeding coolies, you swing along the damp, dark lanes which are too narrow to permit a tree to root. The sewage rolls its noisome tide in the single gutter in the middle of the road. No Chinese street has side gutters. The large square stones of the paving bear testimony to an eternity of years by the deep hollows made by the passing of countless bare feet. At last you come to a court where three streets meet, and where the blackwood cutters guild is located. The shops spread along Tai Sun, Yuck Tsze, and Old Factory Streets. It is the sweetest spot in all foul-smelling Canton. You enter the stone basement and kick your way refreshingly through the fragrant red teak-wood chips, for they are not yet stained the familiar ebony. The men whom you observe carving the legs of chairs will tell you their forefathers carved here, too, when Cabot, Columbus and Da Gama were only dreaming of discoveries. Once a leg carver or a turner of panels, always one. In an adjoining shop, idol carvers are working on images which will be covered with gold leaf and placed before the incense pots of the Tai Fat Tsze Monastery. If you desire a buffet with shelves, lockers, mirror and Yunnan marble like the one you are admiring, it will take Tack Loong and his sons a year before they can deliver it. Kowtow to Tack, for he is an artist who dreams and works while he dreams, over the best product which his Family Academy can evolve. His ancestors executed no better work for mandarins in Kang He's day, when China, first hearing that there was a " *Ta Si Yang Kuo* " (great kingdom of the Western Ocean; i. e., Portugal), declared " then it must come and pay homage to the whole earth's *Shang Ti* (Lord)." In the strength, permanence and pride of such an assurance is rooted a real art spirit, and you behold its flowers in these elaborate teapoys, chairs, screens, stands, tables, and everything that the king of woods can be worked into.

It is the same in Nganking, the capital of Nganwei, with the horn lantern workers; once a lantern maker, always one. Hang a silk net over the lantern, and you have something opal-soft, but light and strong. Think of the patience of artisans who work and stretch horn in a moist heat until it is pliable enough for these designs. It is the same story in Swatow, among the needle workers who execute drawn-work; they are the descendants of those who have been developing their art for centuries.

Or wander along the Sun Tau Lan or the Hin Chan, where you may find old turquoise-blue and gold vases of the Yung Chin period which bring five thousand dollars. Vases of the Ming dynasty are worth as high as ten thousand dollars, and you will find one here if anywhere. A pair of old Chinese large *famille* rose vases, enameled with chrysanthemums, magnolias and cherries of the Kien Lung period, like these you behold, have sold at Christie's for four thousand dollars. A pair of square Kang He vases, tapering in shape with *famille verte* decoration on a black ground, has brought nineteen thousand dollars; a pair of Ky Lin jars, twenty-nine hundred dollars, and a pair of Kien Lung jars eighty-six hundred dollars at Christie's in London, but the Chinese call this extravagance on our part, an affectation in view of our neglect of their present productions. The Manchu conquerors have inspired the production of no porcelain equal to the product of the ancient potteries of the native Ming kings of the fifth century, which answers to China's Augustan age in art. The proportions of the royal ware are fixed: base one-third, bowl one-third, and neck one-third of the height. Even in these more or less decadent days nothing changes in China: the lapis lazuli color of Ming vases and the cobalt blue of the Kang He period are the standards in judging the tones of modern productions. Other vases, showing some ancient imported Greek influence perhaps, are of gourd shape, with a ground of powdered blue, on which are set circular panels, the scrolls being gold and the subjects enameled pylins, branches and birds. Some of these unique vases bring as high as one thousand dollars each.

The most famous Imperial pottery towns with a history of one thousand years in the art, are inland, in Kiang-si Province, and lie along the Kan River. Eastward from Poyang Lake, about thirty miles up a deep valley, where you would rather look for sooty coal, is King Teh Ching, introduced to our verse by Longfellow. The population of these pottery towns once ran as high as one hundred thousand, all engaged in firing the *ping-tu,* or powdered decomposed granite. When twilight deepens fast, you will notice the flames of five hundred kilns brightening into view in the darkening valleys. The fifty pound bricks for the Great Wall, and the enormous yellow tiles for the Nanking Pagoda, specimens of which you will find at the Metropolitan Museum, New York, were fired here. For miles along the shore of Poyang, the junks are loading for ports three hundred miles away along the great Yangtze River, there to distribute to mandarin and white typan the treasures of Gold Medallion; Blue and White Willow; brown water kongs with raised blue panels; Nanking blue barrel-shaped garden seats; brilliant White Ting, the glaze of which you would marvel to learn was produced with the ashes of ferns; pale bluish green Ju; creamy white, trout-scale, crackled Kien Yiu; Tai cups which are realistic water-lilies, the handle being a green sepal; precious cerulean blue Yu Kwo Tien, whose tone is the despair of Europe and broken bits of which are carried about and set as jewels in China; highly colored cinnabar, green and purple-brown Chun ware; paper-thin tea-green and scarlet Mandarin Kuan work with crab-claw pattern; sea-green and gull-gray Ko Yau; Kang He black vases; bright red Hsuan Te with insects rilievo; Cheng Hua ware with life-like figures of fowl; jade green and gold Tsang ware; and the celebrated beef-blood Ming pottery, whose wavy lines of red are formed by intermittent drafts of air being blown into the furnace as the enamel bakes. Only a few of the vases with *rouge de fer glaze* and the *mei* tree with red blooms as motif, exist; one priceless specimen being in the Metropolitan Museum, New York City.

You will notice on old Chinese porcelain merely the

name of the reign. In contemporary output the factory
name is fired as " made at the Harmony Factory," " made
at the Myriad Peaks Monastery," but never the name of
the artist as is the Japanese custom old and new. However, tradition has brought down the name of the family
Lung as the most wonderful of the potters of the sixteenth century. They took to the grave with them the
secret of their inimitable blood-red ware. Something of
praise must then be admitted of the only race which has
reached that artistic extinction of self-consciousness
where the workers are willing to forego their identity.

Porcelain is used for the façade of many of the temples
of the Yangtze Valley, and the effect of the gorgeous
panels and relieved figures in the glistening white space,
together with the sun-bathed colored eaves, is more like
the shimmer of jewels than anything our architecture has
produced. The Hung Shek temple at Wuchow rises
with a perfectly plain wall above colored balustrades and
noble flights of steps, on which large vases are set. This
plainness is intentional, to give effect to the gorgeous
tiling of the towers and cornices. The Chinese is a pro-
founder artist than the Japanese, as he understands the
balance which exists between rich decoration and plain
surfaces. The façade of the Temple of the Black God
in the city of Chow Tung in Yunnan is a solid gleam of
rich porcelains, but the effect is lost in the narrow street.
One-half of China's temples are thus miserably situated.

The famous cloisonee is made as follows. A copper
vase is secured and the design is etched thereon, thin
copper or gold wires being cemented on these lines. The
vase is then fired to anneal the wires. Colored vitreous
pastes of saltpetre, sandstone, oxides, lead salts and rice
water are dexterously filled in the interstices. The vase

is again baked. When cool, a file is applied, after which the vase is again fired. Several polishes are now applied, with limestone used on the lathe, and a polish with charcoal follows. If gilt is to be applied, it is now done by galvanic process, after which there is a final polishing which reveals a work of enduring and enrapturing iridescence. In the firing of large roof and wall tiles and solid shapes for mullions, sills, plinths, lozenged ventilator vents, etc., the potters are as expert as any of our artisans at Trenton or Liverpool, Ohio. Nothing is built up from single bricks that can possibly be fired in one piece.

The coolie and the fisherman however still eat off Hankau iron; camphor-wood deck or plaintain leaf. When they, like any other labor in history, can afford to sit before an earthenware plate and have the wherewithal for renewals when it is broken, there may possibly not be a Manchu on the Yellow Throne. For it is to be noticed that when peasants are able to buy crockery they generally change their minds first and purchase swords to mend their grievances, or retaliate upon those who kept them serfs too long.

In meeting residents of the South and of the North, it is noticeable that among the former the names are soft and flowing, as compared with the sharp and hard names of the North. In looks it is the opposite, the Southerner having the high cheek-bones and harder face, and the Northerner having the oval face. The Manchu is tinctured with the severity of name and manner of the Mongolian and Korean, among which latter people you encounter names like Pak Sok. Compare the southern Fung Kwang Chung with Jen Yuk Gko, or Min Yin with the harsh Hok Ngon. The commonest family name in

China is Chang. It resembles the Smith family in America.

In the ingrafting of American and European inventions among her industries, especially at Han-kau, the Chinese find themselves without means to name the strangers in the arbitrary Wenli or mandarin written speech which dates to B. C. 2500. As an instance the best they could do with an incandescent light was to call it " new moonshine." Wenli is the common speech of the masses only in Honan and Shan-tung. As illustrating the slight differences between the pronunciation of the mandarin Wenli and the Cantonese, the word *loh* in the former is sounded *lok* in the latter; and *yu sha tsze* in the former is *yau sha tsoi* in the latter, which is not as great a difference perhaps as " fo yee ol " of the Kentuckian and " four year old " of the Yankee. There is really only one language in all China, though so many speak the provincial dialects that they have gained an unwarranted reputation as separate languages. These dialects, difficult both to the foreigner and the Chinese from a remote part, have grown up from the isolation of the provinces, as a germ center propagates when not disturbed. It is not because there has not been sufficient pride in the letter, for the Thibet monasteries outdo the performance of the Hotel Rambouillet in a fine frenzy for glossification and formula. Railways will have most to do with the scattering of the dialects and will give the Chinese that unification of speech and resultant dissemination of idea, which have been the main things (and not the lack of Christianity or inventions) that have kept them from moving forward as a very assertive body in the world's polity.

The character or picture system is inadequate for law

or commercial writing, though it floods the mind in their poetry with beautiful suggestions and with instant effect, as compared with the considerable time before the eye can glance along a Latinized sentence, for instance. Into the spoken or provincial dialects, especially in the south (and Cantonese seems to be of greatest antiquity with its soft musical sounds and flowing diphthongs as compared with the gutturals of the Kansu dialect of the North) have crept many phoneticized English words, and English is likewise enriching herself with words formed phonetically from the Chinese character. Historically, the Chinese language, with all its boasted conservatism, has already authority for this intrusion and enrichment, for there are traces of Sanscrit words which were introduced by the Buddhists. A neglected piece of Sanscrit advice however in fever-stricken China is the following: " Keep water in copper, and expose it to the sun, dip in it seven times a bar of hot copper, and filter through charcoal." On July 9th, last, at the parade of the new Chinese Volunteer Corps along the Maloo at Shanghai, it was remarked that Colonel Yu Ya Ching invariably gave the word of command in English. It is to be noticed that the Chinese are more anxious to learn English than we are to learn Chinese. In my experience in Hong-Kong we had a constant procession from the two Kwang Provinces of punkah coolies, 'rickisha pullers, office boys, and comprador's clerks, none staying longer than six months. They were really students of English. When they learned something of the language while being paid the usual laborer's wage of five dollars a month, they resigned suddenly to blossom out at twenty dollars a month, as consul's interpreters, clerks to ship's pursers, and in their own Imperial Customs or importing Hongs. This

interest in the languages was not mutual. In twenty
years history of this Hong, with probably an aggregate of
three hundred staff employees, only one English speaking
clerk acquired Chinese, and it was Portuguese blood in
his veins which stimulated the linguistic interest. The
Chinese are determined to gain more from us than we are
from them. The telegraph blanks in use over China's
thirty thousand miles of wire are printed in English and
Chinese, and have been excellent primers throughout the
land in disseminating an interest in that one type of foreigner, the credit for which is due to the ablest business
man who ever came to China, the indefatigable Irishman,
Robert Hart, the head official, until his retirement recently, of the Imperial Customs.

The dialect, or *hang-tan,* as in every country, is a tone
play on the written word, differing according to locality,
and the tone differences are most minutely drawn. They
are not insurmountable however, as is the belief abroad
concerning them and can be illustrated by the pronouncia-
tion of the name of the town in the Sunglo Hills of Nganwei Province where the best ink is made. In the local
dialect it is Wei-Chow; in Cantonese, Fy-Chow. The
town on the Chang River which distributes porcelain, in
the local Kiang-si dialect is called Kau-Chow; in Cantonese it is Jau-Chow. In the same manner, tea is called
ta at Nanking, and *tai* at Canton. The word for a village headman in Nganwei Province is pronounced *taipoa;*
in Kwangtung Province it is *taipan;* in Singapore it is
towkay. The word for a tael called *liang* at Shanghai is
pronounced *lan* in Kansu Province, while the word for the
ten cash copper piece called *fun* at Hong-Kong, is pronounced *tun* at Tientsin. The word *mapoo* (jockey) at
Seoul is pronounced *mafoo* at Hong-Kong, and *mahong*

at Yunnan. The name of the capital of the oldest province of China, is pronounced by the Shensians themselves
Chian, but a Kwangtung man would call it *Tsian.*
The whisky distilled from rice, which in northern Shensi
is pronounced *somshaw,* is called *samshui* in most southern Kwangtung; *som-jee-o* in Pechili Province and *chom
chum* on the boarders of Yunnan and Tonquin. A foreigner, or literally a " foreign devil," is pronounced *Hung
Kwei* at Peking; *Yang Kwei* in Kansu Province and *Fung
Kwei* at Canton, which invented the term. A head
helper, in charge of a gang, store or pack train, is called
futau in Yunnan Province and *fokai* in Kwangtung Province. *Pai,* which means " white " at Peking, is pronounced *Pek* at Amoy. The Goddess of Mercy called
Kun Yam at Canton is pronounced *Kuan Yin* at Tientsin. *Taotai* which means city governor at Hong-Kong
is pronounced *Tu-ti* at Peking. In Mongolia the late
Emperor's name is pronounced *Kang Si,* while at Peking
it is *Kwong Su.* The Mongol word for wood is *mo-don;*
in Chinese *mu-ton.* *Hung,* which means " red " at Peking is pronounced *hong* by the brilliant and independent
aborigines of Yunnan Province. The great iron Province is called *Hupei* by the Pekingese and *Hupeh* by the
provincials themselves. The poet who wrote the Chinese
Raven ode, which suggested Poe's theme, is called *Ki Yi*
at Canton and *Chi Yi* at Peking. The word for river,
pronounced *kiang* in the Yangtze Provinces is called
giang in Yunnan. The monumental arches erected to
widows who did not remarry, are called *pailou* at Peking
and *pailo* at Canton. The numeral " one " is called *ya*
at Canton and *ta* at Peking. *Jen,* which means " men "
throughout China proper, is pronounced *ren* among the
aborigines of sequestered Hainan Island. The Korean

Copper Mine " Kapsan " is called by the kindred Japanese
" Kosan." The Chinese retort that the Occidental is not
free of suspicion of opaqueness of expression both in the
written and spoken word. A Chinese student in France
pointed out a hospital which bore the name " Hotel Dieu
du Precieux Sang " and asked " Who the blood was precious to," and a student in English added his experience
by inquiring when it would be " right to write to Wright."
and when " March fourth " is a date or a command. To
show that Pidgin-English has no etymological relationship it is only necessary to give an illustration. *Kwai* in
pure Chinese is " quick "; in Pidgin it is " fightee."

A gentleman is marked by his aspirates and tones.
How important these are, can be judged by the greatest
Chinese dictionary issued in 1711, the *Pei Wan Yun Fu*,
one hundred and thirty volumes, which arranges the
words by their pronunciation, and which monument of
its language China owes to the efforts of her literary Emperor, Kang He. A curse and a compliment are differen-
tiated only by the hiss of the lips. *Koot* means good;
shoot means evil. The same word pronounced in
the Doh tone has a vastly different meaning when the Soh
or Me tone is used. *Ta, Erh, San,* are one, two,
three in Pekingese in Soh tone, but you would not
want to be responsible for them in Doh tone. The
character the Roman Catholic missionaries use for God
is " Tien Chu "; if you are not careful to give it the
proper lisp, you will say the " Heavenly Pig." When
you squeal *yu* in a shrill voice you say " fish "; when
you rumble the same word in a base tone you say " rain."
If you say *chi* sharply it means " gas," but if you say
chih with a hiss, it means " red." The same word
in Doh tone means " man " and in Soh tone a " disease."

The reason a Chinese school-room is as noisy as a boiler shop, is that the requirements of the exact tone compel the pupils to study their lessons aloud for their own satisfaction.   Because of the many inflections of tone necessary the speech of a highly cultivated Chinese statesman sounds not unlike a soft song.   It is these finely drawn distinctions of speech which have robbed China of orators and thus kept the people separated.   To speak correctly requires a low tone and plenty of time, ill suited to the storm and strenuousness of the rostrum of American life for instance.   Like the Roman, Chinese abounds in impersonal forms of address, and with historic unconcern winds its cumbrous course along.   Not in these garbs could a Pepys pirouette.   The Chinese involved character or ideogram, which is a built-up tree, every branch adding a condition to the parent character is too cumbersome for business, and some advocates of the new learning are calling even for the phoneticizing into Roman character, of the Wenli.   For purposes of telegraphy the thousands of Wenli ideograph characters have each a number, which latter is transmitted, and the receiver looks up the code to transcribe the message.   There are five thousand distinct characters, and four times as many amended synonyms.

Similar to our abbreviated writing in account books, the Chinese shroffs have invented a careless style called *tsao tsz* or plant writing, which is their nearest approach to a running shorthand.   The characters are certainly arbitrary enough for any system of grammalogues. The difference between the rapid commercial and the more florid styles in writing the character can be at once seen in the word " son."   The commercial style leaves off certain lines and slurs other lines: commercial 丨羊 ; florid ,慎

The *Hing Shu,* or flowing hand, answers to our unabbreviated Spencerian, and is the pride of their decorative scroll work. Books and newspapers are printed in the orthodox *Kiai Shu* form of character. The ancient characters also find themselves too indefinite for expressing the abstruse. The same character acts as noun, verb, or preposition, according to its place in the sentence. The indefiniteness of the present system may be illustrated by the character for a tree, which is a veritable picture of a banyan with two hanging branches dropping to take root. The character representing forest is two of these tree characters run together. The character of three peaks, *shan,* 丩 of course is their word for mountain. One bamboo commercial tally cast down ⌣ represents the figure " one," and three of them parallel represent " three " 彐. As their system is decimal, two tallies crossed mark the first halt ⼲ or ten. The ten cash coin, with this cross of the Christians upon it, was accordingly despised and shown contumely by the Boxers in 1900. Earth is represented as stretching out flat beneath a standing man ⼟. Water is illustrated by sprays arising from an aperture, ⼨. The character ⌒ is the representation of a Chinese gable with heavy eaves and ridge tile. Therefore it stands for the roof of a yamen or academy near a pagoda, where the schools are held. The character 乎 is the picture of a child with arms outstretched and wearing the large grass sun-hat made in Hupeh. Putting the two characters together thus 字 therefore represents the familiar scene of a boy sheltered under the academic roof, studying the classics, and in the language has become the arbitrary for the word " literature." The word *san* (scatter) is the exact picture of a helmeted soldier chasing a fugitive who has thrown away his hat, thus 新瓦. The character for heaven, Tien, represents two roofs, one of the stars and one of the sky, supported by two props or trees 天 . The character for rice (*mi*) represents a man with his arms outstretched, standing in a field on which scattered grain lies, thus 米 . The character for God (Shang Ti) represents a kneeling mortal in the act of making an offering before a Being who hovers over the two roofs of sky and stars, which latter is supported with the trunk and branches of a banyan, thus 上帝. The character 女 is woman; place her under her roof tree, and the arbitrary represents domestic felicity, or the word " satisfaction," 安 .

The Chinese language accordingly can be dissected into roots just as ours can. Punctuation is considered inelegant, but I have seen shroffs in Hong-Kong venture upon the paragraph. The new characters which China calls for, must come. When they do, the old characters, which are the most elaborate and beautiful that language ever designed for its abode, must pass to the select possession of priests and literati. It should certainly always be taught in the universities and monasteries, just as our classic the Greek is preserved from extinction, and it always has a great mission of culture in interpreting those proud riches of China, the works of her unrivaled philosophers. There are on the other hand, moderns in other respects, who declare that the Chinese character will take upon itself both definiteness and elasticity, and be able to grow as lustily as has the Saxon language, which, with its borrowed Roman characters, has fed on every speech, dead and living. While the Wenli character means the same thing all over China, and while the cultured Japanese can read any Chinese book, the Japanese use the character so

differently that the Chinese can not read a Japanese book
or paper. The Japanese have long lapsed from the artistic
freedom of stroke in painting the character, which with
them is a stiffer and more squat ideogram.

As soon as a Chinese boy enters the school-room he
bows in reverence before the tablet that bears the name
of Confucius. Decoratively, tablets in that land take
the place of busts and statuary among ourselves. In the
memorial tablet is said to dwell one of the three souls of
a man, the other two with his death going, one to heaven
(Tien), and the other remaining in the grave with the
sacred body.

The Uigur writing of the Manchus is decidedly grace-
ful in occidental taste. It has only been preserved to
translate Chinese books, as the Manchus have lost any
literature which they once may have had. The constricted literary radius of the Manchu can be compre-
hended at a glance when we say that 'the total library of
these translations amounts to only three hundred books.
There are eighteen consonants and eight vowels. The
alphabet is syllabic in distinction to the monosyllabic
Chinese. As a spoken language, Manchu is retreating
to the fastnesses of Manchuria, and the intruding Japanese purposes to put a quietus upon it there. The decadence of the Manchu in this respect exhibits the
interesting fact that this is the only time in history where
a conqueror has not flourished a sword in one hand and
a pen in the other. This conqueror put both hands to
his two-edged sword and, perforce, in language was conquered by the vanquished in arms. As compared with
the Chinese the Manchu is the more forcible but less
elegant language.

The kindred Mongolian holds its own, especially in the

Oldest pagoda now standing in China. The pentagonal Tien Fung
Tah at Ningpo, 800 A.D. Note the bold gable Che-
Kiang style, of the residence on the right.

Spirited and delicate carving and tile work, Temple of Cho Shing, Canton, South China.

Temple of Five Genii, Canton, South China.

Note spirited treatment of draperies of two Genii on right by Chinese sculptors, who surpass even our St. Gaudens in this respect. Their treatment of the facial expression, not being according to our canons, cannot be criticised.

spoken language which has no dialect, for a Mongol of
Khotan can understand one from Koren. The language
is also alphabetic in distinction to the Chinese arbitrary
character; it abounds in the use of involved adverbial
phrases, wound round and round, like a cocoon's thread,
in the sentence. It is interesting to remember that this
was the writing used by the conqueror, Genghis Khan;
that is to say, it was used by those who wrote for him.
In literature and religion, the Mongols are more closely
allied to the Thibetans than any other of the Chinese
divisions, but the literature, like the Manchu, is mainly
translations of Buddhist books.

Like our own shorthand system, the vowels of the
Mongol writing, with two exceptions, must be guessed.
Thus, the letters N. R. may represent the words pronounced *nara* (sun), or *nere* (name). Curiously, some
Mongol sentences are our exact words, as "*eat I*"
is their expression for "I eat." The Mongolian has no
right and left hand, but rather a "west" and "east"
hand. There is one sacred spot on the Selenga River on
the borders of Siberia and Mongolia where two missionaries of the London Mission, Stallybrass and Swan, lived
in what was then a terrible exile from 1818 to 1841, and
translated our whole Bible into Mongolian characters,
and when the battlefields of Genghis, Kuropatkin and
Kuroki are forgotten, the place where these two men
worked will still be drawing the admiring feet of the
world to see a Mongolia redeemed.

There is a censorship in China, the government im-
primatur being two dragons encircling the name of the
book. One of the new great *Pus* (Boards) is named
' Colonies and Censorship." The government is finding
that the growing press is assertive in the progress of

China. For example, where four years ago Tientsin published four native papers or *Paos*, there are now twenty-three sheets, and this is an illustration of what is going on beyond the treaty ports. Hong-Kong's splendid Chinese sheet is the *Wah Tsz Po*. Even in Lhassa a paper has been started by the head Chinese resident, Tschang Ying. I asked my Chinese humorist if he expected that the morals of his country would be improved when newspapers shall have illumed the whole land, and he replied: " This far at least, we shall be harder to fool." China's organization fulfils many of the historic requirements of modern political power. Over manners, laws and religion, she long ago established a centralized authority. It remains, if her civilization is to be permanent, that a free press shall arise and try by public opinion the strength of every prop of the State, rather than to permit an enemy to do so by arms. The *King Pao*, or Peking *Gazette,* the official organ, has long generously thrown open to foreigners intimate information concerning the government of the realm. You will find copies of the monthly issues, bound in yellow, lying about any taotai's yamen. The censorship covers the remarkable privilege of intimately censuring the Emperor on his expenditures. In times of famine this board has used its influence for the people, inducing the throne to curtail park extensions and expenditures for luxury and ceremony.

The Chinese call what answers to our Elzevir and pocket editions, a " sleeve edition," the sleeve in that country serving for both pocket and basket. The students at the triennial examinations are searched so that they may not carry in these sleeve editions or cribs. There is no copyright protection for authors. At present one person in one hundred is reached by their press. Opinion is not vitalized for quick and concerted action until the proportion is one in ten, as in Europe. America, of course, leads with a proportion of one in four.

Where we place on the street corners boxes bearing the sign: " Throw your papers in here for the Hospital," the Chinese have similar receptacles with the words " *King Sik Tsze Chi*," " Reverence the Written Word, for it is Holy." Their religion teaches that words never die, and prescribes as an offering to the informing Spirit of Light, the burning of the printed Truth, which, after all, is only loaned to mortals, and should be constantly clarified after it has gathered the soil and dross of the earth. It is considered a pious work, even at the Europeanized treaty ports, for natives to gather every scrap of newspaper and take it to the monastery to be consigned to the alembic of the sacred flames. It is quite possible that this bull was promulgated by the astute priests of Hwang Te's reign, in the third century, B. C., in order to bring all books to the monastery for hiding, when that most hated of Chinese monarchs had his prime minister, Le Sze, issue with a will the infamous " Edict for the Burning of the Books," the insane design being to date history from the Tsin dynasty.

Chinese literature is a mine of rare jewels. An address to a Manchu prince is embroidered in blue and red characters on a banner of yellow silk. Attributes of the Diety are accorded him: " Your Majesty's quickening influence! in thy hands are the jeweled greetings from a king's palace; on this happy day of the second month the wheels of your princely chariot are stayed; you come as a glorious cloud and as a downpour of timely rain; your banners descend from Heaven and the longings of your people are fulfilled. As your escort enters the walls, lo! at every door the shouts of the children arise. Oh, King's Son, your coming swells the rice and fattens the meat." All this exalted conception and flowery expression is turned to ridicule by the facetiousness of the closing paragraph: "Dated on a *lucky* day of the second month."

Another petition begins: "For the jewel glance of a mandarin." You can get some of these interesting pamphlets among the book-shops on Liu Li Chang Street, Peking.

When a Chinese writer wishes to express that the wealthy parent of the heroine has set his affairs in order before dying in her favor, his idiom is: "He has settled his plums." "To have plucked the *kwei* (cassia) flower," signifies gaining the Master's degree at the triennial examinations. Their idiom for "Let there be no backsliding" is: "Let there be no absorption of sweat." A runaway wife is said by Liu Chia Chu to "carry her guitar to another door." When you wish to say you have secured a vindication you express it: "My adversary has been forced to paint my front door." When a great man dies they say: "A corner of the city wall has fallen." When a coolie wishes to express his utter detestation of the slow movements of another, he hurls out the following: "Thou egg of a turtle, dost thou dare to race with a leopard." They do not speak of the port or starboard sides of a boat, but of the north, south, east or west sides, so that in all admiralty cases, the essential thing is to ascertain the course which was laid.

On friendship they have this parable. Shun, once wealthy and famous, lost land and health, whereupon every single friend since his boyhood turned upon him in calumny and cruelty, like vultures eager to hurry death. Is therefore mankind incapable of honor, and might a brave man better have a wallowing sow for a friend? No, Shun was a blind fool in his prosperity and youth; his friends were always vultures in disguise, and their presence kept from him those who would have been real friends in admiration of his mind and character. Know that there are those who, when hungry, crawl, and when fed, take to their wings, and remember, also, that when the tree falls, the monkeys flee. A wealthy man, and indeed a man of any estate, never can know friendship, and should justly doubt the depth of every acquaintance. Friendship is alone founded in adversity, for poverty is the test of disinterestedness, as the lamp is the proof of the ruby. When Tien (God) gives thee poverty, He too will give thee a true friend, and if thou wouldst have a friend, famous or rich man, thou must invite or simulate poverty, sorrow and pain in the finding of him. Piteous is that land where there is not the compulsory charities of the clan, for the law is better than the heart of man. Did not Confucius say in the *Lun Yu,* " Have no friend unlike your heart of hearts."

Regarding the virtuous, Confucians poetically say: " Devils once attacked a good man, but the tips of their spears turned into flowers."

The following is a parable of the folly of a policy of injustice. A water-buffalo looked upon an ant and despised it; blew upon it; grunted at it; vilified its ancestors and tablets, boasted to other buffaloes of his hate, and in supreme insolence, made it the center of his manure heap. The buffalo laid down to sleep (as helpless, you will note, as the ant in his needs) in venomous satisfaction of having extinguished the very memory of self-respect in the soul of the ant. Fortified with the poison of the buffalo's own manure, the ant crawled forth and stung the buffalo in one eye, and on the blind side of the ridiculous brute, for ever evades and torments his impotent fury, to the glory of the gods and the vindication of the truth.

A cynic was asked: " How is it that every youth is a hero and flaunts a bribe, and every elder a villain who can be bribed, first with not less than a thousand taels, and afterward with a *tiao string*. Your venal elders are your former heroes. Pale Huan, the youth, finds that his honorability has been his downfall. His self-respecting poverty throughout his youth invited the persecution of those envious of his shining independence of character. He decides at last, as earth's responsibilities grow on him, to suffer no more and to commit no more the compulsory petty sins of poverty in order to live. He thereupon commits the one great sin of the rich and takes Shan's bribe. Oppressed before, as conscience dies, he soon oppressor grows, all through the law of self-preservation, which, in the end, banishes true religion in a wicked world." Again: " There are some so bad that their sins pickle and confirm them in evil instead of rotting them."

Another cynic remarks, " Some people cry over graves only to make the grass of forgetfulness grow the quicker." And again, " There is no one who will not smile to the tickle of a bribe, and do not conclude that it requires long feathers to do the tickling; mankind holds itself very cheap."

A bonze asks, " Of what avail to scold a brother like brass, and pray to Buddh like silver? "

Epigrams are attributed to busy nations, but they happen also to be the favorite form of crystallizing the wisdom of the race which enjoys the most leisure. "Tact," say they, "is the discounting of principle in the mart of expediency." "Success is the greatest good to the smallest number." "When does a statesman descend to be a political trimmer?" "When he takes his flag from the poor, but his wheels from the rich." "The farmer tills the paddy field, but the mandarin tills the people." The maxims of Confucius are terse epigrams. How much this sage has influenced the morals of Europe has not been fully considered. The authorship has not been credited, but many a sermon and essay have drawn their inspiring fire or human pathos from the "Five Classics" of the Orient. The consciousness of inspiration, present in all great teachers, was not unmarked in Confucius. At fifty-five years of age, when driven to the wilds of Wei, he declared: "If it is Heaven's will to reserve me to teach this truth on the earth, the murderous persecutions of these evil men of Kwang will do nothing to me." Wonderful that on the same day, Ezra, the prophet of the true God, who had journeyed from Babylon, stood amid the ruins of Jerusalem and cried also of the Great Help: "Our God hath not forsaken us in our bondage, but hath given us a wall in Judah." A king (Wu Wang), when asked to substantiate his confidence of victory against an enemy numbering ten thousand, replied: "Because they have ten thousand hearts, whereas my army has but one heart."

The most eminent of the Chinese characteristics is displayed in the following conversation. "Shun was very great in his boldness to cut the knot," said a soldier. "Shao was great in his patience to untie the knot," said a bonze. "Therefore Shao was the greater in genius," added a philosopher.

A Chinese satirist rails at those who write lady-like lyrics with a pot of perfume on the table, and at those who spend time in perfecting the splendid sweep of the picturesque *Hing Shu* characters which are painted on large motto sheets. He retires to his Epicurean confession, "The enjoyment of ease is my chief concern; I have lived for Myself."

Another indolent poet, who happens to earn the larger portion of his bread by occupying a menial position in a mandarin's household, exclaims: "I would hie from office cares; by the brooklet I would lie, catch the finny tribes with snares, read my books and dream and think, past to present I would link."

The proverb of the laziest man in China is: "It is easier to know how to do a thing than to do it." A matter-of-fact man, a forerunner of the new Hok Tong scholars, said, "To see it once is better than to read about it a thousand times."

Regarding jealousy they say: "It is easy for two of a guild to hate," and "Nine women out of ten are jealous." "Don't bend the mulberry when it is old," corresponds to our saw not to teach an old dog new tricks. On games of chance "The winning tip is to stay away from the gaming-table." For our *in vino veritas,* they have "*samschu* is the arch-thief of secrets, its bubble is a woman's smile." A cynic rails: "Put not our Holy Books in the hands of a man until he has made his competence, for conscience keeps men poor and the poverty of the virtuous is the opportunity of the unjust oppressor." When a girl has lost her affianced their idiom is: "She has spilt her tea." "To have no

ink in one's stomach" is their expression for lack of
literary ability.   On deceit: "The lips of Buddh, but the
teeth of a snake."   Equivalent to the Greek *hoi polloi*
and our "the masses" is their expression, "the myriad
names," which shows that China has always been con-
scious of her vast population.   A cynic, but withal a
virtuous man, declares "There are only two true things,
God in Heaven and an honest dollar on earth," and of a
gossiping wife, "If a chattering bird be not placed in
the mouth, vexation will not sit between the eyebrows."
A Buddhist cynic answers a Taoist: "The final proof
that men are not gods is that a poor man, suddenly raised
to a position of wealth, immediately becomes as oppressive of the poor as the rich class which previously he
criticized; therefore the arm of evil is gold, but the seed
of it is in man's heart."   Both as a metaphor and as a
moral, the following Mongolian maxim is good enough
for any people: "Cast from thy heart the dog, hog
and serpent, for they are the incarnations of lust, greed
and malice."

On ability, they say: "The world is unsafe when it has
more genius than virtue."   On ambition: "Climb the
pole higher to find how much thinner it is."   On truth:
"If you tell me a lie you must consider me your enemy
and that you are acting under the rule of self-preservation, for the bosom of a true friend is the mirror of one's
self."   On scandal: "A lie is the branch mirrored on
the surface, but beneath how deep the well of true water."
Where we admonish a student to grind or work, they
express themselves: "May you ever perpetuate the fragrance of books in your ancestral home."   Concerning
charity they say, "Benevolence being of the heart, no
rule can be set for its acts," and "You can not call a deed

kind if it is done in the hope of recompense." On exaggeration, "Paint a snake and add legs." They turn the flame of scorn on the soldiers of the old régime: "Your valor is at a chicken's neck." On appearances: "Antics are not always vivacity as the fish on the hook can say," and "A rat may smile, but it is not ivory." On the schoolmaster's rod: "The cudgel is the best polisher." On a wife: "Only her husband speaks of a virtuous woman, but the name of an evil woman grates on all men's teeth." One who is not a gentleman they say "lacks the tenth stroke of the lacquer brush." The inability of a man to keep a secret they express in the *Three States Classic* as follows: "If you do not want anybody to know it, do not even do it." On satire: "His was a golden pen that rayed the shafts of truth."

A philosopher says: "The world is about equally divided between good and bad people; in the good is a small proportion of bad; in the bad is a small proportion of good. This balance of virtue and evil is so perfect that it requires the nicest adjustment of the individual to adapt himself to his environment, and yet remain loyal to his class; in fact, our civilization contemplates the direction of the clan more than the man, and we have at least evolved as a national virtue, the humility of the individual." Their most cynical saying is: "The creator is like a cruel sculptor; he fashions man the statue; he tires of it and chips it day by day with persecutions; then petulant, he smashes it at last into dust."

Their idiom for spending an afternoon is to say, "I *ate* an afternoon there."

A poet who was passing, after enjoying the view, called to thank the owner of many acres. "But I have not given them to you." "You have done better; you give me the pleasure of viewing the scenery, without my being under the burden of paying the taxes on it. As you pay the taxes for my view, I must thank you."

A certain Jesuitical doctrine regarding the end justifying the means, a Chinese philosopher refutes as follows: "If Chang steals Wong's fortune and uses it all in charity, what credit is to Chang? None. The credit will be laid to Wong by the god of Restoration, and Chang must answer for sacrilege to the god of Opportunity." And again, "If Kwok commits but one sin by killing Li's child in envy, but performs ten thousand charities with his wealth, is there any tally for Kwok? None. He answers to two gods; he tries to deceive the god of Vengeance with the property of the god of Benefactions." The Chinese throughout their literature and conversation take the keenest interest in the morals of wealth, and thus predate the twentieth century in America. In their action with the rich in times of famine, they have put in practice the principle of our suggested income and prevailing death taxes, the confiscatory principle being operative above a certain figure. Wealth over a certain number of millions is confiscated for three purposes, the relief of the poor in famine, the extension of education and the larger national exigencies such as dikes and afforestation. The ground taken is that the law must have been evaded, as no individual could honestly secure a fortune which overtopped the State itself. The government on its own part steps into the breach, and for this it has not received due credit, by remitting to the people in times of stress, and emigration to new districts, the land taxes for one or two years.

Examples of Chinese proverbs are: "Opportunities come in cycles, like meteors. "Between the mulberries, plant beans, for two things can not fail." "The mouth of a dumb man and the look of a fool, make a ruler, for the first outwits his inferiors and the latter his superiors." "A child's slap on a plow-buffalo's ear, and a hint to a wise man, are sufficient." "Shave Chang every day, but skin his buffalo once." "Those who chase kites, fall over straws." The Kan Ying Pien homily says: "Happiness and trouble stand at every one's gate; yours is the choice which you will invite in."

The very constitution of the Chinese written character has guided them to think and express themselves poetically. The people along the Yangtze call their great river "The Son of the Sea" because the tides flow upon it. A vast number of people in the eastern section never call their land anything else than *Sze Hai,* "The country of the four seas." Korea is called *Chaosien,* the "Dewy morning land." Shanghai interpreted is "Nearing the sea," and Hong-Kong is "Fragrant streams," because of the damp earth and vegetable odors brought out by the equatorial storms which suddenly leap with wild white manes from the hills in August. Lhasa is "God's Ground." Canton is "The broad city," and Ningpo, within sight of the great bore of Hang-chow Bay, means "Beautiful wave city." China also has her golden gate port, for Quemoy Island at the entrance to Amoy literally is "Golden Harbor." The names of the provinces are similarly poetic: Shan-tung is "East of the hills"; Fu-kien means "Happily established"; Shansi, "West of the hills." Shensi, "Western defiles." Hupeh, "North of the lakes." Szechuen, "Four streams." The oldest known to us, Kwangtung, means the "Broad east." Yunnan is "South of the cloudy mountains" of Thibet. Kansu, where the conquered Mohammedans dwell among the sesamum oil trees, is satirically named " Voluntary reverence."

The names of popular brands of tea are bestowed with literary taste: " Autumn Dew," " Pearl Flower," " Lotus Heart," etc. Even a potato is an " earth egg." The almonds of Shensi Province are an abundant source of food, and it is beautifully suggestive to see the many restaurants all over the land with signs out bearing the legend, " The Almond Flower." Where we would say " May you flourish like the green bay tree," the Chinese idiom is " May you be as full as a peony," for that flower represents wealth in their figure of speech.

The *ming* or given name of girls is often taken from flowers, as " Jasmine " Chung; " Orchis " Choy, etc., and boys have names such as " Moon-shining " Cheng; " Olive Bud " Fong; " Temple Steps " Shun; or " Pagoda of Letters " Yung. Sometimes the family or *sing* names are also taken from nature, as Yuen Chuen, " Sweet Spring." A late ambassador to America who was educated at Yale, would perforce be called in our produce exchange, if his name were translated, " Mr. Millet," and the most progressive viceroy, Yuan Shi K'ai is literally " Mr. Duck."

Where our statesmen refer to the olive branch of peace, they phrase it " may the bamboo wave." The Chinese line of beauty is set forth as follows: " Yang's lids and eyebrow were twin willow leaves above a pearly pool." Where we wish a happy pair the conjugal felicity of two mated doves, they make it " two geese," and at the marriage ceremony the bride kowtows to a pair of the latter. Where we wish age the honors of " cedars of Lebanon," they say " May you be as wide as a chrys-anthemum border," for that flower is their emblem of

longevity. They call age a "candle in a draft." They
could not wish a child to be as pure as a lily, for that
flower is their emblem of death. Their flower of virtue
is the plum blossom. Where we say "as quick as a
shot or a bird," their figure is "with the speed of flames."
Love they call the "oil of the lamp of life."

The Emperor's palace is called "The Palace of
Heaven," and the Empress', "The Palace of Earth's Re-
pose." Although China invented the compass which
points to the South Pole, there is a temple at Peking
dedicated to the "God of the North Star." Not to be
behind the humor of Occidentals who build cathedrals
over the bones of a saint, Peking has erected an obelisk
over a piece of Buddha's skin.

Delightful to a strenuously tired Occidental, Peace is
for ever in their mouths. "The Gate of Heavenly
Rest;" "The Temple of the Eternal Peace of the
Lamas;" "The Gate of Extensive Peace;" "The Hall
of Secure Peace," are all at Peking.

The *Shi King,* a book of three hundred odes, is laden
with lyrics as dainty as are Campion's. "The new wife
is a peach bud. The aged pair entwined wistarias are.
Peace is a bamboo spear in flower. The great man's
soul cried out for God and swept his body like a husk
away. 'The moth-like eyebrows of my moonlight girl'
suggests the universal use of powder by decent women
in China. Fei's step is as light as the lotus on water.
As typhoons sweep the bamboo's sprays, so Death blows
up old Age's sleeve. The white owl hoots of death upon
the stricken poet's sill. Slow as a nut-oil wick her life
departs. His concubine the cold jade-jewel; his first
wife was a true peach flower. Years fly like arrows, one
eager to pass the other to the mark. A forgiving answer

is vernal from the mouth." All of them twine nature so as to adorn some human interest, and the human motive is not read into nature in the affected occidental fashion of our day.

China had its Chatterton in the poet Tu Fu, who starved to death on a temple's steps; its Edgar Allan Poe in Kia Yi, who wrote centuries ago *A White Owl Ode* with the exact plot of *The Raven;* and its Hood in Han Yu, who warns the farmer's son who became a mandarin: " Ne'er forget the chastening ditch that found thee poor and left thee rich." A counterpart of Leigh Hunt is Su Tung Po, who languished in prison for his satires and whose imaginative flights are little short of Miltonic. His poetry best bears translation into English without losing as much of the boquet of the original as other poets suffer in the transition. Li Po was their Ovid in the praise of wine and women; Chuang Tze their Shelley in imaginative flights.

Szma Tsien, who wrote his great history B. C. 100, compares with our Herodotus, and Li Pai with our Horace. Outside of the realm of pure literature, the fifty volumes of Li Shi Chin published in 1590 are at once a Materia Medica and an Audubon. Chinese naturalists describe with surprising exactness the habits of animals, fish and insects. As an illustration of official knowledge on these subjects, note this extract from a late proclamation of the viceroy of the two Kwang Provinces concerning the extirpation of grasshoppers: " During this month great flights have appeared in our adjoining province. At this time our second crop of rice is in the blade. The insects first are seen on the borders of large morasses. They produce their young in hillocks of black earth an inch deep, the hole remaining open. The nests are in colonies. One grasshopper drops ten pellets, each containing one hundred young. At early dawn they can not fly easily from the tender rice as the dew is on their wings. Catch them at the nest and in the morning. At evening when fed they resort to one spot. There dig a trench with wings and fill it with fire, throwing flaming brush over them as they crawl in heaps toward the pit."

That their criticism can be patriotic and sturdy, the following will illustrate. Under the temple bells and the bamboos that whispered of Chinese sages who studied beneath them when Europe and America were fastnesses for the auk and the reindeer, and our warriors wore wolf masks over their heads, a bonze thus accumulated his criticism of us. "The Anglo Saxons and the West deride us. Why? You were great only once and that time is not now. You will never produce a Bible or a Shakespeare again, for used to luxuries as you are now, you will for ever despise the simple poverty that produced the poetry of Elizabeth's time and the manly virtues which evolved the philosophy of Plato's and Paul's day. The asceticism and unselfishness of your Bible gave you sturdy virtues, but now that you have machinery you are looking unto wealth for greatness, forgetting the odium of your despised Crœsus and that your philosophic (so-called religious) literature alone has brought you strong unto the present. You must fall. You ask us to impoverish our thought and our character by a universal debauch of pampering and really ignorant riches. Our State is not reared over a burning mine, for where no individual fortune exceeds half a million (since Li Hung Chang passed) there is no cause for rebellious envy on the part of the unhappy many against the privileged few, and little opportunity for that grinding oppression which breeds undying hate because prominence and selfishness are synonomous.

"Every garment frays first at the hem and every branch dies first at the tip; so your furthest colonization in America shows the first signs of the protest, the denial of justice by the privileged, and the decay of confidence, but the root in England will die too. How inconsistent you are; your society despises the emigrants now reaching you, but you clamor that you are descendants from still poorer emigrants. Anchored to the soil as we are, we will never swing in history, as you will, between the extremes of a tyrannous oligarchy and an unstable, socialistic proletariat. We shall always surpass you in the judgment of universal history and the immemorial God (Tien), and in the production of our Shakespeares and Platos, for our State is founded on an honest poverty which has time to think and courage to be virtuous. We have never enslaved manhood within the State as have your Roman and Saxon, or enthralled alien dependencies to our chariot of pride, as do your Briton in India and your American in the Philippines. When you have retrograded to an opulent barbarism sufficiently savage to attack us, we shall destroy you in the resort to arms, not so much by our strength as from your weakness and the lack of patriotism among your classes. The test will then be whether privilege, or land, makes men.

"There have been peoples as ostentatious as you before, Babylon for instance, and in public monuments the Pyramids are as stupendous as what Pittsburgh makes; yet they stand for a dead race; not so our Great Wall, which stands with a live race. Again I repeat, you are not doing anything new, and you were greatest as intellec-

tual men in Shakespeare's day, and as moral men in
Paul's day. The intellectual decline has been gradual;
next came Milton, and then you dwindled down to Dick-
ens, Longfellow and Carlyle, till now, how thin is your
veneer of letters. Morally, how dead and sad the review.
You are the only race who, powerful enough to retain it,
has given over your religious shrine, Palestine, to an un-
believer, and yet five hundred million of you attribute all
your civilization to the Bible of that land. This astounding sacrilege has eternally amazed us, and we can see no
reverence, love or depth in you. We glory in teaching
Confucius in all schools and in preserving his shrine.
You throw your greatest book out of your national
schools. You were harder to civilize than any race, a
bloody tearing down preceding every building up, as
under Cromwell and in Russia to-day. For every little
law, you have sent your people to their swords to win
it.

"Your whole system is one of objection to improvement and temperamentally you could not accept as a
race a peaceful endowment of civilization such as Confucius bestowed upon us. All your Emperors dress as
generals of war; ours alone as a philosopher of peace.
When we would translate your word Liberty, we perforce
are driven to the character Rebellion, for so you have
won it. We have never flung derision at the constitution
as have your races when the bravoes of Milo and Clodius,
of doges and dukes, made private altercation a substitute
for public pleading. Where each citizen already rules
himself with *Shun* (morality) the State is already clothed
in Liberty. In the adaptation of ourselves to the inven-
tive age you will see that we shall reach the higher planes
without bloody disorganization, as we are a race with

City wall, Ching-tu, capital of Sze-chuen, furthest West province.
The lower part is the oldest city wall in China, contemporary
with the Great Wall. Watchman on water gate. Physician gathering simples. In early times Sze-chuen
was famous for its engineers.

Looking from the Imperial Bank of China toward the British and American quarters, Shanghai, East Central China.

Gondola, and marble revetment walls of lake in Royal Palace Grounds, Peking, North China.

conscience and faith enough to follow what Time, the only test (and test us by it) has proved to be right. Look to yourselves!"

The performance of a theatrical company (Thespians in China are called " Brothers of the Pear Trees ") is extended to the length of a festival.   Great structures of bamboo and mats are erected near the water-front, partly that the lapping waves may be referred to by the gesturing actor in the climax of the play, but particularly in order that the sampan people may have no excuse for staying away.   Historical dramas from their Shakespeare-Jonson-Fletcher collection, the " one hundred plays of the Yuan Dynasty," which take days to perform, are given.   Farces and sketches are interspersed to enliven proceedings.   The titles of the latter are as we might expect: *Ah Bing Selling His Pig; The Congratulations of the Eight Genii; A Visit to the Moon; The Fairy Wife,* etc.   On April 16th, reminiscent of the world's creation, a religious drama is performed, the title being *The Opening of the Peach.*

The two lowest grades of Chinese society, both of whom are debarred from entering the classical examinations, are a keeper of an opium den and an actor.   It can therefore be judged how all China burst into a laugh of derision when there was added in 1906 to the Exempts under the American Exclusion Act, immediately after scholars, who are the highest class, actors, who are diametrically opposed.   Yet priests and actors fraternize sometimes.   At Chowtung in Yunnan, the gorgeous Temple of the Black God has a theatrical stage set up in the court.   This stage displays in perfect proportion the best features of Chinese architecture and is notable.   In the courtyard of the Temple of the God of Riches at Tangyueh, just on the borders of Burmah, a theater is set up, and one can pray or laugh under the patronage of the same bonze. The costumes of the actors are as gorgeous as description can paint, even surpassing the robes of the throne. In passing we might mention that the favorite gown of those who act the part of an empress is of yellow, with a very wide border of purple wistaria. Women do not act. Their parts are taken by men, and the Chinese in whose speech many falsetto tones are in constant use, can dissemble the female perfectly. When applause is expected from the falsetto ladies on the stage, it is given in a chorus of orthodox squeaks. As soon as the curtain is rung up, all the actors troop out and kowtow before the mandarin's box, which sways on its draped bamboos in more apparent than real jeopardy. China has not yet evolved the modern drama, so popular in Japan, where heroes are apotheosized and the doings of gods, mythical warriors and living heroes are woven into a wonder play. When Nogi and Oyama go to the Honchodori Theater the curtain is rung up (or really tom-tommed up) to reveal some slain subaltern of Port Arthur in the act of tearing down a Russian flag, while mythical Kagekio and Terasu present the hero with a sword and a dove.

The Chinese actor is apprenticed for four years and the repertoire of a star consists of about fifty plays. The playwright, just as Shakespeare did, travels with the company as its permanent adapter of the ancient tragedies and traditions, and proving that mankind, whatever the color, has ever been strung to the same chords, he never fails to consign the villain to tortures, the oppressor to accidents sent by the gods, and the hero to recompense, bliss and applause. The Actors' Guild comprises thirty thousand members, and the highest individual earnings are eighteen hundred dollars a year.   As already stated, certain plays are performed in Buddhist temples, the nuns being permitted to dance, but these plays are more popular in the country bordering Siam and Burmah, and if we go over the border to the Wat Chang Temple in Bangkok, we can easily find bold examples of them.

A Chinese city shorn of its street signs would be like a pheasant plucked of its plumage. Rob Heavenly Peace Street, at Canton, or Tung Tan Street, Peking, of their black and gold signs and yellow lanterns, and it would be as though you tore the transforming sunset from the bare loess hills of China. Not only is the beauty of gilt work exhibited, but marvelous creations in alto-rilievo carving are hung out. The signs follow the triple plan of mentioning the name, birthplace and motto. The business is not mentioned, as " Fung Shan, born Sam Shui City,— This is the Abode of Generosity and Light." Sometimes merely the picture of an animal is the sign. The tiger has been adopted by the Clothiers' Guild. With the words " Strength and Courage " added, it is hung out over the tailors' shops which are equipping the new Volunteer Corps. Here is a hasty gleaning of the street names of Canton: " New Green Pea," " Medicine," " Golden Flower," " Plum Lane," and as this is the city which next to jade worships the pearl, we find they have named a street and their river (Chu Kiang) after the latter jewel. A popular name for a city gate is " Entrance of Bright Amiability." The beauty of poetry is not without its humbling fault of humor, a charcoal shop being called: " The adornment of the Eyes," and a pawnshop " Virtuous and Prosperous."

In the rear where the cashier, or shroff, sits behind his

swanpan, the shop is no less gorgeous than the signs.
The front half of the store, where the willow and camphor-wood boxes of merchandise are packed, is paved
with plain red brick tiling or granite blocks, but the rear
portion is divided by a screen of massive and elaborately
carved blackwood, pointed heavily with gold, and overhead is carved a gilded Confucian motto, such as " To
become permanently wealthy, you must exercise the principle of right." The stench of the street is fought back
by burning pieces of sandal and teak woods, and by incense sticks smouldering in the ashes before the ancestral
tablets, for all China, except the *fokis*, lives where it
works. They are only business streets, but the signs
suggest to a stranger the way to a temple, not only by
the religious mottoes, but by the lavish beauty of red,
green and gold lacquer. Chinese signs perforce are
pendant and narrow, for two reasons: because the lettering must be horizontal, and because the streets are so
narrow. There are three characteristic things which we
learn to associate with and love in Chinese cities: first,
the signs, and then the pagodas and lanterns. As the
traveler goes farther north, notably at Liao Yang, it is
noticeable that the signs are not suspended but are elevated upon lacquered posts. The post itself bears the
firm's motto and the arms are given up entirely to decoration. In Kin Chou Fu in Manchuria, the one-storied
khan or inn is marked by a tall lamp post and a long
semaphore arm, from which hangs a string of metal
rings with horse-hair plumes, which flutter out an in-
vitation to the camel drivers from distant Mongolia to
rest a while. Occasionally mine host greets a suspicious
Japanese or a curious Westerner who has the twin habits
of roaming and writing. Rich merchants provide in their

wills for inns, as a public benefaction, and depend upon the monumental gates which front them for their glory.

Other characteristic architectural features are the walls which are built around private residences and compounds; the monumental topes of the dead lamas, and the *pai-loa* arches in honor of widows who would not remarry. The walls are composed of a stucco called *chunam,* generally mauve colored, and a foot from the top is inserted a dainty fretwork of tiling. Set into the stucco at wide intervals are panels of blue and white porcelain. Nothing is crowded in the work of their architects who believe in the beauty of line and the significance of plain masses relieved only a little.

In the middle of the main street at Wuchow stands a noble circular archway which sets the view in a frame. There are two wing arches with smaller circular openings. None of these arches is made to drive through; they must be circumvented. The most pleasing *pai-loa* arch is erected on the shore of the lake in the grounds of the Summer Palace, Peking. In proportions, grace, and just enough of the sumptuous carving, it is altogether a delight to western eyes. As a rule, however, the architecture of arches in the northern provinces, such as Shansi, is Doric in its simplicity, as compared with the more bizarre and ornamented arches of the southern provinces. The most famous arch in China, the most individual arch extant, is that which stands at the entrance to the Ming Tombs near Peking. Five towers crown its five square arches. It is a massive, awesome and triumphant memorial to the great artistic emperors. Napoleon copied Titus' arch; America copied Napoleon's, but the Mings found in themselves the original inspiration for an architectural expression which has never been equalled for balance, power, scope, truth, and singular daring. Standing in the now unpeopled plain over against the mountains of the creator, it seems almost Eternity's monument, magnificent amid the sorrows and desolation of the inhabitants of the earth. See it and be steadied in your taste for ever.

Whatever adverse may be said of Chinese perspective, there are certainly no painters of birds, insects and flowers to equal them. They catch the poise and color to a second. They delight to deceive their larks and short-tailed cats with their canvases. Famous also are the temple scenes of Wu Tao Tsz, which are sought for the royal collections.

For uniqueness, Canton's concentric carved ivory balls can not be overesteemed. How wonderfully the workmen cut one within another! Each one is minutely fashioned into beautiful open tracery so that the partitions left shall show flowers, pagodas, temples and animals. The scalpel which carves the balls is, of course, introduced through the holes of each completed ball.

If anything artistic is found inland, they will tell you it was made at Canton or Nanking, the latter city in addition enjoying a literary fame, and being the center of the book trade. The Chinese have a saying: " You never know what luxury is till you have lived in Canton."

As odd as the native appreciation in medicine of ginseng, for which we have no estimation, is their appreciation of the yuk, or greenish-white jade stone. Nothing can take precedence of it as the chief object of virtu in Chinese taste, in which place it has ruled supreme since the second century, B. C. It is sometimes set as a wheel around a golden hub, and is cut into rings and hair-pins, but generally it is made into a massive seal representing

a monkey or a pear.   The Metropolitan Museum of Art,
New York, has the finest collection in America.   The
stone is softer when first mined than it is after exposure,
when it becomes exceedingly hard.   The polish gives it
a soapy appearance and texture.   The stone is found in
small pieces in river beds in Mongolia, but the chief
source is the mountains of Yunnan, and Yunnan City
and Canton dispute the supremacy for the cutters' shops.
The Yunnan quarries at Tali also supply the cloudy
marble which is carved along the veins of color into fan-
tastic trees, landscapes and animals.

In Kwong Man Shing's and Wing Cheong's jewelry
shops on Queen's Road Central, Hong-Kong, you will
notice that no prices are fixed upon the many gold articles which are worked generally in 20 carat metal.   The
weighing is done before you on a long and short lever
of ebony or ivory, which is notched with minute gradu-
ations.   Jewels are also weighed, as well as examined
before the glass and flame.   The link cuff-buttons, popular with foreigners, always bear the characters *shao* (long
life), and *fuh* (happiness).

Those who have traveled in the Orient will recall the
captain warning them from the rail which has been newly
lacquered while the steamer laid in port.   The varnish
is very poisonous, the gatherers who work at night among
the varnish trees at Ningpo having to protect face and
hands.   The tree is a species of rhus.   The process of
lacquering book covers and objects of virtu is a tedious
one.   It must be performed in a room which is sealed
from wind and dust.   The applications oddly dry best
when it is damp and with a temperature of about eighty-
seven degrees.   Each application of dense black is polished with powdered charcoal and pumice stone.   When

the gold-leaf powder is applied through a sieve which is tied over the end of a bamboo tube, the artist must be sure of his slightest movement, as the gummy surface will not permit the slightest correction. Lighter colors, such as the golden brown and green, are effected by mixing gums of other trees, as well as pig's gall and camellia oil. Gilt flowers are laid between the different layers so that as the lacquer wears, the glorious blossoms rise gradually to the surface, even as a lotus bursts through the dark swamp. This is the idea in the minds of both the artist and the connoisseur. The carving of the thick lacquer paste is a lost art of the Imperial manufactories of the Ming dynasty. The product shone with the brilliancy of a jewel.

Wayside shrines are as numerous as, but far more beautiful than the bizarre specimens that one finds in Mexico or Spain. Sometimes two monoliths with gilt texts artistically applied, support a highly decorated capstone. Sometimes the shrine is a miniature temple of solid blocks, with merely the incense aperture, while others, like the Altar of Heaven in the suburbs of Fuchau, are jewel-like in crimson and gold lacquer, and are equipped with luxurious Nanking porcelain seats and kongs of flowers.

Carved stone lions are the most popular of all statues in a land which has no lions. That in front of the Lama Temple, Peking, is an excellent example, as are also those which decorate the great flight of steps to the temple on Siung Shan Island at Chinkiang. These are all made at Nanking, China's Athens of sculpture.

The vermilion of Canton is a characteristic coloring perfected by a famous secret. The quicksilver which is employed in its preparation at present is largely brought from America, and how the Chinese importers of Des Voeux Road, Hong-Kong, squabble over the elusive globules which have escaped into the hold of the vessel from the long retorts. The basal powder is produced first as a sublimation in contact with sulphur on the sides of the retorts. The Emperor's Great Seal is dipped in vermilion. The native quicksilver mines are far inland in Kweichow, and have been worked since the fourteenth century. The product is transported in pigs' bladders, but poor local transportation has compelled the nation to import for its growing requirements.

VII

MODERN COMMERCE AND BUSINESS IN CHINA

The Shang Pu (Board of Commerce) has pretty well laid out the railway policy. Half of the midland trunk line, north to south, from Peking to Canton, has been completed to Han-kau, a distance of seven hundred and sixty-eight miles, and is known as the Lu-Han Railway. It was built under the direction of Jadot, a Belgian, with a loan of thirty-one millions indirectly from France, and repaid in only ten years. The road is thrown across the shifting Hoang-ho on a notable bridge of one hundred and twenty spans. Han-kau ("mouth" of the Han River as it meets the Yangtze) boasts of a channel six hundred miles to the sea, twenty-three feet deep. It is the emporium of the black tea trade. This city will be the future Pittsburgh of the Orient, as here meet the iron, coal and antimony beds of Hupeh. She has already shipped pig-iron to Brooklyn, N. Y., at a price laid down of seventeen dollars gold a ton, including four dollars and seventy-five cents freight, which speaks portentous volumes for the future. Two things are noticeable at Han-kau: commercial antipathy to the European, and the popularity of the Japanese street hawkers, who have never before come so far inland. Han-kau will grow at Shanghai's expense. The London Homeward Conference (Suez route) has now agreed to charge the same rates from Han-kau as from Shanghai. There is a province-owned steel plant, with an output of one thou-

sand two hundred tons a day, already in operation at
Han-yang (across the river from Han-kau), which is
constantly shipping to Japan and occasionally to Mexico. The ancient method of producing carbon iron,
still followed in opulent Shansi Province, is as follows:
ore and one-quarter of coal dust are mixed in sixty cru-
cibles, eighteen inches by six inches, and with the usual
layers of coal, cinders and clay, are placed in a furnace
which is fired for sixteen hours. Very fine wrought iron
is afterward hammered from the product over a wood
fire.

The railway from Peking to Canton will run almost all
the way over and between beds of iron and coal, the
largest in the world. Every prophecy in this respect of
Richtofen thirty-eight years ago, has been verified, in-
credulous as it seemed at that time. The next largest
area is in Shansi with its fourteen thousand square miles
of anthracite, twenty-two feet thick, and immense bituminous beds besides. Then follows Szechuen with
its fabulous beds which crop out in plain sight even along
the gorges of the Yangtze River. Who would suspect
that China mined twenty million tons of coal last year?
You have hardly left Peking when the old transportation
system appears in strong contrast with the new. At
Paoting Fu, a name of shame because of the murder of
the American missionaries in 1900, shaggy dromedaries
and wheelbarrow trains come down to the railway from
the Shansi mines. The camels are led by a wooden peg
inserted through the nose. They cost fifteen dollars each.
Every driver is a one-time Boxer. At Tsechow, a mountain of anthracite is tilted three thousand feet above the
plain. To reach these deposits a branch would have to be
run thirty miles from the present Peking-Han-kau Rail-

way at a severe gradient. The coal beds on the main line level are flooded with the exfiltration seepage of the Yellow River and pumping is costly. As nearly all the land is a porous loess, drainage, more than grades, is the all-serious problem, and China's cry is for pumps.

A New Yorker, familiar with the small locomotives which used to pull the elevated trains, will be humorously reminded of the old days of jolt and grime, by seeing several of them harnessed on the Canton end of the line to second-class cars, which are merely flat cars with a roof and no sides. The old signal disks which indicated " Sixth " and " Ninth " Avenues are retained on the tops of the cabs, the Chinese engineer explaining with the infinite courtesy of the race: " no wanchee change good luck pidgin." The first derailment occurred at Fatshan when a water-buffalo became patriotic in opposing the effrontery of progress. The delight of the Chinese wrecking crew over the use of the derrick was indescribable. Former Viceroy Chum, burning with zeal for the New China, is advocating the extension of the line from Canton to the deserted deep-water port of Whompoa, ten miles away, and famous for its intercourse with foreigners for three centuries. His plan is a direct challenge of the supremacy of Hong-Kong in the far East. Hong-Kong is hotly alarmed over the possibility of seeing one-third of her vast trade depart. Hong-Kong has the advantage of graving docks but Whompoa will eventually offer cheaper coal from the Pe River and Fa Yuen mines, lower freight rates, and a patriotic sentiment, for this will be their own port for Canton. The first result of the battle has been Shum's removal to another province, and activity in building the Kowloon-Canton Railway with British capital and partly through British territory, but

Shum and those who think like him, are scotched, not exterminated. There is room for both ports in the development of Southern China.

The remaining seven hundred and fifty miles of the Peking-Canton Railway will be financed to an extent by the Hong-Kong government and the Hong-Kong and Shanghai Banking Corporation, with the opium and other revenues of the two Kwang Provinces as security. The road will be partly financed by Chinese underwriters, America having unwisely released this famous concession at a profit to the American holders of six and one-half millions. What's the use of thinking imperially when we can act profitably for our own if not our son's sake? The concession was sold by Morgan and Company to Chang Chih Tung, Viceroy of Hupeh, Chang borrowing four and one-half millions from Montague and Company, London, and their underwriters, on the understanding that Britain would have the veto over any foreigners employed in construction work. The viceroy of the two Kwang Provinces raised the other two and one-half millions of the purchase by a wonderfully popular subscription covering tens of thousands of small lots. Thus the concession which China gave away cost her six and one-half millions to buy back, another lesson in patriotism recited bitterly by the New China party, but partly forgiven when America, led by that Daniel of justice and judgment, Roosevelt, restored a third of the absurdly large Boxer indemnity. Only twenty-eight miles of road had been laid down. China has added forty miles. When the road is opened, it will throw the marvelous gorge scenery of the Upper Yangtze, where the cliffs rise two thousand feet from the river's edge, open to sightseers at a cost of only three days' time from Canton.

Ninety miles from Canton, where the railway passes the Pe River, perpendicular coal seams are prominent, and horizontal mining can be accomplished at little cost. The engineers employed in nearly all Chinese railway construction are Japanese. On the northwest road from Peking to Kalgan, Chinese engineers are employed. This road is being entirely financed from the coffers of the Wai-Wu Pu (Foreign Board). In some cases the *cais* (foremen) are also Japanese. The Canton-Han-kau road, called the Yuet-Han Railway, is at present employing the most famous of the Chinese railway engineers, Kwong Sun Mau. The president, Cheng To Chai, is experiencing difficulty in diking out the provincial political floods which threaten to engulf his financing and construction. It is the old temerity of the South, the world over, to awake and know herself.

The roads from Nanking to Shanghai, and through the silk province from Soochow to Ningpo and Wuchow, via Hang-chow (the ancient capital of the Sung dynasty and the loveliest city of China) are under way through these nursery grounds of Chinese liberty. From Swatow to Chao Chou Fu on the Little Han River, sixty-five miles, a railway is being constructed, and will later be extended to the earthquake city of Amoy. With money withdrawn from Russian schemes, the French plan to build a trunk railway from Hanoi, the capital of Tonquin, four hundred miles through tin and copper territory and elephant fastnesses, to Yunnan City. The mephitic Namti Valley, which this road must cross, and which separates the Red River from the high tablelands, is levying a death toll of seventy per cent. among the workers, and filling the Orient with a growing scandal. It is already impossible to get the Yunnanese to enlist.

Coolies ignorant of the conditions are brought from
Shan-tung, and seventeen thousand of these, the tallest
and strongest of the race, are employed in the Namti Valley alone.   Work is entirely suspended in the primeval
gullies and jungles during the summer rains.   In the cool
season, thirty-five thousand Annamese are brought up to
the work.   This valley is destined to live in history.   No
modern public work ever levied such a toll, neither
Panama, Suez, or the Russian works in southern Turkestan.   It will be four years before Yunnan and Haiphong
can be linked, and the tale of difficulties only asserts the
adage that the Tropics do not write histories of wars
because they are engaged on a more compendious History
of Fevers.

At Yunnan City this French road will connect with the
British concession which comes from Calcutta and Mandalay, thence going northeast as far as Choong King at
the headquarters of the Yangtze, where the soil is so
worked by irrigation that it supports twelve hundred
people to the square mile.   The figures involved in the
opening-up of such teeming provinces are more like the
unreasonable repetitions of a dream than a commercial
certainty of the near future.   This province alone is as
large, as populous, as thrifty, and infinitely richer in
natural resources than France.   At Yunnan will meet
two other roads, one from Bangkok and one from Canton, so that Yunnan City, from a railway aspect, will become a sort of St. Louis, as a midland distributing point.
On account of the altitude of six thousand feet, Yunnan
City, two days from Canton by the railway, will be a new
summer resort for the coastal tropic cities.   The summers are delightful and from October to April the sun
shines from a rare and cloudless sky.   Yunnan is nearly

as rich as Shensi in both kinds of coal, and considering
in addition her gold, copper and salt deposits, she may
be termed the richest in minerals of all the provinces, as
she is also the lowest in intellectual boasts, for here the
mixed races and aborigines abound. Kwangsi, the adjoining province, which the railway will cross, will gather
its freight from unnumbered antimony mines.

The French concession, on account of the hilly country,
is for a narrow gage railway. All the other roads in
China are of the standard American gage of four feet
eight and one-half inches. At present the only transportation from Burmah and Tonquin into China (that by
pack trains) collapses four months annually, owing to the
rains blocking the roads. When this French road is
built, Kwang Se and Yunnan will send to the coast
forty million bunches of bananas a year, as well as valuable cargoes of mangoes and the delightful ruby-red man-
gosteens, which last must have been the apple of Eden,
for it is the choicest fruit known to mankind. A coast
road will eventually run from Canton to Amoy, through
the British territory at Kowloon, and from Wuchow on
the West River a road will run one hundred miles north
to the world's richest quicksilver deposit at Kai Chau.
As these roads have been wisely planned to run at right
angles to the rivers and canals, with the exception of
the road which follows the Grand Canal from Tientsin
to Soochow, the transportation facilities of the empire
will be immediately doubled. The additional wealth
which will be added to the property of Chinese shippers
when the railway supersedes the canal in that hot country,
can be computed when it is stated that it is necessary
now to allow the tremendous waste of twelve per cent. for
shrinkage on grain compared with the allowance neces-

sary in America of only one-fourth of one per cent. These railways are being built at a cost of thirty-six thousand dollars a mile, which is four thousand dollars less than America's cheapest built railway, the Great Northern, cost.

A nation which has erected the greatest, costliest, and most enduring monument ever raised by human hands (the Great Wall, which they call the Wan Li Chang, myriad mile wall) can, when it rises in the same numbers, cover its valleys with a web of railways, and as America held the eyes of the world in the nineteenth century because of her progress, China confidently expects that the twentieth century will likewise be hers, as Africa will take the twenty-first. With all this proposed development, China will even then remain only scratched. There is hardly a word concerning a railway into old Shansi Province, which is as large as Michigan. For hundreds of miles, under the loess deposited on the plateaus centuries ago by the Yellow River and its tributaries, and which can be dragged down with a rake, extend vast veins of anthracite and bituminous coal and iron. The mines have been known for thousands of years to the Mongols, as compared with America's knowledge of anthracite dating back only to 1791. Camel trains of coal, and small articles made of excellent carbon iron, have been sent to the capital of the province and to Peking for many years. Erosion for centuries has been uncovering the seams for the pick of the twentieth century Chinese miner, as he digs his way into preeminent opulence and power. The only thorough mineralogical survey of the inexhaustible coal and iron deposits of the central provinces was made in 1870 by the Russian Richtofen at the suggestion and with funds

secured through the Shanghai American Mr. Cunning-
ham.   In those days American diplomacy was dominant
at Peking through the power of Minister Burlingame.

A railway from the capital, Thai Yuan, would have to
be surveyed along the Fuen River to the Yellow River
and thence to the Grand Canal, and enterprise could readily make the richer portion of this Crœsus province of the
north tributary to Europeanized Shanghai, instead of
Peking, which latter could still supply herself abundantly
from the nearer Ping Ting coal mines in the north section.
It is to be noted that the coal areas of China are generally distributed, while in America the possession of coal
only in the central east has retarded the growth of the
west.   On the railways now in use, especially inland, it
has been necessary to use colored glass in the coaches,
as the coolies, who are unfamiliar with anything besides
shell-lights, in their excitability over the passing scenes,
frequently jam their heads through the windows, whose
existence they are not aware of.   European engine
drivers have been dispensed with, and natives now do
the work at a wage of thirty cents gold a day.   As illustrating what Chinese labor can work for I would say that
at Hong-Kong in 1903 we got the cost of handling cargo
on the American mail ships down to the lowest point
ever reached, of seven cents a ton, against forty cents
in America.   Most of the railway travel is fourth class,
standing room only being provided in gondola cars
(some with a roof but no sides) at one cent a mile.
First-class fare, with a leather seat, is three cents a mile
on the railroads, and one cent for fifteen miles on the
native house-boats where human feet propel the tread-
wheel.   Freight rates on the railroads for rice are two
and nine-tenths of a cent; machinery two and three-

tenths; coal one and eight-tenths of a cent gold per ton
per mile, against an average rate in the United States
of less than eight-tenths of a cent per ton per mile, and
in England of two and sixteen one hundredths cents.
It is not surprising therefore that the net profit of the
Peking-Han-kau Railway in 1908 was thirty-one per
cent. and that the members of the finance Pu (Board)
want more railways. As illustrating the industrial status
of China at present a study of the freight carried by the
Shan-tung Railway reveals coal as the chief factor, followed in order by beans, oil, cotton, straw-goods and
crockery. When the average Chinese makes a shipment,
it is generally a " personally accompanied " one, and the
railway thus secures a third-class fare in addition to
the freight.

In condemnation proceedings, the price paid for land
is about twenty-eight dollars an acre, or five dollars per
mao; and single graves, which are scattered everywhere,
like sage-bush in the desert, are purchased at two dollars
and a half each, including the value of Fungshui! For
earthwork, two and one-fourth cents; and for rock bal-
lasting eighteen cents per cubic yard, is paid to the contractors. Ties of Japanese kuriwood, which last without
creosoting for six years, cost forty cents each. Track
laying is done for about three cents per lineal yard. One
oddity which would appal our railway commissioners,
is the obliteration of class rates when merchants club
together and hire a car. They may put in it any class
of freight they desire, the rate being charged on the basis
of second class.

The advantage accorded and always demanded by the
Japanese is illustrated on the railway from the treaty
port of Swatow to the prefectural city of Chao Chow Fu,

the concession for which was given to Chang Yu Nan, a wealthy local merchant. All material is being supplied by Japanese contractors, no public tenders having been invited. The engineers are all Japanese and the rolling stock was bought through Japanese Manufacturers' Agents.

To summarize the principal railway routes which will be well under way within ten years, imagine a central trunk railway from Ottawa to New Orleans; and routes from New Orleans to Oklahoma; El Paso to Kansas City; Austin to Oklahoma; Galveston to Oklahoma; New Orleans to Tallahassee, and Halifax to New York, and you will comprehend the initial extensive program. What effect China's action in adopting a four foot, eight and a half inch gage will exercise on the Indian and Burmese Railways, remains to be seen. Fifteen thousand miles of railway in India are five feet, six inch gage, and the remaining twelve thousand miles are three feet, three and three-eighth inch gage. From an operating point of view, China should probably have followed the broader Indian gage. When India built her railways, she had steamship connection alone in mind for through business. That the Chinese are not lacking in that imagination which makes countries commercially great, is evidenced by the expectation that the Peking-Kalgan Railway will be extended through arid Gobi Desert, and join Koren through the Kaikhta Pass with Irkutsk, thus saving six days to St. Petersburg as compared with the South Manchurian Railway route, now dominated by the selfish Japanese. It will be remembered that before the opening of the Suez Canal, Kaikhta was the mart through which China traded with Russia. Humanity at large is interested in the rapid extension of Chinese railways,

Prince Ching, who has been the " Power Behind Three Manchu
Thrones." This conservative of conservatives surprisingly
has alone advocated most advanced views for the
education of Chinese women.

Nanking road, principal native shopping district of Shanghai,
Eastern Central China.

The wide streets of the Northern Cities. Street bazaar on Kaiser
road, running from South Gate to Chien Men Gate,
Peking, China.

because it will then alone be possible to rush supplies from the fields of plenty to the famine districts of the three flooding rivers, the Hoang-ho; Han, and Yangtze, and save verily hundreds of thousands of lives each year.

Many may be surprised that the railways came with such a rush, but the way was prepared by the extensive system of telegraph wires which the Danes under Scheirn strung through the kingdom, even crossing Yunnan into Burmah. All the ports are connected, the total wirage being forty thousand miles. The most sensational line of wire in the world probably is that crossing the Gobi Desert in Mongolia, three thousand and five hundred miles through a generally hopeless stretch of blight and immemorial neglect. Over all this expanse of silence; over the ears of the trudging pony and camel and their almost as obtuse drivers; over the solitary shadow of a glacial rock here and there, how the songs of the glad parts of the earth are humming in the dreams of the half-awakened giantess, China. The profit to the government from the wires in 1907 was twelve per cent., and again the Finance Pu wants more of them. Only fifteen feet below the sands of Gobi there is water which, if raised, would turn the earth's saddest desert into the lilac and the buttercup.

The I Chau, or Imperial Courier Service, with its thousands of wonderful runners, and an organization running through four thousand years, will continue long after railways are built, but more like our rural postal service. These runners claim as a regular thing records that surpass Marathon, and it is a pity that some of them were not sent to the Olympic games. A Chinese track victory would win the popular sympathy of the world more than would the bloody laurels of a fleet of war.

From Peking to Canton one hundred miles a day over abominable paths, are expected of the relay runners.

There is already a postal service, called the Min Chu, which radiates from the treaty ports, which was established by the always ready Robert Hart for the Chinese.

Travelers who have enjoyed the comfort of the wide, cool seat of a high-wheeled yellow Macao jinrickisha, once used generally throughout South China treaty ports, will lament the Japanese invasion of China with a lighter, narrower, plum-lacquered 'rickisha, which has already driven out the Chinese vehicle at Hong-Kong and Shanghai. The coolies, who work for public contractors and do not own their own vehicles, will have nothing to do with the heavier Chinese machines, but occasionally, in the Portuguese Colony, pulled along the Praya Grande by her liveried runners, a gentle Macaense, hid beneath her flowing black silk Do-veil, passes you in a 'rickisha of the old period, which rumbles along with its echoes of slower, quainter and courtlier days, which will soon be a memory throughout the whole awakened land. The revulsion which comes over one on first stepping into a human-drawn 'rickisha, will not quickly pass. It is hard for a Westerner to degrade his fellow-man so literally to the position of a driven beast. The Oriental refutes this point of view, and says, "I am the more honest in practising that we all are servants of one another." However, there is no other means of moving about the streets of Japan and the maritime cities of China. Hong-Kong has a tramway, but it traverses only one water street,—their Praya. Manila has a more ramified tram service, but waits are so long that there also the imported Japanese runner and his vehicle are indispensable. The private 'rickishas of Hong-Kong are pulled by one runner and pushed by two, the salary of the three amounting to eighteen dollars gold a month. The rivalry of the owners in equipping their runners with uniforms of conspicuous borders is one of the characteristic features of life on that famous oriental island.

More significant than the 'rickisha invasion was the announcement of President Matsugata of the Kawasaki Dock, Kobe, that his company had purchased ten thousand *tsubo* of land at Shanghai for the purpose of erecting a branch in China, and competing for the ship work of the Yangtze territory. This was going far afield for an unprovoked attack, not only on Chinese but British capital and political sphere. This commercial invasion has not been one-sided, for China has now found in Japan her best customer, selling her last year sixty million taels' worth, mostly of raw material.

The Chinese Imperial Customs duties of five per cent. ad valorem are probably the smallest of all international customs imposts, but this tax at the treaty ports was until lately only the beginning of the load accumulated on imports. An inland tax, under native control, called *li-kin*, which literally means a cash a catty (one-twelfth of a cent for each one and one-third pounds) is generally added despite the treaties with America, Britain and Japan, from province to prefecture about every twenty miles, until the bolt of Fall River arrives at the retailer's hong or store, as a luxury, and a mandarin only can purchase what the rice-tiller needs to comfort his blistered shoulders from the sun. Unifying as railways may be, they will accomplish less than is expected until the *likin* absolutely ceases to keep the provinces disjointed. The great federator of China has therefore yet to arise, and it will be he who positively smashes for ever the whole

pythonic chain of the *likin* system, and thus makes free
inter-provincial trade.   It is curious to note that no *likin*
is levied in Mongolia, probably because the poor camel's
back there has already been broken with the burden of
its debts.   Next in revenue-producing powers to the land
tax, comes the *likin,* and the Imperial Customs following
a long way off with a total of about twenty-five million
dollars.   The necessities of the provinces, owing to an
abolishment of *likin,* could be at once met by a tax on
mines and profits from railways, without adding to the
burdens of the farmer or shopkeeper, one cash more than
at present.

The governor of far Shensi Province has drifted into
the Japanese eddy, and is exploiting the oil wells of Yen
Chang, which employ Japanese engineers.   The oil refines in the highest grade.   The Pennsylvania of China
in coal and oil is that most populous inland province, Sze-
Chuen, where the natural gas flows through rude bamboo
tubes.   The wondering natives, leading it beneath their
salt evaporating pans, have put Japanese matches to it,
and called it " devil's breath."   Encouraged by the success in industrial developments of Viceroy Chang at
Han-kau, China has loaned the governor of Chinese
Turkestan one hundred and seventy-five thousand dollars
to establish a cotton mill in the far eastern corner of the
empire at Turfan to beat out Russian goods.

The nineteen Chinese mints are entirely under provincial jurisdiction, though the central government steps in,
as in 1906, when the Kiang Nam mint over-produced
copper *fun* coins.   It is the viceroy's perquisite, though
he is sometimes followed closely by the counterfeiters,
who smuggle in strips of Australian copper, and export
the " moonshine " stampings for tutenag, into the interior

provinces whose mintings are the lowest. A Chinese shroff in a bank, and the native croupier at a fan-tan game are experts in the ring of true coin. They care nothing for the stamp, whether it be Mexican, Spanish, Chinese, or Hong-Kong, so long as the coin is pure silver. So little respect is paid the provincial coin of the two Kwang Provinces in the south, that banking houses put their " chops " or seals on the dollar pieces, which are dented in their passage into unrecognizable cup-shaped articles. The Hong-Kong government is endeavoring to teach the Chinese respect for the head and inscription on coins of the realm, and will not receive at the post and tax offices any coins of the king which are " chopped."

The sycee of commerce is the perfectly pure silver which is melted at the mint into bars from the Mexican, Spanish, American and Chinese coins that are received in toll at the *haikwan* or custom-house on a bullion basis. The silver bars so produced are officially called *wan-yin* or " fine silver," and colloquially *se-sze* (fine silk), implying that the metal is so pure that it can be drawn out in a thread as fine as silk. The Chinese very naturally fall into the decimal system. Their monetary computation is as follows: ten copper *cash* or *li* (which have a square hole in the center and Chinese characters on one side and Mongolian characters on the other side) equal one *fun;* ten *fun* equal one *tsien;* ten *tsien* equal one *tael,* and a *haikwan* or custom-house *tael* equals seventy-four cents in our money. A string of one thousand cash is known popularly as a *tiao,* and is equal to fifty cents gold. The bar of sycee is sold as being of so many *taels* in weight. The *cash* coin, known as far back as one thousand years B. C., is the most generally coined, and shows the minute economy of the Chinese in their commercial dealings with one another. Their economists argue that if we had a lower coin than the cent, our households would live on half what they do, as shopkeepers charge the poor a cent for what is worth only a twelfth, and the poor in America as well as China of course live from hand to mouth. A Chinese silver dollar and dime piece are coined in the two Kwang Provinces in the south, but their stamp gives them no fixed value. They are only bullion when challenged at the *haikwan*. The Kiangnam mint issued in 1906 *fun* pieces of Yunnan copper, but they were unpopular, and were withdrawn when the markets took them at a discount. At Kashgar in Chinese Turkestan, copper is cast into ingots and used as money alongside of the silver sycee bar.

The notes of private banks, called "flying money," are in wide use, though the advertisement on the back requests circulation only in the guild district or hong street. The bank has to give security to the viceroy for its note issues. There is little counterfeiting because part of the note is written by hand and an impression copy is taken for comparison on presentation. Until 1909, not since 1300 A. D., has the government itself issued treasury notes. These notes have been prepared in America. There was much scandal about abuses when the Mongols issued paper, one being that the government discounted its own obligations. An old government note of the Mings, dated 1368, is on exhibition in New York. It reads in part: "This seal makes this note current anywhere under heaven. Counterfeiters will be executed. Persons giving information will be rewarded with two hundred and fifty taels and all the property of the counterfeiter." Only China and Persia of the greater coun-

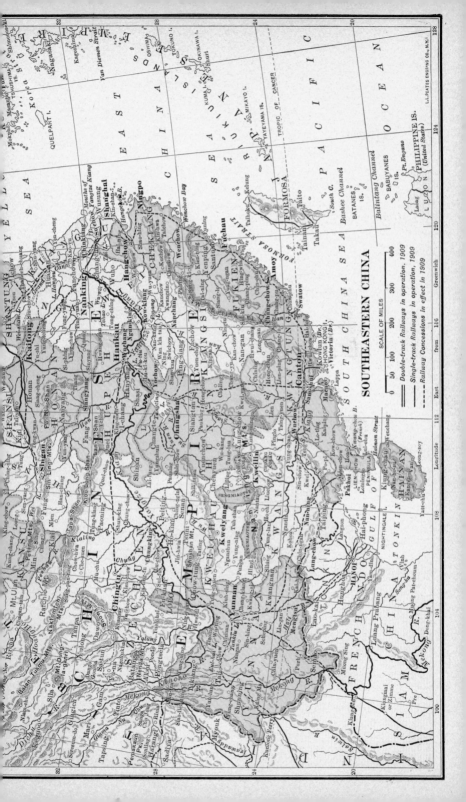

SOUTHEASTERN CHINA

SCALE OF MILES

0   50 100   200   300   400

Double-track Railways in operation, 1909
Single-track Railways in operation, 1909
Railway Concessions in effect in 1909

tries of the world now remain on a silver basis. Gold is not coined. The dust and virgin nuggets, known as "Huang-huo," are washed from alluvial sand in river beds in Szechuen. In Kwangsi, the next province west from Canton, much business is carried on by the barter of cotton yarn. An early Chinese coin was made of porcelain, three and one-half inches across by one-fourth inch thick, bearing the legend, "Eternal prosperity."

As China mines little silver, in times of depression of imports, bolts of silk, blocks of dried tea, Mongol riding-boots, and even baked earth and wooden disks bearing the viceroy's chop, have been the circulating medium. The early Buddhistic writings frequently mention the last named money, as the priests did not like to horde it, both from want of room and want of appreciation, which criticism of theirs naturally made them unpopular with the vice-regal inscriber of the "chop." When railways facilitate circulation, we shall see another oppression wiped away, namely the exorbitant interest rate of four per cent. a month, which obtains at feast times and New Year settlements in February. Besides the *fokis* on watch, the bankers' safe is guarded by five padlocks, each requiring a different key, which is carried by each member of the firm, so that all must be present in order to open the safe. The rate of interest at the pawnshops is thirty-six per cent. a year. To protect these shops in a land where there is little police protection, the penalty for robbery has been made death. Rocks are stored on the roof so that they may be thrown down on an attacking band. The pawnshops are the most conspicuous buildings in the cities; they rise high and square, like forts, over every other roof and pinnacle.

Small native newspapers have cropped up all over,

and Japanese money is being expended to swing this important influence in line with Japanese prestige. On this field of tournament will meet the progressive merchants, traders, and foreign-educated Chinese, against the old-school literati and official classes. Cartoons have a wider circulation and are in systematic employment by secret societies and guilds. A notorious one used during the boycott of 1905 exhibited Americans goading their "god-beast," the buffalo, and on the reverse the same Americans goading a Chinese.

Quail are raised tame by the Chinese, and shipped across the Pacific seven thousand miles. This bird ranks eighth in the heraldic embroideries. It would have been given a higher place were it not trained to fight in the gaming pit. Fish are likewise brought alive across the Pacific, this being a perquisite of the ship's Chinese bo'sun. The beautiful rice-birds, yellow as Hartz canaries, are caught in nets and drowned so that they will not lose weight in struggling. They are hawked around the streets of Hong-Kong. The Cantonese have long been famous for their delicious preserved little oranges, the comquats. They are now exporting pickled olives, which compete in California with the local product. A New Yorker can buy in Mott Street tinned rice-birds from Canton's suburbs.

Over three-quarters of the uplands of China have not been utilized because she has few cattle and fewer sheep. Vast herds of Swiss stock could be grazed on the mountain uplands which at present are given up to scenery for Buddhist temples, or empty glebes for the Fungshui nonsense. Japan is importing blooded stock as rapidly as her thin resources will allow, and as China will do everything Japan does, a vast accretion of China's wealth in herds will shortly ensue. A Canadian imported a flock of sheep and set them free on the islands which guard Junk Bay, Hong-Kong, but the spear grass of the southern sea-coast lacerated the windpipes of the animals. The half wild cattle of the Canton delta, with their pronounced hump, look like diminutive buffaloes. Their faces are even gentler looking than our Jersey breed. A windmill seems a little thing, but China will need a million of them to take the place of the irrigation-wheel treaders who will be called from the fields to the mine pits within the next five years. Will America or Germany supply the million windmills to sing their music beside the Chinese homesteads?

The Manchurians crush vast quantities of beans by donkey-driven rollers. The oil is used for food and light. The cake which remains is used partly for food and partly for fertilizer. Vast as is the quantity of petroleum now imported into China, it has made so little impression on the absorbent ability of the nation, that even yet, everywhere one goes, little else is noticed but the use of vegetable oils,— on the 'rickisha's shafts, on the sampan's masthead, in the huts of the rice tiller and mulberry picker, and at the idol's shrine. The popular illuminating oil is produced from the nut of one species of tea-plant. Ground nuts, or peanuts are crushed in vast quantities for the oil. Two million gallons of nut-oil are imported annually into America for use in the manufacture of high grade varnishes. This rapidly drying, tasteless, but rank-smelling oil, which has no superior for water-proof requirements, is made from the purple-leafed Hwa Tung tree (Aleurites cordata). Szechuen Province cultivates it abundantly in the West. It is a common sight to meet coolies carrying the nuts in bamboo boxes on their shoulders, and not slung between them on bamboos, as is the universal method of carriage in the east. On the coast, Fu-chau is the best known center. The product is there drawn from the gorges of the picturesque Min River. In the next province west, the hills along the Kan River are clothed with the trees, and the capital Nan Chang turns over a busy *cash* in the enterprise. The trees which grow in stony ground, bear in six years, when they reach a height of fifteen feet. Oddly the pressure on the poisonous nuts is not applied by a screw as is done with olives by us, but by wedges, which surprisingly express forty per cent. of the fifty per cent. oil which the nuts contain.

Manchuria promises to become wonderfully successful in the culture of the sugar beet, and with her cheap labor probably will conquer in wider fields across the Pacific. The Manchurian beets contain thirty per cent. of sugar, against a percentage in our country of eighteen per cent.

All of Kwangtung produces that delightful succulent orange, famous throughout the East, known as the "Coolie" orange. It is thin-skinned, slightly smaller, but fully as juicy as our Indian River variety. The skins are sedulously preserved and sold to make a tea to cure fevers. Indeed, in the treaty ports, the fruit is called the "Quinine orange." Mangoes, despite their strong turpentine taste, grow upon the palate. The small-pitted lychee, with its cool, sweet flesh of pearl color, can not be over-praised in a land where the longing for fruit is intense on account of the poor quality of foods available for the use of the white man, and the salicylic acid in imported foods. The yellow-skinned whampee, fragrant as a flower, has a taste between a plum and a grape. The pumelo or giant grape-fruit grows to enormous size, and is preferable to our shard because of its mildness.

The egg-shaped and ink-red persimmons, together with golden limes from Hainan Island, add to the varied colored piles on the fruiterers' stands, in a picture the most welcome that the Orient presents amid all its forbidding dirt and smells.

On the hills around Canton lie the terraces where the succulent ginger root is cultivated. The scene is a pretty one, for not only are the flowers attractive, but the long leaf gleams brilliantly in the sun. The street of the syrup workers in Canton, where the ginger is preserved and candied, affords an interesting excursion. The most notable firm is the Chai Loong, of which Wong Ki Sam is the versatile president.

When some machine shall be invented for taking the gum more cheaply out of the ramie stems, the product will add vastly to China's wealth. This nettle gives four crops a year, producing two and a half tones of fiber to the acre, and the cloth is well known for its silky finish and quality of adding luster when mixed with wool or cotton.

So long as rice continues to be the major staff of life, there is little hope for foreign agricultural implements, and the buffalo continues to wallow through the flooded fields, dragging the wooden cultivator. Hong-Kong has erected its first flour-mill, however, with a capacity of one thousand barrels a day. The grain will be brought eight days by sea from Manchuria, and also imported from Oregon. Electricity developed from reservoirs in the hills back of Junk Bay, eight miles from Hong-Kong's civic center, will be used. Hong-Kong has not supplied Vladivostock and Manchuria since the Russian-Japanese

War. She has been devoting her abilities to supplying South China with a low grade imported Oregon flour at two cents a pound. For the finer festival cakes, the Chinese have of late been importing slightly superior Australian and Alberta flours. The Chinese does not yet appreciate, or at least he could not pay for Minnesota flour. At Chin Kiang on the Grand Canal, there is another native flour-mill which rolls a good product at two cents a pound, and Shanghai has several mills. In the native mills, the nether stone revolves, while the upper is stationary. More mills will certainly be erected, and grain be brought from Manchuria, the West River in the south, and across the Pacific. The former unassailed position of rice, we are glad to say, is now doomed to be attacked. The native cotton-mills, located at Wuchang by Viceroy Chang, are manufacturing all the uniforms for the new Chinese army of the central provinces.

Land is leased from the government, and the right of occupancy is evidenced by a Hung Ki or red deed, but the people exchange land among themselves by a private and unregistered white deed, because they wish to escape the expense of the government deeds. There are few suits over the white deeds, which speaks volumes for the famed honesty of the Chinese peasant. When new land is broken, the government allows six crops (two seasons) to be reaped, before calling for the first taxes, and in times of famine all taxes are remitted. Taxes are never over fifty cents an acre, and descend to ten cents an acre for hill land. China exacts no direct tax in Thibet. She collects yearly a nominal tribute from the central government at Lhassa. Thibet, however, has to support the resident minister sent from Peking. Taxation is not always collected in money, but sometimes in tithing of produce, the rice being stored in government granaries. China is the only country that in this way is repeating the picturesque history of Joseph and the Pharaohs, in the storing of grain against famine by the government. Americans will best remember the five granaries at Canton, and the even larger ones at Peking. The peasants of China do not bear the burdens of those of Japan, where one-third of the revenue goes to the government.

There are few additional sources of revenue. Provincially, the pawnshops' licenses, and the *likin* on transportation help out. The customs, salt excise, and the *loti* (tea export duty) further assist the general government. A citizen of China can boast of enjoying two of the several essentials of liberty, that to be well governed is to hear little of it, and pay little for it. When China's mines are sunk, and her factories are erected, she can afford one of the heaviest budgets in the world, provided the people continue in their individual economic habits and temperance. She owes her vast population to two causes: low taxation and early marriages. A reorganization in the system of collection could yield the government even now two hundred and ten millions from the land tax; the customs yield of about twenty-five millions could be brought up to one hundred millions if *likin* was absolutely wiped out. The *loti,* as well as the *likin* tax should be abolished. Government royalties on mining, and the receipts from railways, could bring up the revenue of China to the enormous amount of five hundred millions a year, without making the poor of the land poorer, and it must be remembered that life is decreed, or a knell sounded, for a state, as it turns on this one problem: will the poor be made poorer or the rich richer? They can not both be made richer and either live, as is the fatuous statement to-day of certain of our "endowed" professors of economics.

There are Building and Loan Associations in China, called *Tei Po Wui* (Spread on the Ground Associations) because the historic founder who first borrowed from his friends was so poor that he had neither hut nor bench where to ask them to sit while the loan should be discussed.

The government's salt monopoly is a great burden upon a people who require so much of the staple for one of their main foods, fish. Indeed, in oriental countries where icing is not yet practical, the necessity of salt and sugar as preservatives is imperative. The cost averages throughout the empire two cents a pound, whereas it should be sold for half that. The monopoly mainly covers evaporation privileges along the sea-coast, and the product being granular, is not so good as the residue from boiling. These sea-water beds are all in the northern provinces. Evaporation is permitted when three inches of water are pumped into the vast basins. The salt is packed in five hundred pound mats. This unpurified salt accounts partially for the rank smells of the dried fish-markets. When the Indian government reduced the salt tax ten millions a year, the progress of India commenced, until her solvency is now assured. Poor China is praying for similar relief. In the toe of northern Shensi Province, is situated the ancient and remarkable walled salt lake, fifty miles square, which supports a Civil Service city of seventy-five thousand inhabitants, who tend the pans for the government. Many more salt and brackish springs could be reclaimed at this point. At similar springs at Fung Tu in Szechuen Province, natural gas is piped in hollowed bamboos to the pans. No salt is imported. The present consumption in the empire is the tremendous amount of one million, nine hundred thousand metric tons. Junks seized in the act of salt smuggling are drawn up on the shore or bank and sawn in twain, as a melancholy deterrent of similar delinquency. The Chinese dearly loves his ethics in pictures, and the government seizes the eloquent opportunity.

Where wood is scarce and paper so necessary, the supply of pulp is becoming a matter of anxiety. Expectation is turned toward the bamboo (*Kam Li*) which grows as much as five feet in a night until a growth of fifty feet is attained in the humid southern provinces. What more need we say for the soil of China? Planted as a hedge between the rice fields, it frames as soft and alluring a scene as the imagination can paint. How wonderful this plant, which furnishes in its tender shoots and seeds, food for man; in its larger growth, poles for his hut and masts for his junks; in its fiber, paper for his kettles and printing press; and medicine in the silicious nodules of the joints! It is split into fibers in Korea, lacquered black, and woven into the astounding hats which the quality of that land wear. It is wound to make the immense hawsers which pull the boats through the Ichang Gorge of the Yangtze, and which suspend the bridges over the gorges between Thibet and Szechuen Province.

The stalks of the two-year-old bamboo, cut into one-inch lengths, are thrown into a pond or clay vat, where they are allowed to decompose for four months. An oily scum collects on the top, which is discarded, but some day it will be purified and used commercially. The pulp is then pounded by hydraulic or hand hammers. A binding material, made from the leaves of the holly-like Actinidia or Lauraceae, is mixed in, and the paper is cut, dried and pressed into the sizes desired. The Japanese have already erected at Toroku in Formosa, an immense modern paper-mill, which uses bamboo entirely as staple. The so-called velvety but frailer " rice-paper," used for those dainty little paintings, with humorous Pidgin verses, at Canton, is only the pith of the Fatsia elder of the Yunnan marshes, the cells of which are cut length-wise and ironed. Into so many lines of industry does the bamboo enter, that lacking as yet the production of iron and lumber, the plant may be said to be the frame-work of China. Throughout Kiangsi Province, it is used to construct the water-wheels of the irrigation canals. Even saucepans and kettles are made of the compressed pulp, which is treated with secret salts. The pans, how-ever, must be kept nearly full of water, which is brought to a boil with surprising rapidity. Medium sized bamboo has been introduced on Bainbridge Island, Washington State, and has reached a growth of five feet. If this at-tempt of the Furuyas firm is successful in furniture making, they will introduce the lumber bamboo, in which America has an opportunity to relieve the destruction of her forests throughout the southern states.

On foot-power looms, in their own homes, the Chinese weave three hundred different patterns of silk and satin goods. Most entrancing are the embroidered goods, on which a woman (often the deserted wife of an opium fiend) will work a month and receive three dollars. The merchant will sell you this mandarin's robe, with its Greek-like spangles of geometrical patterns, or its orna-ments of trellises, chrysanthemums, fruit or butterflies, for fifteen dollars. Were you to sell it in your own land, you would receive one hundred dollars. That robe will be exhibited in homes and galleries. Its pattern will teach industries to our art schools. Over the world the power of its beauty will spread. But whatever commercially results, or æsthetically emanates from the creation, nothing whatever will reach that woman of Hang-chow, who received her all in the three dollars. To the altar of art the women of China have bound themselves that beauty may not die. The world piles up its debts, even though the piling up be done in secret places in neglected lands. The death of a generation can not outlaw them. Some day we shall have to pay that woman of Hang-chow, or her heirs of suffering, what we owe her, just as, for one instance, the labor unions of England are now collecting what their forefathers owed Wat Tyler and his Kentishmen, when they commandeered their arms, their service and their poll-taxed bodies in 1381, without recompense.

The United States does not produce one-third of the wool she requires and she therefore draws on North China for nearly three million dollars' worth a year, which is about China's complete exportation of the product. The export is, of course, through the port of Tientsin.

On the iron hills around Canton and Macao, you will notice drying in the sun, the delightfully soft grass linen which has been dyed with the blue " Polygonum tinctorium." If you wander into the sheds where the silkworms are feeding, they will beseech you to make no noise, this odd requirement being quite necessary in sericulture. If the raising and feeding of the grub are tedious, the procuring of the skein from the cocoon is simplicity itself. Let us enter a reeler's house. There is no unnecessary furniture in the working-room. On the adobe floor lie the bits of charcoal and precious pieces of drift-wood gathered from every nook of the fields and canal. There is the bamboo basket which brought them, and a tray where he assorts the cocoons. The skein itself makes the circumference around two crossed frames which revolve. The fire pot is of stone and is without a door. It rests on a rock. The Han-yang copper pot is wide and shallow. Into it the cocoons are thrown with a wooden spoon. With his right hand the reeler works four or five to the edge, gathers deftly the ends of five wet threads and lets the cocoons drop back into the hot water.

In the ancient Portuguese settlement of Macao you pass the lofty Boa Vista Hotel, with its Renaissance beauty alien enough here, and saunter westward along the Rua de Penha, beneath the hill toward which Portuguese navigators for five centuries have looked for succor. On each side of you are high walls, cut with gates which bear noble white stucco ornaments, and arms above them, and a wonderful iron lamp which looks more like the art of crusaders than the hand-work of Chinese. You pass Fort Bomparto, erected by Lopez Carrasco in 1615. At your feet is a small half-moon bay as blue as Naples; at the other horn is the fort of Sao Thiago de Barra, with its big-bellied cannon, obsolete, but delightfully quaint. There are home-cast copper cannon, too, and blue-domed white sentry boxes, which look more like lighthouses of a miniature past. You are recalling the Dutch invasion which was repulsed on this silver beach in 1622. If you can evade a cordon of yellow chow dogs, every one of which you would like to take home as a prize, you will reach a series of terraces, on each of which are crowded dozens of huts. This is the ancient village of the native fire-cracker makers. Take up some of the torn paper

The Manchu Regent of China, Prince Chun, brother of the late
Emperor, Kwang Su, and father of infant Emperor-
elect Hsuan Tung.

600 miles inland at Hankow, Central China. The Yang-tze and
Han rivers, which meet here, rise forty feet in the spring
floods. Hankow is the Pittsburg of China, for here
meet the opulent antimony, coal and iron beds of
Hupeh province. It is also the center of the
black tea trade, and the head of deep water
navigation on the Yang-tze river.

The busy Metropolis of China, Canton, as seen from the Hong Kong
boat wharf. Canton has had an uninterrupted trade with
foreigners for 450 years, despite the intriguing
of Peking to end the intercourse.

lying about, which is used for stuffing the crackers. The text is in Chinese, and the translation reveals the fulminations of Amos against the heathen, copies of which have been handed out in thousands by the Christian colporteurs. Buckwheat paste is rolled in the fuse; straw and every possible refuse is used to make the cheap paper. Each child or woman prepares two thousand five hundred crackers a day, for which she receives ten cents. More of the earth of China is scattered over the Americas than the soil of all other lands together. Chinese humorists say they are anointing us unto the conquest. The middle and ends of each fire-cracker are sealed with Chinese red clay. In China, however, the fire-cracker is only used in religious ritual, for the purpose of frightening away evil spirits.

Where a stream, now almost dried up, once rushed between the loess foot-hills of Kowloon, across the bay from Hong-Kong, is situated a village of soy-makers. The stream has sunk down from a dozen levels as the forests which fed it have been uprooted at its source, until now it whispers deep in a sunken gorge. From terrace to terrace, the high bamboo water-wheels patiently feed the irrigation bamboo and mud troughs. There are two narrow terraces on each side of the highest level. Above are the hills with their waving camphor-trees. Behind the bamboo fences you will notice the bean poles, and the great earthenware pots, where the bean liquor is fermented, and stirred for two months in the blazing sun until it is black. The beans are skinned and made into a flour, into which gypsum is mixed. Salt and secret things are added to make this appetizing soy, which those who have learned the taste prefer to the flavored Worcestershire, of which it is the base. The soy costs only a trifle, and the workman who earns only ten cents a day will have it at his meal. The wealthy are equally proud of their national " abettor of appetite."

An odd pursuit on the plateaus of western Szechuen Province is the gathering of musk, which is worth more than its weight in gold. The product comes from a gland in the stomach of the hornless deer, which stands only twenty inches high, and whose habitat is never lower than eight thousand feet.

In computing the future of Chinese exports, one must consider the eight million Chinese abroad, who are becoming wealthier, and are sending to their native land for the things to which they have been used, and which they passionately love.

Cornwall and Malay were supposed to contain all the deposits of the world's tin until the mines of Bolivia, ten thousand feet up the Andes, were uncovered recently. It may surprise many that the fastnesses of distant Yunnan Province conceal ancient mines at Kuo Chia, which, working on the most primitive methods in the alluvial deposits formed by erosion, produce to-day one hundred thousand *piculs* a year (13,333,000 pounds), valued at twenty-two cents a pound at the mines, before the payment of the export *loti* imposed by China. These mines are near the Tonquin border and the proposed French railway which will have one Chinese port at Pak Hoi will profit by the carriage of this freight, which now is exported to Hong-Kong. The tin averages as high as sixty-five per cent., there being little wolfram and mispickel in the ore, which is run through sluices after the larger stones have been picked out of the muddy gravel. The metal is run in pigs weighing one hundred and forty-six pounds, which are cut in half for convenience in packing on donkey back. The furnaces consume wood as fuel. The blowing apparatus is most primitive. Each coolie worker is expected to produce one kilogram of tin a day. Some of this tin is used at Swatow in making the celebrated pewter ware, the antimony coming from the particularly rich mines of Hunan. Changsha, the capital of that province, has two native smelting establishments, and Carlowitz and Company, the well known Hamburg firm, run a large smelting plant at Wuchang.

Ten miles from the British military and sanitarium settlement of Wei-hai-wei, five hundred feet above the sea, shafts have been sunk by foreign companies into oxidized ore which carries free gold. The wages paid muckers are fifteen cents gold, and miners twenty cents gold a day. The native miners used to break the ore small by hand, and then throw it into a bean mill under stone rollers. The free gold was panned out by the use of quicksilver. The rocks of the neighborhood are of volcanic origin, traversed by seismic intrusion, and also showing signs of erosion.

How rapidly the spear becomes a share is evidenced already on the Mongolian and Manchurian steppes adjacent to the Siberian Railway. They expect to ship five hundred thousand sheep to St. Petersburg, and even some to London, through the port of Riga this summer. The disbanded soldiers of Kuropatkin are throwing away their buttons, importing Austrian enameled cooking ware, and getting to work between the furrows. And far away in Thibet, where the red banners of Younghusband and the yellow ones of the Lhama made their kowtows, they have begun a modern cart road from the fertile lake regions over the passes to Simla. Bullock and yak wagons, instead of barrows, are now bearing out pashum (fine shawl wool of the Thibetan goat), borax, silk, tea, charras and sulphur.

We have said that the roads of China are only wide enough for a barrow, on which the load is generally five hundred pounds, though in the north of China some barrows carry one thousand pounds. Of several, there is one venerable exception, dating from the third century, A. D., and when there is an exception in China, it is on a gigantic scale. From Peking to Ching Too, the capital of Szechuen, a distance of one thousand five hundred miles through the most populous plain of China, there runs a road built one thousand five hundred years ago. It is fifteen feet wide, and is paved with large blocks of stone, some being five feet square. It is, of course, in wretched condition, taken at spots, but judged as a whole, there lies the great work ready for easy adjustment to the present day. The ancient cedars stand sentinel, pointing piteously to a return to the patriotic public works of yore by taotais, mandarins and viceroys. The *fuyuns* (mayors) are not at fault. The scenery, where this road crosses the Sin Ling range, is on the most stupendous scale, Alpine in its beauty. The engineers cut the road at eight thousand feet, and the snowy peaks tower three thousand feet still higher. If one may judge the religion of the Chinese Buddhists by the condition of the roads, it must be at a low ebb, for one of the most neglected of the Ten Charities is: "He who makes a piece of road cuts off one thousand dots on the debtor side of his record with Buddha." Peking's streets, those sloughs of dust, pitfalls or slime, have lately seen their first steam roller. Shanghai and Hong-Kong, of course, preceded Peking in this respect. In the stone-paved native cities, the sewer is under the middle row of slabs.

As the flow of water is poor, decaying vegetable matter makes a malodorous cry to heaven. The sewers are used for no other filth, however, as all else is carried to the fields in buckets. Chinese civic philosophy is thankful therefor, considering that things would be infinitely worse if the fields did not demand more fertilizer than is available. There is not an American, however, who will believe this, when he is caught rounding a lee corner for the first time. .

Since little glass is manufactured (and that only at Canton), and as porcelain is too costly, and earthenware too brittle to stand the jolting, it may be asked how their *samschu* wine and valuable oils are transported. Large grass baskets, to support one hundred pounds weight, are prepared. These are lined with thick bamboo paper, which is soaked in vegetable oil. Withes of strong grass are twisted about the bundle, and also around the large hood which is placed over the orifice. The coolie takes no risk with this burden, and has it harnessed on a prop, so that he does not have to put the bundle down each time he rests against a wall or tree.

More alleviating even than railways is the institution at last of public utilities in some of the suffering cities. This is really the breaking of the true dawn, the distinct form of the sun of comfort itself seen over the horizon at last. A contract to provide Canton with water-works at Tsang To has been awarded to a German firm. Up to the present, Canton has taken her supply from the polluted river and thousands of city wells, and epidemics would be even more frequent if the Chinese did not take most of their drink in boiled tea. The second city to follow is at the other end of the land, Newchwang letting a similar contract to a British firm, and even old Peking is laying down pipes to bring filtered water from the Sha and Ching Rivers. We know what Lourdes is in relic week as a distributor of disease, but the water of Chinese cities holds a continuous carnival in germs. When the music of the steam water-pumps is heard in the land, how many millions will rise upon their couches and say they have heard indeed the pulsing of the wings of that good angel which shed healing upon the West. The object lesson was afforded by the filtration beds at Tokio, Osaka and British Hong-Kong. Families too poor to pay for a faucet in the house are furnished a key to the street hydrant for seventy-five cents per annum, with the liability of being swooped down upon by the patrolling *lukong* if water is wasted.

Harbors, too, are being improved. It is proposed to prepare the water-front of historic Whompoa for Canton's revived shipping, and the railway terminal which will be located there. Even the dizzy old bund of Canton itself has lately been straightened up before the surveyor's line. But the other day, two towns off the Tung Ting Lake opened their black-barred gates to foreign trade, and the vast hemp fields of sealed Hunan were thus at last brought to one day's steaming from Han-kau.

The foolish pounding on a wooden cymbal by a watchman who noisily dragged along his wooden shoes through the thief-infested shadows is being replaced by the stealthy tread of the uniformed, carbine-armed policeman. Drained boulevards are being broken across the stinking cities from gate to gate. Something more systematic than the visits of the wandering sow is depended upon to clean the streets of garbage. More victorias and automobiles, full of happy painted wives, are seen, as wider roads are macadamized in the suburbs of the treaty ports. Copied from Hong-Kong, the great teacher of the East, the electric car will run before long out of Canton, up the gorgeous West River (Sikiang) country. Honest China has at last allowed her impeccable self to loot the Occident of its inventions, for the sake of the relief it will give her tired sons who were almost buried in the dirt of the centuries.

VIII

CLIMATE AND DISEASES OF SOUTH CHINA

The stricken British island-colony of Hong-Kong has learned to welcome those recognized experts, the Japanese doctors, in the annual visitation of the terrible bubonic plague, called by the Chinese, *Chang-chih*. How its recurrence shrinks history! We read of the curse first in I Samuel, 6.4; in Thucydides, as occurring at Athens in 594, B. C.; and at Rome in the reign of Justinian, A. D., 542. We have even considered Manzoni's description of it at Milan, and Defoe's and Pepys' accounts of the "Black Death" in London in September, 1665, as ancient history. But here is the veritable monster, virulent and steaming, suddenly barring one's path this very day. A Japanese, Kita Sato, discovered the bacillus in the epidemic at Hong-Kong in 1894, and since then, the Japanese physicians have been invited to Canton, Bombay, Singapore and Manila when those ports are visited by their annual scourges. The Chinese of Hong-Kong call it *Wan Yik* (the epidemic), in painful recollection of the blowing up by the British soldiers in 1894 of the vast Taeping Shan section, which hole lies under the beetling brows of Victoria and Davis Peaks.

The most marked contrast between China and Japan, therefore, is not in arms, manufacturing, or shipping, astonishing as have been the achievements in these respects, but in the splendid modernity of the latter nation in sanitary accomplishments. Of a verity, when we

speak of plague, angels have come upon earth and the
Haran of visitation this time has been in heathen Nippon.
China, of course, has never equaled Bombay in the viru-
lence of the plague, although in the 1894 epidemic, thirty-
five thousand died at Canton alone. Even in the cool
season, Canton has never less than forty deaths a week.
In the neighboring province of Yunnan it is probably
raging in many a damp, mephitic valley when the medical
journals are claiming that at last the earth, so far as
newspaper knowledge goes, is enjoying a respite from the
curse, as seemed to be the case between the years 1844
and 1873. Of late Hong-Kong, which has a native population of three hundred thousand, has averaged three
hundred deaths a year, and from January to September,
1906, the Colony suffered nine hundred deaths from
plague. Cases recur among the Europeans of the Colony
every third year. It is remarkable how plague clings to
a house. After a long respite the scourge broke out in
1901 in a beautiful Arcade opposite the Hong-Kong Bank
on Queen's Road, a European being attacked. Do what
the sanitary board will, each year it has returned until
the house has come to be called " The Row of a Hundred
Shudders." Surprisingly the government has permitted
plague corpses to be buried at Cheung Sha Wan on the
slopes of Mount Davis, in immediate touch with the foreign life of the Colony. This cemetery of ten thousand
tiny stakes and round mounds, is just above a section of
the noble Victoria Jubilee Road, which sweeps half round
the island, thirty feet above the water, and winds in and
out of a dozen bays through Pokfulum as far as Aberdeen. Anchored beneath the Chinese cemetery, swings
around her buoy, the white bulk *Hygeïa* (an old war
vessel of Nelson's time), terrible to many a European

with memories of the fevered struggle with the plague, the only alleviation for which seems to be copious drafts of brandy in the intent to stimulate the action of the heart, which is immediately depressed by the poison of the plague. The Chinese administer musk, hoangnan tea and rhubarb, and sometimes lance the bubo. Among the natives ninety per cent. die, but with the more highly vitalized, meat-fed foreigners, seventy per cent. recover. As is to be expected in mixed bloods, one hundred per cent. of the Eurasians attacked, succumb. The first indication is an eruption under the arm pit, or a swelling in the groin. Almost immediately a great weakness ensues, followed by delirium. The only vanquisher of the bacillus is sunlight. A germ has been known to live two centuries at Haarlem in Holland, and at last attack the workmen who opened the tomb of a sailor.

When the plague becomes epidemic the villagers of Kwangtung, following the principle of the segregation of the healthy and not the diseased, desert their houses and make a pitiful pilgrimage to the hills, where they erect bamboo matsheds. Rats, ants, pigeons, cats and fleas, all die of the disease, and spread the bacillus among humans from towels, plates or food, and humans spread it among themselves from expectoration and contact. Above all, the disease-soaked earth of the cities, undrained of filth for thousands of years, breathes out the plague in the dark, rainy and prostratingly hot May days. In Hong-Kong, excavation is prohibited from May till October.

During the prevalence of the plague in Amoy in June, 1907, the inhabitants proceeded to Kulang-su Island, and secured the idol of Shing Hsien Kung, which is named after a famous doctor now canonized by the Buddhists.

The Emperor at the last procession ten years ago, gave the name of "Hsu Chen Jen" (Genuine Fairy Healer) to the idol. You immediately noticed that the procession was not a gala one, by the unusual feature of horsemen being dressed to represent gods. The *taotai* loaned his new military liveried band of drums and fifes, which alternated with the usual strings, tom-toms and horns. Then, of course, followed the characteristic chairs of fluttering silk and glistening tinsel; tables of food for the gods; bribes for the devils most conspicuous of all; and noble umbrellas and day lanterns.

The new method of treating plague clothing, long followed on the hulk *Stanfield* in Hong-Kong harbor, is now practised throughout Japan, on the suggestion of Doctor Hayaki of the Kencho Board. A steam generator and retort with trays are rolled into a house. Steam is forced at great pressure through the clothing and bedding for half an hour. The method is simple, effective and non-destructive, for the natives have few leather possessions to be injured. The loss of clothing and bedding two or three times a year by the former methods came to be a confiscation as much feared as the epidemic itself. Japanese crews, ever insistent that they have rights over other eastern races, have always been rebellious to permitting their effects to be steamed. I have seen them charge the Chinese crew of the *Stanfield* with knives, even under the turbanned brows of British law in Hong-Kong.

The health of these sub-tropical, coastal cities is somewhat ameliorated by the most violent typhonic rain-storms which sink much of the fetid malarial matter or *chang-chi* far into the ground.

White ants work as insidiously as the causes of earthquakes, and as suddenly, when the timbers are perforated, bring the floors tumbling to the earth. In Canton, more care is now being taken to seal the beams and rafters with tin. Ceilings are perforated, often in beautiful designs, as the ants are less destructive where air is admitted between the floors and the ceilings. The pest arrives on the wings of the night like a cloud, and storms your window if the light is burning. The wings are immediately molted and they crawl away on their mission of destruction. At the season of flight, we would set a light in a tub of water and darken the remainder of the house. The pests would stream to this ignis fatuus, and in this way thousands were lured to a moat of destruction, as the flame clipped their wings. The bite of these insects is another feature of their unpopularity, though not equaled by the fright that they reach you on wings and explore your neck and arms as reptiles.

Even within the pale of civilization at Hong-Kong, a pedestrian on Bowen, Barker or Plantation Roads need not be surprised to encounter a five-foot cobra or a green viper, and on the lonelier roads to Taitam and Stanley, twelve-foot pythons make their slimy way up the bank from the ferny undergrowth. The natives on the Kowloon side fear most the six-inch Teet Sien She, which drops on their wide Hupeh hats with a thud from the tiled eaves of the stone houses.

The white man for the tropics is the wiry, lanky, individual. He is already too thin for anæmia. He should look like a veteran of amœbic dysentery campaigns, but be innocent of the experience. He certainly can not grow apoplectic. His complexion should incline to the swarthy, as those best resist the actinic rays of the sun. Squalls of the nerves, and typhonic centers of melancholia, he

will weather, and ride out on an even keel in his third
year. Thereafter, the three rocks he must chart are:
the yellow girl, typanic airs on a number-man's " screw "
(salary), and the reiterated " peg." But perhaps it is
plainer to say that it takes a genius to withstand the
tropics and sub-tropics, and he must be born. The band
who rove the East find their discoveries as melancholy
to-day as did the followers of Camoens' hero, Da Gama,
to whom: " a grave was the first and awful sight of
every shore." Certainly three-quarters of those who adventure float out on the tide again as dead culls. Many
a good fellow's ignorance has stranded him in the melancholy little cemetery at the foot of the White Cloud Hills
at Canton; in the old Portuguese cemetery outside the
West Gate of Peking; in the yellow-walled cemetery on
the Wong Nei Chong (Happy Valley) Road at Hong-
Kong, in casteless comraderie with the blue ghosts of Parsees; behind the fort-like walls of that square graveyard
of the missionaries that crowns the height over the Areia
Preta beach at Macao,— or in a similar banishment of his
white man's soul in the suburbs of many another treaty
port. Unquestionably those who retire come away with
weakened eyes, liver, spleen, or blood, but these disabili-
ties are merely physical; they have gained in heart, in a
broader comprehension of all human kind, " Cingalee,
Chinee, and Portugee "; caste, half-caste, and outcast. It
should be understood, however, that he does not reach all
these conclusions while he is in the turmoil and the chastening sweat, but from the better perspective of his ancient
and native heath, which he a thousand times despaired of
ever reaching. As a Chinese sage says, " Appreciations
come by contrast, and experiences are the ladder of
Truth." I never knew a foreigner in the southern Chi-

nese ports who did not languish for nine months of his first two years in sickness. Saigon and Bangkok have even a less enviable name than Shanghai, Nanking and Hong-Kong. Hong-Kong, with miseries enough of its own, is not, however, productive of the pulmonary troubles that are prevalent farther north at Peking, Ningpo, and even Shanghai, where great changes fall suddenly.

The physicians of Hong-Kong are associated into partnerships and have splendid suites of offices in the large buildings on the Praya front. A large part of their lucrative practice consists in answering messages from foreigners taken ill inland in China, directing them to the proper remedies in their medicine chests to relieve the symptoms which they have telegraphed. There is probably nothing as unique as this in medical practice anywhere else in the world.

It is proposed to segregate the ten thousand slowly rotting lepers of Canton into lazarettoes in the canal-moated territory round about. In the province there are twenty thousand more untended wretches, and in the whole country three hundred thousand. The disease is most prevalent in the damp, hot South, and especially in the silk villages. It does not seem to increase with the population; there have always seemed to be about the same number in the land. Subscriptions are asked for the segregation camps, one *cash* (one-twelfth of a cent) a day being deemed sufficient to keep one person. As it is now, they come into unpleasant proximity to their fellows. I once took a powerful launch and passed through some of the canals south of Canton in the Heungshan district between the Pearl and West Rivers. The water teems with boat life and duck farms. Wending among it all were the lepers, with distorted hands sculling their boats against the tide. A gong was displayed, but it was too difficult to strike it. Some trusted to their appearance to have alms tossed to them. Others held up a cup which was tied to the end of a bamboo. Silently up and down they went, beating out the short, fateful strokes against the hour of death. Those who had no hands or feet to row, laid on the deck, using their eyes or their lungs, but otherwise appearing as castaway, dismembered bodies of breathing humanity, pitiable and revolting to look upon.

A charitable Chinawoman,— a Hakka of the boat class, with unbound feet and wearing a flapping veil on her hat, is seen coming along the tow-path by the canal. A leper has placed his jug in the middle of the path. He has no hands or feet, and rolls and crawls back from the path. The woman approaches, and drops in the alms. The mortal eyes, with supra-mortal gleam because of the spiritual accession which comes of suffering, flash out a thanks and a blessing and an assurance of pity, that he will not roll back to the cup until she is safely passed. When she is gone, he works toward the food, and grasps it in his teeth, feeding like the animal that mortal misery can make of any of us. Where charity is spread thinner in the rural districts of Kwangtung, the lepers have the privilege of accosting funerals for alms, and if they are not paid they jump in the graves until they receive food. The disease is now ascertained to be microbic and is a heritage from times in China which were even dirtier than the present, although popularly it is still said to be a poison communicated by sun-dried unsalted fish.

Along the sea-coast of southern China, in all the large English and French settlements, hot as the climate is, every foreign house must be equipped with a drying room. Here are stowed master's violin and lady's fischu, and in fact once every week all wearing apparel must have its day in the hot room. Shoes collect so much fungus overnight that there is no telling what mysterious growth they would be the center of, were time allowed. Here, therefore, is a people, the political writers moralize, who must keep on the march when they take to leather, and that it will be woe to us when they do. The home-made veneered furniture of the colonizing American who is on his way to Manila, peels like an orange, and a week afterward his glued boxes tumble apart to the touch of unseen hands. When discouraged, go to the Chinese cabinet-maker and watch him make his joints with mortise and screw.

There are no papered walls in the rooms of the palatial residences of foreign exiles in Hong-Kong or on Shameen Island, Canton. Walls are either painted or kalsomined, and the streams of moisture soon make them sorry enough. The effect would be unbearably gloomy were it not that bright native tapestries are resorted to, to hide the oppressive evidence of the melancholy, clammy climate.

Following the American boycott of 1904 the Chinese newspapers trained themselves for something really admirable in the boycott of Indian opium. In whatever manner Chinese life is relieved of the blight, every lover of humanity will welcome the abolition of the abhorrent trade, if it has the sincere accompaniment of the uprooting of the far too extensive Yunnan and Szechuen poppy fields. The Chinese poets have come to lament of it as the " White Dragon of the treaty ports ": " *Kwo Wu Ti Ya Pien*," " Oh, the murderous opium." The

Eunuchs of the late Empress Dowager in the garden arcade, Palace, Peking.

Late Empress Dowager Tse Hsi, carried in her chair by eunuch bearers in Peking's forbidden Palace Grounds.

The lake in Royal Palace grounds, Peking, China. The long revetment wall is built of marble. The pagoda is of porcelain. Patachu hills in distance.

drug has only been in general abuse for seventy years, and it was England which popularized it by force and persistent proffer of it. H. E. Chum, once viceroy of Canton, who is exceedingly unpopular with the Europeans of Hong-Kong because of his tactless patriotism, is especially active in the anti-opium movement. The following is quoted from one of his circulars to officials, published at Canton in April, 1906: " The habit is perhaps excusable in the old and decrepit, but any other officials found to make a habit of opium smoking will be immediately cashiered, as it is a danger to the nation and demoralizing to the individual. The opium eater is one of the dead who is not yet buried." A greater than Chum, the veteran Viceroy Chang Chih Tung, in a passionate appeal, calls the drug: " a worse curse than flood or beasts; destroyer of mind; consumer of substance; transformer into demons and depraved; the only salvation is a Renaissance of learning." The use of morphia is increasing, and for this England's ally, Japan, is to blame. She is flooding China with cheap hypodermic syringes, but American influence will probably encourage China shortly to prohibit the importation of syringes and morphia.

To become disgusted with the mad indulgence, look into the dens along the Leng Thau at Amoy, and at Toulon, Cherbourg and Brest; into the wardrooms of the French warships, or into the smoking-rooms of the steamboats running to Canton and Macao from Hong-Kong, like the *Tai-on*, the *Fatshan*, the *Heungshan*, etc. Couches are provided; the little tin can is feverously opened e'er the steamer casts off. The native, nervous with the *ying* or fiery longing upon him, searches for a prod which looks like a hair-pin; he twirls it around in the can and draws out a moist bead which is heated and rolled, cooled and rolled and heated again. At last its consistency suits. He places the gummy bead on the large flute-like pipe, or *yen siang* (smoking pistol). There is a ravenous, full-mouthed inhalation as the peanut-oil lamp heats the ball into vapor; a mad glare in which brilliant thoughts, like a Chinese Coleridge's perhaps, sweep through the mind. He does not really see you at the window, though he is looking at you now. You are only one of a numerous fairy company which is hovering there, so do not be sensitive or excuse yourself. Then ensues a sinking dream, followed by a wild awakening and craving for a further pipe, which he prepares with sickening impatience. Our own trans-Pacific steamships all have a hidden opium room for Asiatic patrons, or woe betide the revenue of that ship. When a man gets the habit (and about one-fortieth of the population use opium) it takes about three years to use the victim up. In his last days, see how the baggy skin hangs on his bones. How black he is! Such caverns of eyes and how they run with water! Such chills come over him even in the flame of the zenith sun! Such a thirst he has, but not for water! He knows not for what he longs; he only remembers that when he smokes he longs no more. The stupefied effect is produced by the alkaloids being inhaled into the lungs. The drug costs the poor Chinese $122,000,000 a year,— more than their greatest burden, the land tax,— and a sum which if spent for a navy would soon make them omnipotent. It makes among the poor nearly all their criminals, just as whisky does among us. If the religious fear of not having children to worship at their graves and tablet did not operate, more than the one in forty would fall to the vice. The priests repeat the warning: "*Chih yen pu neng yang san tai."* " If you eat opium your sons will die out in the second generation."

Formerly the opium was all imported, but now in faithless Yunnan, which diverts all her rivers into French China, and in the most fertile upland plain of China, Ching Too in Szechuen, in the irrigated valleys which the engineers Li Ping, father and son, laid out in 250 B. C., the glorious rice terraces are being obliterated and the cursed poppy is blooming everywhere. All except the white blooms are weeded out, the white variety being most prolific in opiate juice. So the most populous and happiest province, to which the gods gave five parallel rivers to drag the harvest boats down to the Father of Waters, the Yangtze, becomes the first to be inveigled into the folds of that destructive monster whose pestiferous haunts have heretofore been confined to the seven hundred thousand acres in the upper Ganges Valley. The scene in Szechuen is interesting enough; the land is plowed deep by a wooden share, which is hauled by anything that can pull: water-buffalo, woman, pony or camel; the plots between the raised mud paths are flooded from well or stream; the precious seed is mixed with earth before it is scattered, a most ingenious method to prevent thick sowing and wind waste. In fourteen weeks the heads are cut off and punctured with needles six times successively, and some of the powdered pods are mixed with the juice in preparing the thickened article which is shaped and hardened in molds about the size of a crab apple. These balls are again sun dried and shelf cured.

When opium is banished then will revive indeed in China the golden age of Yau and Shun of which Confucius sang. On June 15th, 1906, the British government intimated to the Wai Wupu that they would agree at a sacrifice to Bengal of twenty-four millions a year, to prohibit the exportation of India morphia to China, provided China ceases to manufacture her own opium or to import from any other country whatsoever. This will cost China a revenue of four million dollars a year duties on the three thousand tons of imported India opium. China lays no special tax on the Yunnan and Szechuen poppy fields, but she taxes the thirty thousand tons of crude opium produced therefrom. John Morley's speech in answer to the prayers of the years rang with the revived Christian statesmanship of Wilberforce: " I am prepared to go all the length of abolishing the opium trade in China at any sacrifice to England or India." The government of the Colony of Hong-Kong is supported to the extent of one third by the tax on the " Opium Farm," which is owned by the Chinese and Parsees. There is accordingly a great to-do in the Colony over the alarming prospect of increased taxation of property, when opiated China sobers up. Surprise is frequently expressed by travelers at the scenes enacted at the Canton Steamboat wharf at Hong-Kong in the name of British law and dignity. Chinese gentlemen are pounced upon by the minions of the local opium farmer and searched. There is far more blackmail than excise in the scheme. These detectives of all colors and records, the " beachcombers " of an occidental civilization tented on remote oriental sands for a season, abuse their authority flagrantly when they conclude that every Chinaman, poor or rich, is an opium smuggler at heart and that his baggage and home can be turned upside down at any hour of the night on the excuse of a suspected caché. The plan of rewarding informers has led to nothing short of a widespread system of fostering the latent secret society and clan spite. The farm is on Ice-House Lane in the center of the Colony, and visitors will know it by the great loads of mango boxes, gunny-covered, drawn to its gate by strings of nearly naked coolies.

A humorous instance of smuggling recently occurred at Bangkok. A coolie wearing an enforced look of faithfulness to his master, and bearing an exceedingly thick gold sign with enormous characters of "*Peace and Honesty*," exhibited eagerness to go ashore. A gimlet was procured and his sign explored. It revealed in its recesses many tins of the muddy opium paste, and Mr. Coolie and his queue were prompt to follow their chagrin over the taffrail.

Large sums of money are being spent at Canton by the New China party in spreading the anti-Opium crusade. Millions of pamphlets and caricatures are distributed. American and Japanese doctors are hired in the sanitariums of the guilds. Lectures are given where distorted and stupefied victims are exhibited as object lessons. Anti-opium Societies are being formed in the villages. The members wear a badge and sign a pledge.

One scene will illustrate the repentance which is sweeping over the land. I do not know how it started, but an iconoclastic penitence was the inspiration of it. Nor do I know why it did not take its way to the park of a sacred temple, to invoke religious auspices. The procession stopped instead at Chang Su Ho's tea-gardens outside of Shanghai for the Burning of the Pipes and the vow of abstinence from opium. Every man carried the evidence of his contrition and the vessel of his shame. Nut-oil lamps of best hammered Nanking brass work; trays of gorgeous Ningpo lacquering; ivory and ebony smoking pipes of best Cantonese carving; jars of fuel for the lamps from Manchuria; cups of the opium treacle from Macao and Yunnan; the burned crooked toasting pins with their precious jewel heads,— were all cast on an oil-soaked pyre, the base of which was made from the lounges and tables contributed by a converted opium shop proprietor. One student withdrew his ebony pipe. There was a sigh and audible prayers begging him to " be a man." But the doubters had not read the vehement fire in his eye. He drew a saw from a nail, cut the costly pipe in two, as though it were cheap white wood, and cast the demolished cause of his sorrow on the heap, to the plaudits of the crowd who from even the roof of the compound-buildings added to this pile of forsaken idols, gathered together in an old nation's new Hezekiah-like strength. Some one from the roof threw a great yellow tile trough upon the mass, and broke glass and ivory ware with a sickening crackle, but it did not draw forth any sighs, or anger, or laughter. Men only looked the sterner, and struck hammers into the head of the mass. A mandarin on behalf of the approving officials, a *tepao* for the people themselves, stepped forth, and all drew back. A singing girl broke through the unconsciously formed circle, and asked to be allowed to add her pipe and powder puff. Then there was no more delay. Oil was called for, and poured from kongs until the stack was soaked, when the flame was touched to seal a company of the people in a vow to the heavens that they would chain themselves no more to the leprous past. A recent regulation is that opium pipes shall be licensed at one dollar, and amusingly: " the license shall be hung on the pipe."

Japan does not look with as much concern as does China on the opium habit. Last March, thirty thousand

new licenses at thirty *sen* each, " good for life " were issued by the Japanese to the conquered Formosans.

The historic destruction in May, 1839, of $11,000,000
worth of Indian opium by the Chinese at Canton has never
had a parallel for voluntary and really philanthropic sacrifice of property, for China ultimately paid triple the
price in war and indemnity. Two hundred chests at a
time were emptied into a trench which was filled with a
mixture of lime and salt water until the twenty thousand
ruined chests were drained into the embrowned creeks
of the Chukiang at low tide. The memories of the
so-called " perfidious Commissioner " Lin Tseh Su and
his Emperor Tau Kwang, whose emotions on this subject at least were on the most exalted plane, both merit
monumental praise. The two memorable letters of Lin's
to Queen Victoria, pleading with her to put an end to
the execrable opium trade, just before the war broke
out, and before China had been taught to grow the poppy,
assume almost the voice of an angel in history, pleading with tears for justice, if one looks at it from the
Chinese side.

The Opium Conference of the nations called by America in Shanghai in 1909 was a failure owing to Hong-
Kong's and India's fear of loss of revenue, but Britain
must yet fulfil Mr. Morley's promises. We shall have
other conferences and America will call them until Britain
keeps her word. The effect of the opium abstinence is
going to add potentially to China's already vast population by the decrease in the death rate.

From Formosa to Tonquin the Chinese coast is fog-
bound during February and March. The warm north-
flowing Japan current, chafing the chilled current of the
Yellow Sea which flows south, foments a heavy mist

curtain which makes the harbors, especially the narrow Lyee-moon entrance to Hong-Kong, impenetrable for days. The coast-line with its many peaks of three thousand feet altitude, is blanketed. There is nothing to do but anchor when iron-bound islands stud the channels. Often the peaks alone are clear and those who dwell upon them for coolness behold glorious effects of a sun-lit fog rolling off and again folding up the spires and towers of a great city from whence still come the distant cries of life. Suddenly a gale rushes down the gullies, and licks up the curtain. In an instant is revealed an active metropolis, colored with the dyes and quaint with the forms of the Orient. Or again the peaks only are hid, and the bearers, as they climb the hills, gradually take you in your mountain chair deeper and deeper into a chilling heaven of milk-white fog, in which the coolies stumble and with difficulty pick out the cement path that leads to *chez vous,* or better *chez moi.*

None is quicker to concede the dangers of his own summer climate than the Oriental himself, inured though he is to it by heredity and habitude. David said: " I will lift up mine eyes unto the hills, whence cometh my help "; the Arab goatherd to-day drives his flock from the plain of Er Rahah to the cooler clefts on Sinai's Peak. The Pekingese officials flee to the heights of Patachu; the Seoul man betakes himself to the Namhan Hills. The Tokio resident retires to Chusenji's mountain lake and splendid heights. The Ningpo people climb Foting Hill on Phutho Island. The Hong-Kongite takes a tram which lifts him in seven minutes fifteen hundred feet above his boiling harbor and he is borne in chairs three hundred feet higher to find a cooling breath brought by the monsoon over the peaks. Or on a still night he slips down the tram; takes a launch and tears around the mountain-encircled bay to create a breeze by motion, but the bow cuts only into molten waves of hot, though magnificent phosphoresence.

It is July; the official heat in the shade is 92, the humidity 90. There has been no rain in six months. How they suffer in number five district of Hong-Kong, where is packed the densest population of the world, one thousand to the acre, against the nine hundred of New York's East Side, and seven hundred of London's Whitechapel! The pigs crawl to the gutter and become molten grease from their own and the sun's heat. The water of the bay shines as metallic as a pan, and radiates the heat like molten steel. The once gray and green war-ships have been painted white again to de-focus the blazing rays. To go to the waters for relief in daytime never occurs to the minds of those experienced in the Orient. There is a mica-like glitter in the blinding atmosphere; it is the sun flashing from the suspended sand and dust particles. Dogs are going mad, for the springs have all dried up, and there is barely enough drinking water for humans. The soldiers in the barracks of this garrison post which is the strongest in the far East lie all day on their backs and cry to the punkah coolies to fan away their curses. The sailors, baking between the steel walls of the war-ships, are ordered to dive overboard on the shady side of the ship after four o'clock. Ale is struck from the rations because heat and alcohol are driving men as mad as a sailor becalmed in the Red Sea. The foreign sick, tossing upon the hot canvas of their cots, bemoan how frightfully far away home is. There is not a breath stirring the Australian eucalyptus trees which have been planted to drive away the malaria breeding Anopheles mosquitoes.

They may talk of a thermometer on a flat roof in Bagdad registering 150 in the sun, but please remember that the Tigris Valley has nothing like the humidity which accompanies heat at Hong-Kong, and it is humidity only which kills, and which tells you of its heartless intent while it is doing the killing. The barometer is scanned at the newpaper offices to see if there is any chance of a typhoon breaking the awful still glow. It is painful to hear a 'rickisha move along at mid-day; what fool can be daring a sunstroke! Every one keeps changes of clothes at the office, for the journey to business in a jolting sedan chair has brought out the perspiration which has wet one's Chifu silk coat through and through. Relays are hired for your punkah-coolie force, who are on night work. You keep your shoes near your bed to throw at a delinquent, who, as soon as he thinks you are asleep, stops pulling the rope of the ceiling-fan, and falls asleep himself, utterly indifferent to the fact that the lack of a breeze will at once wake you up. It is stifling under your mosquito curtain and you tear it down, trusting to the punkah breeze to alarm the flying cockroaches and other winged pests. You raise the temperature of your bath, for your diminishing vitality will not stand the slightly cooled water from the cistern of your home, or the artesian water of the club. Day by day the pavements and walls grow more dazzling in the sun; night by night your head swims and you think you will swoon away for ever. If only you could, and the torture of recoveries not be repeated. You grow terrorized, and the sight of the blue walls of a Christian's cemetery in exile gives you a panic. You are fearing that after all you will not be able to pull through. They are sending the patients who have been operated upon, from the hospitals on the peak by ships to Wei-Hai-Wei and Chifu, as their wounds will not heal here in the south. The barometer lowers and you have high hopes, but still no rain comes. Two days later, a ship arrives, minus a yard and a boat or two; exasperating! the blow swung just clear of the Colony.

You hate the full moon, it only seems like another glaring sun in the stifling, sleepless night. Some of the trees impatient with nature herself are shedding their leaves in a land where there never is frost. The king of blooms, the purple lotus in the public gardens, has closed and gone to golden seed. It marks the height of the tropic season. The reservoirs have lost their purple sheen and are down to the yellow liquid of the muddy bottom, and weeds are beginning to grow down the sides of the basins as a sign of the subjugation of hygiene. The stores have run short, and you send your *foki* out in a sampan to the steamers in the harbor for "Schweppe and Scotch." Religion comes to the gates of nature. The missionaries are praying in the chapels; the bonzes are beating cymbals and dog-skin kettledrums as soon as the day begins; the sampan women are lighting extra handfuls of punk sticks, and even you, an irreligious seven year man, on your second term, are thinking of your mother, and joining the rest in prayer to her God for rain. Again the barometer is sought; it is falling. Men gather round it at the club and the harbor office. The bulletin of rain is announced in the Chinese sheet and credit is given to the dragon for old Faith's sake, though the proof-reader smiles now. But where is that first wind that is to come from a corner somewhere, anywhere, and open the gates of Salvation?

The wind at last rises with the voice of an angel, and the harbor in welcoming joy has leaped up with white arms. It is growing darker even at four o'clock, and the burned hills are not so glaringly red and white. There are shadows spotting them. Coolies come out of their cellar retreats and are gathering at the curbs, a *high-ya* upon their voices and a new soul in their eyes. The fowl on the disease heaps are crowing, and the caged Tientsin larks are singing. How the world to-day worships Heaven in whatever language you pronounce the word, and shows its faith before the gift! Some one declares they have seen a drop on the pavement, and a number have dropped their bamboo poles and are stooping over to make examination. *Hoi Loi* is shouted: Mah tells Kih that he did it with his wet finger and the homely humor explodes the always cheerful native crowd. Of a sudden a darkness, like later evening, closes in. The drops strike like shots on the wide grass Hupeh hats of the coolies and on the starched blue Nankeen blinds of the sedan chairs. It pelts; it comes in spears and sheets; the earth drinks and rises in a glorious perfume. Goats, fowl, pigs, dogs and water-buffaloes break bounds and join master and servant in the street. There is no bond or free, driven or driver, Yellow or White, animal or its superior, for a spell. All stand forth equal in need and gratitude. The curse is ended and there is respite from the sentence of death by the shafts of the sun. How it rains! The gulleys and gorges roar in the night. Thirty inches fall in twenty-four hours. The great white Praya has been converted into a lake, which, as it drains into the sea, makes of the long revetment walls a waterfall of wonderful width. The mounted army officers dash through the flood and remind one another: " How like it is to Calcutta's maidan in August." The unpaved country roads become a viscid pudding and your house coolies at last have a good excuse for delaying the supplies for your dinner.

It is one of the world's wonders to go out into a tropic storm and hear nature take up her clarion in the weed-grown gulleys, and see her hands drive the white torrents over the precipices. It is not the effect of Niagara, which has always been the same; it is the alarm of the unfamiliar, for here you stood yesterday and now you know it not in its mad, new grandeur. Your precious bamboo Venetian blind, that shaded you for so many months with all the faithfulness of the prophet's gourd, has gone like a thing possessed of the hilarious storm soul, fluttering your poster-pictures from its yellow sail. What of it; it is a sign of manumission. The last week of April, 1908, was unprecedented for rainfall in southern China. Fifty inches fell, making seventy inches for the year, which is twice what Shanghai and ten times what Peking gets. Canton and its villages were under two feet of water. The creeks flowing into the Sikiang (West River) rose with their parent and submerged rice fields, trees and huts. Millions die yearly of famine because China persists in a devotion to rice. The riverine fields necessarily are in danger of continual inundation by the flooding of her great rivers whose headwaters are not gradually released by restraining forests. If China would only take to raising grain on higher land!

In August last, Peking, which in winter has as low a thermometer as Albany, reported 105 degrees of heat, and a cholera scourge, with three hundred deaths daily, added to the horrors of a summer residence in the capital. It is impossible under present hygienic ignorance, to restrain the natives from eating green fruit even during cholera epidemics. When the deadly cramps strike them the native expresses himself by saying: " A rat is eating me."

Hong-Kong is the emporium for Manila in cattle and fresh produce, and the United States Marine Hospital inspectors are stationed at the former place with all power to visé exportations. I recall an official excursion with one of the doctors during the prevalence of a cholera epidemic in Manila, to find the impossible: a potato field in the Canton delta which was innocent of the abominable method of using human fertilizer. To prevent the carriage of cholera germs these officials will not visé during certain seasons the exportation to America of the sacred narcissus roots, which are wrapped in Chinese earth. We rest secure at home because our government sleeps not abroad.

A foreigner wonders why his underclothing, which is beaten on stones in streams, should afflict him with spots which burn agonizingly. He soon discovers that the clothes were dried on grass patches which have been used for years for the same purpose, and that he is poisoned with dobie itch. Small white pimples form under the skin wherever there is chafing, and the tortured griffin is transformed into a humorous jumping-jack for the amusement of the veterans of great and little ills.

In the early days of oriental colonies the now familiar dengué fever (then called the Sand) was looked upon as a rapidly approaching stroke of death, as immediate insensibility attacked the limbs, and early writings are full of the amusing fears of travelers. The symptoms are similar to the plague, excepting that there are no eruptions under the arms. There is immediate lassitude, bone-grinding aches, and a delirium of pleasant visions such as opiates produce. The most marked feature is the itch, which attacks the whole body at once during convalescence. The sufferer is soused in hot baths; salves are applied, but do what his nurses may, the victim must stand three days of the most violent itching that imagination can comprehend.

The climate has produced a certain moral effect upon the Chinese of the south. In Europe, heat has made the southern races hot-tempered and tender under trial. In China the heat and humidity have taught the race that if they are to live at all, they must take things calmly, and thus in conquering their bodies so as to endure the climate, they have unconsciously disciplined their minds, as perhaps no other race has, for greatness in a world mission of the future. Their coolness of temperament is reinforced by the philosophies of the schools. The race further steadies itself under discipline, as witness the native regiment raised by the British at Wei-Hai-Wei, and Yuan Shi K'ai's troops,— and with this threefold patience, promises to become a ponderous machine when drilled to methods, whether of modern commerce or warfare. Their equipoise of temperament is possibly best illustrated by an absolute absence of taste for alcoholic stimulant.

It is peculiar that a tubercular diathesis, absent in China, should be the strongest inclination of the race when they emigrate.

An oriental scourge, not so widely written of in these days because it is attacking foreigners less than it used to when ships made slower voyages, is beri-beri, the germs of which are taken from moldy rice, like the Rangoon product, which carries the excrementitious infective matter of a small brown weevil. The damp climate of the south fosters sporadic outbreaks at Canton. Those who live on the ground floor are particularly subject to it. The Portuguese of Macao therefore make of their street floor merely a shed for the 'rickisha and rake. The beautiful stairway leads from the middle of the adobe tiling to the second floor, where the family lives, the choicest situation in the home thus being given up to the necessities of hygiene. The disease only becomes epidemic where vegetables are lacking in the food and where the people are crowded together without exercise, as on shipboard or in camps. As in plague, light keeps down the beri-beri germs. Instead of a swelling of the gland, it exhibits itself by a swelling of the ankle. The mortality is over ninety per cent. The Osaka hospitals had many cases break out among the rice-fed troops who were invalided home from the great war in 1905.

Distant from the town of Victoria four miles through the hills, or ten miles around the island of Hong-Kong, is the deserted settlement of Stanley which first created the name: "The White Man's Grave." The only thing there now which shows the attention of man is the government fence around the graves of the soldiers who fell a prey to the malaria in the forties, when drainage and tropical digging were not understood as they are at present. The mortality was eighty per cent. Even now the admissions to hospital on account of malaria are one-third of the troops on the sick list. The worst feature of the fever is its predisposition to other diseases. Governments may well fear malaria as it costs seven hundred dollars to invalid a soldier home. It is cheaper to keep him well on foreign station, which explains the recent growth of recreation grounds and clubs without canteens, and the increase also in the amount and variety of his work before and after sundown. Mimic war makes for stern health and leaves less time for whisky and worry.

A Chinese emigrant will lift his hat before his mouth to protect his inhalation if you mention the lethal valleys of the Red River in Tonquin or the mephitic Salween in western Yunnan, which the superstitious will cross only in the night. This of course is the worst thing they could do, as the sun exercises some effect in checking the malarious vapors.

Cockroaches are a noisy pest which rummage the whole night. They eat the enamel off your shoes. Every blue covered book on the shelves is attacked. You can not keep them out, for they come in on the wings of the darkness and escape with the wings of the morning. They dash in your face as you turn up the lights, and they dive into your friend's cocktail glass between the time of salute and swallow. When you pursue them they back up under your chiffonier and eye you with a squint. In other words this pest of China is a winged, a wiser, a more traveled and a larger bird than our crawling specimen in occidental cellars.

It is considered brotherly among the natives to use the same basin of water when handing to the guests after a meal a hot wet cloth to wipe the face. This unfortunate etiquette is sowing much of the trachoma which afflicts the race. However the Chinese do not use one water for a family bath as do the Japanese, and suffer from less trachoma and skin diseases. Faces, pitted by small-pox, which they call " Heavenly Flowers," are constantly met. In Hong-Kong the natives offer no resistance to vaccination.

A great deal has been written that the race does not

pursue heavy physical exercises and participates only in light outdoor games.   But it is not to be judged therefrom that the Chinese ignore the importance of physical culture; they differ from us in that their care of the body is by a lighter rule suited to their climate, and their more exhausting day's work.   The leading classic of the nation, the fount of all its morals, *On Filial Piety,* lays down the following as the basic principle of conduct: " The first thing which filial duty requires of us is that we carefully preserve from all injury and in a perfect state, the bodies which we have received from our parents."

Who that has taken his first ride behind the hill-climbing chair coolies of Hong-Kong has not marveled at these splendid specimens of muscular strength?   They are with one exception a sculptor's Greek-like model in the thin ankles and knees; great calves and thighs and fair chest and neck muscles.   The arms however are rather thin.   A rhythm to the quick step is beaten with one arm extended, or the " goose-arm " as the German sailors call it.

A race which believes in the infusion of a young buck's horns, ginseng and cockroaches' wings for a fever antidote may be expected to follow other unusual medical methods.   With no modern knowledge of dissection or the osseous system, a Chinese doctor jabs needles six inches long all over the body and will never hit a bone or an artery.   It is said they practise upon wax figures.   In a wonderfully responsive way they compel the patient to rouse his courage and exhilarate his nerves.   They are decided dietists and bring about therefore many results similar to our own.   Broths are made of bay, honey, carbon, blood, wine and almonds; aperients and hot water flushing are called into service. They attach great importance to the appearance of the tongue. Violent ice douches, exhausting exercise and sudden smotherings are resorted to. The severest kind of pinching osteopathy is used efficaciously for dyspepsia and some cases of massage are so heroic that the athletic physician kneads his groaning victim with his knees as well as hands. They do not study the nervous system, or harden the outer edge of the hand, as do the Japanese, who in ju-jitsu make one blow on a nerve center paralyze a man.

Their diagnosticians believe in microbes, but consider that they are larger than microscopic, and so treat for eggs and worms. In stomach troubles, neuralgia, rheumatism and boils, they are quick to effect a cure. An infusion of crickets' wings is used to reduce obesity. They attach the greatest importance in their diagnosis to the beats of the arteries and claim that there are twelve movements of significance. There are no apothecaries, the physician himself compounding his prescriptions, and the patient, if able, is encouraged to come to the doctor's residence to take his medicine. Their offices are fitted up artistically, the physician claiming that the new and agreeable surroundings have a beneficial influence. A pair of deer's horns (not a mortar and pestle) mark the doors, and crockery jars take the place of our bottles. Butcher shops often add one shelf of medicines to the stock. No physician uses his own 'rickisha; he hires one, and it is customary for the patient's family to pay the coolies on departure. When the fee is finally received, it is wrapped in tissue paper and is called "golden thanks." Withal, zeal is added unto prayer and prescription, for no physician is paid in full if his patient succumbs.

Ginseng (ivywort) is dried over charcoal in Korea. It is cultivated under screens in a valley sixty miles from Seoul. Korea makes six hundred thousand dollars a year from its sale, and America might increase her trade to millions in the really useless root to which the Chinese pin their greatest hopes in sickness. The imports of the root at Hong-Kong in 1908 had dropped to seven hundred and sixty-six *piculs*, as compared with eleven hundred and ten *piculs* in 1900. A sweet-tasting, dark-colored, clean and unbroken wild root is preferred. Korean roots bring the largest price, sometimes as high as twenty-five hundred dollars Mexican a *picul*. While an infusion of the root is general, some of it is preserved in honey. The black-barred, adobe-tiled cellars on Des Voeux Road West, Hong-Kong, where the herb is dealt in, are unpretentious enough places, but the canny dealers there know the pulse of trade and in a moment can judge the valuable roots, picking out faults of weevil, moisture, imperfect roots, the paler cultivated plants, or roots which have been redried. Long as the voyage across the Pacific is, the importers in Hong-Kong will receive the goods only on consignment.

Another skin disease, communicated by the unspotted Culex mosquito, is our familiar " Barbadoes' leg," where the bitten part swells up hard, sore and feverous, and makes the terrified sufferer think his last day has come, for he is sure he has been bitten in his sleep by a heathenish salamander.

Flights of greenish gray locusts are an occasional visitation. They settle on the shrubs with weight enough to break their branches. In three or four hours they will leave a dozen acres as bare of green as though a forest fire had singed the landscape, and then like all plagues

Ladies of Manchu society, Peking, North China.

The old examination park of 12,000 brick stalls at Canton, South
China. No lectures were given; the University
consisted of an Examining Board.

Delicate carving and tile-work, shrine of Temple of Choo Shing,
Canton, South China.

which have accomplished their malign purpose, they are off with the wings of the morning.

But the never-to-be-forgotten thing, when on the subject of the Chinese climate, is her typhoons (Fung Kau) of August and September. Ninety miles an hour velocity has been recorded. I stayed a day and a night at Hong-Kong fifteen hundred feet above the water, during one of these blows. The crescendo shrieks of the wind were terrifying. A crash was heard: it was the brick end of the Mount Austin barracks, four hundred feet above us in the clouds, being blown in. A walk afterward through the town on the lower terraces revealed a desolation of windows and shutters, eucalyptus and banyan trees, like Detaille's painting of *The Defense of Champigny*. A barricade wooden shutter, with a thick typhoon brace, is fitted on these tropical houses, for no glass would stand for a moment. On another occasion I had been out on the auxiliary Japanese cruiser *Nippon Maru* for a trial trip, which was completed in haste at Aberdeen under a rapidly lowering barometer. With full speed, in a lightened ship, riding frightfully high, we returned to the northern anchorage under the shelter of High West Peak at Hong-Kong. The blow had come; it was too dangerous for two days to take a tug boat ashore, even if one were available. Great war-ships steamed against their chains and plowed like Leviathan. White-crested billows vied with the gale in a mad race westward. Behind the breakwater at Causeway Bay, and at Shau-Ki-Wan and Shelter Bays, a forest of junks were hid under the Wong Nei Chong Hills. Now and then, several would be torn out into the path of the storm, like so much seaweed.

Just previous to a typhoon, it is a wonderful spectacle

to see the excited crews and women of the junks,— a dozen on each two-piece fir sweep, sculling to help the steam launches as they pull strings of boats to safety behind some peak. As the storms are circular, a refuge that is safe one night may be the exposed position next morning, and therefore there is much loss of life among the harassed junk people. A typhoon covers a space of one hundred miles in diameter. There is a calm of ten miles in the center, and when passengers on a Pacific liner are congratulating themselves that they have passed almost through death, they can not understand the worried look of the navigating officers, who know that shortly they must run through the other rim of the storm. When things seem the worst because of the perfect deluge of rain and darkness, it is an unfailing indication of a rising barometer and the end of trouble. Fortunately the typhoons give about three hours local warning, as they sweep along the coast northward from the tropics, in a barometer dropping as low as twenty-eight and one-half, a " typhoon-bank," or over bright west at sunset, with a cloudy eastern horizon accompanying, and huge unbroken billows which cast their white wreaths on the shores of a foamless sea. We were warned in the harbor by black baskets (globe, oblong, or cone shaped to indicate direction) being hoisted to the peak on the commodore's East Indian war relic, the hulk *Tamar*. The flag-ship hoisted a red burgee over a white ensign as a signal to steam against anchor chains at three quarter speed. Manila and Hong-Kong are more in touch regarding typhoons than trade, and the former city sends almost daily warnings by cable. I recall the United States battleship *Oregon,* after a fiercer struggle than she experienced in the battle of Santiago, limping through a typhoon into Yokohama harbor in the fall of 1903, with her steel deck plates sprung, and boats gone by the board.

The historic typhoons of China are those of July 21st, 1841; July, 1862; September 22nd, 1874, and September 20th, 1906; and of India that which swept over Calcutta in October, 1864, which last drowned forty thousand people. In the 1874 typhoon the saddest destruction was wreaked along the noble Praya Grande at beautiful Macao. That the unique ruin of San Paulo's façade was saved is attributed by the pious Macaenses only to prayer, as the ruin dominates the city on an exposed hill. The Chinese are zealous custodians of records, and it is quite easy to secure photographs of the great destruction. Up the Canton and West Rivers the storm swept, bombarding everything into ruin and drowning fifty thousand of the boat people in a tidal bore ten feet higher than spring tides. Steamers of eight thousand tons and sailing ships of six thousand tons were hurled up on the stone prayas.

The typhoon of 1906 which destroyed ten thousand people came without telegraphic warning over the southwest peaks of Hong-Kong. The local warning of a vivid sunset the night before was disregarded. Harbor work and shipping were going on as usual in the early morning. The blow began at nine A. M. right on the echo of the observatory gun and was over at eleven A. M. The screams of the wind rose above the cries of death, save now and then in agonizing lulls when death alone spoke. It was impossible to see a yard ahead. The rain came in torrents undermining everything and hurling the rocks down the mountain gulleys as from a Roman catapult. The wind caught up Chinese hats like disci, together with native sign-boards with their wild flash of gilt characters,— palm trees, tiles, shutters, masts and

bamboo sun screens. From the steel walls of the mighty
war-ships which bucked the storm, could be seen a long
procession of two thousand junks, sampans and even
steamers, gale-driven eastward toward Lyee-moon Pass,
and in the lifts of the rain-sheets their crews were beheld bowing to tablets and throwing joss prayer boats
overboard, while their wild faces were torn with terror.
It was possible to help only a few of the thousands, for
death would not tarry or be interfered with. No theater
of Lethe as melancholy has ever been witnessed from the
decks of war-ships and merchantmen, whose captains
had all they could do to save their own craft. When
the rain-veil parted a moment the whole mountain side
was seen to be leaping white with cascades. At noon a
calm came and in the places where it found them, every
Chinese survivor stood up so uncomplainingly that all the
world save themselves was thrilled. Such is the stuff the
Hakka boat people are made of. Almost the entire
Hong-Kong fishing fleet, which was outside when the
disaster came, was lost, and the little Joss-house at Aberdeen (their headquarters) started in to burn for ever
memorial sticks in the sacred ash pots before the shrines.
There are fewer boats now tied to the prayas, and for
a long while those who had never begged before, were
forced to cry against their Hakka pride *cumshaw*
and *Chow-chow* (help and food). The work of
cleaning the harbor was horrible. In the hot waters,
the bodies immediately fell to pieces or were attacked
by crabs. The Chinese abhor touching the drowned.
They say a typhoon is " devil pidgin," and if they touch
the devil's victims he and they will turn upon the intrusive mortal. An hour after the typhoon H. M. famous
cruiser, the *Terrible*, whose guns saved Ladysmith and

turned the tide of the South African war, came in from the east through the Lyee-moon Pass, and a P. and O. mailer arrived through the west passage, both reporting no knowledge of the storm.

Blake Pier, a structure of iron and concrete, boasted of a matshed over its upper end, where every foreigner in the Colony stood at least once a day. The storm struck it with a flip of the wing and it was powdered to dust. Oddly the Sikh's sentry box was unnoticed by the destroyer and defiantly stood. The matshed over Queen's Pier came down like the clap of hands. Over on the Kowloon side, a mile across the bay to the mainland of China (but British territory) hundreds of sampans had crept timorously under the bridge into the Police Basin. Here they were battered to chips as the storm like Hercules leaped into the herd. Scores of bodies floated under the kindling wood. In the heaving of the subsiding waters, heads would look up through the shifting debris and seem to be merely playing hide-and-seek with death. One end of the matshed of the Kowloon wharf became a toboggan into the water. That noblest terrace of ferns in all the world, in front of the Chartered Bank of Australia on Queen's Road Central, was littered with the roots and limbs of banyans which had fallen from the heights above. Under the uprooted boughs you beheld white-uniformed Jackies at the unhandy shore work of hacking out a path. A Spanish steamer lifted her prow from the deep bay, and started overland for the Cosmopolitan Dock. The British cruiser *Phoenix* reared and backed up on the beach of the Victoria Recreation Club, where the famous water polo games are held between the navy and the Portuguese, for treaty-port China boasts of the world's great-

est swimmers. The boats of the *Phoenix* on the
port side had been washed away and from the davits instead was dangling the cage-like cabin of a sampan, the
human occupants having been shaken out, as they themselves used to shake rats out of a wicker trap. In one
hour more damage was done, and far greater loss of life
occurred than Togo effected at Tsushima and Round Island. The smallest, prettiest and bravest of them all,
the white destroyer *Fronde* stood out into the gale with
that brilliant recklessness of the French. There was little room on her curving decks to take a stand and fight.
It was uneven; the storm paused and grimly laughed as
the brave little French vessel was swept past the green
bows of the towering British ships. Then, pitiless, he
came on again. Seven white helmeted sailors, with a
song in their hearts: "*La Rhone et Chine; mes pays; mes
amours, adieu,*" were swept into the obliterating turmoil.

The Japanese mail steamer, *Sado Maru,* came down
the coast on the hem of the tempest. In the heaving seas the Japanese captain stopped his ship twenty
times to rescue eighty junk people, many of whom were
too crazed by exposure to be willing to be saved. The
new tramway on Hong-Kong Island was commandeered
for the gruesome service of rushing rude coffins down
to Ah King's yacht slipway, which had been made into
an emergency morgue. The whole city, stunned as it
was, now rose to the greater fear of a pestilence in a
tropic land, where the safety of the survivors depends
on the dead being entombed on the day they die. Fire
could not be applied to rain-soaked heaps of wreckage
and garbage. The danger must be met; lime was shov-
eled over them for the time being. There was need of
speed, for some said five thousand, and others said ten

thousand had been drowned. Certainly three thousand were found along the prayas, shore and harbor. The veteran emigrant steamer, *Charterhouse,* which, on her last charter had been plying between Hong-Kong and Singapore for fifteen years, raced southward before the storm without avail. She was caught by midnight and turned over like a kettle. Seventy were drowned. The Scotch engineer and twenty-five Chinese crew were picked up three days afterward on a raft which was washed bare of food and water. They endured the agony of seeing the ship's empty life-boats drift just beyond their reach. On the following days, silent junks, like great catafalques of the dead, came drifting back into the harbor, manned by an unseen crew, and spreading terror among others besides the superstitious Chinese. The lower revetment walls of the two European cemeteries fell, spilling graves of the white man's dead into the Wanchai Road, and over the upper walls the Bowen hill tumbled, burying other graves.

The good Anglican Bishop, J. C. Hoare, who was washed in the typhoon from his sail-boat, the *Pioneer,* between Lantao Island and Macao, was a familiar figure to us at Hong-Kong Peak. His efforts in enforced leisure hours to make life mentally tolerable for foreigners by giving lectures, as well as his oratory without notes in the Cathedral, will be held in grateful memory by a long line of English and American exiles in China. His body went down under the cliff where the great pioneer missionary Morrison was buried, and many hope that a landmark to their honor will be erected by those who, whether for religion's or civilization's sake, have come to find bonds about them holding their interest to China.

Thousands of these gyrating storms fortunately die out in the place of their birth, as their progressive speed in the tropics is seldom higher than ten miles an hour. When they meet the funnel of the trade-winds they are given accelerated progress and direction, and reach the higher latitudes with tremendous impetus. The recognized experts on the laws of typhoons are the French Jesuits of Manila, Sicawei, Hong-Kong and Macao, the most famous name probably being that of Faura's, the Padre of the Manila Observatory.

In a country where the light is so bright, sight is prized as Nature's highest gift. When the American boycott was at its height, it was only necessary for the bonzes and *taotais* to cause the statement to spread among the superstitious masses that kerosene was bad for the eyes, in order to bring about a return from the American product to nut-oil illumination. In the religious riots, the fury of the ignorant is most easily aroused by circulating the rumor that the medical skill of the missionaries comes from their compounding in their medicines the eyes of Chinese slave children.

The natives of the South show a diathesis to enlargement of the spleen, on account of the long, hot and moist weather. Foreigners in the treaty ports are heavily fined if they kick or strike a Chinese about the body, as death caused by rupture of the spleen frequently results. The native roustabouts are well aware of this tendency, and duels take place, where the spleen is jabbed with the forefinger only. Training for these murderous contests consists in stabbing bags of rice with the fingers, which grow stiff as iron.

IX

CHINESE RELIGION AND SUPERSTITION

I asked my cook-coolie why he kept a pet hen caged. He replied that he was feeding it for sacrifice day. But would not a dead hen do? " Master, I no wanchee a hundred year dam." The teaching of Confucius has percolated even to the laboring masses that conscience is the ever-present representative of Tien (the Diety). The purgatorial figure is Buddhistic; the lively sense of morals among the people is creditable mainly to Kung Fut Tsze. When we think of China we must not think of a land which is solely superstitious, but one which is largely and interestingly religious.

A pretty superstition at Hong-Kong is the purchase by the Hakka fisher class of red effigy prayer boats. The workmanship is delightfully neat. Loaded with prayer papers, and wafted on their way with scented joss sticks, they are set adrift with a great clamor of devil-chasing fire-crackers, as the sun breaks over the Lyee-moon Hills. The high sterned junks will turn their unwieldy course rather than wilfully run down one of these prayer boats.

A Chinese dearly loves a motto written in black on red paper. If it is the name of his god, or literary ancestor, he hangs it over the family shrine; if it is a maxim of virtue from strenuous Mencius, he places it over his business counter or couch. The larger the lettering and the bolder the individuality in the sweep of the brush, the greater the art.

Among the rice tillers, if sickness strikes a family, it is concluded that the devil must be hailed and decoyed. The Taoist priests come in, and bang cymbals to draw the evil spirit's attentions; then a dog is killed and its blood is caught in cups. Lifting these up, the priests lead the procession to the hills. The sacrifice is set down, and while the evil spirit is supposed to be busy gorging itself, the procession, with a worldly wisdom learned from thieves, scatters to foil the pursuer, the priest returning by a roundabout path to the home, where he labels the door with red slips exorcising the evil one. If, on the other hand, the home of the mulberry grower on the hills is attacked by misfortune, the procession wends its way to the riverside, where decoy boats are set adrift. In strange quarters the evil spirit is supposed to be more easily got rid of. In Korea, two regal red chairs are borne along, the devil being supposed to choose for his attentions the one which has, in place of a passenger, many tempting sweets and pork.

The purpose of the prevailing upcurling cornices and eaves is, of course, that evil spirits, which crawl like snakes on alighting, may be diverted up into the air, and not down to the door where human beings enter. Because of the habit of foxes prowling near the habitations of men, it is believed among Buddhists that souls which decide to return to the earth prefer this animal for an abode. If one who is always striving to follow the best morals, constantly falls into evil fortune, the depressing fatalism is repeated: " the gods are punishing me for evils done in a former life, when my opportunities for good were larger and my riches greater." This belief is constantly brought out as the one morbid touch in their lyrics.

The farthest inland and the most populous province is Szechuen,—the land of waterfalls and mountains,—which has seldom been ravaged by war since the re-peopling, after the Ming dynasty was uprooted. Here Thibetan lamasery influence is now strong. *"Lama su poh sing"* (We belong to the Lamas). But when the railway which the French are building into Szechuen is completed, Canton and Confucianism will rob Lhassa of its power here and the cairns which the crawling pil-grims have raised will go to ballast the path of the great leveler and civilizer. The passes out of Szechuen to Thibet are sixteen thousand feet high and can never be profitably graded. So that far, pounding their long *muh-yu* boards, may the last trains of superstition come with their yaks, to see the tide of progress roll beneath their scorn; the faithful kissing the tail of the Lama's pony to obtain magnetic holiness, and the shamans in maroon canonicals and golden underskirts, muttering ten thousand times: *"Om Mani Padmi Hum"* (Oh! Jewel in the Lotus). You will notice in a spirit of irrelevant western humor that this saintliness does not at all re-press the pony's propensity to communicate magnetic virtue by a quick drive of the back heels.

Let us look for a moment at a temple of the Lamas. Into the plaza around it, turjin poles are stuck, and all the way up the poles little flags, called *Lung Ta,* flutter, wafting to Buddha by his holy wind the names of the dead, for whose early bliss prayer is thus made. The statue over the entrance is flanked by two brass cups, one containing rice, the other oil. On the altar, stand seven cups brim full of water. The flashingly dressed priests carry about drum, sprinkling horn, bell or book. In the dangerous religious gloom, you are very likely to stumble across bones, whether of buffaloes or humans it is hard to say. The stench would be awful were it not for the smoking incense sticks. They are of two colors, six inches long, the *Shi Shang* being black and the *Mong Shang* yellow. Most of them come from my old home in Kwangtung Province, and are made of sandalwood, laka, aniseed, musk, orange peel, ginger, rhubarb, camphor, myrrh, cassia, cloves and putchuck powdered and gummed together. Great as is the altitude of eleven thousand feet, buckwheat, rye, wheat and oats are cultivated, and chickens, goats, and marmots are seen about the dizzy villages.

There might never have been a Dalai Lama, and no abstract dreaming of the Ultimate and Timeless had there been no Himalayas and Snowy and Patroi Ranges (Sacred Mountains as the zealots call them) to cage in this secluded worship, which is really the Saints' or High Church of Buddhism. Reciprocally, so much does Catholicism admire Buddha that he has been canonized at Rome. Where we canonize saints, the Chinese ennoble their ancestors, long dead, when the fruits of their works are apparent. The old Tsung Li Yamen of Peking got the Lamas to accord canonization to two generations back of Robert Hart, our Saxon founder of the brilliant Imperial Customs Service! The similarity of Buddhism and Catholicism, in masses, nunneries, statues, vows, music, exorcism, relics, bells, prostration, incense, and the use of dead Sanscrit as the Catholics use Latin, is worth remembering. There is much religious interchange between Thibet and Shansi Province in the north, the Lamas from the former often visiting the Tai Shan shrines which attract the Ordo and Mongol tribes from sacred Urga. Shansi is even permitted to exhibit a Lama, who is declared to be a partial incarnation, or Gegan, of Buddha. The road from Ching Too to Lhassa, one thousand five hundred miles of peak climbing, must for ever remain, therefore, intellectually the most unlighted road of the earth. Like all mountaineers, the Thibetan carries his drink badly, and tumbles down into Szechuen to disgust the remainder of his race, who abhor even the slightest use of *samschu*. He is the most amiable of the Chinese. Withal, how akin we are; the Lama, paddling his boat along the Kinsha River on his way to the dying, rings a bell, so that the faithful may kowtow and pray for his mission; and the Catholic curé, riding between the firs along the rough roads of the Laurentian foot-hills of Quebec on a similar errand, rings a bell to request a bow and a *Mere de Dieu*. It was among the Buddhists, and in a convent at that, that the Boxer movement germinated, which is evening up for a Christian convert launching the Taeping rebellion.

The members of the Chinese Civil Service throughout asseverate that the Ih Ho Chuan ("United Retaliating Arm," which we have translated into the famous word "Boxers") troubles were precipitated by the action of the Jesuit missionaries in shielding Chinese political prisoners under the cloak of their being proselytes; to be frank, using their converts as "Agents Provocateurs." They also affirm that the outbreaks of 1906, such as that which occurred at Nan Chang where an unfortunate mandarin committed suicide, were caused by the ambitious policy of Catholic missionaries who used government chops on religious documents in order to impress converts with the independent attitude which the Catholic Church could assume toward the heathen Chinese government. In fact, the Catholic Church, known in China as the Tien Chu Chiao, is charged with an ill-concealed ambition to establish an *imperium in imperio,* but if the fault is the Church's, it is the more the impudence of France's political policy in China. Her presumption of protecting all Catholics in China should be exploded, as was proposed by the Pope in 1898. She is only using the Catholic Church as a political tool. The separation will be better for both parties. The same use of government seals had much to do with the bitterness which led to the famous massacre in 1861 at the French convent in Tientsin. In June, 1906, the central government issued a gazette to viceroys and governors, calling attention to the paragraph in the new treaties that missionaries are not to be permitted to interfere in litigation in which converts are involved. The various Chinese ambassadors declare that if this clause is honored conscientiously by the Catholic missionaries, we shall see the end for all times, of anti-foreign and anti-Christian rioting. This point has been again and again brought out by Sir Liang Cheng Tung, himself a Yalensian, in his speeches, and it should be treated by our press with emphasis.

Another vexatious source of altercation has been the insistence by the Catholic missionaries on building their chapels and schools in Gothic architecture on dominating sites, so that the towers shall rise above the surrounding native buildings, which are always low, as is illustrated by the twin steeples of the Pei Tang Cathedral at Peking, and the two white granite spires in Canton's New City. This offends the deepest Taoist superstition of the race,

Fungshui,— that nature worship of high places in hilly country, prominent peninsulas at the seaside, and bends in rivers. It would be wise for the church immediately to abandon the conflict with this innocent and really poetic belief. The Protestant missionaries declare that the constant friction of the Jesuits with the political affairs of China, and their continual demands that the central and provincial governments shall call Catholic missionaries mandarins, are jeopardizing not only all missions, but the safety of life and the future influence of all white men in China.

On the lonely wooded eastern slopes of Pokfulum, one thousand feet above the water, on Hong-Kong Island, facing nine thousand miles wide of lonelier ocean, is the retreat and headquarters of the daring Catholic propaganda in south China. Above the camphors, banyans, firs and bananas, amid the dank smells of ferns, tuberoses and ivy, over the terraced tombs of the Brothers, look the dormer windows of the beautiful Gothic pile (formerly Douglas Castle) of refectory, printing house, chapel, and monastery of the Missiones D'Etrangeres, white and quiet in an alien scene. When the prostrating sun declines, the brothers emerge for exercise. Some wear white topy-helmets, and long coats of alpaca, called soutanes, and the scene is enlivened for others have adopted the queue, felt-soled shoes, and the brighter robes of the natives. The ruling Chinese vastly despise this condescension, but it is popular with the people themselves. In the days of Xavier and Ricci, the Jesuits in China adopted the yellow robes of Buddhist monks, but on being jeered upon the counterfeit, they have since worn the blue and lilac robes of the literati, and in this, and permitting the Chinese to retain ancestor worship, the official

Chinese believe that Catholicism admits that it has not come to establish a new religion, but to add culture and a political system. The Missiones D'Etrangeres is one of the heaviest stock-holders (holding half a million) in the lucrative Tanjong Pagar Wharves and Dock of Singapore.

There is no reason why Protestant missions should not permit the ancestor tablets to remain in the home for memory's sake, in the respect that we hang photographs, but of course the incense stick should be forbidden. When we speak of Protestant missions and Christian literature in China, one name ahead of all comes forward, that of Robert Morrison, the first and greatest Protestant missionary, who lies buried in that little square, high-walled cemetery at Macao over the grand Areia Preta beach. His translation of the Holy Scriptures in twenty-one volumes, completed in 1823, remains the foundation stone of Chinese missions. What a labor that was in surreptitiously chiseling on blocks of tin in the East India Company's local office the thousands of characters, the meaning of which he was almost the first to unlock, and certainly the first so generously to apply. The Nestorians in A. D., 505, and again in 780, and the Jesuits Ricci and Ruggiero in 1580, and Schaal under Shun Che's patronage in 1661, had the same, indeed a better opportunity, but it remained for Morrison to give the Book (the " Way " they call it) to the Chinese, and leave the truth to the consciences of the people, to be watered by their own cares and sorrows. He was wisely willing to let meddlers, not missionaries, in an arrogation of temporal authority, interfere with Rule or Misrule. To his name scholars also bow for his compendious dictionary of Chinese.

It is marked that missionaries receive little sympathy from white men resident in China. In extenuation it is pointed out that this should not be wholly laid to the latter's spiritual condition which remains in a suspended state. The eyes of the alien layman are in the back of his head, looking longingly toward home. He is not enthusiastic on even the letters of China, and hardly in the notable scenery. He is engrossed in a race to make money rapidly against the speeding ravages of an enervating climate. The fact remains that missions must look to America and England for that love which more than money speeds their feet along, in following the path through China first trod by the Apostle Thomas. America should for years send none but medical missionaries to China. The London Mission hospital at Peking is an example of what should be copied throughout the land.

In a corner of Mongolia near Turkestan, at Turpan, in an excavation, old boots have been found which were repaired with kid palimpsests of the third century, A. D., — a literal example of the truth marching into benighted Cathay. On what other Tartar's long boots, borrowed from an Osmanli brother, have been sewed those lost treasures of the West, the palimpsests of Sappho's poems, and the missing chapters of Livy and Cicero? Speaking of relics, the enlightened governor of Shensi headed a procession from an open field outside Sianfu in the fall of 1907, which bore the sacred Nestorian tablet for the first time in eleven and one-half centuries, under a roof within the Peilin Temple of Sianfu. As is well known, the two thousand Chinese and Syrian characters of this stone record the communion with the fifth century Christian Church, and the deposit in the Sianfu library of part of the translated Bible. The notable fact is to be recorded here that this year a replica of the Nestorian tablet was placed in the Metropolitan Museum of New York City.

Thirty miles southwest from Macao lies the island of Chang Chuen, where the pioneer missionary Xavier died. Shortly after leaving Shanghai on the southward voyage you pass Phu Tho on the starboard, to land where would be a task requiring Pauline zeal, for the whole island is given up to a hundred monasteries occupied by thousands of mumbling bonzes. It is to the Chinese what Philæ was to the Egyptians.

The nationalism of China owes everything to Confucianism, with its great teachings of the immortality of the soul's conscience; *Hiao* (filial piety); *Chung* (obedience to virtuous rulers); its eternal insistence on *Shun* (personal character); duties more than faith, and opposition to caste. Ancestor worship was, of course, founded by Confucius, and remains the most unique feature of Chinese customs. Confucianism exempts no position, taking ground as forward as the Roman *Censor Morum*, Commune or Duma, even to the granite seat of the throne: " Vice dethrones the divine right in a ruler." According to a Confucian sermonette: " The seed of Heaven or hell is all sown in this life," and again, the Ming Tsien Chi says: " If you practise good works here you need not worry about your future." These teachings have made the race the eternal adamant it is to-day, founded, of course, on tablets of a different color, but not so much of a different grain from those of Moses; stones indeed of strength and ready to hold the superstructure of whatever new commercial, industrial or religious civilization may be laid upon them. Like the

Romans of the Republic, the Confucians in temples, streets and mottoes exalt the fame of the leading virtues, calling them "Most Excellent Truth"; "Heavenly Aid"; "Beneficent Concord," etc. No weaklings, therefore, such a race. What they are now they have always been, and will always be. We need not fear for their sincerity in the future. Judge of the morals of a people whose business men paste on their shop doors mottoes for the New Year such as: "May I manage my occupation according to truth and loyalty," and "May I uphold benevolence and rectitude in all my trading." Over a temple at Canton is the inscription: "Right and Wrong are blended on earth, but separated in Heaven." Mottoes and empty spirit seats take the place of Buddhistic statues in Confucian temples.

With the advent of modern learning, especially while Japan influences her,— beautiful, dreamy, metaphysical Buddhism of the temples, with its bezoar amulets and its teaching of faith more than duties, will recede into desuetude, and China will adapt for national uses the amended Confucianism. Confucianism will add to its creed that to serve the State is to be sure of immortality, on which latter subject it has previously been as hazy as Buddhism was replete. Confucianism will become picturesque, or humorous in its patriotism (dependent on the oriental or occidental view) and issue bulls deifying its heroes. But all the æstheticism of the classics that has been cultivated in the past will be neglected for the new militant Confucianism, which in this respect alone can be compared to the Shintoism of Japan. The superiority over the more clever Shintoistic Japanese which the Chinese have enjoyed, in that breadth of character which philosophy produces, is creditable to Confucianism. In collecting the philosophy and poetry; in codifying the manners, and in adding to them riches of his own in the Book of History; The Odes; Spring and Autumn Annals, Confucius or Kung (as Mencius unlatinized is Mang), has been the Homer and Chesterfield of the Asiatics, and in the Book of Rites he has been their Moses. As was Plato to Socrates, so was Chu Hi to Confucius, and the sublime academic groves at Nankang in Nganwei Province draw the feet of thousands of religious and literary pilgrims every year. An interesting bit of stoical philosophy of the Confucian school refutes the Occidental's argument concerning prayer:

" God answers no individual. He merely has given a memory to mankind in the aggregate to avenge accumulated wrongs; thus cycle by cycle man achieves his own advancement with the passive approval of God, who forbears ever to interfere after He once created the human mind." Another Confucian said to me: " You Occidentals worship Eternity in the past, we believe in the Immortality of an endless human succession." Then I asked myself if West and East in matters of the spiritual after all may not be going around one circle to a meeting point in the one Judgment of all Virtue, which will weigh these two peoples who come, one from the right hand and one from the left, by the two rules, those from the West by conduct, and those from the East by conscience.

Oddly the religion of Fo or Buddhism, with its censers, crosiers, holy water, extension of hands in blessing and manumission of sins, is the religion of a few daredevil, camel-riding, dirty Mongols of the northwest provinces. While Confucianism puts the stigma of inferiority on women, Buddhism recognizes her religiously

Characteristic Manchuan sign-poles on the wide main street of
Mukden, the birthplace of the reigning dynasty.

Great bell tower, Temple of Five Genii, Canton, South China.

Christian converts herded in the Apostolic Mission during the battle
of Tientsin between the Boxers and the foreign allies.
The converts were unflinchingly loyal to their teachers
and religion, both Protestant and Catholic,
during the bloody days of 1900.

and socially.   Accordingly Buddhism's strength in China
is in the hearts of the women.   It was Buddhism which
brought most of the present art into China, and also
evidences of Greek influence, which we find occasionally
in the architecture of joss houses and the Greek interlocking gold border used on tunics.   Buddhism endowed
China's literature with imagination, and is the mother
of her short novels.   Buddhism has been instrumental in
teaching the masses patience in their poverty, because
in some future life they will receive rewards.   One weakness of Buddhism in China has been that her official
language is Sanscrit.   Not since the twelfth century
have her theological productions been virile.   The poetical mysticism of Buddhism can be judged by its emblem,
the lotus, and the interpretation of its teachers: " It
grows from the slime and expands in glory over the dark,
filthy waters which hold it; so shall we expand in the
blessed Nirvana."

Miracles are believed in; the favorite one recited being of the righteous lad, Wu Mang Tsang, whose poor
mother was dying for the lack of sustenance, which he
was unable to purchase and would not steal.   In his
despair, he went to the bamboo brake to weep.   Although it was winter, pitying Heaven (Tien) made the
tears to bring forth tender shoots of bamboo, which he
brought home and boiled,— a parallel with our Elijah
and the Ravens parable.   Their Virgin Mother, whose
statue shows her outstretching many arms of charity, is
called " Tze Pei Kun Yam," merciful hearer of prayers,
and a notable temple is erected to her honor in Canton.
Buddhist temples are generally known by the name of
" Three Chiefs," referring to the three incarnations of
Buddha.   Buddhist nunneries are not infrequently met

with. Travelers will particularly remember the one in the picturesque Shui Hing gorge of the Sikiang (West River). Strong believers in marriage, the government has never looked with favor on the increase of these institutions. The infants thrown into the baby towers of silence, largely come from their unhallowed halls. The Buddhists always select the most conspicuous sites, and which have been most adorned by nature, for their temples. At Honam, across the Macao passage from Canton, they cremate the bodies of their priests. In a compound of the temple they give a refuge to pigs, which are overfed until a natural death releases them, the intent being to show toward the lowest of animals respect for the principle of breathing life. In Mongolia, after saying his prayer, the Buddhist votary leaves his handkerchief as an earnest of his vows.

Modern books of Buddhist sermons are procurable. Each sermon is divided into eight heads. The homely virtues are wreathed in noble, poetic settings, and the literary beauty and power of some of these homilies are not surpassed by our best products. Characteristic of the democracy of the teacher and his hearers, some sermons close: " This has been a long parable; we'll stop and take a pipe." Our Peoples' Institutes have therefore had forerunners on remote paths we hardly should have dreamed of. Cynics here, too, have their fling at religion, for says one: " When the old cat's eyes close in prayer to Buddha, my cheese is safe."

Buddhism's doctrine of the transmigration of souls, whereby a man may become an animal hereafter, and that the animal before our sight was a man in a former state, is, of course, a most pernicious and immoral teaching. Its half beauty, in that it inculcates love of animal life, is like the iridescence that attracts in the grass, but is found to glitter from a snake's coils.

Taoism, outside of its one brilliant classic, the *Tao Teh King* of Li Erh (who is best known by his cognomen of Lao Tsz, "old teacher") its founder, is as much akin to a folk-lore, like the Scandinavian myths, as to a religion, with its elaborate tales of genii, dryads, goblins, sprites, demons and gods. Their priests are the autocrats of the powerful Fungshui geomancy. If only the Chinese were dramatically musical, they have the libretta in their voluminous mythology for a native Wagner, especially in the great "Hill and River classic." Taoism admits that the world would be pleasant enough as it is, were it not for the terrible rule of the spirits of our dead over us. When an evil spirit is adjured, the north is faced, for that is the way shadows fall. The south, too, has some ill luck phases, for from that quarter are said to come droughts, fires and typhoons.

The sect has a weird ceremony, showing how Buddhism interlocks with their system, called "Breaking Hell Open," where a light is sent to the departed spirit among the Pretas. The priests request the god "to send a procession with streaming banners to show the spirit the way to the golden bridge which crosses over to bliss." The Taoist priests may marry; the Buddhists, of course, may not. The Pope of Taoism resides on Tiger Mountain in Kiang-si Province, and is reputed to be in touch continually with the revelation of wonders; hence the spread of Taoistic superstition, especially in Szechuen and Hupeh. Dark as it is, Tao means the "way." Trees are worshipped; all through Shansi Province in the north you will notice red votive streamers attached to the wide branches of a species of oak. They believe that all kinds of matter have souls, and that a year of our time is a thousand years of the soul's time, so intensely do spirits live. It is remarkable that they have a Prometheus myth, for Sui Jin is said to have brought fire down from Tien (Heaven). Their Adam (Pwan Ku) is represented as coming from Heaven in the form of a giant, and they believe that for a long while there were giants on earth (our Titan myth). The Taoist priests are recognizable by gray and blue robes in distinction to the saffron and pink robes of the Buddhists. The former, unlike the latter, are not shaven. Taoism can hardly be said to have an ethical mission; it is rather a prostration in fear before the wonderful and supernatural. It has done more to depress the courage, alarm the imagination, and make the race impractical than any other influence in China.

If, in one comparison, the religion of the East and Christianity are to be discussed, it may be said that the former prescribes the duty of class; the latter the duty of the individual. One Chinese may indulge in the San Chiao (all three of their religions). They have a saying: "When all is well and you wish it to stay well, be an ethical Confucian; when in trouble, seek the supernatural Taoists; when you die, let the atonement-procuring Buddhists be called in."

In the British alliance with Buddhistic Japan, and what may almost be called a consequent alliance with Buddhistic China, Britain strengthened herself immensely in the affections of Buddhistic India, which has a keen affiliation with the Buddhists of China. She thus raised another arm to keep in subjection India's sixty million Mohammedans, about whose rebel hearts is always folded closest the green standard of the Prophet, which is ready

to unfurl at the first throb, as seen in Armenia in 1909.
No nation knows better the inner spirit of this sect, which
they call Kei Chiao, than the Chinese, for when the government was busy with the great Taeping rebellion, suddenly all Mohammedan Kansu and Shensi arose in the
northwest, and the extirpation of the green fires of the
Prophet's war camps was one of the most vexatious un-
dertakings in recent Chinese history.

In Mongolia, the government has had to use arms
and bribes alternately to keep in check the Mohammedan
Tungani tribes. In Yunnan, the Mohammedan Puntais
called a Ghazi or holy war and no settlement could be
found of the difficulties until every living Mohammedan
was driven into Burmah. Many have now returned to
Yunnan, where they are engaged mainly in the fur trade.

Standing high above the low buildings of Hang-chow
(the bore city) you will notice the minaret of a mosque
whose preservation through the surging times of the
Taepings in 1863 speaks loud for religious toleration
in China, for this coastal city is the farthest removed
from the centers of Islamism. At the north gate of
Canton stands the Kwang Tah minaret, one thousand
years old, a memorial to the Prophet's uncle, whom Canton claims. The numerous Mohammedan tribes of Mongolia have more of a reputation for singing and eating
than for industry. It is an odd sight to see the blue-
capped Chinese muezzins mounting the minarets.

The Great Thanksgiving Day, the ritual climax of
the year, is the Feast of Lanterns, occurring on the fifteenth day of the first moon (February), when the Emperor on behalf of his people goes up those uncovered
altar steps to worship the Imperial God of Heaven
(Hwang Tien). In times of drought, and visitations

of typhoons, the trials of criminals are hurried, lest Heaven should have been offended by delayed justice on earth. The prayer of the Emperor, who is dressed in blue, because he is worshipping the High God who dwells above the cerulean, shows some of the sonorous solemnity of the old Hebrew Prophets: "Oh! Imperial Heaven, looking up I consider that Thy heart is benevolence and love. With trembling and anxiety I would not rashly assail Thy footstool, but would first consider my errors. I would inquire if I have swept away one poor man's field to add to a monarch's park. Have the oppressed had no appeal? For the gluttony of bribes, has the blood of the innocent been spilt? Have the gleaners been pushed into the ditches, by the powerful, to starve? Have our enemies been left to trample on my flock as mire and ashes? Oh, lay the plumb line to my sins and teach me duty. Grant me renovation for the sake of my myriad innocent." This strenuous self-searching, set in rugged poetry, is truly Davidian, Cromwellian, or Rooseveltian, as one's taste may say.

The Chinese are not always patient with their gods, which cost each inhabitant one dollar and a half Mexican a year. If drought continues; if the fisheries are poor; should a bonze become unpopular,— revenge is taken first upon the idol, gilt and fearsome as he is. "Thou pig of a spirit; thou art well gilt, incense-smoked, set firm and high, fed tight as a drum-head, yet thou givest up nothing. Thou wooden thing so impotent that thou canst not wipe off the webs which the insolent spiders spin over thine eyes; thou harborer of filthy rats' nests in thy bowels, we spew thee;" and forthwith the idol is lassoed and dethroned. The bonze is then beaten. The temples are never closed. They crown every prominence.

To the Buddhists alone these poor people give six hundred million dollars a year. Confucianism, which ethically and religiously has done more for the nation, has asked for comparatively nothing.

The dragon is not only the emblem of China, he is a god, the great spirit of mountain and air, the supporter of the Middle Kingdom of this supposedly flat earth. His retreats must not be impiously disturbed, says the Taoist Fungshui geomancy. Our happiness depends upon his somnolence, and his sleep depends upon our virtues, especially obedience to tried and honored customs. In other words, as the Chinese like as few reminders as possible from their rulers, they likewise appreciate their gods most when they hear the least from them.

At Ue Chau, a village on the Rhine of China,— the Sikiang,— four hours by launch west of Canton, an Episcopal mission hall has been raised with a name in conformity with the Chinese taste for the grandiloquent. It is called " The House of the Illustrious Teaching." This slight accedance to Chinese customs is a wise move.

At midnight of the first moon, which begins the New Year, the father leads his whole household to the door. Lanterns are lifted up, and all bow before Heaven and toward earth, in solemn worship of nature's God. Another beautiful nature ceremony is the pouring of libations, when favors are asked for the growth of the grain in the field. At the northern boundary of the farm, whence enter all evil spirits, is placed a statue of Buddha, in the same manner that the Romans set up Terminal statues of deities.

The expressions of mankind the world over, after all, reveal the similarity of the human heart, when its sorrows drive it to poetry. The proclamation of the present Regent employs the following language in reference to the demise of the late monarch: " He who has now gone the Great Journey." Would not this equally well serve as a metaphor for North American Indian, or Caucasian?

By different names, but in a similar worship of patron saints, China accords with the rest of us. As the sailors of Brittany and Marseilles pray before the shrine of " Notre Dame de la Garde," or the raftsmen of Montreal to " Notre Dame de Bonsecours," the fishermen of China, most of whom are Buddhists, for dangerous vocations call for a picturesque faith,— bow to the Venerable Mother Ma Tsu (i. e., Maya, mother of Buddha) for succor. The most conspicuous temple outside the walls of Ningpo is erected to her name, and her worship is principal in the bonze-ridden island of Phu-Tho, in the Chusan group. Throughout sea-faring Fu-kien you come across her shrines. She is the Athena of the Chinese. At Canton she goes by another name, Kun Yam (Goddess of Mercy), a temple on a hill, erected in the fifteenth century, being dedicated to her. The sightseer will not soon forget the great flight of stone steps, both to this heathen temple, and to the Christian ruins of San Paulo at Macao.

Singularly Mosaic is that part of the worship at the Altar of Heaven, when the Emperor commands a bullock which is without blemish to be burned whole upon the porcelain altar as a sacrifice to the God of the Sky. In the case of the bullock brought to the Altar of the Earth, the animal is buried, not burned.

Too little attention has been paid to the vicarious heroism of Chinese morals. A son may offer himself for imprisonment, to free a father, and it is legal to punish relatives where an individual is considered to have placed too great an onus of crime on a community. The family is responsible for the individual's debts, with the result that there are few bankruptcies, the family taking the place of the government in restraining individual defalcation.   Thefts are punished by the family, and not the magistrate,— the clansmen whipping the culprit along the highroad. The principle of "Filial Duty" is not only religious. It is the political and ethical foundation stone of the nation itself.   The mandarin is instructed to act "as a parent to the people." China has possessed an easy-going central government, because it needed little other, so long as it withheld from dealing with the Occident. The ninety million family wheels, all of one pattern, going at one speed, to the same end, and by the same simple impetus, worked in their own circles without conflict, because they did not overlie. There are no billionaire wheels in the State, keyed to a billion-metre speed in conscience and privilege, to upset the balance of the other wheels. It was not desired to produce even great men, much less powerful ones, but rather uncompetitive happiness and uniformity.

Murderers cut off the hand or foot of their victims, and place it in the mouth of the despatched. The superstition is that this prevents the spirit of the dead from following the desperadoes through this life. As near Canton as the defile of Yan Ping, eight of these victims of Hakka brigands were discovered in April, 1907. It is very common to hear among one's native friends at Hong-Kong lament for members of their families who have been kidnapped and probably taken to the defiles of Yan Ping, San Ning or Hoi Ping, while emissaries go to and fro between the capturers and the relatives of the captive, discussing terms of ransom.

As near the vortex of commerce as Bowen Road, which hangs over mountainous Hong-Kong, one may see native women bowing on the open hill before stones in their Taoist faith. You will notice a well-worn path winding up the mount, and a jutting rock which throws its shadow over the road. The sampan women of the Hakka tribe believe that the Being, one-third of whom is resident in prominent stones, has power to affect the fortune and the motherhood of sons. Part of the worship consists in sitting on the stone. The stone is sometimes given a name, and letters are painted on it, but there is no bonze in attendance. While jade is the fashionable jewel and "good-luck" stone, meteorites are worshipped in Pechili and Manchuria, because they come from Tien (Heaven). The same idea of veneration crossed the Aleutians, and is noticeable among the Esquimaux. The immense meteorite of pure iron in the Natural History Museum, New York City, which was brought to the United States by the explorer Peary, shows evidences of having been chipped by the Esquimaux for amulets.

China has its pilgrimage, with a fair adjunct, just as Mecca and Benares have. In Confucius' country, the road to Tai Shan Mount, near Tsi Nan, where the saintly Shun is reputed to have instituted sacrifices to Heaven, is lined with booths, and those who pass by on their knees return erect, to buy and sell. The suppliant who crawls along, begging you in his piety to step on him, will mark you out and drive the harder bargain on his return, for your having done so.

Their art portrays only one being comparable to our

winged angels, i. e., Lui Kung, the God of Thunder, who always appears with wings. We pour ridicule upon the attempts of the Chinese to express their idea of the Creator, and we laud our own Greeks for loftiness and refinement of imagination. Both races are equally in earnest. The Greek tells you that God is an accumulative Greatness, and he makes you the statue of a man five times enlarged, as the Zeus of Phidias, which does not frighten you at all. The Chinese say that God is illimitably vast; that the vastness bewilders the human imagination, and he prepares to show you how unequipped you for ever are to essay the subject. He conceives for you the gigantic Creator Pwan-Ku, with abnormal brain, distorted limbs, terrifying look and awful gesture; or the leaping war demons, Hung and Hah, which hurl thunderbolts and whose eyes burst in flame. It would be hasty to say that the Chinese sculptor is ridiculing God; nothing in his theology, ethics or attitude supports this. He frankly tells you that the omnipresence of God which they express by the word *Shang Ti,* and the vastness of God which they express by the word *Tien Chu,* can not be expressed in sculpture, and in their worship can only be recognized fittingly by falling before the heavens in utter prostration. If anything, the Chinese ridicules you that you should dare to conceive what God is. The art of both races is really reverent, but when it comes to imagination, the Greek is a tame multiplier of his man unit. The Chinese sculptor does not attempt to bring you definiteness or peace of mind; he brings you the terrific, just as the thunder brings it to a child, and this is exactly what his art intended.

The existence of Chinese Jews in Kaifong, where the railway crosses the Yellow River on China's longest bridge, reveals one of those marvelous strandings of history which are the despair of research. A lost tribe they certainly are. They came down from Kansu, just as the original Chinese did, but how they reached that province in the first place, none can say. They retained few rolls of their Scriptures; some they left in Turkestan for mending boots. Their synagogue, or Li Pai Tsz, has vanished, and the sect can only be traced by ferreting out the few melancholy individuals who will probably never be united again to unroll the sacred scroll. The decline of letters, and consequent inability to read and appreciate their scriptures in the original, caused the disbanding, more than did persecution or poverty. What more concrete argument was there ever offered for the all-importance of education? More melancholy from our point of view was the wiping out of the last of the Nestorian Christians among the Chinese by the sword of Genghis Khan in the thirteenth century. Tantay, a village near Amoy, possesses the ancient ruin of a Mohammedan temple built during the reign of the Mings, when Mohammedan bands wandered freely about the empire. The religion of this band has now been lost, but the Arab features are noticeable among the descendants of a lost tribe of the Prophet's.

X

The click of the trigger in the "Thousand Islands" kingdom has ceased, and the land now hums to the noise of the spindle. The Arisaka gun-barrel has been stacked away, well oiled for future use in Manchuria, Luzon and Australia, and the stocky Japanese is instead aiming hammer blows at rivet heads. A larger industrial host than England's is at work, and each man is half a day longer on his "job." It is unromantic but inspiring. What is Japan doing, what is she doing it with, and what will the influence be upon her neighbor and pupil, China?

Her wharves are few; her harbor facilities as yet miserable. They will not always be. At Kobe, for example, I found the sampan journey ashore from my steamer a turbulent one. The ship cast anchor in a wind-swept roadstead, where lightering is on some days impossible. The godown (warehouse) accommodations are as much a problem of congested terminals as in American cities. The government (not the municipality) is erecting vast breakwaters on the Onohama side. The project of digging a channel and bringing ships to wharves is not favored in Japan, except at Kobe. A ship can be loaded by lighter-junks from both sides while in the stream. Yokohama is constricted by a breakwater built too far up the bay. The hills have crowded around Nagasaki's little bay until it is almost smothered.

Fierce tides, like a vengeance for the Russian fleet sunk near-by, tear at the buoy moorings at Shimonoseki and Moji. But whatever the hindrances, they are going to be overcome by vast walls of cement, and the patriotic government has made higher walls of tariffs, so that the cement shall all be Japanese, which means wealth to the cement king Asano, who owns the Toyo Kisen Kaisha Steamship line which plies to San Francisco. It is Mr. Asano's plant which is supplying much of the cement for the new San Francisco.

Osaka is both the city of sculptors, and the Manchester of Japan. Its citizens declare it is destined to surpass Hong-Kong and Shanghai as the leading emporium of the East. The East is for ever hearing the noises of challenges and attacks in the great wars of the ports. Some years ago, twelve million dollars were appropriated for dredging in Osaka Bay, and six thousand ton ships can now reach the once silt-barred port. The Toyo Kisen Kaisha will soon have five home-built fourteen thousand ton ships running. Osaka is now proposing to spend fifteen million more dollars to bring their like within lightering distance of her bunds, and the smoke of a thousand mills tells you why. This is where labor is cheapest, and it is also the unhealthiest part of Japan. Japan for sometime has been sending from Osaka a branch fleet of the Nippon Yusen Kaisha to Bombay for seven hundred thousand bales of raw cotton a year, as compared with imports of four hundred thousand from America, and seventy thousand home grown, used in the mills. These mills ordered fifteen million dollars' worth of looms and spindles from the Manchester and Bolton manufacturers. The Bombay cotton is carried five thousand miles for three dollars and twenty cents a ton, which

shows how cheaply the Japanese can run boats, and pres-
ages, whether we like it or not, their approaching marine
triumph in the China coastal and trans-Pacific trade,
where the white man's unsubsidized ships have to charge
two and one-half times greater freight rates per mile to
pay expenses.   The Japanese, by paying low salaries to
navigating officers, run their ships at fifty per cent. less
wages (even though a large part of the white man's crews
on the Pacific are Mongolians), and still pay their stock-
holders never less than twelve per cent.   The largest
steamship company, the Nippon Yusen Kaisha, paid fifteen per cent. in 1906, and in the panic year of 1908 it declared twelve per cent.   The standard freight rate by
American ships on flour in quarter sacks across the Pacific
varies from eight to five dollars; on the Japanese lines,
which are not in the conference, it runs from three dollars
to one dollar a ton, depending on competition.   A ton of
coal is carried from Moji to Yokohama, seven hundred
miles, for thirty cents gold, on Japanese ships, whereas we
would lose money in carrying a hundred weight at that
price.

The British have complained; later the Germans
grumbled; and last the ambitious China Merchants' Line
objected, that the Japanese should enter the coast trade
of China.   The Japanese reply was that they won the
perpetual right to the Yellow Sea when they destroyed in
the thirteenth century the two armadas of Kublai Khan,
that famous digger of the Grand Canal, whose fleets
sailed from the now silted-up port of Chin Cheu in
Fu-kien.   Japan reaches results rapidly in modern days.
She took only ten years to put on the seas the world's
most victorious navy.   She boasts that in five years more
she will control the mercantile marine of the Pacific, and

in ten added years, have purchased and copied enough
machinery to make her industrial production so vast that
it will conquer on both sides of the Pacific. Japanese
commercial flanking movements at sea have recently been
as sudden as those famous appearances of Kuroki on
land. This year they drove the Boston Steamship Company of America into liquidation. It paid its stock-holders nothing. There were three ships averaging eight
thousand tons.

For a decade the North German Lloyd have enjoyed
what they first well won, the monopoly of the Bangkok-
Swatow service. Japan clapped alongside of it one
sunrise a competing line, and a running fight was made
over the whole course and back again, until the Lloyds
capitulated in a division of the service and concessions
on another route. The next to be attacked were the
lines long run by the ancient and honorable Scotch
houses of Jardine and Butterfield, on the Yangtze, and
latterly the service of twenty-seven vessels of the North
German Lloyd between Shanghai and Tientsin. In the
thick of the former fight the Japanese used methods
which they declared would not exactly prove to be hara-
kiri ones, of carrying cargo and passengers free between
Shanghai and Han-kau, a distance of six hundred miles.
Winning a position accordingly in the center of China,
they did one commendable thing in instituting a new line,
where even the Germans did not think of going, between
Han-kau and Changsha, through the famous Tung Ting
Lake. Modern steamers, drawing only four feet, effectively perform the service. For the due upkeep of
this fleet in the Yangtze region, the Yokohama Dock
Company have bought certain *tsubo* of land at Shanghai
for a branch dock and ship repair yard; a double invasion

therefore, of even her friend Britain's "sacred Yangtze rights." It would never do to fatten the shares of the British-owned local repair yard. Perfide Nippon! the share-holders of Farnham-Boyd's cry. But why recriminations over so unheroic a matter as business, the cold Japanese retort. A few years ago the Japanese had not one vessel stemming the yellow current of the Yangtze. To-day they have forty steamers on the river, operated as a branch of the Nippon Yusen Kaisha, capitalized at six millions, and receiving from the Japanese government a subsidy of four hundred thousand dollars gold. If anything ever leads to the annulment of the Anglo-Japanese alliance, it will be this act. Not even the Holy Sea of Europe is sacred from their attack, for 1909 opens with a Japanese line on the Mediterranean Sea from Port Said to Trieste.

A word backward. The first Japanese steamship company, the Yubin Jokisen Kaisha, founded in 1872, was naturally a small affair. The Cunard of Japanese shipping arose in 1874 in the person of the great Samurai, Yataro Iwasaki, who founded the more pretentious Mitsui Bishi Kaisha. In ship-building nothing was done until the daring subsidy law of 1896 gave birth to the great shipyards at Kure, Kobe, Yokohama, and the baronial Mitsui family's dock at Nagasaki, which are now building fourteen thousand ton merchant ships to join the vast steam tonnage of 1,200,000 tons, accumulated mostly in the last ten years, which is a fleet therefore as imposing as the world's largest line, that of the Hamburg American Line. These fourteen thousand ton passenger ships, which are for the Toyo Kisen Kaisha's San Francisco run, will burn oil as fuel, thus being the world's pioneers in this respect. Twenty million barrels of California oil have been contracted for, to be delivered within the next three years. The oil will be refined in Japan at refineries being erected at Kobe, Moji and Yokohama. Only twenty per cent. duty will be levied on crude oil against forty per cent. on refined oil. The oil will be carried in five subsidized tank steamers, now being built at Nagasaki. The Toyo Kisen Kaisha will not carry the oil in its mail steamers as the heavier traffic on the Pacific is westbound, and the space is all needed for merchandise. By touching at Vancouver with these eighteen knot ships, the Japanese expect to bring the allies at London and Yokohama within twenty-one days of each other.

This year will see the Nippon Kisen Kaisha in operation under the presidency of Baron (of course a Baron, for business is now a matter of privilege, just as war used to be in the feudal days) Shibusawa, with a tonnage of two hundred thousand, including lines to Chili for fertilizers; Bombay for cotton; Java for sugar; Saigon and Bangkok for rice; Brazil for leather, wool and quebracho, and Canada for flour and lumber. Japan will grant a subsidy only to a line which brings raw material. She wants also to enjoy the freight on the manufactured material, to be returned in her own bottoms to the producer of the raw. When the St. Paul road reaches the Pacific, it will invite over the Osaka Shosen Kaisha as its trans-Pacific connection.

The plan is eventually to buy out the choicest American ships on the Pacific, and the Anglo-Japanese Bank has a standing offer to loan twenty millions at five per cent. for the purpose. This contemplates the purchasing of the Pacific Mail and Hill fleets of eight eight-year-old ships, averaging eighteen knots and fourteen thousand

In quaint Mukden, the birthplace of the reigning Manchus. The famous Drum Tower gate, which sounded the alarm when the
Russian and Japanese armies passed each twice down the
wide main street of the northern capital in 1904.
Note the peculiar shop signs. The boy is carrying hair switches, which are used to
drive flies from his master.

The future battleground of Chinese, Russians and Japanese: the country near Mukden, Manchuria. Japanese infantry charging the Russian trenches, 1905.

The Great Wall of China with parallel lines and redoubts climbing the first range of hills, 2500 feet high, as it leaves the sea at Shan Hai Kwan, Pechili province.

gross tons. They expect then to have only one remaining battle on the Pacific, but a hard one because the same weapon will be used, viz.: subsidy against subsidy,— in the case of the eight steamers of the Canadian Pacific service.

Until recently the Japanese mail lines to America and England have employed foreign masters, mates and pursers, partly because white passengers were thus attracted to their boats, and partly because the foreign insurance companies demanded it. But as Japan has entered the insurance field this has all been changed on the Nippon Yusen Kaisha, the premier line. Captain Yagi now takes the fine ship *Aki-maru,* and Captain Kato the *Sado-maru* to and from Seattle. The experiment was also introduced on the London line, when Captain Mie took out the *Iyo-maru.*

In addition, there is a modern sail tonnage of four hundred thousand tons which is crowding back to the fisheries the cumbersome but picturesque, high-sterned junks. Japan's modern steam and sail, and old style junk tonnage aggregates 2,500,000 tons.

China has few natural harbors, which are good. They are generally where a river meets the sea, and her problems of siltage are similar to that of our Mississippi at New Orleans. Afforestation at river sources is to be tried. China has one great coastal steamship line, the China Merchants', which has in its directorate some of the Peking official set, and she has spasmodically run a line financed by Hong-Kong Chinese merchants, from Hong-Kong to San Francisco and Mexico. Foreign loans and subsidy are to be tried, in the Japanese fashion, to foster a national mercantile marine, and particularly to furnish a reserve for a navy. China has had for years tens of thousands of Cantonese sailors serving on foreign ships. Coastal shipping laws will also be adopted to drive out the foreign carrier, but Japan will declare war on China over this venture, if America does not befriend China.

The trouble with the whole American subsidy question is that the rich railroads are allowed by government to drive the American flag off the seas by making contracts with foreign ocean carriers. If the freight were in patriotism and in appreciation of the valuable government protection which has made the roads a success, refused to foreign owned steamship companies, the whole complexion of things would change. The railroads would own their own trans-oceanic lines and see that they paid without anything more than a just mail allowance. Extend the jurisdiction of the Interstate Commerce Commission and among other joys we shall have a transport service always ready to impress and save the nation in peril, which was not the case when we fought the Spanish for the liberty of a neighbor.

The formidability of Japan's labor can be understood when it is stated that a dock for the Mitsui barons was recently cut at Nagasaki out of the solid rock large enough to put on the blocks a twenty-two thousand ton battleship. The cost per cubic yard for hand-drilling, blasting and removing was only fifty cents. The highest wages paid to artisans in the empire are one hundred *sen* (fifty cents gold) a day given ship-builders. In textile industries the maximum rate is fifty *sen*. Police receive eighteen *yen* (nine dollars) a month and sergeants twenty-five *yen* a month. Into the world field of labor steps the Chinese, with figures which beat the Japanese by one-third, for we got the cost of labor on cargo on American mail ships at Hong-Kong down to seven cents a ton, against twenty cents in Japan and forty cents in America.

Japan has conquered the eastern coal markets with exports of six million tons a year, laying down coals as far south as Singapore for three dollars and a quarter, against the cost for English and Australian coals of five dollars. The famous oily coals all come from Kyushu, the southern island, and much of the mining is done under the sea, American electric turbines providing the power. The northern island, Ezo, also produces bituminous, but of a harder quality, known as Muroran. Japan mined fifteen million tons last year, and produced eighty million gallons of petroleum. As a gift of the war, she will now develop the product of the famous Entai mines of anthracite in Manchuria, which come in good stead, for Chinese anthracite coal has been costing ten dollars a ton at Newchwang on account of the expense of transport. Machinery, a mining policy on the part of a progressing government, the abolition by edict of the Fungshui superstition, and branch railways, will before long uncover much of China's vast wealth in coal, and her undeveloped deposits are the richest in the world. With hampered facilities and disconnected transit she now mines half what Japan does. We are now beginning to notice Chinese coal offered in competition with the foreign article at Canton, Han-kau and Tientsin. The successful cotton and iron mills erected by Viceroy Chang in the middle provinces burn native coal.

The little empire of Nippon, which is smaller than Scotland, and supports far more people than the British Isles, perforce uses many unique footholds. Swamps, which are too poor to raise rice, are put under toll to produce the matting rush. In one prefecture, Okayama, which faces the Inland Sea, four hundred thousand rolls a year, worth over a million of dollars, are woven for export. These old industries, with a lingering sentiment, are yet retained to the clans, which have immemorially worked them.

China's largest matting swamps lie off the romantic West River, near Canton. German middlemen control the product, which moves in the fall. Only the cheapest labor and steamship rates make possible the export of the product, which will probably rise in price, following Japan's example. The Chinese matting is superior in strength but inferior in design, as compared with the Japanese matting.

Here is the reverse of the shield. In many instances it was humorous, yet it was mendacious. I found large numbers of our copyright labels pirated on Japanese inferior canned and bottled goods, offered throughout Japan, Korea and Manchuria, despite all international agreements and conventions. A shameful authority until recently for national theft was Article Two of the Japanese patent law, by which if the Japanese Patent Bureau published the description of any foreign invention it became Japanese public property and could not be patented by the foreign owner. In this way Japan has stolen ten thousand foreign inventions for the benefit of her people, and she has given exclusive right to Japanese firms and individuals to collect royalty on six thousand additional foreign patents. When the Israelites left Egypt with the borrowed valuables of their taskmasters, their thefts did not at all equal the debts their enslavers owed them, and therefore the unbecoming spectacle was not an altogether reprehensible embezzlement from the view-point of equity. The Patent Bureau of Japan has neither Isis or Moses, and only the frenzied god of Ambition on its dishonored shrine, and the Samurai must eventually come forward and do some shop-cleaning for his weaker commercial brother, if Japanese progress is to be permanent and live in the smile of the nations. Japan can not too earnestly consider history's eternal lesson that moral strength is prerequisite to armaments in conquests of herself and her enemies.

The editor of the Tokio *Nichi* introduced a bill in a recent session of the Diet to prevent newspapers copying telegrams without the consent of the paper which had paid for the telegram, but the House of Representatives, on the suggestion of Mr. O. Oka, editor of the Tokio *Shimbun*, threw out the bill, so that if the Japanese steal patents from the world, they are also pirates of copyright and Press Agency right among themselves. It is risky to lend an ambitious Japanese student your book; he will translate it; he will have it published in his name, leaving yours off, of course, and immediately his fame as a scholar is enhanced in the eyes of his ducal patron. If you expostulate, he asks if he is not the author of the Japanese version, and offers you a glorious dinner at the tea-house when he receives an appointment in the Civil Service as the protégé of the said duke, who also has his reasons for affecting literature. The Japanese apologists are sufficiently patriotic to be blind to every national criticism, but they are lavish enough in reviling their betters in the homely virtues, who dwell across the yellow water. To quote the smart Mabuchi, as far back as the seventeenth century: "The Chinese, bad at heart, are good only on the outside. The Japanese being straightforward can do without moral teaching; the Chinese have theoretical morals; the Japanese have practical, up-to-date morals."

Comparison in the case of China is comforting, for China protects foreign patents.

Japan was winning some wonderful commercial victories years before she sighted her arms for war. She was and is selling America twice what she buys from America, which is probably the most significant achievement of the island kingdom to date. Every Japanese propogandist who is trained to write articles for the American press, purposely ignores this fact. Until 1905 America was Japan's best customer, but now she sells China more than she does America, which is distinctly in line with her ambition. Immediately after the war closed, her imports decreased five million dollars a month, and her exports increased by the same amount, all because the soldiers of Oyama went back to the silk and cotton looms, the porcelain kilns and the matting sheds, which they had deserted for a while.

As eastbound freight is the lesser, it will not be surprising if timber from the war-won Yalu is freighted in larger quantities by the Japanese steamers to the Pacific coast of America. They have formed the Japan-China Timber Company, and expect to cut three hundred rafts a year at a profit of six hundred thousand dollars. Already they are laying down at Guaymas, Mexico, two million ties from Manchuria at fifty-six cents gold each. These virgin forests have never before been desecrated with saw or ax. The Japanese railways buy their chestnut (kuri) ties for twenty-five cents gold each, which shows the latent resources and the economy of production of the wonderful little kingdom. Japan's lumber is produced mainly on volcanic Ezo Island in the far north. The foot-hills have been enriched with an ashy and charred deposit over the marshes. On this soil *kashiwa* (oak) *senn* (elm) and ash grow to a sturdy girth, but not to a great height. The lumber is faulty and twisty. In the great heat of the summers an undergrowth of bamboo grass, ten feet high, springs up. Winter is severe during three months. The stream courses are precipitate, and the whole country is cut into canyons and fissures, which make logging difficult, but the indefatigable workers overcome everything and produce at the low cost already detailed. Every sprig of wood is used as carefully as in France or Palestine. The waste is burned into charcoal, if nothing else. Every living Japanese, male, female and child, I think, smokes cigarettes, and the cost in forest fires is something deplorable, which the little country can not and will not long afford. Her forest policy will add a total abstinence adjunct. Not only into lumber exporting, but furniture making, Japan is going, and she has a fashion of lifting her goods into any country where the tariff wall is not too high for such little brown men. Pitiable, deforested China possesses no timber, except in Manchuria, and Japan will block the export of lumber from that province to the sea via the South Manchuria Railway until the Chinese, overcoming the vast diplomatic difficulties which have been raised recently against them, parallel that line to Newchwang. The rival yellow men are now at swords' points over this development, and you can put it down as the cause of two future wars.

Seven years before the Japan-Russia war Japan unfolded her serious designs upon China by soliciting ten thousand Chinese students to come to Japan. Thirty thousand are this day in Japan. Of course no other country can now hope to equal Japan's predominant influence, evidenced for one thing in the overthrow of China's most ancient institution, her Classical Examinations. It would pay the four white nations chiefly concerned to set apart five million dollars a year to secure Chinese students for our schools, shops and universities. No other commercial plan can be so effective, for the students are in the fore of the New China already. Particularly should Chinese from the southern provinces be solicited, and not Manchus, for the Manchu is only one-twentieth of the population, and he will in the end only bend to the opinions of the majority. The Japan-China trade, largely as a result of this educational policy, has developed wonderfully in the last few years. In 1903 the imports and exports of the two countries amounted to twelve million *yen* only. In 1905 the total had risen to fifty-two million *yen*, and this year it was eighty million *yen*. This year Japan sent to China for twenty million *yen* of raw material, and returned the goods in manufactured form, charging China forty-five million *yen*. Until 1897 the smooth bores glistening from armored sides compelled Japan to admit the manufactures of the nations at a duty of not more than five per cent. ad valorem. The China war showed the nations what Japan could do, and the five per cent. condition was annulled. The real victory of the Russian war is a more extended one, in that the nations now consent that Japan may raise her ad valorem duties to fifty per cent. unless a *quid pro quo* is given. Statistics of the peace years demonstrate two things, that a smaller number of Occidentals visit Japan than one would suppose, and that Japan is becoming the Mecca for Orientals in increasing numbers, who, marvelous to say, leave in the country half as much per capita as does the Occidental. Here are the figures of tourist arrivals:

	ORIENTALS	OCCIDENTALS
1902 ..	4,950	8,759
1903 ..	6,418	8,810
1905 ..	9,237	7,293
1906 ..	12,500	8,000
1907 ..	20,000	7,000
1908 ..	40,000	6,000

Of the Occidentals, Russians predominate, with Americans and British following in order.

Cheap labor is Japan's greatest industrial asset. Japanese industry, in order to overwhelm competition, has adopted a new slavery, that of long hours for operatives. Mill hands work from daylight till dark, or thirteen hours, for forty *sen* (twenty cents gold) a day. The departure of tillers from the field to factory and mine has increased the cost of living seventy per cent. against a wage increase of forty per cent. The enormous reserve which this people can discover is illustrated by the work, mainly performed by women during the war. Seventy per cent. of the war necessities was produced within the empire itself. When Britain, a similar island manufacturing nation, fought in Africa, only forty per cent. of the war's necessities was produced at home. That taxes are not to be lowered, can be judged from the figure in Prince Ito's (by the way, a common name in Japan) speech, in which he said: " No Daruma, with his fairy gold-producing hammer, is likely to appear in Japan; there is nothing for it but our own diligence. If others do not drown who are lower down than we, you may be sure we are still swimming." How he loves to rap China's " submerged civilization," and how China hates him for it, just as the Koreans do!

You will be struck by the dangerous width of the cars which run over the main lines of three feet six inches gage. On this account the fastest expresses do not make over forty miles an hour. The railways carried one hundred and forty million passengers last year, with only thirty deaths. The government had to take over the railways, as only government credit in such a country could standardize gage through the numberless tunnels, culverts, bridges and grades of this difficult country, where nature has tried to delay the feet of beauty, and not to speed the car of commerce. As in China, so in Japan the merchants club together to secure carload rates, the ratio of this " consolidated " traffic assuming the very large proportion of eighty-six out of one hundred tons shipped. Ninety-five per cent. of the passengers travel third class, and only five-sixteenths of one per cent. travel first class. The average train load is sixty-three passengers, and length of journey twenty miles. How opposite is the tale, and the luxurious habits it reveals, in America! The average freight train load is three hundred and eight tons, and average haul sixty-one miles. Gross earnings averaged sixty-two hundred dollars a mile, fifty-five per cent. of this being applicable to net earnings. The average monthly compensation for all railway employees is seven dollars and a half, against forty in America. Engineers get forty cents a day.

China is entering upon a railway policy under better auspices, and with less physical obstruction than Japan, and the result will accordingly be more gratifying in all directions. Already the Chinese mileage is greater, and is rapidly increasing.

That commerce in America and Japan is respectively on a peace and war basis could not be better illustrated than by the railway policy. Government control of railways in America so far is only desired in respect of

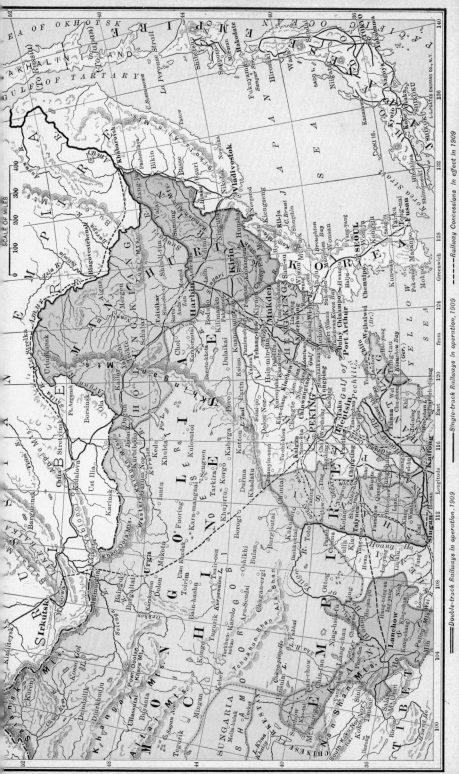

SCALE OF MILES
100 200 300 400

— Double-track Railways in operation, 1909
— Single-track Railways in operation, 1909
----- Railway Concessions in effect in 1909

NORTHEASTERN CHINA

rates. Japanese control was primarily desired in respect of operation. It was found that the operation of the Japanese railways during the war was not satisfactory for the movement of troops, and nothing to compare with the wonderful work which the Siberian Railway performed in carrying and feeding nine hundred thousand troops, five thousand and five hundred miles from their base. Russia won only one victory, but that was a signal one, and a monument to America's pupil, Prince Khilkoff, the maker of the Trans-Siberian Railway. On a single track line, with rails only forty pounds per yard, twenty trains at a speed of sixteen miles an hour were passed in the twenty-four hours. Compare this with the best performance in India of thirteen trains daily. Japan has not been slow to admire and follow. The first 125,000,000 *yen* have been transferred for the purchase of all roads authorized by both houses of the Diet in March 1906, and the following roads have already entered government operation: The scenic Sanyo from Kobe to Shimonoseki; the Kokkaido; Tanko; Kobu; Nippon; Ganyetsu, and Nishinari "Tetsudos," or railways. Under the new Japanese tariff, Germany now supplies the largest amount of locomotives and Britain the largest amount of cars to Japan. Considering the money America loaned Japan during the war, she should be in second instead of third place. When the contracts were made our navy was at home.

Weight is computed by the *Kin* (one and one-third pounds), and *Kwamme* (eight and one-fourth pounds); measure by the *Go* (pint), *To* (one-half bushel), and *Koku* (five bushels); and for precious metals the *Momme* equals our fifty-eight grains troy. Land is surveyed by the *Tan* (one thousand and eight hundred square feet), and *Cho* (nine thousand square yards). China was not behind in an irregular system of weights and measures, understood differently in the various provinces, until the Peking Board of Revenue recently advised a decimal system, the unit of length, *Tchi*, being equivalent to thirty-two centimeters; unit of capacity, *To*, equivalent to 10.35 liters; the unit of weight, *Lian*, equivalent to 37.30 grams. It will take some time before the people are taught the new system.

The mortgaging of real estate in Japan was only permitted as late as 1906, and brought into the country forty million foreign dollars each year since, which has been immediately put into mines and manufacturing. The Japanese government is encouraging the investment of Lancashire capital on long leases (the same as the Hong-Kong crown leases) in the cotton-mills of Osaka, just as Dundee capital went to India and developed the jute factories. Prior to the passage of the real estate law, manufactories paid as high as nine per cent. for their loans. China is yet behind in the security she gives the foreign investor. Therefore the viceroys borrow on provincial account, with taxes as security, and like Chang of Hankau erect their own provincial cotton, iron and coal plants.

As might be expected in so volcanic a country, where there are fifty-four active and one hundred and ten extinct volcanoes, sulphur is largely produced in Japan, generally as in Sicily, in the district of the active volcanoes. Fifteen thousand tons a year are exported from Hakodate. These Ezo mines are owned by the ducal Mitsui family. Work is interrupted for five months by snow. Japan was thus happily in a position to produce her famous Shimoso explosive for the " Great War," as they call it, and naturally her matches (a government monopoly) are all-conquering in China and the far East. They affect the use of a gloomy-colored box patterned after the Swedish. The superior richness of the Japanese ore can be judged by comparison with the ore of Sicily, the figures being fifty per cent. against twenty per cent. The yearly output of sulphur is seventy million pounds. Salt and tobacco manufacture are also government monopolies, so that Japanese conservatives are not eloquent on Trust-smashing. China follows suit in the respect of making salt a government monopoly, but she knows her people will not stand for much repetition of this system.

In Formosa Japan is eagerly developing gold mining at an increase of about twenty per cent. each year. In 1908 one and one-half millions of bullion were produced at the Kyufun, Kinkwaseki and Botanko mines. There are even successful placer workings at this late date. Sulphur, coal and petroleum mines are now being developed near Kilung in Formosa. Since Japan has shorn China of Formosa, China's old port of Amoy, which once controlled Formosan trade, has fallen into bitter desuetude. Put it down, too, in these days of awakening national conscience and restitutions, that China must have Formosa back, of course paying Japan the tutor bill.

When the silver above the line of oxidation worked out in the Kosaka mine in the north of Nippon Island, copper was discovered, and seven thousand and five hundred tons are produced yearly. The ancient Ashio mine, in a hill near the sacred temple town of Nikko, turns out like clock-work, with its eight thousand employees, seven thousand tons yearly, and the Besshi mine adds another six thousand tons. So Japan takes pretty good care of herself in this other war and electrical requisite. Before the Great War the steel industry was in a languishing condition, not twenty thousand tons a year being produced. The war changed things, the Government putting $12,000,000 into the furnaces at Wakamatsu, near Inaka Lake, in the north of Nippon. Note that it is the government initiative in all this progress. The works there, and new works at Muroran, in Ezo Island, are turning out one hundred and fifty thousand tons a year, and in two years the government expects to meet one-eighth of the requirements of the country, which are about eight hundred thousand tons a year. At present Japan is drawing pig-ore from Han-kau, China, where most of Japan's supply will come from in future. Speaking generally of copper, silver and gold mines in Japan proper, the ore is of low grade, but great profits are made because every member of the family works at the lowest wages. There is also little expense for pumping, as the drifts are cut horizontally into the hills. The finest machinery and complete electric plants minimize the cost of operation. Last year Japan proper produced seven thousand and five hundred pounds of gold, and two hundred thousand pounds of silver. Japanese galleries are protected less carefully than in America, and the proportion of deaths is therefore heavier. The health and education of operatives are sacrificed to production, and Japan has many an uncomfortable sociological problem on her hands.

Let us take a glance at " Outer Japan," for so we must learn to call it. She is finding it hard as flint to conquer the spirits of the sulky Koreans in their stream-webbed land of the " Morning Calm," who want neither to rule themselves in a modern sense, nor to be ruled.

Their emblem, the Tageuk — two comets involved and for ever impeding each other — is a sign not without significance. The Japanese affront their pride on every occasion. For instance, they have turned over an important precedent in compelling political prisoners to submit to their hair being cut off. The Japanese intend that the Koreans shall remain a subject and dying race and not be absorbed, the government having prohibited the Japanese colonists to intermarry with the natives. Japanese statesmen are emphatic that Lincoln made a mistake in giving the negroes equality with the whites. This unmistakably shows how they mean to rule in Korea, and the trend of their influence in Manchuria (and in China when they arrive)! The conceit of it, you say. In her new era of colonization Japan means to follow Roman more than British methods. Simple Korea of the past! In the style of his home, the Korean exhibits his exclusiveness, each house being entirely surrounded with the servants' compound. It is a green and white land, the houses and garments being the latter color. The valuable gold bodies belonged to the Imperial household. They have been confiscated for the benefit of Japanese baronial houses, or " Titled Trusts." The Japanese have completed the railroads running the length of the peninsula five hundred and fifty miles, and also across the country from Seoul to Gensan, one hundred and sixty miles, according to program laid out five years ago. They will be operated by the government, which also retains the coal deposits, to work chiefly as a war reserve. In a word, the peninsula is to be a repetition of Egyptian occupation, but the Kohim Hoi (Society of Daily Progress) declares the Japanese will not find the Korean as docile and extinguishable as the Fellahin. For the East, the sickly East, the climate is a joy. The summer rains are somewhat heavy. The winters are of the Canadian type, dry and bracing. Spring and autumn are as green and gold as the maple leaf. China of course sympathizes with the Koreans in what appears to be their commercial and national extinction.

While the sovereignty of China in Manchuria, which the Committee of white Shanghai merchants called a " second Manitoba," is reiterated by the Japanese well organized press agency, and the irregular " American agreement," you hear little of it along the wonderful valley of the Liau Ho, which the Chinese call their " Thousand Mile View." Baron Saionji has formed a trust, called the Minami Manshu, with $75,000,000 capital, restricted to a Japanese majority subscription, for the development of the deposits of five hundred million tons of coal in the Mu Tsi district, and connecting them by branch railways with the old parent line to Port Arthur. The scheme is a Manchurian Development Company with a very broad charter and comprehensive aims under distinct Government patronage. On the railway which the war gave her in Southern Manchuria, Japan is seeking a loan of $150,000,000, which will be reloaned to finance these Government-Baronial Development Companies. The railway is to be broad-gaged so as to exchange traffic with the Chinese railways coming from the south and west, rather than to look for trade with the broader gaged Siberian Railway at Kwang Chau Fu. Exclusive of the revenue from military transport the South Manchuria Railway is already earning $3,000,000 gold a year, or nineteen dollars gold a mile per day. The operating expenses are forty-five per cent. China is fighting Japan bitterly to parallel with the Fakumen Railway the

Japanese South Manchurian Railway from the Russian railways down past Mukden to tidewater in Liaotung Gulf. China, with America's support, can on this question eventually force Britain to aid China and break the unholy alliance with Japan. The Yokohama Specie Bank is intrenched through government assistance, though the Chinese take their notes at four per cent. less than the Mexican silver dollar, which they are used to. An odd feature of the wharves of Newchwang are the piles of Japanese and Russian shell fragments, which have been gathered from the battlefields by the indefatigable Chinese and brought down the Liao in junks. What would we think if similar hands had commercialized the glory of Plevna, Metz, Vicksburg or Alexandria? But the Chinese have never thought war was glory.

Another knotty problem for the future in Manchuria is the question of taxation in the railroad zone. The Russians control the largest part of the Chinese Eastern Railway. The Japanese own as a war legacy the South Manchurian Railway. Now, if the Americans, British and French have a right to levy taxes in the settlements of Shanghai, Tientsin, etc., why have not the Russians and Japanese the same right in the railroad zones in Manchuria? The foreign occupation of the ports is ancient history and does not cut a province in two. Again, if the Russians and Japanese have the taxation right, when will they ever concede China's ancient right to Manchurian sovereignty? I recommend that the Manchurian question be treated solus, and that Russia and Japan have a limited police privilege per mile, but not the tax right within the zones, and that otherwise there be sincere evacuation of the province by the Russian and Japanese arms. At present, the Russians admit Chinese sovereignty, and the right to divide the taxes within the railway zone, and the Russians still keep the wedge in by holding a municipal district at Harbin, all of which will encourage Japan to invent similar claims in South Manchuria, to the distress of other foreigners and of China.

The Japanese cotton merchants of Osaka, who are driving America's cotton trade from Manchuria, also despite the " American agreement," have organized into a guild, and appointed the baronial house of Mitsui as Manchurian Agents. The latter have obtained from the government an advance of 6,000,000 *yen* at four per cent. and the merchants are extended this rate for four months upon their shipping bills. There is no wonder therefore that America's cotton trade with Manchuria of four million *taels* a year should be throttled, and although Japanese consuls disguise it, Japan's entire business (railway, export and manufacturing) is becoming nationalized into the largest aggregation of baronial-government trusts which commerce has ever experienced. To speak the clear truth, there are very few privileges granted in Japan unless the southern Satsuma and Cho Shin baronial families, who placed the priest-Emperor over the political-Shoguns, are first asked what they want — the former in navy affairs and the latter in army and commerce. The members of the Imperial family are heavy stock-holders in the largest Japanese steamship company. The baronial or daimio families number two hundred and fifty. Japan owes half a billion to America and Britain; she borrowed as much from her own people. Her railways cost her $200,000,000. Cotton, tobacco, matches and other monopolies cost the government another $100,-000,000. So it can easily be figured what the government has to earn to live. When their jingo " Progressives "

Monster statues along the avenue to the Ming tombs, near Peking,
date 1330 A.D. The rocks on the elephant statues
have been thrown there by irreverent tourists
who were not of Oriental blood.

Monster statues on the road to the tombs of the Ming dynasty, near Peking. Date 1330 A.D. The sheep of North China furnish the largest part of America's wool supply.

A prophecy in fertile Manchuria, the future granary of China, Japan and the Western United States: an American cavalry horse discarded at the Peking siege; a Chinese waterbuffalo; a Mongol burro and a Manchu pony, all hitched to a draft vehicle which carries imported American cotton.

froth, many among us are beginning to cogitate that, as in the case of the head of the Musselmen, the only way to keep Japan from marching upon our toes is to keep her in debt. A fever of speculative promotion of companies has seized upon Tokio from time to time, among the incorporations being the Anglo-Japanese Bank, 20,000,000 *yen,* formed by Okura, the J. Pierpont Morgan of Japan; Ojigawa Electric Power, 13,000,000 *yen;* the Kyoto Electric, 6,000,000 *yen,* and so on to a total of 160,000,000 *yen* in industrials. The banks' names as a rule are tersely businesslike, merely " Sixty-fifth Bank," "Eighteenth Bank," etc.

On exports to Manchuria, the subsidized steamship lines, which so far are in private control, have been compelled by the government to reduce rates fifty per cent. During the first year after the war the government charged on its Manchurian Railway half rates on Japanese goods, which alone came duty and *likin* free through Tairen (Dalny), on the flimsy pretext that Russia, which is not a manufacturing nation at all, had no custom-houses on the Manchurian border. This duty preference amounted on cotton goods to four *yen* a bale. The duties and freight rates on the South Manchurian Railway have now been equalized by our diplomatic compulsion, but government loans at a nominal rate, Japanese police throttling the competing junk trade on the Liao Ho, reduced steamship rates on Japanese goods carried in Japanese bottoms, and preference car supply to Japanese shippers from Tairen up-country, are beating the foreigner just as effectually as ever in the race to the Chinese bazaars of Mukden, which, by the way, are portable ones manufactured in Japan. In Mukden alone there are three thousand Japanese traders. At least, they say they are, though they carry a " Banzai " and a dirk under their vests. In the controversy over the question as to how the foreigner shall be treated in Manchuria, Viscount Hayashi has represented the diplomatic side against the exclusive militarism of Marquis Yamagata, on whose heart is written a vow against the Russ, " Back to Baikal," and doubtless writing against others of us, judging from what preceded the retrocession of Newchwang in December 1906. China looks to America chiefly to get her justice in her own province of Manchuria, and this must be settled ere many years pass. The Japanese desired that under one pretext or another their brands or " chops " should have two years' start of the foreigner. Another question being asked is what connection Sir Robert Hart's withdrawal from the Chinese Imperial Customs will have with a Chinese tariff compulsorily favoring Japan. The latter feels she must win back somehow in the next ten years the $600,000,000 she spent in the war. The Chinese indemnity robbed her of the zeal for that chastening experience of Pitt and Talleyrand in paying battalions to reap glory only. Fifty thousand Chinese a year are leaving Shan-tung Province for Manchuria. The Japanese are sending among them free, battan weaving looms and teaching their use, so as to encourage the importation of Japanese cotton yarn. Japan argues that if India with three million hand looms can produce two-thirds of her needs in cotton fabrics, Manchuria is not too poor to buy Japanese yarn and get to work in clothing herself in something less humorous than sheep-skins.

The Bureau-bossing malady in Japan's methods has also extended to finance, the government assuming the power of suspending any bank on the pretext of driving undesirable persons from influence, and of ejecting from any exchange any broker or listed bond. The government controls the Yokohama Specie Bank and the Bank of Japan. Before the war the Japanese banks did everything possible to attract foreign money, which raised not a little suspicion. I recall that the branch of the Yokohama Specie Bank in Hong-Kong paid throughout 1903 seven per cent. to depositors against five and one-half per cent. which they paid in Japan. No other bank in Hong-Kong paid more than four per cent. Loans were made in Japan at as high a rate as nine per cent. A Japanese bank will shortly be opened in Brazil to assist Baron Shibusawa's new Nippon Kisen Steamship Company.

China is far behind Japan in banking. The first national bank is barely established, and its working has not been tested, but it will of course slowly be successful and copied.

The war table, under canvas, on a rough field, furnished withal some choice crumbs, one being the $100,-000,000 Manchurian Railway. Another was the extension of Japan's fishing privileges into Siberian waters. They expect to take $10,000,000 a year in salmon, trout, cod and herring, and incidentally to enlarge their naval reserve tremendously. One of the first indications of the new rights was the creation of a fleet of fifteen steam whalers, with a home port on Ezo Island. A species of menhadden herring is also pursued for oil and fertilizer. Watch for the schools is kept from baskets erected on poles on shore. The nets are hauled on the beach and the fish thrown into bamboo yards until they can be tried out in the brick ovens. About sixty per cent. of the oil is drawn out by the fire and five per cent. by wooden presses. The oil is soldered up in old Standard Oil kerosene cans.

The residue is spread in the sun and dried. In famine it is used as food, and in good times it is powdered up for manure. The drying process, however, costs the product the stored phosphorus. The government is expected to step in at any time and stop the fishing, as the menhadden attract food fishes to the coast.

The production of crude iodine is rapidly increasing. Two hundred thousand pounds were exported last year, averaging one dollar and eighty cents a pound. Divers gather it. The primitive methods of burning it still continue.

Cricket bats, tennis rackets and nail brushes have all won the market in Australia, despite the prejudice there against the Nipponese. Osaka is producing menthol crystals from distilled dried mint. The plants are raised on the hills around Nagasaki.

The growth of the press can be judged by the production of paper. In 1894, the year of the Japan-China war, the Oji and Fuji mills produced thirty million pounds. Last year they produced three hundred million pounds and had to move their factories to Ezo (now Hokkaido) Island for the pulp supply. In addition, Japan imported twenty-five million pounds. China as yet knows little, save in the matter of forestry, of the policy of conservation of national resources, such as stocking fisheries, etc., but she will learn from Japan.

A touch of the sentimental still crops out in Japanese business, especially in some of the decisions in equity. The courts decided that the insurance companies need not pay in full fire losses which were occasioned by the Peace-News rioters, but that a compromise payment should be made on the understanding that it was " money of sympathy."

'As it was to be expected, now that war has ceased, and one hundred and fifty thousand soldiers lie about idle, the Japanese courtezans have made Port Arthur and Tairen (Dalny) like the hem of a Roman triumph with the moral flotsam and jetsam strewn along the course. Their 'rickishas, parasols, gaudy gowns and faces have brought unquestioned color to what before was a somber enough scene. The Peking *Times* is insistent in its criticism, and the brave *Kirisu Sekai* of Tokio has bordered on *lese majeste* in its worthy strictures. The great difficulty is in reaching the barons and wealthy political families who have long patronized the geisha, and taken many as secondary wives from that class. From a geisha to a courtezan is more of a difference in age than a distinction in morals. You may ask what place this has in a business article. Only this, that Japan makes the feature a branch of the Government Intelligence Service in every port of the East, from Hong-Kong's " Ship Street " to Saigon's and Singapore's " Yoshiwari " balconies in the suburbs, and every one of these Delilahs knows how to write, and not to drink too much saki from the stone bottles.

Eastward the tide of Nippon dares to take its way, and as illustrating more important branches, let us cite the unexpected line of saloon-keeping in Honolulu. Travelers have long complained of the high price of liquor in the islands, cocktails being twenty-five cents and beer ten cents a glass. Japanese who learned English on the plantations have come to the city and opened bars where cocktails cost ten cents and beer five cents. Again in Hong-Kong and Canton I found printing presses and pianos copied from American models by the Japanese, set up at prices which neither New York nor London, with their lowest " export prices," could approach. Now, whether it be bars or more serious endeavors, Japan would like to do the same thing on both sides of the Pacific, and mix a potion equally sweet and extinguishing for his commercial rival. He lost his temper a little at San Francisco, and surprised himself more than he did us; but he never loses his design.

China, with her economic, able and exhaustless labor, will learn some of the apter yellow brother's ways. She has more latent power and our assurance is that she has more latent character in the approaching business competition, first for the Pacific, and later for the world field.

XI

China alone of the races existing to-day traces its unbroken line back to the first evidences of history. She was broad in her culture and stable in her institutions when Egypt was a ruin. The Egyptian went west from Syria and in due time collapsed because the nation was an inverted social pyramid, balanced alone on aristocratic wealth and arrogance. The Aryan went south to India and lost his mind for a season in vapid philosophies brought on by the climate. The Chinese went northeast into Turkestan; scribbled his hieroglyphics at the same time that Egypt was burying hers; left his hieroglyphics there; rose, said like Joseph "let us build granaries instead of monuments," and betook himself through the Kansu gate to his future home, from whence he was never to look back, or owe to any one a renewed light from the lamp of knowledge, for he kept his own vessel unbroken. Only the rear-guard of the race kept in any touch with the Syrian past. There are only, however, etymological evidences. The Mongol written language shows its relationship to the Hebrew and Syriac, for like them it uses only two vowels, i and o. The other vowels must be guessed. Though we can find no ruins or records (largely through Emperor Tsin's mad incendiarism) dating back to the pyramids and hieroglyphics, China has incomparably the longest history as a cultured nation, which is probability enough that the race went back farther than Egypt in her formative years of thinner culture spent in Turkestan. The Devanagari, Uigur and Niu-chih characters cut on the Ku Yung gate in the Great Wall are not ancient, but the work of Mongol sculptors in 1345, and the inscriptions on the rocks near Oorga in Gobi Desert were cut in 1215 B. C. by the Mongol men of Genghis Khan.

It is there in Turkestan, among the relics of the annual fair camps of Mongols, Shans, Miaotszes and Lolos, that archæologists must look for the China which parallels Rameses, if that is considered worth the digging for. The numismatist may assist in these scrapings of old camp fires and mortuary mounds. There exist coins which were used in China when David reigned in Jerusalem, which are exactly the same as the common *cash* coin of to-day, with the exception that to-day both the Mongolian and the Chinese characters repeat the expression, " current coin of the realm," and the name of the Emperor. Then how far back before David did lost coins go? But if we desire to make moment of the argument, which seems immaterial, we can easily surpass the hieroglyphics of Egyptian history, going back to 7000 B. C., for diggings in Szechuen Province and in Eastern Turkestan have furnished similar stone adzes of the palaeolithic age, in company with bones of extinct mastodons. Even if we had hieroglyphics, a more popular argument of the age of a race is based on a comparative study of the formation of the social organization, and literary product. If it took from Moses until now, about four thousand years, to reach our Western social and mental development, and the Chinese had an equal development, lacking constructive sciences, in 723 B. C., when Confucius wrote and ruled, we can easily follow the race back to times contemporary with the Pyramids.

The Great Wall climbing Liao Hsi (Iron Mountains), North-
Eastern Pechili Province.

The Great Wall crossing the plain between the sea at Shan-Hai-
Kwan and the Liao Hsi mountains, Northeastern
Pechili Province.

A ruined fort on the old wall of Canton, South China. Tartar cavalry patrol the top of the wall, which is built of
sandstone and brick.

This lack of science, remember, was a heroic abnegation on their part, for every principle of hydraulics, transportation, navigation, construction, propulsion and refining was invented by them, but for the sake of the existence of the many (and they instructed the national conscience to see that there would be many), they chose the rural and trading life as better suited to their mental and social peace than a manufacturing organization. They blazoned on their scutcheon: "To live well, not wealthy," and because of this faith, eternal national life has been given them alone, of which their absolutely independent art is the most unique manifestation. Literature, giving an account of the creation, has come down more or less correct from writers contemporary with Moses, which would be 1491 B. C., and the Chinese Shu King history takes dynastic chronology back to 2200 B. C. in Shensi alone. Their earliest writings discussing creation show philosophic calm and create no mythology, which is another proof of the long formed and steadied nation. The superstition of the race that it is unlucky to repair anything has allowed thousands of monuments to pass out every thousand years.

But enough of the past is within reach to satisfy the hungriest antiquarian. We have the rubbings of the Mount Hang tablet relating the inundation in tadpole characters, which tablet went to pieces in 1666 A. D., after a known life of eight hundred years. These tadpole characters were in use by certain priests of the Hia kings in Shensi Province in times contemporary with Noah. In the Confucian temple at Peking are the hieroglyphic stone drums relating history of the Chou kings, and which is more than remains to-day from Solomon's Temple, which was executed at the same time. Near

Ichang on the Yangtze River stand the Yien-tung (literally smoke towers), which were erected as beacons during this same dynasty. These towers were not used to burn fire at night, but to display smoke from burning manure by day. In present day ideograms, we have the poet Han Yu's song of the creation and deluge, which he wrote when the unpoetic Assyrians were taking to Nineveh two of Thebes' obelisks on a stone boat, over a constantly moving bed of portable stones, which they had laid over the sands.

You can wander through Yunnan Province to-day among the downtrodden Shan tribes and observe the heel of oppression on a dispossessed race, for the conquering Chinese beat them down here from the Great Plain when the Ethiopians were doing the same thing to dying Egypt, and Syria was likewise treating shamed Israel under Ahaz.

A blight then came on China in the rise of Taoism with its depressing theology, at the time when far away the most sonorous voice and most archangelic poetry that a human being ever sounded, were hurling lightnings among the shadows of men's thoughts, in the words of Isaiah.

That section of the Grand Canal (literally " grain-carrying ") north of the Yangtze River to the Wei River, one hundred and fifty miles, was being dug when Nebuchadnezzar was cutting his Royal Canal at Babylon by gangs of captive Jews, whom his chariots had dragged from desecrated Zion.

The worlds, West and East, were now reaching momentous hours. It was to be decided whether the far West was to be a shambles, or if white mankind could turn in peace and face the sun of knowledge. Marathon

decided it and Athens endowed us of the West for ever
with liberty and light.   On that same day China reached
the iron coast of Shan-tung and she, too, turned her face
toward the sun of knowledge, while Confucius wrote
what she saw.   His original manuscripts were lost; many
succeeding copies were lost, but the succession was sure.
His words were good and mankind was sure to hold
them fast.   Antiquarians, however, can handle something age-damp of this period in the *Bamboo Books,* dating back to 300 B. C., found in a priest's tomb in Honan
at the time when Zenobia was shining in the West with
that barbaric beauty which has dazzled history, which
was only too willing to record such things for a race
that liked them.

Events now cluster in our little western world.   Philip
of Macedon and Demosthenes exchanged the enginery of
javelin and anathema.   The Colossus of Rhodes was
built from the wreckage of Athenian and Egyptian defeat.   Ptolemy Philopater, the fratricide, overran Bible
lands and sowed salt under the heels of his spurning.
Hannibal challenged the Roman Republic and Rome re-
taliated upon the walls of Carthage.   Destroyers these
were, so that all we have to-day safe from their hands
is the little Magna Mater temple at Rome and at Edfu
that nearest perfect example extant of an Egyptian temple.   Untutored by all this, not wotting of it, over the
misty iron Roof of the World, yea, onward a year's journey to the Yellow Sea, we find the Giant Mason of all
time pacing up and down before a clay model of the
known earth; pushing his engineers aside and drawing
his trowel-sword across the models of mountains six
thousand feet high, and decreeing " there it shall go."
The Giant Mason was Tsin Chi.   He had a palace and

a throne besides, but they were his toys. Work was his hobby, and that hobby the Great Wall of China, the most marvelous monument ever erected by man, and standing for your wonder and mine even to-day and for ever. He was a grim humorist, too; when vassal lords of rebellious eye and mien visited him in his capital, Hienyang, he was wont personally to conduct them to a little object lesson in the back yard: toy replicas of the palaces of rebellious princes whom he was compelled to annihilate. He told these same vassals he would see them in a year, but he suddenly dropped in on them in six months and increased the tribute.

He was always up and down his kingdom at the head of armies, and he built great roads, for we do not learn that any successful rebellion got under way before his armies arrived back. He exacted mercenaries, just as Carthage was then doing across the Roof of the World. He extended the Grand Canal, because he was collecting grain for a work which should surpass even the superlatives of his soothsayers. He was here an adopter; there an originator. Other princes had raised protecting walls against his inroads. He took them; added to them; combined them into a Wall Trust. He was the first great Incorporator, Amalgamator, Financier, Despot and Trust King, and he boasted of the faults and virtues of them all. As he grew older, he believed occasional war was invented to achieve accumulated peace. He believed in trade, for he didn't tax his highways. He taxed luxuries, aristocrats, and rebels. He has for all time given the name of his dynasty to his country because of this monument, and history says it at least is worthy.

The wall is fifteen hundred miles long and has the appearance of a mighty dragon encircling the world, and hugging it deep in vale, and high over hill.   Some bricks weigh sixty pounds.   At the base it is twenty-five feet across; it is twenty-five feet high, and fifteen feet wide at the top.   Towers every mile or so stand twenty feet above the wall, and they are often built as redoubts on an independent base.   At places the wall mounts fifteen hundred feet in the sky.   Twenty thousand soldier masons labored at it for ten years.   Four hundred thousand soldiers protected the twenty thousand trowel men from the Turkestan Mongols, whose "cousinly" ambitions and traits Tsin Chi well knew.   Twenty thousand more soldiers were in the Commissariat Department, which farmed as it moved.   Thirty thousand more men were in the Army Service and Transport Corps, which had a Potter's and a Quarry Department.   China was then a nation of sixty millions.   Tsin was a peace-maker, for these manœuvers kept four hundred and seventy thousand men for ten years at harmless play, and away from their brothers' throats.   Indeed, in this way he peopled the Mongol plains and made possible the later Tartar invasions and dynasties, irony though such a result is, and he as well made it to come to pass that Russia should be largely Oriental in blood and taste.

He was a sane and beneficent ruler until he finished parts of the Wall.   He was a mighty ruler as he watched them grow, but it is not good for man to contemplate too long things done.   He went mad over the possibilities of what he had conceived when it should be completed. When the Pharaohs built the Pyramids, they immured their hieroglyphic records in them, and probably, too, went as mad, and destroyed everything that praised a lesser or a rival being.   Tsin Chi decreed history should date from his day, and popular readers may agree with his wishes, for perhaps we are all getting tired of these antiquarian chapters, which take every race wading through the flood to times contemporary with Luxor and Babylon. He ordered the destruction of the books and records, which has made it so difficult for the sinologue who essays personally to conduct to the Ark. Even five hundred priests, most famous for their memorizing of history in a land where memorizing reached its perfection, were burned. It is not impossible that the Great Wall will give up, as the years go by, tablets surreptitiously and ironically put there by rebels to this insane edict, and thus link us back to times in Turkestan contemporary with Rameses, which would only be from the Shu King books, contemporary with Noah, back two thousand three hundred years. The Great Wall has been copied in walls about every city. Enough labor has been wasted in such work to have girded the land with permanent highways and lock-canals which would be floodless. Only a land which has teemed with millions of people, even back to Noah's time, could have stood the waste. Say that there are six hundred cities, averaging fifteen miles around each; here are nine thousand more miles of wall. It was largely this waste of labor, values, money and mental patience, which robbed the toil-driven Chinese of the desire to carve monuments, strike coins, cut ideograms into stone, metal and porcelain, and load tombs with archæological treasure, so that here Tsin Chi has made us poorer because of his mad vanity-Trust. There are other records of Tsin Chi's work. In the records of the far western province of Szechuen, which were rewritten as the old copies wore out, it is inscribed that the first three miles of the present wall of the capital Chingtoo were erected in his reign.

The last of Egypt and mock-Egypt had been seen, and
Manetho in 270 B. C. composed an epitaph upon its culture and arms in a history written in the Greek language.
China, ever renewing itself independently of all outside
influences, was even more refulgent than usual in social,
martial and literary glory. When Roman Republicanism
fought for its franchise, and Sulla offered it a halter on
the way from Nola to Rome, Szma Tsien was writing his
great history of one hundred and thirty chapters, which
flooded twenty-two centuries with the light of returned
day. You would not call his style ponderous like Gib-
bon's, or classically pure like Macaulay's, but vivacious
like Green's or Herodotus'. Largely through Szma
Tsien's influence, literature was established for all time
as the key to political preferment, and the classical examinations became universal.

When Christ was born, the Emperor of Peace (Ping
Ti) of the Han Dynasty was reigning in China. For
thousands of years China had been fully civilized. The
rich brine and natural gas wells at Tsz-liu-tsin in Szechuen, which are still worked, are mentioned in the writings of the Taoist priest, Lunghusan, first century. Here,
then, is a vast enterprise, producing one hundred thousand
tons a year of salt, with a continuous history of twenty
centuries, contributing its share to reveal the ancient commercial stability of this people. No other country in the
opening century of the Christian era had such a commercial development. Religion had long consisted of a litur-
gy for the honoring of ancestors and the practice of a decided moral life on the part of a man as individual and
citizen. The Christian apostles, and the Buddhists of India, at the same time started to preach their gospels to the
long-forgotten, the new-discovered eastern world, which

now reached its fullest extension by absorbing Cochin, and St. Thomas, or a disciple, is reported to have reached Canton. Buddhism was more largely equipped and was widely successful in the north of China. Heathen Rome was then erecting the Colosseum for Titus, and followed it by Trajan's superb column. They liked toys more than philosophies, those cringers to tyrants, our Latin forefathers. The cycles rolled and ever accumulated pagodas, like the luxurious Flower Pagoda yet standing in Canton, as well as balustrades, and monasteries, until the sweet Nestorians came with a faint second echo of Christianity, and that dear melancholy tablet, cut in 781, the most precious stone existing in all the world, which lies in a temple compound in Singan, the first capital of the united Chinese.

Then followed the Mohammedans, matching minaret against pagoda, until the arm of the law like a wedge has driven the remnant of their rebellion only to the north and south of the kingdom. Mohammedanism challenged Buddhism to renewed art, and the latter responded with the hexagonal seven-storied " Tien Fung " pagoda at Ningpo, which is still standing. But grander still, the gem of Chinese art remaining to-day, she fashioned the falcon-like curves of the Loong Wah pagoda, when the best that Europe was doing was the dreary wooden huts of Charlemagne, disconsolate perhaps after losing his Roland at Roncesvalles. These two are but a salvage from thousands of such monuments which were erected in the next two hundred years. When Canute the Dane scourged our barbarian English, who retreated into path-less forests and resigned their huts to his firebrand; when the new Russian nation on the one hand and the new Arab nation on the other, rivals for the term " World's

Iconoclast," were in turn trying to knock down the walls
of Constantine's palace at Byzantium; when the earlier
Popes drew a longer sword than a ready prayer; — sane,
steady, artistic China had not deviated from the immemorial paths of magnificent peace and culture, as sayeth still
that grand witness, some of the stone piers and bulwarks
of the "Ten Thousand Ages" bridge at Fu-chau.
There was nothing but truth in this art, and the national
spirit was truth, and the truth was freedom. It owed
nothing to any other race. It came before them and lived
after them, and while conceding its beauty of curve and
carving, none has been strong enough to copy.

It mattered little if a wilder kindred tribe took for a
season the mace and crown. The people ruled themselves each in his own place by a conscience that brooked
no rebellion or impatience or lack of faith. They knew
that those who broke in roughly among them for honors,
or out of ignorant intrusion (for they accumulated not
wealth save for their need from day to day), would soon
by the preponderating example of virtue be as obedient
to patriotism as themselves. So we soon find the Mongol Genghis building canals, marble summer palaces in
the Gobi Desert between Kalgan and Urga, and those un-
opened grave mounds at Kalgan; and his grandson Kublai building national fleets. But Europe thinks more of
the latter, not because he took the Master's course at the
hands of his subject-tutors, but because he entertained
one Polo, a Venetian. That he entertained him with
breeding which was a revelation of wonders, let the same
Polo say through a thousand noted pages, which taught
the western world its first manners. The men of Genghis made graves as follows: The body was taken into
the open, surrounded with dried dung (argol), twigs

and anything burnable, and burned. Then each one of the host flung a stone and relics on the ashes. As time went on, sand and earth made a mound of this cairn.

Art overcame arms, as it always will in refined China. The encyclopedia writers, the potters, the elder brothers of the purple people themselves, came back into their own in the famous, delightful Mings, the last reigning house of the pure Chinese. You know that grandest arch in the world, so wide, airy and free, at the entrance to the four-mile amphitheatre twenty-five miles from Peking, and the Herculean statuary of twenty-two figures or more, solemn distances apart in the open plain: warriors; horses; elephants; tigers; camels; lions, standing and recumbent in pairs, and then the tombs of the Mings, with acres of silence between each. Gorgeous in life he is the plainest in death, Yung Loh, who thought this haven of the soul all out. Marble bridges, green and yellow-tiled pailos, painted and chiseled inscriptions, take up the broken theme of woe as you wander on from hillock to hillock, and disturb alone the meadow lark, the grasshopper and your memories. Considering it is eternal China, there is no antiquity here, but for us Westerners it was the day of Notre Dame and the first part of the Louvre, and these, too, were a gorgeous curtain across the passing of royalty.

When King James' translators were at work upon our Protestant Bible, an unfamiliar band of Manchus were setting up that Temple of Literature at Mukden, which you can enter to-day, and which the Japanese spat upon, for they have found a different key to life, and sixty-three miles east on the Tsz-yun Mountains these same Manchus were putting in order another tomb for one now unpegging his felt Bao tent, who would come home either as a dead shepherd, or as the conqueror of the earth's widest throne, to pay thanks and vows to his father's faithful manes.   Comparatively modern as is the beginning of this Tsin (pure) Dynasty in China, it is still hoary with age as compared with the oldest thrones of our white man's world.   The exploits of arms, and by sea, of Richelieu in France and Cromwell in England, covered a puny space as compared with the hosts and distances with which their contemporary, Shun Chi, the next Manchu king, had to deal in his work of organization. It was the following sovereign, Kang He, who reigned, keeping company with Louis XIV. all along fifty-four years of royal road, who was the grandest of this present Manchu dynasty, which may flutter like a candle flame and die before long.   Its greatest mind, but weakest arm, was the beloved Kwang Su, deceased as a martyr only yesterday by sinister causes, and on whose inspiring edicts of 1897 the present blessed constitutional hopes of China are based.

THE END

INDEX

INDEX

433

6232